Get ISO 27001 Certified

This book offers a clear, practical, and well-structured guide for implementing ISO 27001 in real organizations. Written for managers, consultants, auditors, and Information Security Professionals, it goes beyond theory to explain what the standard requires, why it is important, and how to implement it step by step.

Instead of seeing ISO 27001 as mere paperwork or compliance, the book emphasizes building an effective Information Security Management System (ISMS) that works in practice. Each clause is clearly explained, with real-world examples, practical advice, templates, checklists, quizzes, and tools that readers can customize to their specific needs.

The book is designed to simulate a guided classroom session, helping readers grasp leadership responsibilities, risk management, documentation, audits, continual improvement, and certification preparation with confidence. It also connects implementation with certification readiness, making it suitable for both first-time adopters and organizations preparing for audits.

Whether the goal is certification, regulatory compliance, or stronger information security governance, this book helps readers transition from understanding ISO 27001 to applying it effectively and sustainably.

Dr. Swapan Purkait is an information security expert with over 30 years of experience in teaching, consulting, and auditing. He has trained more than 25,000 professionals and has supported ISO 27001 implementation projects across various sectors, including central banks, telecom companies, government agencies, and critical infrastructure providers in over 20 countries.

He holds a PhD in Information Security from the Indian Institute of Technology (IIT) Kharagpur, India, and has contributed to initiatives that help local law enforcement agencies understand cybercrime and digital risks.

Known for his discussion-based and highly relatable teaching style, he uses everyday analogies and real-world examples—often inspired by his travels to over 60 countries—to simplify complex ISO standards, making them practical and easy to grasp.

Based in Kolkata, India, he values work–life balance. Outside his professional work, he enjoys cooking as a hobby chef. He is an avid rower who travels to row with local crews in different countries and is also an amateur 10-meter air rifle shooter.

Through this book, he reconnects with his first passion—writing. Drawing on decades of experience, he presents ISO 27001 in a clear, practical, and conversational manner, helping readers feel as though they are part of an engaging discussion rather than reading a technical manual.

Get ISO 27001 Certified

A Practical Roadmap to Implementing ISO/IEC 27001:2022 in Any Organization

Dr. Swapan Purkait

CRC Press
Taylor & Francis Group
Boca Raton London New York

CRC Press is an imprint of the
Taylor & Francis Group, an **informa** business

First edition published 2027
by CRC Press
2385 NW Executive Center Drive, Suite 320, Boca Raton, FL 33431

and by CRC Press
4 Park Square, Milton Park, Abingdon, Oxon, OX14 4RN

CRC Press is an imprint of Taylor & Francis Group, LLC

ISBN: 9781041249023 (hbk)
ISBN: 9781041249030 (pbk)
ISBN: 9781003744139 (ebk)

DOI: 10.1201/9781003744139

Typeset in Sabon
by Newgen Publishing UK

To
Ma and Baba

Contents

Acknowledgments xi
About the author xiii
AI statement xv

Introduction 1

1 Bridging the gap: Why ISO 27001 isn't just for techies 5
About this book 6
How to use this book 7
Why are you here? And how this book can help 9

2 ISO—Order in a chaotic world: Why ISO exists, and why ISO 27001 has become so important 11
ISO: A short history 12
How ISO standards are born 12
What ISO standards really do 13
Types of ISO standards 14
The one that protects them all 16
Quiz #1 17

3 Building an ISMS that works: How ISO/IEC 27001 became the framework of choice 18
What is information security (really)? 18
What is an information security management system? 20
What makes an ISMS work? 21
Key principles that support an effective ISMS 22
Why organizations need an ISMS 22
How ISO 27001 fits in 23
Why ISO 27001 matters 24
Brief history of ISO 27001 25
Meet the family: ISO/IEC 27000 series 25
Know the standards, use them well 27
Quiz #2 28

4 The backbone of ISO/IEC 27001, structure and strategy: How harmonized structure, process thinking, and risk focus shape the standard 29
Introduction: So far, so good? 29
Why structure matters in standards 29
The harmonized clause structure 30
A little secret about all ISO standards 31
Why Clauses 4–10 matter so much 32
So, why are these clauses so important? 32
You can't pick and choose 32
Not all clauses are created equal 33
Process-based thinking: Seeing the bigger picture 35
Why does this matter for ISO 27001? 36
PDCA and the process approach: The engine behind the ISMS 36
A quick trip back in time: Meet Mr. Deming 36
PDCA in ISO 27001: The hidden map 37
PDCA + process thinking = Your ISMS in action 37
Risk-based thinking: The real reason ISO 27001 exists 37
Follow the risk, not the routine 38
So, what is risk-based thinking? 38
Risk is not just a section—It's the theme 39
Quiz #3 40

5 Terms you'll hear again and again: Clarifying the core terms that shape an effective ISMS 41
ISO/IEC 27000: The vocabulary standard 41
Core ISMS terms you'll encounter often 42
Quiz #4 52

6 What you must deliver and document: Understanding ISMS requirements and documentation needs 53
Where do ISMS requirements come from? 53
Requirement ≠ Documentation—But one often leads to the other 56
ISO/IEC 27001:2022—Mandatory documents you need 57
Building your ISMS documentation framework early 59
The danger of copy–paste compliance 60
Clause 7.5.2: Documented information that works 60
Clause 7.5.3: Controlling what you create 63
ISMS documentation template 67
Quiz #5 73
Answer key: Implementation Task 1 74

7 From Gap to Gantt, your ISMS project starts here: Assess where you stand—Then plan the journey with purpose 75
Why Gap Analysis is the first real step 75
Gantt chart 85

Quiz #6 88
Case 1: The data fortress in Nairobi 89

8 Clause 4—Understand your world before you secure it: Mapping context, interested parties, and scope for a strong ISMS foundation 92
Introduction 93
Guiding principles for every clause 93
Why context matters in ISO 27001 94
Clause 4.1: Understanding the organization and its context 94
Clause 4.2: Understanding the needs and expectations of interested parties 99
Understanding the climate-change amendment 104
Clause 4.3: Determining the scope of the ISMS 105
Clause 4.4: Information security management system 109
Quiz #7 111
Case 2: Monsoons, markets, and messy Chennai politics 111

9 Clause 5—Leadership isn't optional: Setting direction, roles, and commitment for information security success 114
Clause 5.1: Leadership and commitment 114
Clause 5.2: Policy 117
Clause 5.3: Organizational roles, responsibilities, and authorities 121
Quiz #8 127
Case 3: Leadership on the line—Abu Dhabi 127

10 Clause 6—Plan your risks, control your future: Mastering risk management and the statement of applicability 130
Beyond this chapter: Where to learn more about risk 130
A quick refresher: Risk management 131
Clause 6.1: Actions to address risks and opportunities 135
Clause 6.1.2: Information security risk assessment 138
Clause 6.1.3: Information security risk treatment 151
Clause 6.2: Information security objectives and planning to achieve them 166
Clause 6.3: Planning of changes 170
Quiz #9 175
Case 4: Planning in motion—Singapore 176

11 Clause 7—Empower your people, manage your info: Building competence, awareness, and communication for a strong ISMS 178
Introduction 178
Clause 7.1: Resources 178
Clause 7.2: Competence 181
Clause 7.3: Awareness 188
Clause 7.4: Communication 195

Clause 7.5: Documented information 204
Quiz #10 206
Case 5: Culture, calls, and quiet change—Hyderabad 206

12 Clause 8—Put your ISMS into action: Implementing controls and avoiding common pitfalls 209
Introduction 209
Clause 8.1: Operational planning and control 209
Clause 8.2: Information security risk assessment 217
Clause 8.3: Information security risk treatment 220
Quiz #11 223
Case 6: Risk, rollouts, and reality—Lagos 224

13 Clause 9—Is it working? Evaluate and improve: Measuring performance, auditing, and management review 226
Clause 9.1 Monitoring, measurement, analysis, and evaluation 226
Clause 9.2 Internal audit 233
Clause 9.3 Management review 250
Quiz #12 257
Case 7: Wheels, audits, and wake-up calls—Kigali 257

14 Clause 10—Get better, stay better: Handling nonconformities, corrective actions, and continual improvement 260
Clause 10.1 Continual improvement 260
Clause 10.2 Nonconformity and corrective action 264
Quiz #13 274
Case 8: A loop of fixes—London 274

15 Preparing for ISO 27001 certification: What auditors want and how to pass with confidence 277
Why consider ISO 27001 certification? 277
Choosing the right ISO 27001 certification body 279
Understanding the ISO 27001 3-year certification cycle 281
Your ISO 27001 journey—The road ahead 285

16 Practice paper: Test what you've learned 287

17 Quiz compass 302

18 Case answer key and reflections 310

19 Practice paper: Answers and explanations 314

Bibliography 321

Acknowledgments

I would like to sincerely thank my editor, Gabriella Williams, for her guidance, patience, and thoughtful feedback throughout the development of this book. I am also deeply grateful to my wife for her constant support, encouragement, and understanding during the long hours of writing and revisions that made this work possible.

About the author

Dr. Swapan Purkait is a seasoned ISO trainer, consultant, and educator with over **30 years of professional experience** in the fields of **information security, network security, risk management, privacy, artificial intelligence and business continuity**.

He began teaching and training in information security as early as **1999**, long before it became a mainstream concern for organizations. Since **2006**, he has been deeply engaged in implementing, auditing, and training organizations on **ISO standards**, particularly ISO/IEC 27001.

Dr. Purkait holds a **PhD in Information Security** from the prestigious **Indian Institute of Technology (IIT) Kharagpur**, where his research focused on phishing and its countermeasures. He is also a **certified Lead Auditor in six ISO standards**. He has delivered hundreds of training programs and consulting engagements across **20+ countries**, including India, Singapore, Netherlands, Qatar, UAE, South Africa, Nigeria, and more.

As the **Founder and Director of Nettech Private Limited**, he has led ISO implementation and training projects across a wide range of sectors—including **central banks, telecom operators, oil and gas enterprises, mining companies, airlines, government agencies**, and critical infrastructure providers.

He is also associated with BSI Group as an Associate Tutor, delivering specialized ISO training courses to professionals around the world. In addition to his role as a trainer, he is entrusted with developing delegate materials for BSI's official ISO programs—a mark of distinction that speaks to his technical expertise, clarity of instruction, and content development skills.

What sets Dr. Purkait apart is his **discussion-based, highly relatable teaching style**. Known for using everyday analogies and real-world examples—often inspired by his travels to over **60 countries**—he makes complex ISO standards practical, memorable, and easy to apply. His sessions are known for being interactive, engaging, and free of unnecessary jargon or PowerPoint overload.

Over the years, he has conducted **hundreds of seminars and webinars** for university students and professionals alike, helping demystify the world of standards and information security.

In short, **Dr. Swapan Purkait doesn't just teach standards—he lives them, applies them, and makes them accessible to everyone.**

AI statement

Please note that I used Grammarly Pro to review the manuscript for clarity and consistency. All ideas, content, interpretation, and final wording remain entirely my own.

Introduction

Before we explore clauses, controls, and audits, let's pause to get oriented.

This book is not intended to overwhelm you. It's meant to guide you.

Get ISO 27001 Certified is presented as a practical, classroom-style roadmap for anyone involved in building, managing, or supporting an Information Security Management System (ISMS). You don't need to be highly technical or have a background in information security. What you do need is curiosity, patience, and a willingness to apply ideas in a way that makes sense for your organization.

This book aims to bridge a long-standing gap. On one side is the ISO 27001[1] standard, written in formal, precise language. On the other side are real organizations trying to implement it, often with limited resources, mixed skill sets, and a lot of uncertainty. This book serves as a bridge, translating requirements into clear actions while staying aligned with the standard.

This book is written for:

- Managers, implementers, coordinators, and team leads responsible for ISO 27001
- Risk, Compliance, Audit, HR, IT, and Operations professionals
- Organizations preparing for ISO 27001 certification
- Readers who want to understand ISO 27001 beyond theory and jargon

If you're seeking shortcuts, ready-made documents to copy without thinking, or a guarantee of certification with minimal effort, this book isn't for you. But if you want to learn how ISO 27001 really works in practice, you're in the right place.

How the book is structured: The book follows the PDCA framework used by ISO 27001:

- Plan phase: building the foundation and understanding requirements
- Do phase: operating and implementing what you planned
- Check phase: monitoring, auditing, and reviewing performance
- Act phase: improving, correcting, and strengthening the ISMS
- Each clause is explained using the same practical rhythm, so you always know what to expect as you move through the book. The goal is simple: turn understanding into action, without losing alignment with ISO 27001.

For every clause, we work through it in four consistent parts:

- **What the clause expects:** A brief, high-level summary of what ISO 27001 requires. This helps you understand the intent of the clause quickly. It does not replace the

DOI: 10.1201/9781003744139-1

standard, so whenever you need the exact wording, always refer to your copy of ISO 27001.

- **How it works in real organizations:** The requirement is clearly explained and supported with practical, real-world examples. This shows how organizations actually put the clause into practice, beyond just theory.
- **Implementation guidance:** This provides step-by-step instructions on how to apply the clause, including recommended actions, responsibilities, and documentation. The focus is on maintaining the ISMS's effectiveness, manageability, and alignment with daily operations.
- **Toolkit and resources:** Sample templates, checklists, and tools you can adapt to your organization are provided here. These are intentionally generic and meant as starting points, not final answers. They should always be reviewed, modified, and tailored to fit your business context. Avoid copy-paste thinking; continual review and adaptation are what make your ISMS work in the real world.

This consistent structure is intentional. It lets you spend less time decoding the standard and more time building an ISMS that truly works, passes audits, and promotes continual improvement.

How to use this book: You don't have to read this book cover to cover in one go.

- If you're new, read sequentially to build understanding step by step
- If you're implementing, use it as a working reference
- If you're preparing for certification, focus on evidence, controls, and audits

Each chapter stands on its own, so you can revisit sections as needed.

Throughout the book, you'll find:

- Short quizzes to test understanding
- Realistic scenarios based on actual implementations
- Practical tasks you can try inside your organization

At the end of the book, you'll find a full-length practice test to help you review everything you've learned. Answers and explanations are provided separately, so you can reflect honestly before reviewing.

The templates included in this book are for reference only. They are not meant to be submitted exactly as they are. Every organization is unique, and ISO 27001 expects your ISMS to reflect your specific context, not someone else's documents. Use these templates as a starting point, then customize them to suit your environment.

Icons are used throughout this book to make reading easier and to highlight important ideas, practical tips, warnings, and real-world insights. These visual cues help you navigate the content quickly, especially when revisiting chapters during implementation or audit preparation. A quick explanation of each icon and how it's used is provided in Chapter 1.

One important reminder before we proceed: this book serves as a practical guide and reference, not a replacement for the ISO 27001 standard itself. To work effectively and accurately, you should always have your own official copy of ISO 27001. The standard can be purchased directly from the official ISO website, and I strongly recommend doing so if you are serious about implementation or certification.

A final note before we start: This book aims to support you, not judge you. ISO 27001 isn't about perfection. It focuses on structure, consistency, evidence, and ongoing improvement. Take your time, ask questions, and thoughtfully consider new ideas.

With this foundation in place, let's start where most misunderstandings begin. Chapter 1 addresses the biggest myth of all: that ISO 27001 is only for technical experts.

Chapter 1

Bridging the gap

Why ISO 27001 isn't just for techies

This isn't just a book about implementing ISO/IEC 27001:2022. It's your roadmap, your classroom, and your companion on the journey to creating a truly secure organization, without the jargon overload.

My journey with ISO 27001 started in 2006 during my PhD at the Indian Institute of Technology (IIT) Kharagpur, one of India's most renowned institutions. My research focused on phishing attacks and their countermeasures, aiming to understand how attackers manipulate trust and, more importantly, how organizations can defend themselves against these evolving threats.

But I wasn't immersed in academic theory or buried in lines of code. I was out in the field, talking with businesses of all sizes across different industries to see what "information security" really looks like in practice. That's when I first came across ISO 27001.

Not just the standard itself, but also the confusion surrounding it. The fear. The persistent myth that "ISO 27001 is only for hardcore tech teams."

Fast-forward nearly 20 years, with hands-on work across 20+ countries—from Africa to the Middle East, Asia to Europe—and deep involvement in sectors like banking, government, telecom, aviation, and more. My journey has been anything but academic. I've learned about information security by rolling up my sleeves and handling the nuts and bolts of implementation in the real world. Yet, even today, I still face the same raised eyebrows.

- *"Is ISO 27001 just for IT people?"*
- *"Do I need a technical background to understand this?"*
- *"Can I implement it without hiring an expensive consultant?"*

You're not alone. These questions sparked the inspiration for this book.

I wrote *Get ISO 27001 Certified* to bridge a gap I've seen for years—the gap between the complex language of standards and the real-world people trying to implement them.

ISO 27001 doesn't have to be intimidating, overly technical, or just for information security experts with years of experience. Many successful ISO 27001 implementations I've seen were led by business managers, HR professionals, and compliance officers—people who understood their organization's goals and were eager to learn.

This book is my way of making the standard more relatable, helpful, and even enjoyable.

It's designed to guide you as you navigate ISO/IEC 27001:2022. Whether you're leading an implementation, supporting a certification effort, or simply trying to understand what ISO 27001 means in practical terms, this resource will walk you through the process with clarity and confidence.

DOI: 10.1201/9781003744139-2

I've kept things as practical as possible—focusing on what matters most, avoiding unnecessary jargon, and breaking down complex clauses into easy-to-understand parts. Throughout the book, you'll find real-world examples, reusable templates, and helpful tools that you can adapt to your organization.

While this book isn't a substitute for formal training, it aims to empower you, especially if you're starting or working without a whole security team. If you're serious about expanding your knowledge, I highly recommend pursuing a recognized course, such as the ISO/IEC 27001:2022 Lead Implementer certification. It's a wise investment that can improve your skills, boost your resume, and increase your credibility as a security leader.

Above all, I hope this book helps you take the first step—or the next step—toward building a stronger, more innovative, and more secure organization.

ABOUT THIS BOOK

Let's be honest—ISO 27001 has developed a particular reputation. For many, it feels like a fortress guarded by IT teams, filled with people who speak fluent tech jargon and dream in risk matrices.

Over the years, numerous books have been written about Information Security Management Systems (ISMS) and the ISO 27001 standard. While many are detailed and well intentioned, they often fall into two extremes: either too technical for non-experts or too superficial to be truly helpful. If you don't have an information security degree or an internal team dedicated to security, you often end up confused—or, worse, simply giving up.

At the other end of the spectrum, some "quick start" guides promise shortcuts that seem tempting but lack depth, accuracy, or real-world experience. Following oversimplified or outdated advice can leave your organization more confused—or dangerously exposed.

And then there's the fatigue. Yes, ISMS fatigue is real. Buzzwords, media panic, recycled checklists, and contradictory expert opinions contribute to it. No wonder many people feel overwhelmed before they even open the standard.

That's when this book comes in.

Get ISO 27001 Certified is written for all of us—the planners, managers, implementers, and the curious. Whether you're responsible for compliance, operations, leadership, or risk, this book is designed for you. You don't need a technical background—just a willingness to learn, ask the right questions, and take action.

Here's what you'll get:

- A clear understanding of what ISO/IEC 27001:2022 is truly about
- Practical steps to develop and enhance an ISMS
- Templates and tools you can customize for your organization
- Real-world examples that make complex concepts easier to understand
- Guidance you can use right away—whether you're pursuing certification or just improving security

Each chapter is self-contained, so feel free to jump around. Already familiar with a topic? Move ahead. Something feels new. Take your time and explore. I've designed this book like one of my workshops—interactive, approachable, and focused on real-world results.

This isn't a textbook. It's a practical guide—without the dull slides, mandatory quizzes, or stiff language. And yes, you can even read it with your coffee.

To make ideas memorable, I've used everyday analogies and simple examples. Just remember: these are meant for learning, not copying verbatim. Your organization's size, culture, structure, and risk landscape will influence how you use them. So, adapt, interpret, and make it your own.

This book also supports your personal growth. If you're preparing for a professional qualification such as the ISO/IEC 27001:2022 Lead Implementer, this guide provides a strong foundation. However, just to be clear, it's not a replacement for formal training or certification. Think of it as your starting point, not the destination.

Information security isn't a one-and-done task. It's a continuous journey. Like any important journey, it helps to have a map, good tools, and someone rooting for you from the sidelines. That's what this book is here to be.

HOW TO USE THIS BOOK

This book is designed not only to inform but also to guide, challenge, and actively involve you in understanding and applying ISO/IEC 27001:2022. Whether you're a first-time implementer, an aspiring Information Security professional, or someone supporting your organization's compliance journey, you'll find this book structured to help you progress at your own pace—from concept to certification readiness.

You don't need to read it cover to cover all at once. Each chapter covers a specific stage or requirement of ISO 27001. You can:

- Read it straight through if you're new to the topic and want a complete overview.
- Jump to particular chapters if you're seeking details on a specific clause or activity.
- Use it as a reference manual while working on your implementation project.

📝 Quizzes, Case Scenarios, and Practice Activities

Throughout the book, you'll come across short quizzes, reflections, and practical case scenarios. These are designed to help you:

- Test your understanding of key ideas
- Apply concepts to real-world situations
- Strengthen your confidence before implementation or audit
- Think like an ISO 27001 practitioner, not just a reader

At the end of each chapter, you'll find a short case study with related multiple-choice questions. These cases are meant to feel realistic—situations you may actually face while implementing an ISMS.

Once you complete the full book, you'll also find a 100-question practice exam at the end. This will help you review everything you've learned in one place, just like a final mock assessment.

The answers and justifications for all quizzes, case questions, and the final practice exam are provided at the end of the book. Please avoid jumping to the answers before attempting the questions—the real value comes from thinking and reflecting first.

Take your time, enjoy the process, and treat every question as part of your learning journey.

❗ **Tip:** For the best experience, keep a notebook or digital document handy to write down your answers, thoughts, and any ideas you want to revisit later.

Toolkit and Resources
You'll also find sample templates and documentation examples used in ISO 27001 implementation. These are provided as illustrative references only. Please don't treat them as "ready-to-submit" forms. Your organization's size, industry, risk profile, and context will require you to adapt and customize each document. Think of these templates as scaffolding—they give you structure, but what you create should reflect your environment.

Be Curious: Google Is Your Friend
Some terms or topics might spark your curiosity—and that's exactly what I hope for. While this book simplifies ISO 27001, information security remains a broad and constantly changing field. If you encounter something unfamiliar, take a moment to look it up, explore related resources, or even dive into the ISO standard itself. This book is just a starting point for your journey of discovery and learning. Learning isn't about memorizing—it's about making connections in a way that makes sense to you.

Icons Used in This Book
To make the book easier to follow and more practical to use, I've included a set of icons throughout. You'll find a simple overview of these icons and their meanings in Table 1.1.

You'll notice these icons appear alongside key points throughout the book—think of them as visual signposts to help you stay oriented and engaged.

Table 1.1 Icons used throughout the book

IconLabel	Purpose
Tip	Helpful ideas or shortcuts to make implementation easier.
Remember	Key points to keep in mind—often useful for audits or documentation.
Quiz	Self-check questions to test your understanding of the section. Answers are at the end of the book.
Toolkit and Resources	Indicates a sample document or form you can refer to and modify for your own needs.
Caution	Highlights common mistakes, risks, or things to avoid during implementation.
Implementation Tool	Used to highlight practical actions, step-by-step guidance, or tools you can apply directly while building or refining your ISMS.
Real-World Insight	Relatable scenarios or practical industry examples that connect ISO concepts to everyday life. This icon bridges the gap between theory and practice.
Author's Note	A personal insight, reminder, or suggestion from me to help you connect theory with real-world implementation.
Key Takeaway	Summarizes the core lessons or outcomes from a chapter to reinforce what truly matters.
Website Reference	A helpful website, official link, or resource you can explore further for research or validation.

Author's Note: This book is here to support, not overwhelm. Take your time. Reflect. Re-read if needed. And above all, make it your own. The goal isn't just to get ISO 27001 certified—it's to develop a security mindset that makes sense for your people, your operations, and your future. Let's make it practical. Let's make it yours.

WHY ARE YOU HERE? AND HOW THIS BOOK CAN HELP

Let's take a moment to ask the obvious question: Why are you reading a book on ISO 27001? Is it because someone at work said, "Hey, we need to get certified—figure it out!" Maybe you're a compliance officer trying to understand the requirements. Perhaps you're a team lead who just got "volunteered" to lead an information security project. Or maybe, just maybe, you're here because you're genuinely curious. If that's the case, then you are my favorite kind of reader! Whatever brought you here, welcome. You're in the right place. This isn't a book filled with rigid academic theory or dry policy templates. It's a conversation between you and me about how to protect your organization's information, meet stakeholder expectations, and build trust with clients, customers, and colleagues.

🧭 **What You'll Walk Away With**
By the time you finish this book, you will be able to:

- Understand what effective information security management looks like throughout your entire organization, from top leadership to daily operations.
- Break down ISO/IEC 27001:2022 into practical, real-world actions—no buzzwords, no fluff.
- Build a solid foundation for your own ISMS—even if you're starting from scratch.
- Use practical, ready-to-apply policies, procedures, and processes that can be customized to your specific needs.
- Prepare your organization for a successful third-party ISO 27001 certification audit—with confidence that you're addressing what matters most.
- Support your professional growth by developing the knowledge and skills needed to earn a recognized personal certification, such as the ISO/IEC 27001:2022 Lead Implementer credential.
- Foster a culture of information security awareness and responsibility across teams and departments, making security everyone's business.
- Protect what's most important: your data, your stakeholders' trust, and your organization's reputation.
- Promote continual improvement and lifelong learning—both in your role and throughout your organization.

🛠 **How This Book Will Help You Do That**

- I'll guide you through the key concepts and clauses of ISO 27001 as if we're in a workshop together.
- You'll see examples, templates 📄, tips 💡, and a few fun analogies (because even clause 6.1.3 can be explained using coffee and cake).
- You'll find quizzes 📝 and exercises to help you test your understanding—no exam pressure, just self-check moments.
- And yes, I'll warn you ⚠ when you're approaching common pitfalls.

💬 **Author's Note:** Don't worry if this is your first time learning about information security. You won't be judged. This isn't about being perfect—it's about improving each day. If you're here, you're already doing more than most.

Information security doesn't have to feel overwhelming. With the right approach—and the right guide—you can make your organization safer, smarter, and prepared for today's challenges.

If you've ever thought, "This standard is not for me," this book is here to prove otherwise. So, take a deep breath, grab a coffee (or tea), and get ready to build something valuable—one chapter at a time.

Let's get started.

Chapter 2

ISO—Order in a chaotic world

Why ISO exists, and why ISO 27001 has become so important

Welcome to the start of your journey! Before we explore the standard itself—officially known as ISO/IEC 27001:2022—it's helpful to step back and learn about the global organization that created it: the International Organization for Standardization (ISO).

From now on, when we mention ISO 27001, we refer to the current, official version: ISO/IEC 27001:2022. It is the globally recognized standard for developing and managing an effective emphasizes building an effective ISMS—and your guide to safeguarding information, building trust, and strengthening your organization.

Did You Know?

- ISO is not an acronym. It originates from the Greek word "isos," meaning "equal"—ensuring the name remains consistent across all languages.
- ISO was established in 1947 after a meeting in London with 25 countries, and it continues to be the world's leading non-governmental standards organization.
- As of 2024, ISO has approximately 170 member countries, publishes over 25,000 international standards, and functions through more than 800 technical committees (TCs).
- Each year on October 14, ISO observes World Standards Day—celebrating the collaborative efforts of the global standards community.
- ISO's headquarters is in Geneva, Switzerland, right in the heart of Europe. From this neutral base, ISO helps shape global standards that promote consistency and quality across industries—from energy and toys to information security.
- Standards are not created in a boardroom—experts are the ones who develop them. ISO develops its standards through over 800 TCs and subcommittees, where thousands of professionals, scientists, engineers, and regulators volunteer to shape the future.
- Every ISO standard takes years of international collaboration. Before publication, it must undergo multiple drafts, national reviews, public comments, and consensus voting to ensure it is technically sound and globally relevant.
- ISO has one vote per country, regardless of size. Whether it's the United States, Bhutan, or Brazil, each member body has an equal say. It is one of the few genuinely democratic systems in international standard-setting.
- ISO standards are reviewed every 5 years. They are not set in stone. Each standard is periodically reassessed to remain aligned with new technologies, evolving risks, and global needs, which explains why we now have ISO/IEC 27001:2022 rather than the 2013 version.

DOI: 10.1201/9781003744139-3

⚠ **Caution:** Sometimes readers confuse ISO (the organization) with being "ISO-certified." ISO creates standards—third-party certification bodies issue certificates. Therefore, saying "ISO certified" is a common but incorrect shortcut.

ISO: A SHORT HISTORY

- **Predecessor (1926–1942):** Started as ISA—the International Federation of National Standardizing Associations
- **Founding (1946–1947):** Delegates and the UN's Standards Coordinating Committee met in London, establishing ISO in February 1947
- **First Standard (1951):** ISO/R 1 set a reference temperature of 20 °C for measuring instruments—still used today under ISO 1:2016
- Growth: ISO introduced significant standards like ISO 9001 [2] (quality management, 1987), ISO 14001 [3] (environmental, 1996), and eventually ISO 27001 (information security, 2005; updated 2013 and 2022).

📌 **Why the "IEC" in ISO/IEC?**
You might be wondering—what's with the extra letters? Why not just call it ISO 27001 and be done with it?—Good question.

IEC stands for the International Electrotechnical Commission. Founded in 1906, the IEC is the world's leading organization for developing and publishing international standards for all electrical, electronic, and related technologies. These are collectively known as "electrotechnology." The IEC unites nearly 170 countries, with about 30,000 experts working together on the global IEC platform to ensure products operate safely worldwide. For specific standards—especially those related to IT and information security—ISO and IEC jointly publish them. That's why the standard's official title is ISO/IEC 27001:2022.

💡 **Tip:** Whenever you see a standard labelled ISO/IEC, it indicates it was developed collaboratively by both organizations. For simplicity, we'll refer to it as ISO 27001 in this book. Now you understand where the "IEC" comes from, and yes—it does matter in the world of formal documentation!

💬 **Author's Note:** Suppose ISO provides the "what" and "why," while IEC often delivers the "how"—especially when it concerns technical precision and systems integration. Together, they form a powerful partnership that gives standards like ISO 27001 both global credibility and practical relevance.

📌 **Remember:** ISO isn't just about documents—it's a worldwide, volunteer-driven organization that promotes consistency, trust, and shared understanding across industries. From temperature references to information security frameworks, it has helped shape how the world measures, protects, and improves. With ISO and IEC working together, you're not just following rules—you're building on a legacy of reliability.

HOW ISO STANDARDS ARE BORN

Understanding how ISO standards are developed helps you appreciate their credibility—they're not created behind closed doors by just a few people. Instead, they result from a global, collaborative, and organized effort.

Creating an ISO standard is like conducting a worldwide symphony. ISO functions as the conductor, with expert representatives from national standards organizations, industry, consumer groups, academia, and government serving as the musicians. Together, they craft standards that address real-world needs.
Here is how it typically works:

Step 1: Market Need Sparks the Process: A new standard doesn't start with ISO deciding, "Let's make one." Instead, it begins when a clear market need is identified, often by industries, government agencies, consumer groups, or other stakeholders. These needs are communicated to ISO through national members.

Step 2: Setting Up a (TC): Once a proposal is accepted, a TC—a global group of experts—is formed or assigned to it. These committees are the main force behind ISO standards. They often include representatives from over 160 countries, bringing together diverse sectors, perspectives, and areas of expertise.

In the field of information technology, ISO and IEC have created a joint TC—ISO/IEC JTC 1—specifically responsible for developing, maintaining, and promoting international standards in this area.

Step 3: Drafting and Discussing: The committee develops a Working Draft (WD) that defines the scope, terms, and technical elements. It goes through multiple rounds of discussions, refinements, and reaching consensus. In many cases, Subcommittees or Working Groups (WGs) are also formed for highly specialized topics.

Step 4: Consensus and Public Review: The draft then becomes a Committee Draft (CD) and, if consensus is reached, advances to the Draft International Standard (DIS) stage. This is where it becomes more democratic—all member bodies review it and vote. Comments are gathered, discussed, and incorporated.

If necessary, a Final Draft International Standard (FDIS) is issued for a final voting round.

Step 5: Publication: Once approved, the final document is published as an official ISO standard. Typically, this process takes around 3 years from proposal to publication.

Bonus: Standards Aren't Static
Every ISO standard is reviewed every 5 years to keep it relevant. Based on global input, it may be confirmed, revised, or even withdrawn.

Author's Note: When you implement ISO 27001 in your organization, you're not just checking off a list. You're accessing a shared global knowledge built through years of discussion, compromise, testing, and validation. That's what makes these standards credible and reliable.

WHAT ISO STANDARDS REALLY DO

ISO standards aren't just academic; they're influential—they serve as powerful tools that shape industries, foster trust, and promote tangible change. Let's explore the benefits that matter most:

1. **Build Trust in Products and Services:** ISO standards guarantee that the items you depend on daily—from medical packaging to electronics—are safe, reliable, and of high quality. They also set the standard for ethical and sustainable business practices.

In essence, they combine performance with responsibility, making your everyday choices feel a little greener and far more dependable.

2. **Empower Small and Medium Enterprises (SMEs):** ISO standards help SMEs outperform expectations. They simplify regulatory compliance, reduce expenses, and unlock access to international markets. For smaller businesses with limited budgets, standards level the playing field and enhance competitiveness.
3. **Support Smarter Policy and Regulation:** Governments and regulators around the world depend on ISO standards as unbiased, expert-backed benchmarks. These standards simplify lawmaking, lower market barriers, and facilitate trade agreements, helping markets operate smoothly across borders.
4. **Keep Consumers Safe and Informed:** ISO prioritizes customer interests. Whether protecting toy manufacturing or ensuring food packaging quality, ISO standards incorporate consumer feedback to develop products that address actual needs and safeguard vulnerable groups.
5. **Drive Business Efficiency and Cost Savings:** Standards help organizations improve efficiency, minimize mistakes, and cut unnecessary work. They are proven drivers of productivity, playing a significant role in global GDP growth and workforce output.
6. **Promote Environmental Protection and Safety:** Environment-related standards such as ISO 14001 help organizations reduce waste, conserve energy, and reduce pollution. These actions lower costs while also providing benefits to the community and ensuring regulatory peace of mind.
7. **Foster Innovation and Interoperability:** Standards establish common platforms and shared languages. This promotes innovation by simplifying the integration of products and services—from medical tech to innovative city solutions—that "just work" together.

Author's Note: When you implement an ISO standard in your organization, you're drawing on decades of expert consensus, not just checking off requirements. You're joining a tradition of trusted, tested frameworks that function across industries, borders, and time. You're not merely following rules; you're embedding proven best practices that boost trust, efficiency, safety, and innovation.

TYPES OF ISO STANDARDS

ISO offers a range of standards tailored to different needs, from mandatory rules to helpful guidance. Understanding the differences helps you apply exactly what your organization needs. Here's a breakdown:

1. Requirement Standards ("Shall" Standards)

These standards use "shall" to indicate mandatory rules. Failing to meet a "shall" requirement results in a non-conformity (NC)—similar to being stopped at immigration without valid documents.

Example:

- *ISO 27001* requires you to implement and maintain an ISMS.
- Think of it like your *passport*: you *must* have it, and the immigration officer checks it every time you travel. If it's invalid or missing, you're not going anywhere.
- Similarly, auditees who don't meet "shall" requirements receive an NC, and that prevents certification.

These standards serve as a benchmark for certification and define organizational compliance.

📌 **Connecting Points**

- "Shall" = Must do
- You don't do a "shall" = NC issued
- Certification depends on meeting all "shall" requirements

2. Guidance Standards ("Should" Standards)
Guidance standards recommend "should" as best practices—not mandatory, but strongly advised.

Example:

- *ISO 19011:2018* [4] guides you on how to conduct audits effectively.
- Think of "should" like *packing luggage for a trip*: no rule says you must, but without it, you'll struggle when you land.
- Auditors won't issue NCs for not following guidance, but ignoring it could leave you unprepared or inefficient.

These are not for certification, but they are invaluable for doing things well.

3. Vocabulary and Terminology Standards
These offer definitions that establish a common language, ensuring everyone understands ISO terms consistently.

Example:

- ***ISO/IEC 27000*** [2] defines ISMS-related key terms.

Think of them as an official glossary—crucial for clarity and consistency.

4. Sector-Specific or Technical Standards
These adapt the core ISO requirements for specific industries or technologies.

Examples:

- **ISO/IEC 27007** [3]: Provides auditing guidance tailored to ISMS
- **ISO/IEC 27002** [1]: Offers a detailed catalogue of security controls that support ISO 27001; can also be considered "guidance"
- **ISO 13485** [4] is tailored to medical-device quality management.

They help standardize best practices across industries with common terminology and frameworks.

💬 **Author's Note:** Think of requirement standards as the official recipe—one that must be followed precisely. If you skip an ingredient or alter a measurement, the outcome won't meet the standards, and just like an auditor, the inspector may reject your work with a big red NC stamp.

Guidance standards, on the other hand, are like grandma's handwritten notes—helpful tips passed down through experience. You don't have to follow them, but you'd be much better off if you did. They won't disqualify you, but ignoring them could make things more complicated than necessary.

Vocabulary standards serve as your glossary, making sure everyone understands the difference between baking, broiling, and blanching. And sector-specific standards? They're regional spice blends that customize the main dish to local tastes, regulations, and industry quirks.

When in doubt, follow the recipe, heed the notes, consult the glossary, and season it for your sector.

THE ONE THAT PROTECTS THEM ALL

With over 25,000 standards under its scope, ISO influences nearly every part of modern life. However, among them, a few have become mission-critical standards that not only guide how we build things but also how we protect them.

💬 **Author's Note:** If ISO standards were a giant toolbox, ISO 27001 would be the lock on the cabinet that protects all the other tools. In today's digital age, information is wealth, and reputation is everything. Whether you're running a small startup or a nationwide bank, securing your data can make or break your organization. That's where ISO 27001 steps in. It's more than just a technical checklist. It's a structured approach to managing risk, responsibility, and resilience.

In the next chapter, we'll zoom in on this powerful standard:

- where it came from,
- why it matters more now than ever,
- and how it can help your organization build trust in a world full of uncertainty.

🌐 **Website Reference**

Interested in learning more? Visit the official websites of ISO and IEC—they're filled with reliable information, from the history of standards to how international cooperation influences global frameworks. These sites provide detailed insights into their missions, member organizations, and TCs.

🔗 www.iso.org
🔗 www.iec.ch

🧭 **Key Takeaway—What You've Learned**

- ISO is not an acronym—it originates from the Greek word isos, meaning equal, symbolizing global standardization across languages and regions.
- ISO was established in 1947 to promote order and consistency in industrial practices through voluntary, consensus-based standards.
- IEC collaborates with ISO, especially in the domains of information technology.
- ISO standards are created through a formal process involving worldwide experts, national bodies, and stakeholders from industry, academia, and consumer groups.
- ISO standards come in various types:
  - Requirement standards (e.g., ISO 27001) include "shall" statements—they are certifiable, mandatory, and failure to comply can result in a nonconformity.
  - Guidance standards (e.g., ISO 19011) contain "should" statements—helpful but not compulsory, serving as support references rather than for certification.

- Vocabulary standards define common language and interpretations (e.g., ISO/IEC 27000 series), while sector-specific standards adapt ISO concepts to a particular industry.
- ISO standards are reviewed at least every 5 years to stay updated with changing technologies and global needs.
- A global standard like ISO 27001 gains authority from the diverse and inclusive TCs (e.g., ISO/IEC JTC 1 for information security).
- ISO is headquartered in Geneva, Switzerland, and operates worldwide through over 160 national member bodies.

QUIZ #1

⚠ **Caution:** This is your first real quiz in the book, so let's establish the ground rules. No peeking at the answers yet! They're at the back of the book for a reason. Be honest with yourself. These quizzes are not exams, but they are meant to make you stop, think, and reflect. If you rush through or glance at the solutions, you'll miss the opportunity to learn. Use the space in the book if you want, or jot down your answers in a notepad—physical or digital, whichever works best for you. What matters is the habit: pause, apply, and check. If you follow this approach, you'll gain much more than just a certificate; you'll build confidence, clarity, and practical skills. This is the only time we'll include this reminder. From now on, I trust you'll take every quiz seriously—and keep going strong.

True/False statement

Sr.	Statement	True/False
1	ISO is an acronym.	
2	The first ISO standard was published in 1951.	
3	ISO 27001 was released before ISO 9001.	
4	ISO standards are developed only by government regulators.	
5	ISO standards help make trade between countries easier and fairer.	
6	ISO Standards can be adopted as national standards by member countries.	
7	ISO standards are developed through a consensus-based process involving experts from around the world.	
8	One of the goals of standards is to ensure that products and services are safe, reliable, and fit for purpose.	
9	ISO/IEC 27001:2022 is a guideline standard.	
10	An organization can get certified against ISO 19011:2018.	

Chapter 3

Building an ISMS that works

How ISO/IEC 27001 became the framework of choice

WHAT IS INFORMATION SECURITY (REALLY)?

We often assume we know what information security is—passwords, firewalls, locked cabinets. But at its core, information security is about protecting the right information in the right way, so it's accessible to the right people when needed.

According to ISO/IEC 27000, information security is defined as the "preservation of confidentiality, integrity, and availability of information." These three core principles—often called the CIA triad—form the basis of all information security practices. The aim is to keep information protected from unauthorized access, ensure it remains accurate and complete, and make it available when needed by those with proper authorization.

Let's review the three main principles that form the foundation of information security.

Confidentiality

🔒 *If unauthorized people access it, confidentiality is broken.*
As defined in ISO/IEC 27000:

> Confidentiality is the property that information is not made available or disclosed to unauthorized individuals, entities, or processes.

Let's clarify that. Confidentiality is about preventing sensitive information from falling into the wrong hands. Whether it's your organization's financials, customer records, or trade secrets, unauthorized access breaches confidentiality.

📌 **Example:** Think of your email password. If only you knew it, your account is secure. But if someone else gets hold of it—even accidentally—confidentiality is lost. In an organization, this could mean an employee accessing salary data they aren't authorized to see, or an outsider intercepting an unencrypted email containing business contracts.

🌍 **Real-World Insight:** Remember the last time you called your bank's customer service? Before sharing any account details, the agent probably asked you a series of personal questions—your full name, date of birth, maybe the last transaction. It might have felt annoying, but here's what's really happening: the system is verifying that you are the authorized person. That agent isn't just being difficult—they're part of a process meant to protect the privacy of your sensitive financial information. That's confidentiality in action.

DOI: 10.1201/9781003744139-4

⚠ **Caution:** A breach of confidentiality doesn't always originate from a hacker. It can occur through misplaced files, overheard conversations, or even sending an email to the wrong person.

Integrity

⌛ *If the information is tampered with, integrity is compromised.*

As defined in ISO/IEC 27000:

> Integrity is the property of accuracy and completeness.

In simple terms, integrity guarantees that information stays accurate, unaltered, and trustworthy—whether it's stored, in use, or transmitted. It's not just about stopping malicious changes; it's also about safeguarding data from accidental modifications.

📌 **Example:** Consider a financial report in your company. If someone changes a key figure—intentionally or accidentally—without proper authorization or a clear record, the report's integrity is at risk. Even a small decimal mistake can cause serious issues.

🌍 **Real-World Insight:** Now imagine this in a hospital setting. You walk into an emergency room, and the doctor pulls up your electronic medical record. That record shows your blood type, allergy history, current medications, and past surgeries. If any part of that information is wrong or incomplete, the treatment could be dangerous—even fatal. This is why integrity matters so much in healthcare. A corrupted medical file—whether due to a system glitch, a careless edit, or a cyberattack—can have life-threatening consequences. Ensuring the integrity of this information means that every doctor, nurse, or pharmacist can trust that the data they receive is accurate.

⚠ **Caution:** Loss of integrity isn't always caused by foul play. System glitches, weak controls, or even human errors—like copying the wrong file version—can result in inaccurate information being stored or used.

Availability

⌛ *Even secure and accurate data is useless if you can't access it when required.*
As defined in ISO/IEC 27000:

> Availability is the property of being accessible and usable upon demand by an authorized entity.

In simple terms, availability means that authorized users should be able to access the information or systems they need when they need them. It's not enough for data to be secure and accurate; it also must be accessible at the right time to support operations and decision-making.

📌 **Example:** Think about your organization's payroll system. Suppose employees cannot access their pay stubs or HR cannot process payments because the system is down on payday. In that case, it's an availability failure with serious consequences for employee trust and operational efficiency.

🌍 **Real-World Insight:** Let's consider something most of us in India can relate to—filing income tax returns online. Suppose you wait until the last date (as many do), log into the government's official portal ... and it's down. Now, this isn't a data breach. Your records may be secure and intact, but they're not accessible. The system failure means you can't file your taxes on time, which could lead to penalties or legal issues. From an information security perspective, this is a classic availability problem. That's why organizations—and governments—invest heavily in redundant servers, backup internet lines, cloud availability zones, and disaster recovery plans. It's not just about keeping systems operational; it's about making sure you don't lose users' trust when it matters most.

⚠ **Caution:** Availability isn't limited to large IT systems. Even a misplaced key to a physical file cabinet or an expired software license that locks users out can cause availability failures.

💬 **Author's Note:** You can think of these three as the three legs of a tripod. If one leg is weak or missing, your information security collapses. You don't just protect data from hackers—you make sure it remains confidential, accurate, and available at all times.

WHAT IS AN INFORMATION SECURITY MANAGEMENT SYSTEM?

Let's start by grounding ourselves in the official definition of a management system. According to ISO/IEC 27000:

> **Management system**—A set of interrelated or interacting elements of an organization to establish policies, objectives, and processes to achieve those objectives.

That might sound abstract at first, but here's how you can think about it:

A management system is like the engine room of an organization—it's where planning, controls, and feedback loops occur. It guarantees that decisions are consistent, responsibilities are clear, and actions align with organizational goals. Whether managing quality, safety, or security, the system transforms intent into consistent action.

Now, extending that idea:

> **Information Security Management System (ISMS)**—Part of a management system about information security.

In simple terms, an ISMS is the organized framework your organization establishes to safeguard the confidentiality, integrity, and availability of information.

Think of it as a framework that ensures:

- You know what needs protecting
- You understand what could go wrong
- You put appropriate safeguards in place
- You monitor and improve those safeguards over time

An ISMS is more than just a document or a checklist. It's a systematic method for managing how your organization secures its information—digital, physical, or even spoken.

But here's the catch: it's not just about installing firewalls or enforcing strong passwords. Those are tools. An ISMS is about developing a repeatable system where information security becomes a core part of your organization's DNA—from hiring practices to vendor contracts to IT access controls.

💬 **Author's Note:** In my classes, I always emphasize: "It's not you doing the thing—it's the system." It's not about one person handling security well—it's about a system that guarantees the job gets done, even if that person is on vacation. An ISMS is built so that security doesn't depend on any single person, tool, or good day. It creates a repeatable process that ensures:

- If someone is sick or leaves, their responsibilities remain
- If one control fails, others are in place to detect the issue
- Everyone understands what's expected—even the new employee on their first day

You don't create an ISMS for today—you build it so that tomorrow's team can still protect yesterday's data, using processes that make sense today.

A Simple Analogy
Imagine your home is your organization. You've installed locks, alarms, maybe a camera. But more importantly, you've taught your family:

- Keep doors locked when leaving
- Don't share the Wi-Fi password with strangers
- Check who's at the door before opening

Even if you're away, the system holds.

That's the ISMS mindset—your information remains protected not because you remembered everything, but because you've built a system that ensures it.

WHAT MAKES AN ISMS WORK?

At its core, an ISMS is more than just a collection of documents or technical tools. It's a structured, risk-oriented approach to safeguarding your organization's most important information assets—including customer data, internal records, intellectual property, and financial systems.

An ISMS consolidates the policies, procedures, guidelines, resources, and actions necessary to protect information assets. Think of it as the operating system that directs how your organization manages information security—from strategy to everyday operations.

It's not just about reacting to incidents—it's about establishing a system that helps prevent them from happening and respond effectively when they do.

The ISMS functions by:

- Identifying information-related risks
- Assessing the level of risk the organization is willing to accept
- Applying appropriate controls to reduce those risks to acceptable levels

In practice, this involves constantly analyzing what needs protection, selecting the right tools and safeguards, and making sure people understand their roles in the system. It's not a one-time setup—it's a living system that grows with your business.

KEY PRINCIPLES THAT SUPPORT AN EFFECTIVE ISMS

A strong ISMS is built on the following principles. These may not be obvious, but they form the core of a successful implementation:

- Understanding why information security matters at all levels of the organization
- Clearly assigning responsibility for security roles and actions
- Visible leadership support and addressing stakeholder expectations
- Supporting broader societal values like data privacy and ethical conduct
- Using risk assessment to guide control selection
- Incorporating security-by-design into systems and networks from the beginning
- Actively preventing and detecting security incidents, not just responding to them
- Taking a comprehensive, organization-wide approach rather than isolated efforts
- Continually improving by regularly reviewing and refining the ISMS

Author's Note: When organizations overlook these basics, their ISMS becomes merely a document collection instead of a dynamic, evolving system. I always say: *you don't secure your information with a PDF policy—you do it with awareness, action, and accountability.*

Remember:
- ISMS = a living, breathing management system, not a one-time task.
- It's about identifying and managing risks so they don't interfere with your objectives.
- It's designed to sustain security over time, regardless of who is present or what changes occur tomorrow.

WHY ORGANIZATIONS NEED AN ISMS

We live in a world where data is the new oil, and like any valuable asset, it draws attention from all the wrong places. Hackers, fraudsters, insiders, natural disasters, and accidental errors—the list of threats continues to grow, evolve, and become more unpredictable. It's no longer enough to have security tools. What organizations need is a comprehensive system—a structured, flexible way to manage and protect their information across all departments, teams, and time zones.

That's precisely what an ISMS provides. An ISMS isn't just a single document or a firewall setup. It's a comprehensive management framework—policies, procedures, people, tools, and practices—that works together to identify, assess, and manage information-related risks.

Let's take a step back and ask: Why does an organization require this level of structure?

Because information security is no longer just an IT problem, it has become a business issue.

From sensitive employee data to intellectual property, from cloud backups to mobile devices, every part of the business creates and depends on information. And when that information is compromised, the effects go beyond system downtime. It can lead to a loss of trust, lawsuits, regulatory penalties, or lasting damage to your reputation.

Author's Note: Think of your organization as a house. Without an effective system, you might lock the front door—but leave the back gate open, the windows unlatched, and the keys under the doormat. An ISMS helps you systematically examine every entry point, assign responsibilities, and continuously monitor everything.

📌 **Why Else Is an ISMS So Vital?**
An ISMS isn't just about managing threats—it's about creating a structured, reliable, and future-ready approach to information protection. Across industries and sectors, whether public or private, an ISMS adds real value by helping organizations:

- Build trust with employees, customers, partners, and regulators
- Identify, assess, and address security risks proactively and systematically
- Protect critical assets from a wide range of evolving threats
- Ensure consistency and control across global supply chains and interconnected systems
- Enable secure communication, digital transformation, and e-business initiatives
- Demonstrate organizational responsibility and maturity in managing information
- Meet legal, contractual, and regulatory requirements with greater confidence
- Replace scattered, reactive security responses with a strategic, repeatable approach
- Foster a culture where security is integrated into daily operations and decision-making

Most importantly, an ISMS provides peace of mind, helping your organization safeguard its most valuable information not just for today's challenges, but for tomorrow's unknowns.

🌍 **Real-World Insight:** Ever booked a flight online and received your ticket, payment confirmation, and baggage policy—all within seconds? Behind that smooth transaction lies a carefully coordinated system of processes, data, and third-party integrations. Your personal and payment information is securely handled, stored, and exchanged among multiple parties—from the airline to payment gateways and even travel insurance providers. That level of coordination doesn't happen by accident.

It's possible because of structured policies and controls, often governed by an ISMS. Each system understands its role, the risks to monitor, and how to respond if issues arise. That's the key difference: without an ISMS, organizations rely on guesswork and scattered solutions. The result? Gaps in protection, wasted resources, and inconsistent user experiences. With an ISMS, the approach becomes more streamlined, risk-aware, and aligned with business goals, ensuring your data and the trust it represents are managed carefully at every stage.

💬 **Author's Note:** In class, I often remind my students that security isn't just about buying the best tools—it's about knowing what to protect, how to protect it, and how to demonstrate it when asked. That's what an ISMS helps you do. And it's not a one-size-fits-all solution. Your ISMS should be customized to your organization's structure, goals, risk appetite, and stakeholder needs. A multinational bank won't have the same system as a regional hospital, but both need a system. The goal is to create a framework that fits your specific context and can evolve.

HOW ISO 27001 FITS IN

By now, you understand what an ISMS is—a structured way to protect your information, ensure consistency, and manage risk. But here's a critical question:

How Do You Build and Run One?

This is where ISO 27001 comes into play. Think of it as the blueprint—the "how"—for putting your ISMS into action. ISO 27001 is the globally recognized standard that outlines the requirements for establishing, implementing, maintaining, and continually improving an ISMS. It doesn't just tell you to "protect your data"—it provides a clear, structured path to follow, with specific steps, controls, and expectations.

WHY ISO 27001 MATTERS

- ***It Provides Structure:*** ISO 27001 helps you avoid ad-hoc, reactive decisions about security. Instead, it establishes a well-organized system—from identifying risks and assigning responsibilities to selecting controls, all the way to auditing and enhancing the ISMS.
- ***It Encourages Accountability:*** A key strength of the standard is that it clarifies roles and responsibilities. Whether you're the CEO or a helpdesk staff member, you understand your role and what's expected of you when it comes to protecting information.
- ***It Aligns with Global Best Practices:*** Developed by experts worldwide, ISO 27001 isn't just "one way" to do things—it reflects consensus-based knowledge gained from years of real-world experience across industries and regions.
- ***It Builds Credibility and Trust:*** When your organization conforms to ISO 27001, it demonstrates to partners, customers, and regulators that you are committed to safeguarding information. Even if certification isn't your ultimate goal, following the standard improves your internal procedures and risk management.

Many organizations—especially small and medium-sized businesses—believe they can "do security" with just a few tools: an antivirus here, a firewall there, and a password policy written five years ago. But these components don't communicate with each other, and no one's sure who's responsible if something goes wrong.

ISO 27001 replaces this patchwork with a single, unified system. It's like moving from random home remedies to a complete health plan—coordinated, proactive, and adaptable over time.

Tip: According to the ISO Survey of Certifications 2023, over 79,000 sites worldwide have achieved ISO 27001 certification. That's a clear signal—organizations across industries and continents depend on this standard to protect their information assets and demonstrate credibility. If you're building an ISMS, you're in good company. And you're not starting from scratch—ISO 27001 offers a tested and trusted framework that thousands already use.

Website Reference: *ISO Survey of Certifications to Management System Standards (2023): This official ISO page offers comprehensive global statistics on certifications for various ISO standards, including ISO 27001, making it a valuable resource for tracking adoption trends across regions and industries.*

www.iso.org/the-iso-survey.html

Author's Note: Imagine you've decided to build a house—your ISMS is the house. You know you want it to be secure, well-lit, and comfortable. ISO 27001 is the architect's blueprint—it guides you on where to put doors and windows, what materials to use, where to install security cameras, and how to ensure the place is safe and livable in the long run. Without a blueprint, your house might still stand, but it's likely to be inconsistent, inefficient, or even unsafe.

📌 **Remember:**

- ISO 27001 is the standard for establishing an ISMS, not merely a checklist of tools.
- It provides structure, accountability, and global recognition.
- It helps organizations integrate security into their culture, not just their IT department.

BRIEF HISTORY OF ISO 27001

Before ISO 27001 became the leading international standard for information security, it had a long history—and it all began in the UK.

- ***1995—BS 7799 Is Introduced:*** The British Standards Institution (BSI) released BS 7799, the first official standard for information security management. It established best practices and control objectives—an essential step in encouraging organizations to adopt structured information protection.
- ***2000—BS 7799 Becomes ISO/IEC 17799:*** The guidance section of BS 7799 (Part 1) was adopted as an international standard by ISO and IEC and published as ISO/IEC 17799. It laid the groundwork for harmonizing global information security practices.
- ***2005—Introduction of ISO/IEC 27001:2005:*** This was a significant milestone—ISO/IEC 27001:2005 officially replaced BS 7799 Part 2 and introduced the requirement-based framework we recognize today. Organizations can now earn certification to prove compliance with an internationally accepted ISMS.
- ***2013—Update to 27001:2013:*** The 2013 version aligned with the harmonized structure (Annex SL), simplifying the process for organizations to integrate ISO 27001 with other standards, such as ISO 9001 (Quality Management) or ISO 14001 (Environmental Management). It also made the risk assessment approach more flexible and better suited to the organizational context.
- ***2022—Latest Revision:*** The ISO/IEC 27001:2022 update reflects today's changing threat landscape—including remote work, cloud environments, and supply chain risks. It aligns control references with the updated ISO/IEC 27002:2022 and introduces more explicit language, fewer control categories, and greater flexibility in grouping and applying controls.

MEET THE FAMILY: ISO/IEC 27000 SERIES

When we discuss ISO 27001, we are referring to just one part of a much larger group. The ISO/IEC 27000 series is a set of standards all about information security, each serving a different purpose in helping organizations plan, implement, assess, and continually improve their ISMS.

Think of ISO 27001 as the main standard—the foundation. But just like a successful team needs more than a captain, this family includes guidance documents, technical tools, sector-specific advice, and even standards for the people who evaluate your system. Let's get to know the key members of this family—and how they all work together to support your information security journey.

ISO/IEC 27000 [2]—*The Glossary and Guidebook:* This standard introduces the basics. It explains what an ISMS is, offers an overview of the entire family of standards, and defines the terms you'll see throughout the series. Think of it as the glossary that helps everyone speak the same language.

ISO/IEC 27001 [1]—*The Main Framework:* **The centerpiece.** This standard outlines the formal requirements for establishing, implementing, maintaining, and improving an ISMS. If you want certification, this is the standard you need to follow. It guides you in managing risks and applying the proper controls to keep information secure.

ISO/IEC 27002 [4]—*Your Control Handbook:* 27002 expands on Annex A of ISO 27001. It offers detailed guidance on each security control—the why, what, and how. If 27001 is the blueprint, this is your instruction manual.

ISO/IEC 27003 [2]—*Getting Started with ISMS:* Need help starting your ISMS journey? 27003 provides practical guidance to interpret the requirements of 27001 and assists organizations in understanding the implementation process.

ISO/IEC 27004 [3]—*Measuring What Matters:* Security isn't just about implementing controls—it's also about verifying they function correctly. 27004 provides guidance on monitoring, measuring, analyzing, and evaluating the performance of your ISMS.

ISO/IEC 27005 [4]—*Risk Management Guide:* This piece focuses on risk. It provides guidance on managing information security risks, helping organizations determine where to focus their efforts and apply controls most effectively.

ISO/IEC 27006-1[6]—*For Certification Bodies:* Not for your average reader—this standard is intended for organizations that audit and certify others against ISO 27001. It ensures they possess the necessary competence and reliability.

ISO/IEC 27007 [3]—*How to Audit an ISMS:* If your organization is planning to carry out internal ISMS audits, or if you're a consultant assisting others with them, 27007 is your essential guide.

ISO/IEC TS 27008 [7]—*Auditing the Controls:* While 27007 focuses on the system, this document helps you assess the actual implementation of information security controls to ensure they're functioning as intended.

ISO/IEC 27009 [11]—*Sector-Specific Add-Ons:* Different sectors have different needs. 27009 explains how to customize ISO/IEC 27001 for a specific industry without changing its core purpose.

ISO/IEC 27010 [12]—*Secure Information Sharing:* This standard supports organizations that need to share sensitive information across different sectors or between companies, such as critical infrastructure providers or international alliances.

ISO/IEC 27011 [9]—*For Telecom Providers:* Designed for telecom companies, this standard offers additional guidance tailored to their information security requirements.

ISO/IEC 27013 [14]—*Aligning with IT Service Management:* If you're already using ISO/IEC 20000-1 for IT service management, 27013 demonstrates how to incorporate it with your ISMS—saving time and preventing duplication.

ISO/IEC 27014 [15]—*Governance of Information Security:* This document is intended for senior leadership. It offers guidance to boards and top management on assessing, guiding, and overseeing information security efforts.

ISO/IEC TR 27016 [10]—*Information Security Economics:* What's the cost of protecting your information? 27016 helps organizations understand the value of their information assets and how to allocate resources effectively.

ISO/IEC 27017 [11]—*Controls for Cloud Services:* A must-have for cloud service providers and customers. This standard extends 27002 to cover cloud-specific risks and controls.

ISO/IEC 27018 [12]***—Protecting Personal Data in the Cloud:*** Focused on privacy, 27018 offers controls to protect personally identifiable information (PII) processed in public cloud environments.
ISO/IEC 27019 [13]***—For Energy Utilities:*** A sector-specific standard for the energy industry guides safeguarding industrial systems such as smart grids and metering infrastructure.
ISO/IEC 27021 [20]***—Competence for ISMS Professionals:*** Not all security professionals are identical. 27021 outlines the skills and knowledge needed to manage an ISMS effectively, which helps in hiring, training, and certifying professionals.

KNOW THE STANDARDS, USE THEM WELL

The ISO 27000 family isn't just a list of publications—it's your comprehensive toolbox for developing a mature, well-functioning information security program. Each standard adds specific value to your ISMS, from planning and implementation to performance measurement and governance.

While this book is your friendly guide, it's important to remember that ISO 27001 is a copyrighted standard. To build or maintain a compliant ISMS, you'll need to obtain your official copy—either from ISO.org or from your national standards body. This ensures you're working from the most accurate, up-to-date requirements.
Depending on your role, I highly suggest you also explore:

- **ISO/IEC 27000**—A helpful glossary and overview that introduces the ISMS family and aligns your team's terminology.
- **ISO/IEC 27002**—A practical guide to implementing each control listed in ISO 27001 Annex A.
- **ISO/IEC 27004**—For assessing how well your ISMS and controls are performing with relevant metrics.
- **ISO/IEC 27005**—For applying a structured, risk-based approach to decision-making in information security.

Author's Note: I always remind my students that having a dependable toolkit is half the job done. These standards serve as that toolkit. This book will help you understand and apply them, but your true strength lies in referring to the official documents. Start with ISO 27001—and as your system develops, let the other standards support you where necessary. You don't need all of them right away, but knowing what's available helps you make smarter decisions as you grow.

Key Takeaway—What You've Learned

- Information security is based on the CIA triad: Confidentiality, Integrity, and Availability.
- Each principal safeguards different parts of information—who can access it, its accuracy, and whether it is accessible when needed.
- An ISMS is a structured, repeatable system that protects information according to business goals and risks.
- ISMS is not just about tools; it's about people, processes, and governance working together over time.
- ISO 27001 offers the internationally recognized blueprint for creating and maintaining an ISMS.

- ISO 27001 belongs to a broader family—the ISO/IEC 27000 series—which provides more detailed guidance on implementation, risk management, performance measurement, and sector-specific needs.
- To develop or sustain an ISMS that aligns with ISO 27001, it is essential to own the official standard—this book serves as a guide, not a replacement.
- Other necessary standards like ISO/IEC 27000, 27002, 27004, and 27005 support various aspects of your ISMS journey.

QUIZ #2

True/False statement

Sr.	Statement	True/False
1	Confidentiality means preventing unauthorized access to information.	
2	Integrity is only affected by malicious attacks, not by human errors or system faults.	
3	Availability ensures that information is accessible only to IT teams.	
4	An ISMS is a one-time project that focuses mainly on technical controls.	
5	ISO/IEC 27001 provides detailed implementation steps for every security control.	
6	ISO/IEC 27002 is a helpful guide for understanding and implementing the Annex A controls of ISO/IEC 27001.	
7	ISO/IEC 27005 supports organizations in applying a structured approach to information security risk.	
8	ISO/IEC 27004 helps organizations measure the effectiveness of their ISMS controls.	
9	An ISMS is only helpful for large enterprises and not for small organizations.	
10	ISO/IEC 27000 offers definitions and explanations for terms used across the ISMS family.	
11	Loss of confidentiality can occur through careless handling of physical documents.	
12	A firewall alone is enough to meet ISO/IEC 27001 requirements.	
13	ISO/IEC 27001 certification is optional, but following the standard strengthens internal practices.	
14	Information security is only the responsibility of the IT department.	
15	The purpose of an ISMS is to align security controls with organizational risks and business objectives.	

Chapter 4

The backbone of ISO/IEC 27001, structure and strategy

How harmonized structure, process thinking, and risk focus shape the standard

INTRODUCTION: SO FAR, SO GOOD?

If you've reached this chapter, that says a lot.

First, you're still with me—and I'm glad. That means the journey hasn't scared you off yet. Second, you're probably starting to understand what ISO 27001 is really about: not just a certification badge, but an innovative, strategic approach to managing information risks in the real world.

We've discussed the origins of ISO. We've explained what an ISMS is. Hopefully, we've removed some of the confusion about what ISO 27001 requires from you.

Now, let's dive a little deeper.

Before we examine the individual clauses (don't worry, we'll address them one at a time later in this book), we need to understand the framework—the foundational structure that gives ISO 27001 its shape. This structure isn't random, and it's not unique to this standard either. It's part of something larger—a shared framework that links multiple ISO standards and allows organizations to align their management systems under one umbrella.

In this chapter, we'll examine that structure, now officially named the Harmonized Approach (though many still call it Annex SL). We'll also introduce two powerful concepts that run throughout the entire standard: process-based thinking and risk-based thinking.

Think of this chapter as laying the foundation before building each room of your ISMS house. Ready? Let's start with a simple question: Why did ISO bother providing a common structure in the first place?

WHY STRUCTURE MATTERS IN STANDARDS

You might wonder, why do standards even need a structure? Can't they just give us a list of things to do?

Here's the thing—ISO standards aren't just checklists. They're management systems. And that means they emphasize how an organization organizes itself to reach goals and manage risks, not simply on ticking boxes.

Imagine a library with no sections, no labels, just thousands of books piled up randomly. You might eventually find what you're looking for, but chances are you'll give up halfway through. Now imagine a library that's organized—fiction, non-fiction, science, history—with a clear index that helps you locate what you need in minutes.

That's the idea behind ISO's harmonized structure. It offers a consistent, logical framework so every ISO management system standard feels familiar, and implementation becomes easier, especially when you're working across different fields.

DOI: 10.1201/9781003744139-5

The harmonized approach was first introduced through Annex SL in 2012. It's outlined in the ISO/IEC Directives, Part 1, which is reviewed and updated every year. Annex SL itself was revised in 2021 to strengthen this unified framework. Honestly, it's been a game-changer. Whether you're implementing or auditing a system, this change has made things much easier.

Instead of managing separate structures for each standard, you can now create a single Integrated Management System (IMS). No more handling three different policies—one for quality, one for environment, and one for information security. You can have a unified, well-aligned policy that covers all of them—no more guessing which standard has how many clauses or switching between different formats. Now, they all follow the same flow and logic.

The harmonized approach includes:

- A high-level structure that applies across all ISO management system standards
- Consistent clause and subclause titles that form the backbone of each standard
- Core text that is common to all standards
- Shared terms and definitions (unless a standard has a valid technical reason to deviate)

THE HARMONIZED CLAUSE STRUCTURE

Here's what the harmonized structure looks like. These ten core sections generally appear in the same order across most ISO management system standards:

1. Scope
2. Normative References
3. Terms and Definitions
4. Context of the Organization
5. Leadership
6. Planning
7. Support
8. Operation
9. Performance Evaluation
10. Improvement

Each standard, including ISO 27001, then establishes specific requirements within this framework.

Why is this useful?

- It helps organizations unify multiple standards, such as ISO 9001 (quality), ISO 14001 (environment), or ISO 45001[24] (occupational health and safety).
- It reduces duplicated effort—you don't have to reinvent the wheel for each standard.
- It enhances clarity—once you understand the structure, it becomes easier to navigate any ISO standard.

So, this structure isn't just there for ISO's convenience—it's meant to make your job easier. Especially if you're trying to combine or streamline your systems, this harmonized structure helps you work smarter, not harder.

A LITTLE SECRET ABOUT ALL ISO STANDARDS

Let me share something with you that I usually keep for the classroom—my ISO "trade secret," as my students like to call it.

If you learn ISO 27001 thoroughly—if you go through this book, complete the activities, and understand how the clauses connect and what they require from you—you're already halfway to mastering any other ISO management system standard.

Why? Because ISO standards that follow the harmonized approach are based on the exact blueprint.

Think of it as a template.

Once you understand how the template functions, you can easily grasp almost any ISO standard—ISO 9001 for quality, ISO 14001 for environment, ISO 22301 [24] for business continuity—and it will feel familiar. The structure, clause numbering, and terminology all follow the same logic. It's like learning one language and realizing many others share the same roots.

Here's how I explain it to my students.

Suppose you want to learn ISO 22301, the standard for business continuity. After mastering ISO 27001 from this book, refer to Clause 8: Operation in ISO 22301. What you do under Clause 8 will differ—naturally—because business continuity and information security are not the same. However, the structure? The logic? The flow? Remain almost identical.

Here's a quick example:

From ISO 27001 (Clause 7.3):

> Persons doing work under the organization's control shall be aware of: a) the information security policy...

From ISO 22301 (Clause 7.3):

> Persons doing work under the organization's control shall be aware of: a) the business continuity policy...

See what happened there? Only one phrase changed—from "information security" to "business continuity." The rest is identical.

That's the strength of the harmonized approach. It creates consistency. It minimizes confusion. It boosts confidence.

Here's a simple task for you—and I do this in my workshops too. Once you're comfortable with ISO 27001, pick another ISO standard you like. Flip through it. You'll see the same structure: Clause 4, Clause 5, all the way to Clause 10. Then choose any clause—say, Clause 4 (Context of the Organization)—and compare it to what we discussed here. You'll begin to notice the pattern. And once you recognize the pattern, you'll know how to develop the rest.

This realization—that the standards aren't as different as they seem once you understand the template—is often a turning point for learners. I love seeing their expressions when it clicks. That "aha" moment. That smile of clarity.

Here's the real bonus: by working through ISO 27001 in this book, you're not just learning one standard—you're understanding how ISO standards work. That opens the door to quality, environment, health & safety, privacy, artificial intelligence, business continuity—and more—with just a bit of domain-specific learning.

📌 **Remember:** You're not just learning a document; you're learning a language. And once you're fluent, you can speak ISO in any situation.

WHY CLAUSES 4–10 MATTER SO MUCH

📌 **The Non-Negotiables of ISO 27001**

Let me share another moment I always include in my training sessions—and it usually raises a few eyebrows. I ask the class to open the ISO 27001 standard and read a specific section. Not in the middle. Not at the end. Right at the beginning, in Clause 1.

Here's what it says:

> Excluding any of the requirements specified in Clauses 4 to 10 is not acceptable when an organization claims conformity to this document.

Now, take a second and let that sink in.

You can't skip any part of it. You can't cherry-pick the sections that seem effortless. You can't say, "Let's just focus on the Annex A controls and leave the rest for later." Because ISO is clear—if you're claiming compliance with ISO 27001, then Clauses 4–10 are mandatory.

SO, WHY ARE THESE CLAUSES SO IMPORTANT?

Here's something most people don't realize at first:

The well-known Annex A—the 93 controls—isn't the main course. It's the side dish. Clauses 4–10? That's your main course.

They're the foundation of your ISMS. They're where your management system resides. The controls in Annex A support it, but they don't replace it.

Let's examine what these clauses do:

- Clause 4 guides you to understand your environment—who your stakeholders are, what they expect, and what issues might affect your ISMS.
- Clause 5 requires leadership commitment—not just in words, but through actions.
- Clause 6 involves planning—risks, goals, and actions.
- Clause 7 provides the tools—resources, competence, and communication.
- Clause 8 puts your plans into action.
- Clause 9 directs you to assess what's working and what isn't.
- Clause 10 completes the cycle—improve it all and repeat.

This is your ISMS engine. If you skip even one clause, the system won't operate.

YOU CAN'T PICK AND CHOOSE

In class, I often compare this to putting a car together.

Let's say you're following instructions to build it. The guide says: install the engine, attach four wheels, add brakes, connect the steering, wire up the lights, and so on.

Now, imagine someone says, "We'll skip the brakes. The rest is enough to make it move."

Sure, it'll move. But would you drive it?

Without all the essential parts, you don't have a safe, working car—you have a disaster waiting to happen.

That's precisely what happens when organizations overlook or neglect parts of Clauses 4–10 in ISO 27001. You might think you've created an ISMS, but if you leave out context, risk assessment, or internal audits, then it's not complete. And if it's incomplete, it's not compliant—and certainly not resilient.

That's why the standard is evident in Clause 1. You don't get to choose your favorite parts of ISO 27001. You either build the entire system or you're not building one at all.

Same here.

Without Clause 4, you miss your context.

Without Clause 5, you lack buy-in.

Without Clause 6, you're not managing risk.

And without Clause 9, how do you know what's working?

That's why ISO says you must include all of them. Because together, they form the system.

🌍 **Real-World Insight:** I've seen organizations that dedicate all their effort to Annex A. They have excellent documentation and beautiful controls. But when the auditor asked, "How did you determine your scope?" or "Where are your objectives and monitoring data?"—they had no clear answers. The result? Non-conformity. Not because they lacked controls, but because they ignored the framework that makes those controls meaningful.

📌 **Remember:** If Annex A is what you do to protect information, then Clauses 4–10 explain why, how, when, and who. You need both. But without Clauses 4–10, you don't have a management system—just a checklist.

NOT ALL CLAUSES ARE CREATED EQUAL

Now that we've discussed the overall structure of the standard, here's something important I always emphasize when teaching ISO 27001—especially to those preparing for audits or trying to map their documentation.

Clauses 1–3 are not requirement clauses. Yes, they're there. Yes, they're essential. But no—they are *not auditable*. You won't be asked to "show evidence" of these in your ISMS implementation.

Let's take a quick look:

Clause 1: Scope

This explains what the standard covers—establishing, implementing, maintaining, and continually improving an ISMS. It reminds us that the standard applies to any organization. Most importantly, it states that you cannot exclude any of the requirements from Clauses 4–10 if you want to claim conformance.

> It also states that the standard isn't only for tech giants or multinational banks. It's for any organization—big or small, public or private, startup or legacy enterprise. The standard clearly states that its requirements are general and apply to all organizations, regardless of type, size, or sector. That means it can be just as relevant for a small neighbourhood coffee shop that runs a customer loyalty program and wants to protect personal data, as it is for a global airline managing millions of passengers' records across continents. The beauty of ISO 27001 is its flexibility. Whether you're managing a few spreadsheets or an

extensive cloud infrastructure, this standard provides a framework that can grow with your needs.

Clause 2: Normative References

Let's keep this simple—Clause 2 acts like a signpost, meaning the documents listed here aren't just optional. They are crucial for properly understanding and applying the standard. If a document is included in this clause, it's considered part of the standard by reference. You're expected to use it. It tells you, "If you're going to work with this standard, there's something else you need to read too."

In ISO/IEC 27001, clause two lists one reference:

ISO/IEC 27000, the official vocabulary and foundational guide for the entire ISO 27000 family.

Author's Note: Other ISO standards might list several normative documents here. ISO 27001 keeps it minimal—just one document, but an important one.

Remember: Clause 2 doesn't include any specific requirements. It's not something you directly implement or are audited on. However, it plays an important background role by guiding you to the supporting document that helps interpret everything else in the standard.

Clause 3: Terms and Definitions

Let's be honest—sometimes standards seem like they're in a language all their own. That's exactly why Clause 3 exists.

The main goal of this clause is to make sure everyone understands the same terminology. Whether you're implementing ISO 27001, undergoing an audit, or just reading this book, words should mean the same to all involved—no guessing, no confusion. Essentially, Clause 3 serves as your reference for definitions.

But here's the interesting part: ISO 27001 does not list all the definitions directly. Instead, it simply refers you to another document—ISO/IEC 27000—which contains the official vocabulary and foundational concepts used throughout the ISO 27000 family of standards.

Why Does This Matter?

Well, if you misinterpret a term like "risk owner," "organization," or "information security event," you could incorrectly apply a requirement or overlook its true intent. That's risky, and not just from a security standpoint—it can also cause issues during audits.

Here's what Clause 3 helps you achieve:

- **Establish a Common Language:** Everyone—implementers, auditors, and stakeholders—uses the same definitions, reducing misinterpretations.
- **Promote Consistency Across the Board:** Whether you're a coffee shop or a multinational bank, the term "information asset" means the same thing. That's the power of standardization.
- **Support Accurate Implementation:** When you understand the exact meaning of a term, you're far more likely to apply the requirement correctly.
- **Improve Communication:** Clear terms lead to clearer collaboration between departments, teams, and external parties like auditors or consultants.
- **Help with Documentation:** Your policies, procedures, and even training materials become more coherent when they use ISO-aligned language.

Don't worry, we'll go over the most important terms and definitions in the next chapter, explaining them in simple language so you can feel more confident before moving forward.

💬 **Author's Note:** I've often seen organizations redefine terms or interpret them in their own way. This causes confusion, implementation gaps, and misalignment during audits. Clause 3 (and ISO/IEC 27000) is your best guide here; refer to it.

📌 **Remember:** Clauses 1–3 are not about requirements. You won't be audited on them directly, but you'll rely on them throughout your ISMS journey. Auditable requirements start with Clause 4 and go through Clause 10. That's where the real work takes place—and what your ISMS will be evaluated on during an external audit.

PROCESS-BASED THINKING: SEEING THE BIGGER PICTURE

If you've made it this far, you now realize something that many people overlook—ISO standards aren't random rules, and they're not just paperwork. They are structured, logical, and designed around how organizations operate.

And this leads us to one of the key concepts behind ISO 27001—process-based thinking.

So, let's create a bridge from what we just talked about.

Now that you understand standards follow a common structure, the next big question is: how are you supposed to operate within it? And the answer is: through processes.

Not departments. Not job titles. Not isolated tasks. Instead, processes represent the actual flow of work.

Let me explain.

Imagine your organization as an orchestra. Different players—IT, HR, compliance, operations—each have their instruments. But what creates the music isn't just individual performances; it's how they play together, in rhythm, with a shared goal and good coordination. That flow, that coordination—that's your process.

Too often, we think in silos:

"This is IT's job."

"That's HR's issue."

"Only compliance needs to worry about that."

But an ISO standard doesn't view it that way. ISO focuses on interactions. It asks:

- Where does the process start?
- What activities are involved?
- Who owns what?
- What inputs go in?
- What outputs come out?
- How do we check if it worked?

Let's say you're onboarding a new employee. Is that solely HR's responsibility? Not really.

- HR does the hiring and paperwork.
- IT sets up email and access.
- Security ensures policies are signed.
- Compliance checks if training is done.

That's not just a checklist—it's a process. For your ISMS to succeed, you need to think this way. Across different functions. Across various roles. From start to finish.

WHY DOES THIS MATTER FOR ISO 27001?

Because every control you implement—every security measure, every policy, every audit—must be part of a process. Otherwise, it's just a document floating in space.

When you adopt process-based thinking, three powerful outcomes occur:

1. **Clarity:** You see how things flow, where they break, and who's responsible.
2. **Control:** You can measure and improve performance instead of just reacting to issues.
3. **Compliance:** You don't just meet ISO requirements—you embed them into daily business operations.

💬 **Author's Note:** I've seen organizations fail audits not because they lacked policies, but because they couldn't demonstrate how those policies are integrated into actual processes. The ISO auditor would ask, "When someone leaves the company, how do you revoke access?" and no one had a clear, process-based answer. That's what ISO cares about—not just what you do, but how you do it, reliably and consistently.

So, as we continue, try to shift your mindset:

- Not just "What do we do?"
- But "How do we do it—step by step—and who's involved?"

Process thinking helps you create systems that don't break down when someone's sick or leaves the company. Systems that function because the process is effective.

PDCA AND THE PROCESS APPROACH: THE ENGINE BEHIND THE ISMS

If you're like most of my students, by now you're probably wondering: "Is there some kind of method to this madness?"

Yes. There is. And this is where it all comes together.

Let me introduce you to something simple—but incredibly powerful. It's called the PDCA cycle—short for Plan, Do, Check, Act. You might not see this phrase printed prominently in the ISO 27001 standard, but it's there in spirit. Instead of PDCA, the standard discusses:

Establish, Implement, Maintain, and *Continually Improve.*

But trust me, it's the same dance. Just a different tune.

A QUICK TRIP BACK IN TIME: MEET MR. DEMING

The PDCA model was popularized by W. Edwards Deming, the man who almost completely reshaped quality management in post-war Japan. He didn't invent the cycle from scratch, but he refined it and made it well-known.

The core idea?

If you want to do something better—whether it's running a company or baking a cake—you don't just wing it. You Plan, you Do, you Check what worked and what didn't, and then you Act to improve it.

Rinse. Repeat. That's PDCA.

PDCA IN ISO 27001: THE HIDDEN MAP

So even if ISO doesn't highlight it very loudly, the entire ISO 27001 standard is quietly following this exact cycle. If you look at Table 4.1, mapping the PDCA cycle to ISO 27001 clauses, you'll see how each phase of PDCA aligns neatly with ISO's own language and clauses.

Table 4.1 Mapping the PDCA cycle to ISO 27001 clauses

PDCA Phase	ISO 27001 Language	Key Clauses That Support It
PLAN	**Establish** your ISMS based on risks, context, and needs	Clause 4 (Context) Clause 5 (Leadership) Clause 6 (Planning) Clause 7 (Support)
DO	**Implement** what you planned—risk treatment, controls, resources	Clause 8 (Operation)
CHECK	**Maintain** your system by measuring, auditing, and reviewing.	Clause 9 (Performance Evaluation)
ACT	**Continually improve** based on audit results and reviews	Clause 10 (Improvement)

Author's Note: Even though the standard is written in clauses, don't fall into the trap of thinking they're meant to be followed in order. The ISMS isn't a recipe—it's a system. All parts are working all the time. You plan and do, but you also check and continually improve.

PDCA + PROCESS THINKING = YOUR ISMS IN ACTION

Now that you know what PDCA is and how your ISMS is built around it, here's the big win:

This approach helps you:

- Understand what your ISMS is doing and why
- Manage interrelated activities as a whole
- Focus on performance and not just paperwork
- Drive continual improvement—not just box-ticking

And here's something worth remembering: Your ISMS isn't just a document. It's a living system composed of people, processes, and decisions.

Whether you're writing a policy or setting up an awareness session, you're part of the PDCA cycle—always making progress.

Up next, let's discuss something that connects all this—Risk-Based Thinking. Because if there's one thing ISO 27001 is designed to help you manage, it's risk.

RISK-BASED THINKING: THE REAL REASON ISO 27001 EXISTS

Let's be honest—ISO 27001 wouldn't exist without risks.

If information was never lost, leaked, stolen, or corrupted—if people never made mistakes and attackers never became more clever—we wouldn't need an ISMS at all.

But the truth is, risk is everywhere. And ISO 27001 is completely built around managing that risk.

Everything you read in the standard—from setting objectives to defining policies, from selecting controls to conducting audits—is viewed through the lens of risk.

- Why do we assess threats and vulnerabilities?
- Why do we select controls from Annex A?
- Why do we document incidents or run internal audits?

Because of risk.

💬 **Author's Note:** I always tell my students—ISO 27001 isn't a to-do list; it's a flashlight. That flashlight represents risk. You shine it across your organization and ask, "Where could things go wrong?" Then, you direct your focus onto the areas where the light uncovers danger.

FOLLOW THE RISK, NOT THE ROUTINE

Here's something interesting: please review Clause 9.2.2 on Internal Audit Programs. It states:

> When establishing the internal audit programme(s), the organization shall consider the importance of the processes concerned and the results of previous audits.

Consider what that implies. You're not meant to audit everything equally. If a process is crucial—like your user access management or your cloud service setup—it warrants more frequent and thorough audits. If something failed badly last time—perhaps your backup recovery test didn't go well—that area should be reviewed again sooner.

Why? Because these are *risk hotspots*.

⚠ **Caution:** You're not just auditing to fill a calendar. You're auditing to locate where the risk is. This is ISO's way of saying: Don't waste time checking boxes. Focus on what matters most.

SO, WHAT IS RISK-BASED THINKING?

Let's keep it simple. Risk-based thinking means:

- You identify where things could go wrong (risks)
- You understand what's at stake (impacts)
- You take action to address it (controls)
- You verify that what you did actually worked (monitoring)

Let's take a daily life example:

You're going on a road trip.

- You check the weather: risk of rain.

- You check your tires: risk of puncture.
- You plan your route to avoid risky areas.
- You keep a spare tire, just in case.

That's not paranoia. That's *risk-based thinking*—and you're already doing it in life. ISO wants you to bring that mindset into your organization.

RISK IS NOT JUST A SECTION—IT'S THE THEME

You'll find this theme *everywhere* in ISO 27001:

- Clause 4: Identify external and internal issues (aka risks)
- Clause 6: Plan risk assessment and treatment
- Clause 8: Implement controls based on those risks
- Clause 9: Monitor where the risk could increase (through incidents, poor audits, or missed Key Performance Indicators (KPIs)).

💬 **Author's Note:** ISO encourages you to consider risk daily, not just annually. Whether you're storing files or assigning admin rights, the key question is: "What could go wrong here, and what are we doing about it?"

Risk-based thinking is what keeps ISO 27001 adaptable. It means you don't protect everything equally. You prioritize. You adapt. You focus on what matters.

That's not just smart information security—that's visionary leadership.

📌 **Remember:** This chapter isn't just about structure. It's about seeing the big picture. You're not memorizing clauses—you're learning how to think like ISO. You're developing the ability to view your organization the way an ISO standard does, and once you do, everything else begins to fall into place.

🧭 **Key Takeaway—What You've Learned**

- ISO 27001 is not just a checklist—it's a management system based on logic, structure, and strategy.
- The harmonized approach (formerly called Annex SL) provides all modern ISO standards with a shared structure, making them easier to learn, implement, and integrate.
- Once you understand this structure, you've already opened the door to mastering other ISO standards—you need to learn the subject-specific parts.
- The PDCA cycle (Plan-Do-Check-Act) is the driving force behind ISO 27001. Everything in your ISMS is connected to this continual improvement cycle.
- Process-based thinking helps you manage work as a flow instead of isolated departments. It strengthens resilience and clarity.
- Risk-based thinking is at the core of ISO 27001. Every decision, control, or audit activity exists because of risk, not routine.
- Clauses 4–10 contain the actual requirements. Those are what get audited. You must include all of them to claim compliance.
- Clauses 1–3 are not auditable—but they are still vital. They define scope, references, and terms to ensure you understand what you're doing.

QUIZ #3

True/False statement

Sr.	Statement	True/False
1	Process-based thinking focuses on how different departments perform their individual tasks.	
2	Risk-based thinking should only be applied during the initial risk assessment phase of an ISMS.	
3	ISO/IEC 27001 allows organizations to skip Clauses 4–10 if they feel those clauses are not relevant.	
4	One benefit of the harmonized approach is that it helps in building IMS.	
5	Understanding ISO/IEC 27001 deeply can help you learn other ISO standards more easily.	

Chapter 5

Terms you'll hear again and again

Clarifying the core terms that shape an effective ISMS

Before we get further into implementing an ISMS, it's important to pause and understand the language used in ISO/IEC 27001:2022.

Terms and definitions in ISO standards are more than just formalities; they are vital in creating a common language. This ensures that everyone, regardless of organization size or industry, interprets and applies the requirements uniformly. By reducing ambiguity, this shared vocabulary enhances communication, simplifies decision-making, and boosts the overall effectiveness of your management system.

In this chapter, we'll review the key terms you'll often encounter. For each one, I'll start by quoting the official ISO definition and then explain what it means in plain language, just like I would in a classroom or workshop. When relevant, I'll include real-world context or quick examples to help make the concept clearer.

Think of this chapter as setting the foundation. Once we clarify these basic terms, the rest of the standard will become much clearer.

ISO/IEC 27000: THE VOCABULARY STANDARD

As we discussed in the last chapter, if you can obtain a copy of ISO/IEC 27000, I strongly recommend it. This document accomplishes two important things:

1. It gives you a broad overview of what an *ISMS* is, and
2. It defines the key terms that show up repeatedly across the ISO/IEC 27000 family of standards.

Having a standard vocabulary isn't just about tidiness—it's about ensuring everyone speaks the same language, whether you're a consultant, an auditor, or part of an internal team. When terms like "risk," "control," or "audit" come up, you want everyone to understand them consistently. That's what this document helps accomplish.

Now, a quick clarification: ISO/IEC 27000 covers commonly used terms, but not every term you'll encounter. It doesn't restrict the rest of the 27000-series from defining new terms as needed. And yes, it's designed to be relevant for organizations of all types and sizes—from tech startups and hospitals to banks and government agencies.

Think of ISO/IEC 27000 as your ISMS terminology guide—not exhaustive, but vital for clarity and consistency.

DOI: 10.1201/9781003744139-6

CORE ISMS TERMS YOU'LL ENCOUNTER OFTEN

ISO/IEC 27000, the vocabulary standard for ISMS, defines over 75 terms. But don't worry, we're not going through all of them here. That would only slow us down and probably overwhelm you.

Instead, I've selected the terms that truly matter at this stage—especially those related to the management system side. These terms will help you understand how ISO 27001 works in practice and navigate the standard with clarity and confidence. You'll notice that we're not diving deep into IT-specific jargon or highly technical terms—and that's intentional. If you're looking for detailed explanations of firewall rules or encryption algorithms, there are excellent technical books available.

Here, our focus remains firmly on the non-technical, management-system–oriented terms—the ones you'll encounter repeatedly as you establish, implement, or maintain an ISMS.

Author's Note: This section is organized differently from the ISO standard. I've arranged the terms in a way that flows naturally, especially for those learning this for the first time. Each term includes plain-language explanations, relatable contexts, and, when helpful, practical examples.

Let's get started—one term at a time.

Organization

The very first term you will encounter in Clause 4 is "Organization."

Here's the official definition from ISO/IEC 27000:

> *A person or group of people that has its own functions with responsibilities, authorities, and relationships to achieve its objectives.*

Now, let's break that down. In simple terms, an "organization" isn't just a company in the traditional sense. It could be a sole proprietor, a government agency, a university, a partnership, a nonprofit, a department within a larger entity, or even a combination of these. The definition is intentionally broad to include all types and sizes of entities.

Tip: Don't assume the term "organization" always refers to the entire company.

For example, if only the IT department of a multinational company is implementing ISO 27001, then the IT department itself is considered the "organization" for the ISMS, not the entire corporation.

It all depends on the scope, which we will examine in greater detail later.

Top Management

Next, we have "Top Management"—a term you'll see frequently throughout the standard.

According to ISO/IEC 27000, it is defined as:

> *Person or group of people who directs and controls an organization at the highest level.*

Now, let's explore that a little more.

Top management isn't always the CEO; it depends on the scope of your ISMS. If your ISMS only covers part of the organization—such as just the IT department—then top management refers to the person or group who leads and controls that segment. For example, in this case, the IT Director may be considered top management.

❢ **Tip:** Top management refers to the individuals ultimately responsible for decision-making, setting the direction, allocating resources, and supporting the ISMS—within the defined scope.

📌 **Remember:** Top management is sometimes called executive management, which can include roles like CEO, CFO, CIO, or similar positions. In other organizations, especially those with more collaborative governance, it might refer to a management team, an ISMS steering committee, or a dedicated security leadership group.

Documented information

This one is important and often misunderstood.
The ISO/IEC 27000 standard describes documented information as:

> *Information required to be controlled and maintained by an organization and the medium on which it is contained.*

Let's analyze that.

> *Documented information isn't just about printed files stored in a cabinet. It can be anything—paper, digital, audio, video, or handwritten notes—as long as it needs to be controlled and maintained. In other words, it's not about how it's stored; it's about what it represents and why it matters to your ISMS.*

❢ **Tip:** An organization can choose to go completely paperless or continue using traditional physical files. Both options are valid. Just remember—the ISMS protects information, not just digital assets.

📌 **Remember:** That dusty file in a steel locker with a coffee stain might still be valid documented information!

Now, here's where it gets more interesting. "Documented information" is a broad term. It encompasses two main categories:

- ***Documents***, and
- ***Records***

Let's simplify:

Documents = *Living information*

These can be reviewed, updated, or modified. Think of your ISMS Policy—version 1.0 in January 2025, then updated to version 2.0 six months later. That's a document. Whenever

ISO uses the phrase "maintain documented information," they mean documents—policies, procedures, plans, etc.

Records = *Fixed evidence*

These show what has happened—evidence of actions taken or results achieved. You don't update records. You keep them exactly as they are. Think birth certificates, audit logs, training attendance sheets, or access control logs. If you try to change these, you're not updating—you're falsifying.

📌 **Remember:** Whenever the ISO standard states, "retain the documented information," it refers to records. The keyword here is retain, meaning you must preserve that log, certificate, or result exactly as it was created, serving as evidence of your operations or work done.

⚠ **Caution:** Mixing up documents and records can cause audit problems. Always ask yourself:

> *Is this something I can change later (document)? Or is this something I need to keep safe as proof (record)?*

Internal Context

According to ISO, *internal context* is defined as:

> *Internal environment in which the organization seeks to achieve its objectives.*

Think of internal context as everything happening within your organization that can influence how your ISMS is planned, implemented, and improved. It's not just about the systems you use—it's about how your people work together, how decisions are made, what values you share, and how roles and responsibilities are organized.
Internal context can include:

- Governance, organizational structure, roles, and accountabilities
- Policies, objectives, and the strategies to meet them
- Capabilities in terms of time, people, resources, and technologies
- Information systems, communication flows, and how decisions are made (formally and informally)
- Perceptions, relationships, and values of internal stakeholders
- Organizational culture and behavior
- Adopted standards, guidelines, or models (e.g., COBIT, ITIL, and Agile)
- Internal contracts or agreements (e.g., service-level agreements between departments)

📌 **Remember:** We'll revisit this topic in more detail when we get to Clause 4.1 later in the book. By then, you'll learn how to identify and document your organization's internal context as part of your ISMS foundation.

External Context

The ISO definition of external context is as follows:

> *External environment in which the organization seeks to achieve its objectives.*

If internal context is what you can control and shape, external context is what you need to understand—even if you cannot influence it. It's the environment outside your boundaries: the conditions, expectations, and influences you must navigate to meet your information security goals.

External context can include:

- Cultural, social, political, legal, regulatory, financial, technological, economic, natural, and competitive conditions—whether local, national, or global
- Key drivers and trends that affect your organization's objectives (like climate change, digital transformation, or shifts in market demand)
- Relationships with, and expectations, perceptions, and values of, ***external stakeholders*** (e.g., customers, regulators, suppliers, and industry groups)

📌 **Remember:** You cannot control your external context, but your ISMS must take it into account. This helps you create a system that's resilient, relevant, and realistic. We'll explore how to analyze this in Clause 4.1 properly.

🌍 **Real-World Insight:** For example, a change in data privacy laws, such as the General Data Protection Regulation (GDPR) in Europe, is part of your external context—and it could significantly impact your ISMS planning, even if you operate from a country outside Europe.

Interested Party

According to ISO, an *interested party* is defined as:

> *"A person or organization that can affect, be affected by, or perceive itself to be affected by a decision or activity."*

In simple terms, this means anyone—individual, group, or organization—who has a stake in what you're doing. That might be because ISMS directly impacts them, or because they believe it could. Either way, they are essential.

📌 **Remember:** In ISO 27001, *interested party* and *stakeholder* mean the same thing.

Interested parties can include both internal groups (such as employees, top management, and other departments) and external groups (such as regulators, customers, suppliers, and the public).

We'll explore more about identifying relevant interested parties and understanding their expectations later in the book, specifically in Clause 4.2. But for now, keep this in mind: if someone believes they are affected by your ISMS or your operations, they are considered an interested party.

Author's Note: In practice, managing relationships with interested parties is a crucial aspect of operating a successful ISMS. Their needs and expectations can influence your policies, objectives, and even your response to incidents.

Management System

According to ISO, a *management system* is:

> *A set of interrelated or interacting elements of an organization to establish policies and objectives and processes to achieve those objectives.*

Let's analyze that.

A system is a group of interconnected parts that function together. So, when we refer to a management system, we mean a coordinated approach to guiding how an organization sets goals, plans to achieve them, and tracks progress—all through clearly defined roles, responsibilities, structures, and processes.

Tip: Think of a management system as the engine room of your organization—it keeps everything running smoothly, goals clear, and everyone aware of their roles and responsibilities.

Now, if you're managing only one discipline, such as information security, the system you'll create is called an ISMS—the very thing ISO 27001 focuses on.

However, if you are addressing multiple disciplines together, such as information security, environment, and quality, you may implement an Integrated Management System (IMS).
A typical management system may include:

- Your organization's structure
- Roles and responsibilities
- Strategic and operational planning
- Documentation and controls

Remember: The scope of your management system can differ. It might include:

- The entire organization
- A specific function, such as the IT services function
- A particular department, like the IT Department

We'll define the scope of your ISMS in Clause 4.3, but for now, understand that a management system is your organization's organized way to reach its goals—with purpose, discipline, and traceability.

Process

According to ISO, a ***process*** is: "*A set of interrelated or interacting activities that use inputs to deliver an intended result.*"

We've already covered ISO 27001's process-based approach, so this concept is key. A process is simply a series of activities working together to take in something (an input) and turn it into something useful (an output). That proper result might be called an output, a product, or a service—depending on the situation.

Inputs typically come from the output of other processes, and the output of one process may feed directly into another, creating a chain of value. When multiple processes are linked this way, ISO may even refer to them as a single process in context.

An organization may have well-established processes that employees consistently follow, even if they are not formally documented. If these processes can be *explained to auditors* and demonstrated in practice, they are considered valid.

The same principle applies to *procedures*, which ISO defines as the *"specified way to carry out an activity or a process."* In simple terms, a procedure is a step-by-step way of completing a task. Again, while documentation is proper and often suggested, it isn't always required unless specifically mentioned by the standard.

In the next chapter, we will examine which documents are required under ISO standards and how organizations can identify what needs to be formally documented or recorded.

Risk

According to ISO, ***risk*** is defined as: *"Effect of uncertainty on objectives."*

Let's break that down—because it's a deceptively short definition.

The effect refers to any deviation from what's expected—and that can be either positive or negative. Risk is typically described in terms of potential events and their outcomes (or both).

In the context of an *ISMS*, we focus on *information security risks*, which typically involve threats exploiting vulnerabilities in information assets and potentially causing harm to the organization. But that's not all.

Think of risk as what happens when things don't go exactly as planned—that deviation could be positive (opportunity) or negative (threat). In an ISMS, we're focused not only on reducing the negative—such as breaches or service failures—but also on spotting opportunities to improve our processes, strengthen controls, or better support business goals. ISO 27001 explicitly asks us to identify the risks and opportunities that need attention. Why? Because both can affect the achievement of information security objectives, either by disrupting them or by helping us reach them more effectively.

We'll explore risk, the risk assessment process, and risk treatment in more detail later when we dive into Clause 6.1.

For more details on systematically managing risk, see ISO 31000 [5], the international standard for risk management.

Let's talk about two often-confused terms: **Correction** and **Corrective action.**
According to the ISO standard:

- **Correction** is *"action to eliminate a detected nonconformity."*
- **Corrective action** is *"action to eliminate the cause of a nonconformity and to prevent recurrence."*

Sounds similar? It's not. I'll make this more straightforward for you.

Think of correction as making the wrong right. For example, if one of your servers has a RAM failure, don't overthink it—replace the faulty RAM. Problem solved. The server is backed up. That's correction.

But now comes the second part—the more important one: corrective action. After you've fixed the RAM, take a step back and ask, *"Why did this happen in the first place?"*

Was it poor-quality hardware, overheating, or a lack of monitoring? This is where you perform a root cause analysis. Once you find the actual cause, you take action to prevent it from happening again—not just on this server, but across your environment. That's your corrective action.

Author's Note: I'll let you in on a secret—I've seen hundreds of organizations stop at correction and never take it further. That's a big mistake. Failure to implement proper corrective action is a common cause of nonconformities (NC) during audits.

We'll revisit this in more detail when we discuss Clause 10.2—Nonconformity and Corrective Action—later in the book.

⚠ **Caution: Don't confuse corrective action with preventive action.**
Corrective action involves steps taken after something goes wrong to prevent it from happening again. Conversely, preventive action is a proactive measure taken before issues arise to stop problems from occurring.

Here's something important: in the older ISO/IEC 27001:2005 version, there was a specific clause on preventive action. But in the 2013 update, that was replaced by the concept of risk and opportunity. So instead of waiting to prevent problems individually, we now ask: *What could go wrong? What risks do we face?* And then we act, we implement controls, and treat those risks before they become incidents.

Author's Note: We'll revisit the concept of risk-based thinking when we cover Clause 6.1 later in the book. That section discusses risk identification, risk treatment, and how to capitalize on opportunities as part of your ISMS strategy.

Let's now look at the term **continual improvement.**

ISO defines it as a *"recurring activity to enhance performance."*

At first glance, this might seem simple, but trust me, it's often misunderstood. I've seen hundreds of people make the same mistake—they say continuous improvement instead of continual improvement. While the words sound similar, they don't mean the same thing in a management system context.

Remember: In ISO standards, we promote continual improvement—not continuous.
Here's the key difference:

- Continual improvement occurs in cycles. You implement something, then pause, reflect, evaluate its effectiveness, and decide on the next step. It's an intentional, step-by-step process aimed at gradual improvement over time.
- Continuous improvement implies an ongoing, never-ending flow of changes. While that may sound ideal, it's not always practical or sustainable, especially for a management system.

Author's Note: Think of continual improvement like climbing a mountain. You move forward, then pause to check your map, evaluate the terrain, and decide your next step. This cycle of act–review–improve–repeat lies at the core of every good ISMS.

We'll talk more about this when we cover Clause 10.1—Continual Improvement—later in the book.

Privacy

In the latest version of ISO 27001, information security is now closely aligned with privacy protection. This is a significant and welcome change, especially in today's world where personal data is constantly collected, shared, and analyzed—often without individuals even realizing it.

While ISO standards don't always give a single, dictionary-style definition, privacy can generally be understood as:

> *The rights and obligations related to the collection, use, retention, disclosure, and disposal of personally identifiable information (PII), ensuring individuals maintain control and autonomy over their personal data.*

Now, let me be honest—I've met brilliant people, from academia to senior corporate roles, who still struggle with what privacy really means. Let me share a real story to make this more straightforward.

🌍 **Real-World Insight:** During the COVID-19 pandemic, a government-supported health app was launched to track infections. It required users to input large amounts of PII—health data, location, contacts, and more. Concerned, I raised the issue on a public forum of a major academic institution.

To my surprise, a respected professor responded dismissively: *"People post everything on social media anyway—what's the harm if a health app collects their data?"*

That right there is a common misunderstanding. Privacy isn't about hiding your life; it's about having the right to control who can access what. I may choose to share my vacation photos on Instagram, but that doesn't mean I've permitted a health app to collect my medical details without my knowledge or explicit consent.

⚠ **Caution:** When individuals are not given the option to opt-in or opt-out, or are not clearly informed about how their data will be used, their privacy rights are being violated, even if the intention is well-meaning.

Before we finish this chapter, let's discuss audits, some important terms related to them, and why they really matter.

If one of your goals is to get your organization ISO 27001 certified (and I'm guessing it is!), then understanding audits isn't just useful—it's vital.

Audits form the backbone of the certification process. They demonstrate that our ISMS isn't just theoretical but a functioning, real-world system. Whether they're internal audits to maintain integrity or external audits leading to certification, this process helps identify what's effective, what isn't, and where improvements are needed.

In short, audits aren't just about passing—they're about improvement. We'll explore them in more detail in the upcoming chapters, but for now, remember: a strong audit process is one of your most valuable tools in the ISO 27001 journey.

ISO defines an **audit** as a *"systematic, independent and documented process for obtaining audit evidence and evaluating it objectively to determine the extent to which the audit criteria are fulfilled."*

Sounds formal, right? But here's what it means in simpler terms: an audit is a structured way to check whether your ISMS is functioning correctly and meets the commitments you made.

There are different types of audits:

- **First-Party Audit:** These are internal audits, done by or on behalf of your organization.
- **Second-Party Audit:** These are external audits done by customers or you as a customer assessing your suppliers.

- **Third-Party Audit:** These are formal audits conducted by independent certification bodies. These are the ones that lead to ISO 27001 certification.

Author's Note: If you want to learn more about how audits are planned, conducted, and reported, I recommend referring to ISO 19011—it's the go-to standard for auditing management systems.

Certification

Let's begin with the term certification itself. Simply put, certification involves obtaining a formal, written confirmation from an independent organization that your system, product, service, or process complies with specific, recognized standards. In our case, it pertains to your ISMS meeting the requirements of ISO 27001.

This type of evaluation is known as a third-party conformity assessment because an organization outside your company or customer base conducts it. It is important to remember that ISO does not issue certificates; its role is to develop standards. External certification bodies handle the actual certification process, which we will discuss next.

So, who gives you the certificate?

Let's break it down.

A certification body is an independent organization that conducts your third-party audit and, if everything goes well, awards your ISO 27001 certificate. They evaluate whether your ISMS meets all the requirements of the standard.

Now here's the next question—who makes sure that the certification body is qualified and reliable? That's where the accreditation body steps in.

An accreditation body is the organization that authorizes and oversees certification bodies to ensure they comply with international standards.

Let's understand certification and accreditation with a straightforward analogy.

Think of certification bodies as colleges or training institutes. Their role is to evaluate whether you (or your organization) meet the required standards, like how colleges test students with exams. If you pass, they give you a certificate—like a diploma or degree—confirming, "Yes, you've met the standard."

Now, who ensures these colleges are legitimate and not just handing out diplomas? That's where accreditation bodies come into play. You can think of them as national universities or regulatory agencies. They evaluate and approve certification organizations to follow strict quality procedures and assess fairly. Essentially, they make sure the 'college' is deserving of issuing degrees in the first place.

If you're aiming for ISO 27001 certification, always select a certification body accredited by a reputable accreditation organization. Just as a degree from a well-known university carries more weight, a certificate from an accredited body enhances your certification's credibility with clients, regulators, and partners.

For example, in the United Kingdom, the national accreditation body is the United Kingdom Accreditation Service (UKAS). In the United States, it's the ANSI National Accreditation Board (ANAB). In India, it's the National Accreditation Board for Certification Bodies (NABCB).

So, if your selected certification body is accredited by one of these national authorities, you can trust that your ISO 27001 certificate will hold real value—recognized both locally and internationally.

Nonconformity

Let's now discuss a term you'll encounter during audits: nonconformity. According to ISO, nonconformity means the "*non-fulfilment of a requirement.*" In simple terms, it indicates you're not meeting a standard requirement, and the auditor will flag it.

There are two primary types of nonconformities you should be aware of:

Minor Nonconformity

As per ISO, this is a *"nonconformity that does not affect the capability of the management system to achieve the intended results."*

In other words, your ISMS is still working, but there is a minor issue that needs to be fixed before it becomes a bigger problem.

Example: *ISO 27001 requires you to maintain competency records for all employees involved in your ISMS. If an auditor finds that two or three employees are missing documentation while the rest are fully documented, it's considered a minor nonconformity. You will need to perform a root cause analysis and implement corrective actions to ensure that no competency records are skipped in the future.*

Major Nonconformity

ISO defines this as a *"nonconformity that affects the capability of the management system to achieve the intended results."*

This is more serious. A major nonconformity usually means:

- There's significant doubt that your process is under control, or
- A product or service may not meet required expectations, or
- Multiple related minor issues point to a *systemic failure.*

Example: *Imagine you've implemented your ISMS, but you haven't conducted any monitoring or measurement activities for a long time. This means you're not checking whether your system is functioning correctly; you're skipping a critical part of the PDCA cycle—the Check step.*

This would be flagged as a major nonconformity. It indicates a breakdown in the system and could even lead to suspension or withdrawal of your certification, depending on the situation.

Key Takeaway—What You've Learned

- ISO 27001 uses precise language—understanding key terms is crucial for correctly interpreting and applying the standard.
- Many definitions come directly from ISO/IEC 27000 and should be reviewed carefully.
- Terms such as information security, risk, control, incident, asset, stakeholder, and objective have specific meanings within ISO language—avoid relying on everyday interpretations.
- Recognizing the difference between a requirement, policy, procedure, and record helps establish a strong ISMS.

- Privacy and PII are more prominent in the latest version of ISO 27001—be clear about your responsibilities.
- Accreditation and certification bodies serve distinct roles in ensuring credibility and compliance.
- An ISO certificate isn't just a piece of paper—it's a reflection of proper understanding, application, and ongoing management.

QUIZ #4

True/False statement

Sr.	Statement	True/False
1	In ISO/IEC 27001, "information security" only refers to keeping information secret.	
2	A risk is defined as the possibility of something bad happening.	
3	The term "control" in ISO/IEC 27001 refers to any action, process, or mechanism that modifies risk.	
4	A document becomes a "record" only when it provides objective evidence of an activity or result.	
5	An "asset" in the ISMS context only includes physical devices like laptops and servers.	
6	A "requirement" is something that must be met or fulfilled.	
7	ISO/IEC 27000 series provides definitions and vocabulary for ISO/IEC 27001.	
8	A stakeholder is only someone outside the organization who is affected by the ISMS.	
9	PII is a general term and not clearly defined in any ISO standard.	
10	Certification bodies assess organizations for compliance, while accreditation bodies assess the competence of certification bodies.	

Chapter 6

What you must deliver and document

Understanding ISMS requirements and documentation needs

Before we start implementing or drafting any part of your ISMS, let's pause and look at the big picture. Why? This chapter explains exactly what ISO 27001 requires you to deliver. Whether it's a policy, a procedure, an objective, or a control, each one comes from a specific requirement in the standard—and understanding these requirements beforehand will save you a lot of frustration later.

This chapter is not just about theory—it's about clarity. Once you understand *who wants what and why* (the standard, the law, your customers, even your internal teams), everything else begins to fall into place.

We'll also closely examine Clause 7.5: Documented Information, which forms the foundation for the structure, control, and consistency of your ISMS documents. You'll understand why it's essential to define elements like:

- Standard document headers
- Revision history
- Ownership
- Access controls
- Retention and disposal rules

Getting these fundamentals right from the start means that as you go through the rest of the implementation, you won't be stuck revisiting, reformatting, rewriting, or re-approving things repeatedly.

Author's Note: Think of this chapter as preparing your workshop before the actual building starts. From now on, whenever you need to create a new ISMS document—like a risk assessment policy or an incident log—you'll already have a clear, approved structure and template to use. That's not just good practice; it's how you keep your ISMS efficient, auditable, and easy to maintain.

Let's get started.

WHERE DO ISMS REQUIREMENTS COME FROM?

Before effectively managing information security, you need to understand what's expected of you—which means knowing where your ISMS requirements originate. These expectations don't just appear out of nowhere; they come from various sources, which I usually categorize into five main groups.

DOI: 10.1201/9781003744139-7

1. **Legal Requirements:** Let's talk about something you can't ignore: **the law.**

   Every organization, regardless of size, must comply with the laws of the country in which it operates. These are not suggestions—they are requirements. If you fail to comply, the results can be serious. Your business could face fines, restrictions, or even shutdowns by government authorities.

   Now, here's the catch: legal requirements don't always stop at your borders. If you serve customers in other countries, you may need to comply with their laws as well. For example:

   - If you handle personal data from individuals in the European Union, you need to comply with the GDPR.
   - If you work in healthcare in the United States, Health Insurance Portability and Accountability Act (HIPAA) applies.
   - If you operate in India or manage data of Indian citizens, the Digital Personal Data Protection Act (DPDP Act) is relevant.

   So, what does this mean for your ISMS? It means you need to identify the laws that apply to your business and ensure your information security practices meet them. Sometimes that involves documenting how you collect and protect personal data. Other times, it might mean establishing clear procedures for handling customer complaints or reporting incidents.

   The bottom line is straightforward: if the law requires you to do something, your ISMS should assist you in doing it—and provide proof that you are doing it.

2. **Regulatory Requirements:** While laws come from governments, regulations are set by industry-specific authorities. These rules help keep your sector safe, fair, and trustworthy—and they often match legal requirements.

   Think of it this way: if you work in banking, healthcare, education, or telecom, there's probably a regulator watching your activities. And they don't just monitor your finances or customer service—they also care about how you protect sensitive information.

   Here are a few examples to make it real:

   - If you're in the banking or finance sector in India, your ISMS may need to align with regulatory requirements from organizations like the Reserve Bank of India (RBI) and the Securities and Exchange Board of India (SEBI). These often include mandates on data protection, incident reporting, cybersecurity controls, and outsourcing risk management.
   - In the UK, financial institutions must consider the Financial Conduct Authority (FCA) and Prudential Regulation Authority (PRA) of the Bank of England, especially regarding operational resilience, incident response, and third-party risk.
   - For those operating in the United States, frameworks like the Federal Financial Institutions Examination Council (FFIEC) Cybersecurity Assessment Tool and compliance with Gramm-Leach-Bliley Act (GLBA) requirements for safeguarding customer data are essential.
   - In healthcare, regulators like the National Health Authority (NHA) in India or the Food and Drug Administration (FDA) in the USA may require strict controls over patient records and medical systems.
   - If you're in telecommunications, organizations like the Telecom Regulatory Authority of India (TRAI) or the Federal Communications Commission (FCC) in

the United States may establish standards for protecting user data and maintaining network security.

These regulations are mandatory. Not complying can result in penalties, license revocation, or damage to your reputation. In some instances, regulators might even suspend your operations until the problems are fixed.

So, what does this mean for your ISMS? It means your security framework should align with the rules governing your industry. You need to understand who your regulators are, what they expect, and how your systems and processes can meet those expectations.

Your ISMS isn't just about data protection—it's about demonstrating to regulators that you operate correctly.

3. **Contractual Requirements:** Not all requirements originate from governments or regulators—some come from your business partners.

   Clients, partners, and suppliers often specify information security obligations in contracts. These can be found within service level agreements (SLAs), vendor agreements, or project scopes. If you've agreed to uphold specific controls, perform regular audits, or maintain a minimum system uptime, those commitments become part of your ISMS.

   Here's Why These Matters: Failing to meet a contractual requirement isn't just a technical issue—it's a trust issue. If you don't deliver what you promised, it can lead to:

   - **Reputational Damage:** Information about a business failing to protect sensitive data or meet standards spreads quickly.
   - **Loss of Future Business:** Clients might choose not to renew contracts or give new assignments.
   - **Legal Consequences:** Breach of contract can lead to financial penalties or legal disputes.

   In the realm of information security, this means your ISMS should help you track and fulfill all security-related commitments made to external parties. That includes documenting responsibilities, monitoring performance, and demonstrating compliance when required.

   Your reputation and future business depend on how well you fulfil your information security promises.

4. **ISO Standard Requirements:** ISO 27001 isn't just a framework—it's a source of precise requirements, and some of these are non-negotiable. Thanks to the Harmonized Structure (which we mentioned earlier), certain documentation expectations apply across all ISO management system standards. However, ISO 27001 also introduces its own specific must-haves—like the Statement of Applicability (SoA), risk assessment results, and risk treatment results.

   These are not optional. If you're seeking certification, they need to be addressed.

   Clause 7.5.1(a) of ISO 27001 clearly states that your organization's ISMS must include documented information as required by ISO 27001.

   In simple terms, if the standard requires you to have documented information—whether it's a policy, procedure, or record—you must have it available and ready for audit. No guessing. No skipping steps. These are the minimum requirements, and if you're pursuing certification, they must be met.

   We'll explore these mandatory documents in detail in the next section.

5. **Internal Requirements:** Don't underestimate the impact of your organization's own decisions. ISO 27001 acknowledges that internal policies, procedures, and operational practices—once documented and approved—become essential parts of your ISMS. These internal requirements are where you turn "what the standard says" into "how we do things here."

   Clause 7.5.1(b) of ISO 27001 emphasizes this flexibility. It states that your ISMS must include documented information identified by the organization as necessary for the effectiveness of the information security management system.

   This means your organization has the freedom—and the responsibility—to determine what additional documentation is necessary to ensure your ISMS works effectively. Depending on your business context, risk environment, and operational needs, you might choose to document specific processes, procedures, or controls that aren't explicitly required by the standard but are vital for your success.

   For example, you might document onboarding procedures for new employees, detailed access control workflows, or escalation protocols for incident response. These aren't mandated by ISO 27001—but if they support the effectiveness of your ISMS, they become part of your documented information.

   In short, ISO 27001 allows you to customize your documentation to fit your specific environment. The important part is to ensure that whatever you decide to document is meaningful, kept up to date, and aligned with your ISMS objectives.

Tip: These requirement types typically don't conflict with each other. In my consulting experience, I've never seen one set of requirements instruct you not to do something while another insists you must. They're usually complementary; some provide more detail or cover additional ground compared to others.

Author's Note: Many people, even professionals, often confuse laws with regulations. Let's clarify that. Laws are generally made by the government or passed by Congress—they form the legal foundation of a country. For example, in the banking sector, the United States' GLBA requires financial institutions to implement safeguards to protect the security and confidentiality of customer information. Non-compliance can lead to legal action and substantial fines.

Regulations, on the other hand, are more specific and are usually created by regulatory agencies—organizations often established under the authority of a law. They provide detailed guidance or rules for particular sectors. For instance, the RBI and the Bank of England are regulatory agencies that issue financial or data-related regulations for banks and financial institutions in their respective countries.

In short, laws tell you what must be done; regulations tell you how to do it in a specific context.

REQUIREMENT ≠ DOCUMENTATION—BUT ONE OFTEN LEADS TO THE OTHER

One of the most common misconceptions during ISO 27001 implementation is the idea that every requirement must be documented. Let's be clear: Not all requirements require documentation. However, many do, and some definitely must.

Before we proceed, let's refer to the official standard: Clause 7.5.1 of ISO 27001, which states that your ISMS shall include:

1. ***Documented information required by the ISO 27001 standard itself***, and
2. ***Documented information determined by the organization as being necessary*** for the effectiveness of the ISMS.

So essentially, there are two types of documentation you'll deal with:

- Mandatory documents specified by the standard.
- Context-driven documents that your organization determines are necessary for smooth and effective operations.

Author's Note: ISO 27001 was never designed for any specific sector, size, or type of organization. Its requirements are intentionally broad, meant to apply to any organization—whether you're a small startup, a government agency, or a global corporation. Over the years, I've often seen people in my classes or during implementation projects argue that a particular document is "mandatory" or that "every organization must have it." But that's not how ISO 27001 functions. The standard clearly states a few mandatory documents. Beyond that, it's up to you to decide which documentation is necessary based on your organization's context, complexity, and capabilities. In other words, your ISMS documentation should be fit for purpose—neither more nor less. Keep it practical, relevant, and effective, and you'll align with both the intent and spirit of the standard.

Let's examine a good example. Clause 4.1 states that the organization shall identify internal and external issues relevant to its purpose and its ability to achieve the intended outcome(s) of the ISMS.

Notice the wording carefully—it says "*determine*," not "*document*." That means it's a *requirement*, but it may not be documented.

Is it wise to document what you've identified for Clause 4.1? Definitely! Especially when an auditor asks how you found those internal and external issues, having it written down makes things easier. However, from the standard's point of view, it's not required to document that specific part.

Author's Note: Just because something is required doesn't mean it needs to be documented—but having documentation is often the smart, traceable way to prove you've done the work.

We'll examine this more closely in the next section, pointing out which clauses require mandatory documentation—and how to manage them effectively and practically.

ISO/IEC 27001:2022—MANDATORY DOCUMENTS YOU NEED

This is where we get to work. It's time for your first implementation task.

We're about to examine how ISO 27001 explicitly requires certain documents and records. Yes, some documented information is mandatory—if you don't have it, you'll face a nonconformity during your audit. This is not a scare tactic; it's a clarity checkpoint.

I'll walk you through a few clauses to demonstrate how the standard sometimes uses unambiguous language—phrases like "*shall retain documented information*" or "*shall be available as documented information.*" These are your *must-haves*.

Let's examine the first three clauses of the ISO 27001 standard to see if they require any documentation.

Starting with **Clause 4.1—Understanding the Organization and Its Context,** you'll notice that it requires the organization to **determine** internal and external issues that affect the intended outcomes of the ISMS. However, it remains **silent** on whether this determination needs to be documented.

Moving to **Clause 4.2—Understanding the Needs and Expectations of Interested Parties,** this clause asks the organization to determine:

1. which interested parties are relevant to the ISMS;
2. the relevant requirements of those parties;
3. Which of those requirements will be addressed within the ISMS?

Again, while these are essential steps, the clause **does not explicitly require** this information to be documented.

Finally, in **Clause 4.3—Determining the Scope of the ISMS,** the organization is asked to determine the boundaries and applicability of its ISMS. Importantly, this clause ends with an explicit instruction:

The scope shall be available as documented information.

This means that if the scope is not documented, it will lead to a nonconformity (NC) during your audit. With that in mind, let's look at Table 6.1, which provides an example summary of ISO 27001 clauses and where documented information is mandatory.

Table 6.1 Example summary of ISO 27001 clauses and mandatory documented information

S. No.	Clause Number	Clause Summary / Details	Mandatory Document Required (Yes/No)
1	4.1	Determine internal and external issues relevant to the ISMS	No
2	4.2	Determine relevant interested parties and their requirements	No
3	4.3	Determine the scope of the ISMS—must be available as documented information	**Yes**

Author's Note: The example given in Table 6.1 doesn't mean you shouldn't document Clause 4.1 or 4.2. It just indicates that the standard doesn't specifically require it. However, I strongly recommend documenting them. Why? Because written clarity supports better training, easier onboarding, and greater consistency—especially as your organization expands or changes ownership. Remember, ISO/IEC 27001 is designed to be scalable. It applies to both a national bank with thousands of employees and a small consulting firm with just five experts. So, if you're a small organization and have thoughtfully considered your internal and external issues—but haven't documented them—that's still okay. As long as you've genuinely reflected on them and they guide your actions, you remain compliant with the standard.

Now, it's your turn.

Implementation Task 1: Spot the Mandatory Documents

This is where your journey shifts from theory to practice.

Get your copy of ISO/IEC 27001:2022 and carefully review Clauses 4 to 10. Don't skim—read as if you need to explain it to a coworker tomorrow. The aim isn't just to read but to understand how the standard communicates its requirements.

Your Task:

For each clause, ask yourself one key question:

Does this clause require documented information, like a formal document or record, or is it simply asking for action without specifying documentation?

As you go, jot down:

- Clause number
- A summary of what it covers
- Whether documentation is explicitly required

Please keep it simple and organized. You're training your eye to identify documentation requirements—a skill every information security professional must master.

A Gentle Reminder: Please don't jump directly to the answer section at the end of this chapter, at least not yet. Remember, this isn't a test—it's a learning opportunity. The true value comes from engaging with the material directly, interpreting its language in your own way, and improving your ability to identify what genuinely needs documentation.

Yes, the answers are there for you, but I encourage you to resist the urge to peek too early. By working through the task first, you'll gain much more insight and confidence. Then, when you compare your approach with the guidance at the end of the chapter, you'll clearly see where you're strong and where you can improve your understanding.

You might be surprised by how much clarity and confidence you can gain from just one task.

⚠ ***Caution:*** *Missing even one of these mandatory documents during a certification audit will be flagged as a nonconformity. That's why this exercise is so important.*

BUILDING YOUR ISMS DOCUMENTATION FRAMEWORK EARLY

Before we go through the standard clause by clause, let's pause for something critically important: how you handle documentation itself.

You might wonder why we're jumping ahead to Clause 7.5 before discussing Clause 4 (Context of the Organization). Here's why—and it's important. We've already seen that ISO 27001 requires several formal documents and records, and how you manage these will influence your entire implementation. Without a clear structure from the start, you'll spend unnecessary time revising documents to meet consistency or control requirements. That's a waste of time and energy.

So we're changing the approach. Instead of waiting to discuss documented information later, we're addressing it now while your ISMS is still in its early stages.

Clause 7.5 outlines the rules for documented information: how it's created, controlled, updated, accessed, and disposed of. This is where your ISMS starts to feel real and operational. From headers and footers to version control and retention periods, these basics lay the foundation for everything that follows.

By establishing a clear documentation structure early, you create a reusable system that saves time, reduces errors, and makes future audits easier. Whether you're writing your first policy or preparing evidence for certification, you'll already have a format that's approved, aligned with the standard, and ready to use. Think of this as setting up your workspace before construction begins. With approved templates and a consistent structure in place, every document you produce from now on will be aligned, auditable, and simple to maintain.

This isn't just a practical shortcut; it's a strategic move that ensures your ISMS grows accurately, not patchily.

THE DANGER OF COPY-PASTE COMPLIANCE

If you're planning to download a template from the internet—or even use the templates provided in this book—and apply them mindlessly to your organization, stop.

This section offers practical tools, checklists, and templates to simplify implementation. But here's the truth: a template is only a starting point, not a finished product.

I've seen numerous ISMS failures when an information security manager mindlessly downloaded and used templates from the internet without reviewing, customizing, or questioning if they fit their business needs. The result? Policies that no one follows, procedures that don't align with actual operations, and systems that break down during audits or real incidents.

> *What works for someone else might not work for you. Your risks, stakeholders, processes, technologies, and culture are all unique. That means your ISMS should reflect your specific environment—not someone else's.*

Here's my advice:

- Use each template in this book as a starting point, not a final answer.
- Read it, question it, and adapt it.
- Make sure it fits your business needs, regulatory requirements, and operational context.
- Involve the right people during customization—including IT, HR, legal, and business teams.
- Keep it simple, realistic, and easy to use.

Author's Note: The goal of ISO 27001 is to create a management system that benefits your organization—not to impress auditors with generic paperwork. If a template doesn't help people do their jobs better or reduce real risks, it's not effective.

Now that you know how to use them wisely, let's explore the requirements of clause 7.5 in detail and begin creating templates we can use throughout our ISMS implementation process.

CLAUSE 7.5.2: DOCUMENTED INFORMATION THAT WORKS

Let's discuss how you create and update your ISMS documents—because Clause 7.5.2 emphasizes getting that process right from the very beginning.

Before you begin writing policies, procedures, or records, establish a clear and consistent approach for how your documentation will be structured, reviewed, and maintained. This isn't just about making things look organized; it's about ensuring your documents are valid, consistent, and reliable as your ISMS develops.

According to clause 7.5.2 of ISO 27001, when your organization creates or updates documented information, it must ensure three key things:

1. **Identification and Description:** Every document should be clearly identifiable. This means giving it an appropriate title, date, author, or reference number so everyone knows exactly what it is and which version they are viewing. No one should ever have to guess which "Policy_v3_final_final.docx" is the correct one!
2. **Format and Media:** Decide how your documents will be created, stored, and accessed. Will they be electronic or on paper? Are they written in one official language or multiple? Will you use a shared drive, document portal, or ISMS software? Format choices impact not just readability but also security, accessibility, and consistency.
3. **Review and Approval:** Every document should go through a formal review and approval process to ensure it's appropriate and sufficient. In simple terms, this means the document does what it's intended to do and is accurate, complete, and authorized before it's shared or used.

Tip: You don't need a complicated workflow. A straightforward process that records who drafted, who reviewed, who approved, and when is sufficient—as long as it's applied consistently.

Author's Note: Clause 7.5.2 may seem bureaucratic, but it's really about trust. When people use an ISMS document, they should be sure it's the most recent, approved version—not an outdated or unverified one. A bit of discipline here can go a long way in building that trust.

Start with a Solid Documentation Framework

Here's what you should set up before creating any ISMS documents:

- Decide on a standard structure for all your documents.
- Create templates for different types—such as policies, procedures, forms, or logs.
- Assign responsibilities for who writes, reviews, approves, and publishes each document.
- Define a revision and approval process to ensure documents remain accurate and relevant over time.

This framework helps you prevent duplication, connect related documents, and stay organized in one place.

What Every Document Should Include

To make your documents easy to identify and manage, including these essential details:

- **Type:** What kind of document is it? (e.g., Policy, Procedure, Guideline, Plan, Form, Log, Record)
- **Title, Purpose, and Scope:** A clear name, why the document exists, and what it covers.
- **Date of Publication, Version Number, and Revision History:** Track when it was created, updated, and what has changed over time.
- **Classification Level:** Define sensitivity (e.g., Public, Internal, Confidential, Restricted).
- **Reference Number or Unique Identifier:** Helps with indexing, cross-referencing, and retrieval.
- **Author, Owner, and Approver(s):** Who wrote it, who is responsible for maintaining it, and who approved it.
- **Location or Storage Path:** Where the official version is stored (e.g., SharePoint link, folder path, Document Management System (DMS) ID).

- **Review Frequency or Next Review Date:** When the document should be reviewed next—helps prevent outdated content.
- **Related Documents or Cross-References:** Link to other relevant documents (e.g., related policies, procedures, or logs).
- **Tools or Systems Referenced:** If the document depends on specific software, platforms, or tools, mention them.
- **Audience or Intended Users:** Who is expected to read or use this document (e.g., All Staff, IT Team, HR).
- **Format and Language:** Specify file format (PDF, DOCX, etc.) and language if multilingual versions exist.

These details help you monitor changes, assign responsibility, and ensure everyone understands the document's purpose.

Format and Media Tips

Your documented information can take many forms—paper files, PDFs, web pages, databases, and even audio or video. No matter the format, ensure you:

- Select appropriate file types and software versions for your team.
- Decide where the document will be stored—on paper, in a shared drive, or in a document management system.
- Write in a style suitable for your audience. A technical procedure for IT staff will look very different from a policy intended for all employees.

Keep It Fresh: Review and Approval

Don't let your documents go out of date. Schedule regular reviews to ensure they stay accurate and valuable. You can base your review plan on:

- *Time* (like every 12 months)
- *Content triggers* (like changes in regulations or after an incident)

And when it's time to update, ensure that changes go through a proper approval process. If necessary, establish a formal document approval workflow. This way, you can confirm the document remains correct, relevant, and accurate for those who need it.

One Last Tip: Avoid Copy-Paste Chaos

Avoid duplicating content across multiple documents. Use cross-references instead to keep your documentation DRY (Don't Repeat Yourself). This approach makes things cleaner and easier to maintain.

Author's Note: Let me take you into the field for a moment. I was once leading an ISMS implementation project for a central bank in a West African country. Sounds big already, right? Well, it came with significant challenges too. Every department had its way of doing paperwork—different fonts, sizes, styles. Some memos had a colorful logo; others were black-and-white. One logo looked like a sumo wrestler, another like a marathon runner—slim and sprinting! It was a formatting jungle.

I knew right then that before we could talk about security, we had to talk about structure. So, I started small: standardizing fonts, logo sizes, paper margins, and document sections. I even went so far as to define the minimum grams per square meter (GSM) for printed paper—yes, that's how deep the inconsistency ran.

It took time. It took convincing. It took climbing a bureaucratic mountain. But in the end, we had a clear, consistent, professional document system that everyone could follow. Looking back now, I smile and say, "Job well done." Order matters—even in the most minor details.

CLAUSE 7.5.3: CONTROLLING WHAT YOU CREATE

Managing documented information isn't just about storing files—it's about making sure they stay usable, secure, and accessible to the right people at the right time. Every document in your ISMS has a lifecycle: it's created, reviewed, used, updated, and eventually retired or deleted.

In simple terms, managing documented information means treating your ISMS documents as active assets—not just static files stored in a folder. You need to ensure that the correct version is accessible where and when it's needed, protected from unauthorized changes or access, and safely removed when it's no longer relevant.

Reasonable documentation control isn't about bureaucracy; it's about clarity, confidence, and continuity. When your information is usable, secure, and in the right hands, your ISMS runs smoothly, your team works efficiently, and your organization builds lasting trust.

Once your document is approved, the next question is: who needs to see it, and how will they receive it? Whether it's a policy, a procedure, or a simple form, your documented information must be:

- Available where and when it's needed
- Protected from unauthorized changes or misuse
- Maintained with integrity and confidentiality

According to ISO 27001 Clause 7.5.3, organizations must control documented information to make sure that:

1. **It Is Available and Suitable for Use:** meaning the right people can access the correct information, when and where they need it.
2. **It Is Adequately Protected:** meaning documents are safeguarded against unauthorized access, loss, alteration, or misuse.

To make this work in practice, ISO 27001 expects you to think through a few essential control activities, depending on your context. I've summarized the most common ones in Table 6.2.

Table 6.2 Key control activities for managing documented information

Control Activity	*Purpose and Explanation*
Distribution, Access, Retrieval, and Use	Specify who can view, download, or modify each document. Ensure that people know where to find the latest version. Use access controls or permissions if necessary.
Storage and Preservation (Including Legibility)	Store documents securely—whether in digital repositories or physical files—and ensure they remain readable over time. Old formats or damaged media shouldn't render information unusable.
Control of Changes (Version Control)	Track updates, revisions, and approvals. Always be able to identify which version is current, who made changes, and when. This avoids confusion and assists during audits.
Retention and Disposition	Decide how long to keep each document or record, and how to dispose of it securely when it's no longer needed. Only retain what's necessary for effectiveness and compliance.
External Document Control	Identify and manage documents from external sources that your ISMS depends on, such as laws, regulations, or supplier documents. Please make sure they are up to date and accessible.

Tip: When ISO 27001 states "as applicable," that doesn't mean optional. It means you should apply the activity where it is relevant to your ISMS. For example, if you use only digital documents, physical storage controls might not apply—but access control, versioning, and retention will.

Real-World Insight: In one organization, two versions of the same document were accidentally circulating—one in SharePoint and another in a department folder. During an audit, both were presented as "the latest." The problem wasn't a policy failure; it was a version-control failure. The team later centralized all policies in a single portal, with proper permissions and version numbering. The issue disappeared overnight.

Author's Note: Clause 7.5.3 isn't just about organizing documents—it's about safeguarding information trust. Your ISMS documentation shows your organization's commitment to security and consistency. When people access a document, they should be confident it's the most recent, approved, and trustworthy version. That confidence is only built when documentation is strictly managed.

Let's Break It Down: What Does Control Mean?

When ISO 27001 discusses controlling documented information, it doesn't mean just paperwork for the sake of paperwork. It's about making sure that your information—whether it's a policy, a form, or an email template—is accessible, accurate, authorized, and secure throughout its entire life cycle.

In simple terms, control means knowing:

- Where each document lives,
- Who can use or change it,
- How long to keep it, and
- What to do with it when it's no longer needed.

Here's how you can make that happen step by step.

1. Use a Structured Document Management System

Begin by establishing a structured document library—this could be your intranet, shared drive, SharePoint site, or a document management platform. The specific tool isn't important;

what matters most are consistency, easy access, and effective version control. Documents should be simple to locate, with clear titles, version numbers, and approval details.

❢ **Tip:** A central document library minimizes confusion and showcases control during audits.

2. Classify Your Documents
Every piece of documented information should be categorized based on your internal classification scheme, such as:

- **Public:** Safe for external sharing
- **Internal:** For internal use only
- **Confidential:** Limited to specific departments or roles
- **Restricted:** Highly sensitive, strictly controlled

This classification decides **how** the document is stored, accessed, and shared—and how it must be protected.

For example, a public policy might be posted on your website, but a restricted incident report must stay in a secure ISMS repository with access logs.

3. Apply Change Control
Only authorized personnel should be permitted to modify or release documents. Every update must undergo a change management process—reviewed, approved, and distributed through predetermined channels.

Maintain a log of who made changes, when, and why.

This ensures the validity and authenticity of your documented information.

4. Control Distribution and Access
Not everyone needs access to every document.

Identify your interested parties for each type of information and determine the access methods. And distribution.

For example:

- Internal policies → Intranet (read-only)
- Supplier contracts → Secure portal (restricted access)
- Regulatory reports → Encrypted email or official upload portal

The goal is simple: the right people, the correct document, at the right time—securely.

⚠ **Caution:** Never share classified documents using public links or unsecured drives. Distribution must always comply with your information classification rules.

5. Store and Preserve Information Properly
Your documents must remain readable and intact for as long as they are retained.

If you use digital files, make sure they are in accessible formats and protected from accidental deletion or corruption. If you keep physical records, store them in a clean, secure environment.

❢ **Tip:** Periodically verify that digital formats stay readable—especially if systems or software versions are updated.

6. Define Retention and Disposition Rules

Every document has a lifespan. Decide how long to keep each type of document—considering legal, regulatory, or operational needs—and determine what happens once that period ends. For example:

- Incident logs → Retain for 2 years after closure
- Supplier contracts → Retain for 5 years after termination
- Awareness materials → Retain for current year only

When the retention period ends, dispose of the document securely—shred paper copies and securely erase or archive electronic ones. This helps ensure compliance and keeps clutter to a minimum.

7. Manage External Documents Too

Remember that some of your documented information will come from external sources, such as regulators, customers, suppliers, or partners. These must also be identified and controlled, especially if your ISMS relies on them.

For example, a regulatory circular, a supplier's compliance certificate, or a customer's information security requirement document.

Please ensure they are current, accessible, and properly labelled as external documents.

📌 **Remember:** You only retain documented evidence as needed for the effectiveness of your ISMS. Avoid over-documenting; keep it simple and practical. If there are business requirements, consider creating a "Documented Information Control Procedure" that covers all the key points—including document lifecycle steps, roles, classification handling, retention schedules, and access controls.

💬 **Author's Note:** Over the years, I've seen firsthand how well-designed document control procedures can completely fail—not because of a lack of structure, but due to a missing culture. Let me share a few moments that left a lasting impression on me.

During an ISMS audit at a commercial bank in Africa, I came across a cabinet marked "Public File." But when I opened it, to my surprise—and concern—it was filled with confidential documents. Just think about that for a moment. A label screaming "public," but the contents were anything but. Imagine the consequences if someone less responsible had stumbled upon it.

On another occasion, I was visiting a large telecom company in East Africa. It was lunchtime, and I was in the staff canteen with the ISMS Manager, grabbing a quick bite. Across from us, a senior executive was enjoying his coffee while flipping through a few files. Then he got up to refill his cup, leaving the documents wide open on the table. Out of curiosity and concern, I walked over. It was a confidential tender document, complete with sensitive pricing data—just sitting there, unattended, in a public dining space. The executive returned a few minutes later, chatting casually with a colleague. When he saw me standing by his table, he froze, quickly gathered the papers, apologized, and left in a hurry.

And then there was the time I was auditing a multinational organization based in Saudi Arabia, visiting their Singapore operations. During a walkthrough, I saw torn pieces of paper in a trash bin. Upon closer inspection, they were parts of a confidential document—still readable. The shredder? Just a few steps away, around the corner.

These stories aren't shared for shock value. They're reminders. You can have the most detailed documentation framework and control processes in place, but if your people don't respect or understand the rationale behind information-handling rules, the system fails.

⚠ **Caution:** A robust ISMS needs more than just documents and controls—it requires a culture of security awareness ingrained in daily actions.

ISMS DOCUMENTATION TEMPLATE

Now that you've finished this chapter, it's time to shift from understanding to action. Below is a generic ISMS documentation template you can use as a starting point for showing compliance with ISO 27001's clauses.

How We'll Work through These Templates
We'll go through each item in a clear numbered list, starting with 1, Document header. For each element, you'll get three things:

- ***The name of the component*** (e.g., Title, Version, Classification Level)
- ***A brief explanation*** of its purpose and relevance within the ISMS framework
- ***A practical example*** to illustrate how it might be used in a real-world context

Think of it as a guided checklist rather than a rulebook, allowing you to customize each section to fit your organization's needs. Follow the steps, fill out the fields, and you'll end up with consistent, audit-ready documents without any guesswork. Use this template to shape your structure, not to limit your flexibility.

1. Document Header
Purpose: Think of the document header as the document's ID card. It tells you what the document is, who owns it, and whether it's still current. Without a proper header, people end up opening files just to check if they're relevant or up to date. Table 6.3 provides an example of document header fields for ready reference.

Table 6.3 Document header fields for ISMS documentation

Field	*Description*	*Example*
Document Type	Type of document	Policy / Procedure / Guideline / Plan / Log
Title	Clear and descriptive title	Information Security Policy
Reference Number	Unique ID for tracking	ISMS-POL-001
Version Number	Current version of the document	1.2
Date of Publication	Date the document was issued	2025-08-01
Next Review Date	Scheduled date for review	2026-08-01
Classification Level	Sensitivity level	Internal / Confidential
Document Owner	Person responsible for the document	Head of Information Security
Author	The person who created the content	Dr. Swapan Purkait
Approver(s)	Final approver(s) of the document	CISO / Compliance Manager
Storage Location	Where the document is stored	SharePoint > ISMS > Policies
Intended Audience	Who should read or use the document	All Employees / IT Team
Total Page Numbers	Total number of pages in the document	12 Pages
Language	If applicable, document language	English
Related Documents	Cross-references to related docs	ISMS-POL-002 (Access Control Policy)

2. Document Title

Purpose and Relevance: The document title is the first thing people see—it sets the tone, clearly indicates the document's purpose, and helps prevent confusion. Within the ISMS framework, a clear, descriptive title allows everyone to identify the document's subject without having to open it or read it thoroughly. A precise title also makes searching, cataloguing, and auditing much simpler.

Example in Practice: If you are publishing a company-wide policy that defines the rules for protecting data, a vague title like *"Security Guidelines"* may confuse. Instead, use an unambiguous title such as:

"Information Security Policy—Data Protection and Access Control"

This immediately tells employees, auditors, or regulators exactly what to expect.

3. Purpose Statement

Purpose and Relevance: The purpose statement explains why the document exists. The ISMS framework provides the context, defines the problem the document addresses, or states the goal it aims to reach. This is important because it makes sure everyone—from employees to auditors—understands the document's intent in the same way. Without a clear purpose, documents can become vague, misused, or misunderstood.

Example in Practice: For an *Access Control Policy*, your purpose statement could be:

This policy outlines the rules and responsibilities for granting, reviewing, and revoking access to company information systems, ensuring protection against unauthorized use or disclosure.

A good purpose statement is concise, specific, and aligned with organizational and regulatory standards.

4. Scope

Purpose and Relevance: The scope outlines the document's boundaries and applicability. The ISMS framework clarifies where, when, and to whom the document applies. This helps prevent confusion, maintain consistency, and stop people from mistakenly thinking a policy or procedure doesn't apply to them—or, worse, from ignoring it. A clearly defined scope is also crucial for audits, as it demonstrates that the organization understands the operational and geographical extent of its controls.

Example in Practice: For an *Access Control Policy*, your scope could be:

This policy applies to all employees, contractors, and third-party service providers who access company-managed IT systems, applications, and data — whether on-site or remotely — across all global offices.

The scope should be broad enough to cover all relevant areas, but not so vague as to invite misinterpretation.

5. Definitions and Abbreviations

Purpose and Relevance: Clear definitions ensure everyone understands terms in the same way. In an ISMS, words like "Incident," "Asset," "Risk Owner," or "Confidential" often carry very specific meanings that differ from everyday language. The same applies to abbreviations, especially when technical or regulatory terms are used across teams, locations, or even countries.

Table 6.4 Definitions and abbreviations used in ISMS documentation

Term / Abbreviation	*Definition*	*Example in Context*
Risk Owner	The person accountable for managing a specific risk	"The IT Director is the risk owner for data center outages."
PII	Personally Identifiable Information	"PII must not be emailed without encryption."

To keep things simple and consistent, it's always a good idea to capture these in one place. Table 6.4 provides an example of how definitions and abbreviations can be documented for easy reference. Trust me, this becomes a real lifesaver during audits—it removes ambiguity and avoids those uncomfortable "That's not what I thought it meant" discussions.

💡 Tip: If your organization is in a regulated industry, you can also link terms here to the legal or compliance definitions from relevant laws, standards, or frameworks.

6. Responsibilities

Purpose and Relevance: This section clarifies who is responsible for what in relation to the document's subject matter. In the ISMS world, unclear roles quickly lead to chaos—everyone assumes "someone else" will handle a security incident or update a policy. To avoid that, responsibilities should be stated clearly and in writing. Table 6.5 shows an example of how roles and responsibilities related to ISMS documentation can be defined. Doing this creates accountability, ensures timely action, helps auditors verify ownership, and prevents both conflicts and duplicated effort.

💡 Tip: For large organizations, include a **Responsibility Matrix (Responsible, Accountable, Consulted, and Informed or RACI chart)** if the roles are complex—it helps clarify who is *Responsible*, *Accountable*, *Consulted*, and *Informed.*

Table 6.5 Roles and responsibilities related to ISMS documentation

Role	*Responsibility*	*Example in Context*
ISMS Manager	Maintaining and updating the policy as per ISO 27001 requirements	"Reviews and updates the document annually or after major incidents."
IT Manager	Implementing the technical controls mentioned in the document	"Ensures access control systems are configured as per policy."
All Employees	Following the requirements of the document and reporting incidents	"Immediately reports suspicious emails to the security team."

7. Core Content

Before you start writing, remember that Core Content is just a placeholder title in this template. You should replace it with the actual name of the section that reflects your document's subject. For example, if this document is about resetting user passwords, change the heading to "Password Reset Procedure." If it's a policy on acceptable device use, title it "Acceptable Use Policy." You can also repeat the document title here for consistency. This approach helps readers immediately understand what the section is about without having to scroll back to the document header.

Purpose and Relevance: This is the core of your document—the part where you describe the actual requirements, rules, or step-by-step procedures. The content here must be clear, concise, and actionable. In an ISMS context, this section directly supports the implementation of ISO 27001 controls, policies, or processes. Well-organized core content helps readers easily follow and comply with the intended requirements, reducing ambiguity and the risk of security incidents.

Example in Practice:

Title: *Password Reset Procedure*

Section 1—Scope and Applicability:

This procedure applies to all employees, contractors, and third-party service providers needing access to the company's network.

Section 2—Step-by-Step Process:

1. User identifies the need for a password reset and contacts the IT Helpdesk.
2. IT Helpdesk verifies the user's identity according to the "Identity Verification Guideline."
3. IT Helpdesk starts the password reset process in the system.
4. User receives a temporary password through a secure channel (SMS/Encrypted Email).
5. User changes their password during the first login..

Section 3—Exceptions:

If the system is inaccessible due to an outage, IT will follow the *Disaster Recovery Access Procedure*.

8. Risk

Purpose and Relevance: This section highlights the consequences of noncompliance with the document's requirements. It reminds readers that certain lapses may not just be operational mistakes but could also lead to nonconformance with relevant standards, regulatory issues, or business impacts. Stating the risk upfront helps raise awareness and promotes compliance.

Example in Practice: Failing to perform the risk assessment as required by ISO 27001:2022 Clause 6.1.2 may result in non-conformance during certification audits, leading to audit findings, possible loss of certification, and higher vulnerability to unmitigated security threats.

9. Compliance with This Document

Purpose and Relevance: Every ISMS document is only as effective as its implementation. This section makes it clear that following the directives is not optional—it's an expectation from top management and a crucial part of the organization's governance. This reinforces accountability within the defined scope.

Example in Practice: The organization's top management expects all employees, contractors, and third-party service providers within the ISMS scope to follow the requirements outlined in this document strictly. Regular internal audits will verify compliance, and any non-compliance will be addressed through the disciplinary process.

10. Waiver Criteria

Purpose and Relevance: Sometimes, operational realities require deviations from documented requirements. This section ensures such exceptions are not made arbitrarily but are well controlled, justified, and time-limited. It also guarantees that risk is evaluated before approval and that exceptions undergo periodic review.

Example in Practice: Any exception to the Access Control Policy must be officially documented, assessed for risks, approved by the Chief Information Security Officer (CISO), and re-evaluated each year. For example, if a specific legacy application cannot support Multi-Factor Authentication (MFA), then an exception may be granted, as long as compensating controls are implemented.

11. Document Revision History

Purpose and Relevance: This section offers a clear record of how the document has changed over time—what was updated, when it was updated, and who was involved. It promotes transparency, traceability, and accountability, especially when documents evolve after incidents, audits, or management decisions. Table 6.6 provides a simple example of a document revision history used in ISMS documentation. In ISO 27001, maintaining an accurate change history is a key part of document control and is extremely helpful during audits, because it clearly shows that changes are reviewed, approved, and managed in a controlled manner.

Table 6.6 Document revision history for ISMS documentation

Version	*Date*	*Description of Change*	*Changed By*	*Approved By*
1.0	xx-xx-xxxx	Initial draft of Information Security Policy	xxx	xxx
1.1	xx-xx-xxxx	Updated password complexity requirements	xxx	xxx

12. Access and Distribution

Purpose and Relevance: Defines who can view, edit, or share the document and through which channels. Properly managing document access prevents unauthorized changes and ensures sensitive information is only shared with those who need it. This complies with ISO 27001's requirements for information classification and access control.

Example in Practice: This policy is stored on the organization's secure SharePoint site and is accessible to all employees for reading. Editing rights are restricted to the Information Security Team. Distribution outside the company requires the CISO's written approval.

13. Retention and Disposal

Purpose and Relevance: Defines how long the document must be retained, where it should be stored, and the secure method for disposal once it is no longer needed. This helps prevent outdated information from lingering, reducing risk and supporting regulatory compliance.

Example in Practice:

Retention Period: Current version + previous two versions.

Disposal Method: Shred paper copies and securely delete digital copies using certified data erasure software.

14. Format and Media Requirements

Purpose and Relevance: Specifies the acceptable formats and media types for creating, storing, and sharing the document. This ensures consistency, readability, and compatibility across the organization, while also supporting secure handling.

Example in Practice: Documents must be prepared in Microsoft Word (.docx) or PDF (.pdf) formats. Approved storage methods include the secure corporate SharePoint repository and encrypted USB drives for offline use.

15. Approval
Purpose and Relevance: Identifies the ultimate authority or authorities who must approve the document before it becomes official. This guarantees that all content complies with organizational, legal, and compliance standards before distribution.
Example in Practice:
Approved by:

- **CISO:** Final authority on ISMS documentation
- **Compliance Manager:** Confirms regulatory alignment

16. Distribution List / Intended Audience
Purpose and Relevance: Clearly specifies who should have access to the document. This ensures the correct people are informed, responsibilities are clear, and sensitive material is not unnecessarily exposed.
Example in Practice:
Distribution List:

- All full-time employees
- IT Security Team
- Third-party service providers with contractual access to ISMS processes

17 References and Related Documents
Purpose and Relevance: This section acts as a guide for your reader, directing them to other documents, standards, or resources related to what they've just read. In an ISMS, no document stands alone; a password policy might refer to an access control procedure, and an information security continuity plan could cite a disaster recovery procedure. Listing these references saves time, promotes consistency, and helps ensure compliance with ISO 27001's traceability requirements.
Example in Practice:
If you are writing an Information Security Policy, you might include:

- **Access Control Policy:** ISMS-POL-003
- **Incident Response Procedure:** ISMS-PRO-002

18. Annex / Appendix (Optional)
Purpose and Relevance: Provides a space for supporting materials—such as tools, checklists, diagrams, or sample forms—that help implement the requirements described in the document. While not always required, including an annex can make it easier for readers to apply the guidance practically. In ISO 27001 documents, this section helps connect to other templates or forms needed to implement the policy or procedure.
Example in Practice:
For an Access Control Procedure, the annex might include:

- **User Access Request Form (Template):** used by managers to request new access rights for their team members.

- **Quarterly Access Review Checklist:** to ensure all user accounts are still valid and appropriate.
- **Sample Access Log:** showing what records should be kept.

🧭 **Key Takeaway—What You've Learned**

- **Understanding the Source of Requirements:** ISMS documentation requirements should originate from various sources, including ISO 27001 clauses, legal and regulatory obligations, contractual demands, and specific business needs.
- **Documentation Is Not the Requirement Itself:** Having a written document does not automatically mean compliance; it's about demonstrating how the documented processes are implemented effectively.
- **ISO/IEC 27001:2022 Mandatory Documents:** You have reviewed the list of documents explicitly required by the standard, and we have emphasized identifying them.
- **Framework Before Filling:** Establishing a documentation framework early on prevents disorganized, inconsistent, and redundant records later in the ISMS lifecycle.
- **Avoiding Copy-Paste Compliance:** Using generic templates without customizing them to your organization's reality can create risks during audits and daily operations.
- **Clause 7.5.2 in Action:** We have discussed how to create documented information that is practical, user-friendly, and aligned with business operations.
- **Clause 7.5.3 in Action:** You have learned how to manage documented information so it remains accurate, accessible, and secure over time.
- **Comprehensive ISMS Document Template:** We have provided a detailed template covering key elements, including document headers, responsibilities, risk management, compliance, annexes, and more.
- **Customization Is Key:** Use the template as your starting point, but modify it to fit your specific operational and organizational requirements. Add or remove items as needed to ensure relevance, adequacy, and suitability for your ISMS.

QUIZ #5

True/False statement

Sr.	*Statement*	*True/False*
1	All ISO/IEC 27001 requirements must be documented in writing to be compliant.	
2	The source of ISMS requirements can include laws, regulations, contracts, and internal business needs.	
3	Copying someone else's ISMS documents without customization is a good practice to save time.	
4	Clause 7.5.2 focuses on creating documented information that is practical and usable.	
5	Clause 7.5.3 addresses controlling documented information to ensure it remains accurate, accessible, and secure.	
6	ISMS document template should be used exactly as provided, without changes.	
7	Including a "Risk" section in ISMS documents can help link content to ISO 27001 controls and objectives.	
8	"Core Content" in a document is the section where the actual policy requirements or procedural steps are written.	

Sr.	Statement	True/False
9	An Annex or Appendix can be used to add supporting materials, such as checklists or forms.	
10	A well-structured document framework can help prevent scattered and inconsistent ISMS records.	

ANSWER KEY: IMPLEMENTATION TASK 1

Table 6.7 lists the mandatory documents and records that an organization must retain to demonstrate conformance with ISO 27001. These are the items the standard explicitly requires as documented information—meaning if any of them are missing, it will almost certainly be raised as a nonconformity during an audit.

That said, there's an important nuance to understand. Just because ISO does not explicitly say "document this" does not mean you shouldn't. The standard deliberately leaves room for judgment. If documenting a process, decision, or activity adds clarity, consistency, or makes training and handovers easier, then it's worth documenting. Always remember—ISO 27001 sets the minimum requirement. What you add on top should be driven by what works best for your organization's size, complexity, and culture.

Table 6.7 Mandatory documented information required for ISO 27001 conformance

S. No.	Clause Number	Clause Summary / Details
1	4.3	ISMS Scope
2	5.2	Information Security Policy
3	6.1.2	Information security risk assessment process
4	6.1.3 (d)	Statement of Applicability (SOA)
5	6.1.3 (e)	Information security risk treatment plan
6	6.1.3	Information security risk treatment process
7	6.2	Information security objectives
8	7.2	Evidence of competence
9	7.5.1 (a)	Documented information required by ISO 27001
10	7.5.1 (b)	Documented information determined by the organization as being required for the effectiveness of the ISMS.
11	7.5.3	Documented information of external origin determined by the organization to be necessary.
12	8.1	Information to the extent necessary to have confidence that the processes have been carried out as planned
13	8.2	Results of information security risk assessments
14	8.3	Results of information security risk treatment
15	9.1	Evidence of monitoring and measurement results
16	9.2.2	Evidence of the implementation of the audit programme(s) and Audit results
17	9.3	Information as evidence of the results of the management reviews
18	10.2	Information of the nature of the nonconformities and any subsequent actions taken, and the results of any corrective action.

Chapter 7

From Gap to Gantt, your ISMS project starts here

Assess where you stand—Then plan the journey with purpose

Welcome to the stage where ideas become action.

By now, you've understood the requirements, explored what must be documented, and even laid the foundation for creating those documents. But an it by introducing Gap Analysis as the first practical step in building an ISMS isn't a "start anywhere, finish anywhere" journey; it's a structured process. And like any good trip, you need to know your starting point before you can plan your destination.

That's precisely where Gap Analysis fits in. It acts as a bridge between "knowing the standard" and "implementing the standard." It not only shows where you fall short but also highlights what's already working in your favor. When done correctly, it transforms a vague idea of compliance into a clear, prioritized, and actionable plan.

Think of it as your ISMS reality check—a practical assessment that lays the foundation for creating your project plan (yes, that's where the Gantt chart will come in later). Without it, you risk pursuing tasks in random order, wasting time, and overlooking critical requirements. With it, you'll have a roadmap tailored to your organization's actual state, not a generic template from the internet.

In this chapter, we'll examine why Gap Analysis is your initial essential step, how to perform it effectively, and how to turn your findings into a clear, trackable project plan.

WHY GAP ANALYSIS IS THE FIRST REAL STEP

Before beginning implementation of an ISMS, you must answer two essential yet impactful questions:

1. Where am I now?
2. Where do I want to be?

That space between your current reality and your desired outcome is the gap. Gap Analysis is the process of identifying it—honestly and with enough detail to make it meaningful.

Think of it like building your dream home. You wouldn't just start hammering nails on day one. First, you'd check the land, look at what's already built, and figure out what's missing—is it just the roof? The walls? Or do you still need the foundation? Only then would you create a plan to finish the build and finally invite everyone over for a big housewarming party.

Or, think about pizza (because everything in life can be explained with pizza). Imagine you're making your signature pizza for friends. Before you start, check your kitchen: do you

DOI: 10.1201/9781003744139-8

already have the dough? Sauce? Cheese? Or are you missing the oven altogether? This quick check saves you from realizing halfway through that you forgot the mozzarella.

For your ISMS, Gap Analysis does the same thing. It helps you:

- **See what you already have**—controls, processes, or documents that are already in place.
- **Spot what's missing**—areas where you fall short of ISO/IEC 27001 requirements.
- **Prioritize what matters most**—so your implementation plan focuses on closing the most significant gaps first.

Without it, you're basically attempting to reach your destination without knowing where you're starting from—and no GPS can assist with that.

Why Gap Analysis Matters

In my experience, I have never seen any organization start its ISMS journey from absolute zero. Even the smallest businesses usually have some form of a management system—a policy here, a process there, maybe even a few controls already in place. And that's a good thing. You don't have to discard what you already possess. Instead:

- **Use Them:** Keep the documents and processes that already work.
- **Review Them:** Make sure they're still relevant and practical.
- **Update Them:** Align them with ISO/IEC 27001 requirements where needed.
- **Create the Missing Ones:** Build what's not there yet.

This approach saves time, prevents unnecessary rework, and maximizes the investments you've already made. I've noticed that clients value this—it shows you're not reinventing the wheel for no reason, but building on what already works.

How to Conduct a Gap Analysis

Now that we understand why a Gap Analysis is essential, let's discuss how to perform it. Remember—this isn't about seeking perfection; it's about getting a clear, honest picture of where you currently stand. You're not aiming to impress anyone; you're collecting facts to create a plan that fits your organization.

If you find something missing, that's not a failure; that's exactly the purpose of this exercise. It's better to identify gaps now, when you can fix them, rather than be caught off guard later during an audit or, worse, during an actual incident.

And one more thing before we dive into the steps: I've included a comprehensive Gap Analysis Checklist in the next section for your reference; the same one I use every time I begin an ISMS implementation project.

Step 1: Gather Your Blueprint, Tools, and Crew: Before identifying the gaps, you need to clearly understand what you're measuring against—and you can't do it alone. Begin by having the latest ISO/IEC 27001:2022 standard open on your desk (or on your screen). This serves as your blueprint, the master plan for your ISMS "house."

Next, gather your tools—policies, procedures, records, and any existing management system documentation. But more importantly, bring in your team: department heads, IT/security managers, and other key process owners who understand what's happening in their part of the "house."

Why It Matters: Without the standard, you don't know what "good" looks like. Without the right people, you're only seeing part of the picture—like trying to inspect a house without asking the electrician where the wires run. The goal is to understand the current state before you start planning upgrades.

Step 2: Map Out the Scope of Your ISMS: Now that you have your blueprint, tools, and crew, it's time to mark the construction site. Clearly define which part of your organization the ISMS will cover. Is it just one "room" (a single office), an entire "wing" (a business unit), or the whole "mansion" (your global group)? Draw clear boundaries before you start measuring and making improvements.

If you're still uncertain about your ISMS scope, here's a tip—pause and finish defining the scope in Clause 4 (discussed in the next chapter) before proceeding with the Gap Analysis. It's like deciding which property to renovate before checking for cracks in the walls.

Why It Matters: If your scope isn't clear, you'll either overlook important areas or spend time on parts of the organization that aren't in scope—like fixing the neighbor's fence instead of your own.

Step 3: Inspect What's Already Built: Before tearing down walls or ordering new materials, carefully assess what you already have. Review your current policies, procedures, and controls. Talk to department heads, IT managers, and anyone else familiar with the "plumbing" and "wiring" of your organization. You might be surprised—some areas may already be strong, others might just need a fresh coat of paint, and a few may be missing altogether.

Why It Matters: No one starts from nothing. Even the smallest organizations have some systems in place—like an HR policy, an access control process, or an incident log. Maintaining and improving what already works saves time, money, and headaches. Plus, your team will appreciate knowing you're building on what they already trust, rather than discarding good work.

Step 4: Compare What You Have with What You Need: Now comes the real detective work—comparing your current ISMS "as-is" with the ISO 27001 requirements. You don't need to start from scratch; remember the Mandatory Documents List we created in the last chapter? Use it as a quick checklist to see which of those documents you already have in place.

Take a further step—retrieve the ISMS Document Template from Chapter 6 and verify if your current documents comply with the document control requirements of Clause 7.5. This will instantly show you which policies and procedures are ready for an audit and which ones need updating or drafting from scratch.

Besides reviewing the documentation requirements, remember to check the requirements that aren't documented as well. For example, ISO 27001 doesn't specifically require a documented "awareness program," but it does require awareness. Ask yourself: Do you hold awareness sessions? Do employees understand their information security responsibilities? These intangible practices are just as important as written documents in closing your gaps.

Imagine walking through your half-built house with the blueprint in one hand and the materials list in the other—checking off what's done, flagging what's missing, and noting where the quality isn't up to standard.

Why It Matters: This is the core of the Gap Analysis—the moment you clearly see where your ISMS is strong and where it has gaps. Without this comparison, you're just guessing what needs fixing. And in ISO 27001 projects, guessing often leads to missed requirements, failed audits, or last-minute scrambling to patch holes.

Step 5: Capture Evidence, Not Just Opinions: When you mark something as conformance, don't just rely on "We do that." Show it. Provide the actual proof—whether it's a signed policy document, a meeting record, a screenshot of a system setting, or even a training attendance sheet. Evidence can take many forms: review the documentation, take a sample, interview a few executives, conduct site visits, or observe whether people are doing in practice what they claim to do. The ISMS world is built on evidence-based thinking, and this is where it begins.

Think of it like building your house again: if the contractor says, "Oh yes, the foundation is solid," you'd still want to see the inspection report, rather than just taking their word for it. In the same way, for every ISO 27001 requirement you claim is met, make sure you have something tangible to support it.

Why It Matters: Auditors don't trust warm smiles and verbal assurances; they rely on objective evidence. Evidence is your safety net—it not only supports your claims but also protects you if there's a dispute later. Without it, you're building your ISMS on unstable ground.

Step 6: Identify the Gaps and Prioritize Them: After comparing your current state with ISO 27001 requirements, you'll compile a list—some items will be okay, some will need improvement, and others will be missing entirely. That's your gap list.

But here's the trick: not all gaps are the same. A missing Information Security Policy? That's a significant one. A minor adjustment needed in your supplier evaluation process? Probably less urgent. Prioritize based on risk, business impact, and how fundamental the control is to your ISMS. Remember the risk-based approach we discussed in Chapter 4.

Another method, if you're unsure how to prioritize, is to go through the standard clause by clause. This method also works well because ISO 27001 is written in a logical sequence, created to provide a smooth, organized implementation process.

In house-building, if your roof leaks, fix that before repainting the kitchen. Likewise, in ISMS, tackle high-risk, high-impact gaps first. This ensures your most critical vulnerabilities are addressed early, while less urgent improvements can be scheduled later.

Why It Matters: Without proper prioritization, you'll spend too much time on "easy wins" while significant compliance gaps stay unaddressed—risking failure in an audit and leaving your organization vulnerable.

Step 7: Turn the Gap List into an Action Plan: By now, you've identified where your ISMS stands and where it gaps. The next move? Move from analysis to action. Take your list of gaps, assign each to a responsible owner, set realistic deadlines, and decide how you'll track progress. This is when you start shaping your actual ISMS project plan.

It's just like building that house — you've walked around, identified the missing walls, loose wires, and unpainted rooms. Now it's time to bring in the right contractors, set a timeline, and keep checking until the job is finished.

Why It Matters: A Gap Analysis stored in a folder is just a report. Turning it into a living action plan is what shifts you from "knowing" to "doing." This is where momentum starts—and without momentum, your ISMS will stall before it even begins.

Implementation Tool: Gap Analysis Checklist

In this section, I've provided you with a ready-to-use Gap Analysis Checklist tool—the same one I've tested on numerous ISMS projects. It's built to help ensure you cover all aspects and turn insights into actions. Use it to evaluate your organization's current readiness and identify exactly what still needs to be done to achieve full conformity with ISO 27001.

This checklist covers all Clauses 4–10 of the standard. It's comprehensive, practical, and reusable—ideal for tracking your ISMS progress over time. Each item in the tool prompts you to evaluate your organization's status based on its maturity or conformance level.

To make things easier, I've provided three different scoring scale options. Why? Because no two organizations are at the same level of experience, maturity, or internal competency. You have the freedom to choose the scale that best fits your team's current ability and the depth of analysis you want to conduct.

If you're not sure which one to start with, here's my suggestion:

- Begin with **Option 1** if you're in the early stages and want a clear, simple picture.
- Move to **Option 2** as your ISMS matures and you need more detail in your assessment.
- When you're getting close to your certification audit, switch to **Option 3** for a deeper, more precise evaluation.

After all, this is your implementation project—I want you to stay the final decision-maker at all times.

Option 1—Binary + Partial (0–2 scale): Table 7.1 shows a simple binary and partial scoring scale that you can use to assess ISMS conformity at an early stage.

Table 7.1 Binary and partial scoring scale for ISMS conformity assessment

Score	*Meaning*	*Example*
0	No work done / Non-conformity	No documented process for handling incidents
1	Partial conformity (some work done, but gaps remain)	Incident handling is documented but not tested
2	Full conformity (meets the requirement completely)	Incident handling documented, tested, and evidence available

Pros

- Very easy to use and explain
- Gaps are apparent because a **zero** stands out strongly
- Quick to total and see progress

Cons

- Less detail than bigger scales (doesn't capture "almost done" very well)

Option 2—Expanded Readiness Scale (0–3 Scale): As your ISMS grows and your understanding deepens, a slightly more detailed scale can be helpful. Table 7.2 shows an expanded readiness scoring scale that allows you to distinguish between awareness, partial progress,

Table 7.2 Expanded readiness scoring scale for ISMS assessment

Score	*Meaning*	*Example*
0	No work done / Nonconformity	No risk assessment performed
1	Awareness stage (requirement known, but no formal work started)	The team is aware that risk assessment is required, but it has not yet been initiated
2	Partial conformity (work started, in progress, or an informal process exists)	Risk assessment started but was not finalized.
3	Full conformity (requirement fully met, evidence available)	Risk assessment completed, documented, and approved

and full conformity. This is particularly useful when teams have started work but are not yet fully consistent or evidence ready.

Pros

- Gives credit for "awareness" even before formal action
- Motivates progress because early work scores something
- Keeps 0 for truly untouched areas

Cons

- Slightly more judgment calls when deciding between **1** and **2**

Option 3—Maturity Level Scale (0–5): This scale is adapted from ISO 21827 [27], Information technology—Security techniques—Systems Security Engineering— Capability Maturity Model (SSE-CMM). I've customized it to suit ISMS Gap Analysis in a practical, real-world context. It uses five recognized capability levels—from initial and ad-hoc practices through to optimized and continually improving processes—with an additional Level 0 (Not Started) added to reflect where many ISMS journeys realistically begin. Table 7.3 shows this ISMS maturity level scoring scale.

Table 7.3 ISMS maturity level scoring scale

Score	*Meaning*	*Example*
0	Not started	No asset inventory exists
1	Initial/ad-hoc (unstructured, reactive)	Asset inventory is updated only when new assets appear
2	Repeatable (informal consistency, some documentation)	Basic asset list is maintained but inconsistently updated
3	Defined (formal process documented)	Asset inventory process documented and followed
4	Managed (measured and monitored)	Asset inventory is regularly reviewed and verified against actual assets
5	Optimized (continual improvement in place)	Automated asset tracking system with continual updates and process improvements

This has been my go-to scale for Gap Analysis work because it doesn't just show where you stand today; it also makes progress over time visible and measurable, which is far more useful than a simple pass-or-fail view.

Pros

- Gives a richer picture of ISMS maturity
- Can be reused later to measure improvement after remediation

Cons

- Needs clear guidance to avoid scoring inconsistencies
- Can feel heavy for beginners

Table 7.4 is your ISO 27001 Gap Analysis checklist—a practical tool you can use to assess your organization's current level of conformity with ISO 27001 requirements. Here's how to get the most value from it:

- **Start with What You Already Have:** Gather your existing evidence, whether it's formal documents like policies, procedures, and meeting minutes, or informal practices that are "how things are done" in your organization.
- **Rate Your Maturity:** Use the **0–5 scale** from *Option 3—Maturity Level Scale* (or your preferred scale) to assess each task honestly.
- **Watch for the Asterisk*:** Any task marked with an asterisk means **documented information is mandatory** under the ISO standard. These are non-negotiable, so give them special attention.
- **Add It All Up:** Once you've rated every task, total your scores to see your overall maturity level.
- **Review Your Summary:** At the end of the table, you'll find a summary section to help you interpret your results and decide where to focus your improvement efforts for your ISMS journey.

Table 7.4 ISO 27001 Gap Analysis Checklist

Sr.	*Checklist Question*	*Current Evidence / Notes*	*Rating*
1	**4.1—Understanding the Organization and Its Context**—Has the organization undertaken a review to determine external and internal issues relevant to its ISMS?		
2	**4.2—Understanding Needs and Expectations of Interested Parties**—Has the organization identified internal and external interested parties, understood their relevant needs and expectations, and decided which become legal or other requirements?		
3	**4.3*—Determining the Scope of the ISMS**—Has the organization determined the ISMS boundaries and applicability by considering internal and external issues, the needs and expectations of interested parties, and dependencies, and ensured that the **scope is available as documented information**?		
4	**4.4—Establishing the ISMS**—Has the organization established and documented its ISMS, including all necessary processes and their interactions?		
5	**5.1—Leadership and Commitment**—Has top management demonstrated leadership by aligning the ISMS with the organization's strategic direction, providing resources, and promoting continual improvement?		
6	**5.2*—Information Security Policy**—Has an information security policy been established, **documented**, communicated, and made available to relevant interested parties?		
7	**5.3—Roles, Responsibilities, and Authorities**—Have roles and responsibilities for the ISMS been clearly assigned and communicated, including responsibility for system performance and compliance?		
8	**6.1.1—Actions to Address Risks and Opportunities**—Has the organization considered the issues identified in 4.1, requirements in 4.2, and ISMS scope to determine relevant risks and opportunities?		

(*Continued*)

Table 7.4 (Continued)

Sr.	*Checklist Question*	*Current Evidence / Notes*	*Rating*
9	**6.1.1—Risk and Opportunity Action Plans**—Have actions to address identified risks and opportunities been implemented, and monitored for effectiveness?		
10	**6.1.2*—Risk Assessment Methodology**—Is there a consistent, **documented** process for identifying, analyzing, evaluating, and prioritizing information security risks?		
11	**6.1.2—Application of Risk Assessment**—Is the defined risk assessment process applied consistently and approved by relevant stakeholders?		
12	**6.1.3*—Statement of Applicability**—Has the organization selected appropriate controls, prepared a **Statement of Applicability, and documented reasons for control inclusion or exclusion?**		
13	**6.1.3*—Risk Treatment Plan**—Has a **documented plan** been prepared, approved by risk owners, and tracked to completion?		
14	**6.1.3—Residual Risk Acceptance**—Has the organization obtained approval from risk owners for any residual risks remaining after risk treatment?		
15	**6.2*—Information Security Objectives**—Has the organization established measurable information security objectives that align with the ISMS policy, supported by plans detailing responsibilities, timelines, and evaluation methods, and ensured these **objectives are maintained as documented information?**		
16	**6.3—Planning of Changes**—Are ISMS changes planned, with risks assessed, resources allocated, and impacts on other processes considered?		
17	**7.1—Resources**—Has the organization provided adequate human, technological, and financial resources for the establishment, implementation, maintenance, and continual improvement of the ISMS?		
18	**7.2*—Competence**—Has the organization determined the necessary competence for individuals performing work that affects ISMS performance, taken actions to achieve and maintain that competence, and **retained documented information as evidence of competence?**		
19	**7.3—Awareness**—Has the organization ensured that all persons working under its control are aware of the ISMS policy, their contribution to its effectiveness, and the consequences of nonconformance?		
20	**7.4—Communication**—Has the organization established processes for internal and external communications relevant to the ISMS, including what will be communicated, when, with whom, and by what means?		
21	**7.5.1*—Documented Information Requirements**—Has the organization established, maintained, and controlled documented information required by ISO 27001 and deemed necessary for effective ISMS operation?		
22	**7.5.2—Creation and Update of Documented Information**—Has the organization defined a structured process for creating and updating documented information, including format, identification, review, approval, and version control?		

(Continued)

Table 7.4 (Continued)

Sr.	*Checklist Question*	*Current Evidence / Notes*	*Rating*
23	**7.5.3—Documented Information Control**—Are documented information controls in place to ensure documents are available where needed, protected from loss, unauthorized access, or improper use, and kept up to date?		
24	**7.5.3*—Control of External Origin Documents**—Has the organization identified **documented information of external origin** necessary for ISMS operation and ensured appropriate control measures are applied?		
25	**8.1*—Operational Planning and Control**—Has the organization determined, planned, and implemented the processes needed to meet ISMS requirements, including criteria for their operation and the application of controls, and **retained documented information** sufficient to demonstrate that these processes have been carried out as planned?		
26	**8.1—Control of Planned Changes**—Has the organization established a process to plan and control changes that could affect ISMS performance, ensuring unintended changes are reviewed and mitigated?		
27	**8.1—Outsourced Processes Control**—Has the organization ensured that externally provided processes, products, or services that can affect information security are controlled and meet ISMS requirements?		
28	**8.2*—Information Security Risk Assessment**—Has the organization established and maintained a process to ensure information security risk assessments are conducted at planned intervals or when significant changes occur, and **retained documented information of the results of these assessments?**		
29	**8.3*—Information Security Risk Treatment**—Has the organization implemented the risk treatment plan, evaluated its effectiveness, and **retained documented information of the results of the risk treatment?**		
30	**9.1*—Monitoring, Measurement, Analysis, and Evaluation**—Has the organization determined what needs to be monitored and measured, along with the methods, frequency, and responsibilities, to evaluate ISMS performance and effectiveness, and **retained documented information as evidence of the results?**		
31	**9.2*—Internal Audit Program**—Has the organization planned, established, implemented, and maintained an internal audit program for the ISMS, considering process importance, previous audit results, and ensuring **documented evidence of both the program and audit results?**		
32	**9.2—Audit Criteria and Scope**—Has the organization defined clear audit criteria and scope for each internal audit, and selected auditors to ensure objectivity and impartiality?		
33	**9.2—Reporting and Management Review of Audit Results**—Has the organization ensured that internal audit results are formally reported to relevant management for review and follow-up actions?		

(Continued)

Table 7.4 (Continued)

Sr.	*Checklist Question*	*Current Evidence / Notes*	*Rating*
34	**9.3—Management Review**—Has the organization conducted management reviews of the ISMS at planned intervals, ensuring they evaluate its continuing suitability, adequacy, and effectiveness while addressing opportunities for improvement, necessary changes, and overall ISMS performance?		
35	**9.3—Management Review Inputs**—Has top management ensured that the management review includes **all inputs required by ISO 27001**, such as the status of previous actions, changes in external and internal issues, updates to the needs and expectations of interested parties, trends in nonconformities and corrective actions, monitoring and measurement results, audit findings, progress toward information security objectives, feedback from interested parties, results of risk assessments, the status of the risk treatment plan, and identified opportunities for continual improvement?		
36	**9.3*—Management Review Outputs**—Have the **results of the management review been documented**, including clear decisions on continual improvement, any required changes to the ISMS, and the allocation of necessary resources to achieve intended outcomes?		
37	**10.1—Continual Improvement**—Has the organization continually improved the suitability, adequacy, and effectiveness of the ISMS, based on monitoring results, audits, management reviews, and other relevant inputs?		
38	**10.2*—Nonconformity and Corrective Action (Identification and Response)**—When a nonconformity occurs, has the organization promptly reacted to control and correct it, addressed any consequences, **and documented the nature of the nonconformity**?		
39	**10.2—Cause Analysis and Prevention**—Has the organization reviewed the nonconformity, determined its cause(s), checked for similar or potential nonconformities, and taken action to prevent recurrence?		
40	**10.2*—Action Review and Records**—Has the organization implemented necessary corrective actions, reviewed their effectiveness, updated the ISMS if needed, and **maintained documented evidence of actions taken and results achieved**?		
Total Score			

Author's Note: Treat this checklist as a learning exercise, not an exam. The aim is to understand your current position clearly so you can plan your next steps with confidence.

Interpreting Your Gap Analysis Score

Your total score is more than just a number; it's a snapshot of your ISMS maturity at this moment. Think of it as a navigation tool that helps you decide where to act first and how fast to move. The maximum possible score is 200 (40 tasks × 5 points each).

Table 7.5 shows how to interpret your Gap Analysis score and what each score range really means in practical terms. Use it to understand your current position and to prioritize your next actions with clarity.

Here's how to read your results:

Table 7.5 Gap Analysis score interpretation guide

Score Range	*Maturity Level*	*What It Means for You*	*Suggested Focus*
0–50	Initial	Your ISMS is in its early stages. Controls, processes, and documentation are either missing or very limited.	Start with foundational policies, basic risk assessment, and mandatory documentation. Build awareness within the organization.
51–100	Developing	Some ISMS elements are in place, but gaps remain in coverage, consistency, and evidence.	Strengthen risk management, formalize processes, and close compliance gaps. Prioritize areas with mandatory documentation.
101–150	Established	Core requirements are met, with evidence in most areas. However, there is room for improvement in integration, monitoring, and continual improvement.	Focus on embedding ISMS practices into daily operations, improving measurement, and enhancing staff engagement.
151–180	Managed	Your ISMS is well structured, integrated, and consistently applied. Weaknesses are minor but worth addressing for resilience.	Refine advanced controls, perform regular reviews, and prepare for a smooth certification process.
181–200	Optimized	Your ISMS is not only compliant but also delivers substantial business value.	Maintain momentum through continual improvement, explore automation, and benchmark against industry best practices.

Author's Note: Your score is not a pass or fail. It's a living metric. A low score means you have greater opportunities for improvement. Even a high score doesn't mean you stop—ISO 27001 is about continual improvement, not a finish line.

From Gaps to Project Plan

You've completed your Gap Analysis and scored your ISMS maturity, so now you have a clear picture of where you stand and what's missing. The best part? You're no longer working on assumptions. The next step is to turn those gaps into a practical, structured plan that fits your organization's reality.

This means deciding exactly **what** needs to be done, **who** will do it, **how long** it should take, and **how** you'll know it's complete. If you're unsure about any of these, don't guess—get professional input. Talk to department heads, your IT managers, or anyone directly responsible for the areas in question to set realistic timelines.

Think of it like drawing up the blueprint for your ISMS house. You've already surveyed the land and taken measurements. Now it's time to map out the build—complete with a clear timeline and trackable milestones—so you can move from plans on paper to a fully built, working ISMS.

GANTT CHART

Once you've listed your tasks and agreed on timelines, the next step is to see the whole plan in one place—and that's where a **Gantt chart** comes in.

Think of it as your ISMS construction schedule. In our house-building example, some jobs (like installing wiring) must wait until earlier steps are finished, while others (like finishing the exterior) can run alongside other work. A Gantt chart lets you see all of this at a glance. It's a simple visual timeline showing tasks on the left and dates across the top, with horizontal bars representing the duration of each activity.

The benefits are hard to ignore:

- **Clarity:** You see the whole plan in one view.
- **Dependencies:** You know which tasks rely on others being completed first.
- **Realistic Scheduling:** Helps prevent bottlenecks and wasted time.
- **Progress Tracking**—You can check how you're doing against the original plan.

You don't need fancy tools to create one. Many people use Excel for quick, flexible charts (I do this myself), while others prefer Microsoft Project or online tools like Trello or Asana. The point isn't the software—it's the discipline of mapping out the work so you can deliver your ISMS step by step, without surprises.

Planning the Build: A Gantt Chart Example

Now that you understand what a Gantt chart is and why it's useful, let's make it more tangible with a simple, non-ISMS example. Imagine you're building a house. You start with a list of tasks, each with the number of days required to complete them, and a logical sequence in which they must happen. Some tasks can run in parallel, while others can begin only after specific steps are completed. For example, you can't lay the foundation until the site is prepared, and you can't install the roof until the roof framework is in place. Table 7.6 shows a sample task sequencing and duration breakdown using this house-building example. This illustration is purely for understanding the concept, but it mirrors exactly how you would plan and structure your ISMS implementation using the same logic.

Table 7.7 shows an example Gantt chart for a house-building project. It's purely for understanding, but it clearly illustrates how tasks overlap, where dependencies exist, and how a project moves forward over time. The goal is to help you visualize your ISMS journey in the same way—clear, transparent, and easy to track, just like watching a house take shape step by step.

Table 7.6 Sample task sequencing and duration breakdown (house-building example)

Task	*Duration (Days)*	*Sequence*
Prepare lot	2	(1)
Lay foundation	3	(2)
Wall frames	4	(3)
Roof frames	3	(4)
Install plumbing	4	(4)
Install wiring	2	(4)
Cover roof	2	(5)
Exterior walls	3	(6)
Interior walls	3	(6)
Finish interior	3	(7)
Finish exterior	2	(7)

Table 7.7 Example Gantt chart for a house-building project

<table>
<tr><th colspan="2">Building a House</th><th colspan="19">Number of Days</th></tr>
<tr><th>#</th><th>Job Breakdown</th><th>1</th><th>2</th><th>3</th><th>4</th><th>5</th><th>6</th><th>7</th><th>8</th><th>9</th><th>10</th><th>11</th><th>12</th><th>13</th><th>14</th><th>15</th><th>16</th><th>17</th><th>18</th><th>19</th></tr>
<tr><td>1</td><td>Prepare lot</td><td colspan="2">2</td><td></td><td></td><td></td><td></td><td></td><td></td><td></td><td></td><td></td><td></td><td></td><td></td><td></td><td></td><td></td><td></td><td></td></tr>
<tr><td>2</td><td>Lay foundation</td><td></td><td></td><td colspan="3">3</td><td></td><td></td><td></td><td></td><td></td><td></td><td></td><td></td><td></td><td></td><td></td><td></td><td></td><td></td></tr>
<tr><td>3</td><td>Wall frames</td><td></td><td></td><td></td><td></td><td></td><td colspan="4">4</td><td></td><td></td><td></td><td></td><td></td><td></td><td></td><td></td><td></td><td></td></tr>
<tr><td>4</td><td>Roof frames</td><td></td><td></td><td></td><td></td><td></td><td></td><td></td><td></td><td></td><td colspan="3">3</td><td></td><td></td><td></td><td></td><td></td><td></td><td></td></tr>
<tr><td>5</td><td>Install plumbing</td><td></td><td></td><td></td><td></td><td></td><td></td><td></td><td></td><td></td><td colspan="4">4</td><td></td><td></td><td></td><td></td><td></td><td></td></tr>
<tr><td>6</td><td>Install wiring</td><td></td><td></td><td></td><td></td><td></td><td></td><td></td><td></td><td></td><td colspan="2">2</td><td></td><td></td><td></td><td></td><td></td><td></td><td></td><td></td></tr>
<tr><td>7</td><td>Exterior walls</td><td></td><td></td><td></td><td></td><td></td><td></td><td></td><td></td><td></td><td></td><td></td><td></td><td></td><td colspan="3">3</td><td></td><td></td><td></td></tr>
<tr><td>8</td><td>Cover roof</td><td></td><td></td><td></td><td></td><td></td><td></td><td></td><td></td><td></td><td></td><td></td><td></td><td colspan="2">2</td><td></td><td></td><td></td><td></td><td></td></tr>
<tr><td>9</td><td>Interior walls</td><td></td><td></td><td></td><td></td><td></td><td></td><td></td><td></td><td></td><td></td><td></td><td></td><td></td><td colspan="3">3</td><td></td><td></td><td></td></tr>
<tr><td>10</td><td>Finish interior</td><td></td><td></td><td></td><td></td><td></td><td></td><td></td><td></td><td></td><td></td><td></td><td></td><td></td><td></td><td></td><td></td><td colspan="3">3</td></tr>
<tr><td>11</td><td>Finish exterior</td><td></td><td></td><td></td><td></td><td></td><td></td><td></td><td></td><td></td><td></td><td></td><td></td><td></td><td></td><td></td><td></td><td colspan="2">2</td><td></td></tr>
</table>

🛠 *Implementation Task 2: Creating Your Gantt Chart*

Now it's time to convert your Gap Analysis into a structured Gantt chart. This will act as your roadmap from the "current state" to a fully implemented ISMS. If you're unsure about the exact sequence, follow the order in your Gap Analysis checklist. Begin with Task 1 and proceed to Task 40, adjusting the durations, dates, and responsibilities based on your organization's situation.

Your Gantt chart should show realistic timelines, consider resource availability, and assign responsibilities for each task. This visual timeline will help monitor progress, manage dependencies, and communicate status clearly with stakeholders.

Table 7.8 shows an example project plan using the first three tasks from the ISMS Gap Analysis Checklist. Use this as a reference format for building out the rest of your project plan.

Once you've set up the first few rows like this, continue expanding the rest of your Gantt chart using your task list from the Gap Analysis. You can do this in Excel (quick and flexible), MS Project, or any specialized project management tool. Even a simple spreadsheet will give you a clear visual of how your ISMS implementation will unfold over time.

Table 7.8 Example project plan using first three tasks from the ISMS Gap Analysis Checklist

Task No.	*Task Description*	*Duration (Days)*	*Start Date*	*End Date*	*Responsible Owner*
1	**4.1—Understanding the Organization and Its Context**—Review to determine external and internal issues relevant to the ISMS	3	01 Jan	03 Jan	ISMS Manager
2	**4.2—Understanding Needs and Expectations of Interested Parties**—Identify internal/external interested parties, understand needs/expectations, and decide which become legal or other requirements	4	04 Jan	07 Jan	Compliance Officer
3	**4.3—Determining the Scope of the ISMS**—Define ISMS boundaries and applicability, considering issues, interested parties, and dependencies; ensure scope is documented	5	08 Jan	12 Jan	ISMS Manager

Key Takeaway—What You've Learned

- Start with a reality check—perform a Gap Analysis before taking any action. Understand your current state so your plan addresses fundamental gaps, not imagined ones.
- Bring the right people together: the ISO text plus process owners equals an honest, practical assessment.
- Clearly define your ISMS scope—unclear boundaries lead to unnecessary audit and implementation efforts.
- Review existing processes and keep what works—avoid discarding proper processes or documents just because they are not perfect.
- Gather evidence, not just claims: every "we do this" statement must be backed by verifiable proof like records, screenshots, meeting minutes, or logs.
- Prioritize based on risk and impact—fix the urgent issues before tackling less critical tasks. High-risk, high-impact gaps should be addressed first.
- Convert gaps into actionable steps: assign owners, set realistic deadlines, and monitor progress. A stored-away Gap Analysis does nothing.
- Create a Gantt chart to visualize sequences, dependencies, and timelines—this helps prevent bottlenecks and keeps everyone aligned.
- Plan proportionately—small organizations need lightweight processes; larger ones may require formal change or project controls.
- Maintain an audit mindset: internal audits, management reviews, and evidence collection should inform your plan and demonstrate readiness.
- View the Gap Analysis score as a navigation tool, not a pass/fail test—low scores highlight opportunities, high scores call for ongoing vigilance.
- Maintain momentum: assign responsibilities, communicate consistently, and avoid "stalled in planning" syndrome.
- Remember: implementation is an iterative process—build, test, measure, refine, and repeat. Continuous improvement begins now, not after certification.

QUIZ #6

True/False statement

Sr.	*Statement*	*True/False*
1	A Gap Analysis Checklist should only include clauses that require mandatory documentation.	
2	The maturity score in a Gap Analysis reflects how well an organization has implemented a control or requirement.	
3	A Gantt chart is only useful for tracking large, complex projects and is not necessary for smaller ISMS implementations.	
4	In the ISMS implementation process, every task in the Gap Analysis Checklist must always be completed in the exact same sequence for all organizations.	
5	A Gap Analysis helps you stop working on assumptions by showing exactly where you stand and what's missing.	

Before you continue, there's something important I'd like to share. Starting from this point, you'll find short case studies at the end of selected chapters. Each case is based on realistic scenarios—full of practical decisions, challenges, and situations you might experience in a real ISO 27001 implementation. After reading a case, take your time with the six multiple-choice questions that follow. These aren't meant to be rushed. They're designed to help you pause, think, and apply what you've learned.

At the back of the book, you'll find the answers and justifications for all the case questions. To get the most learning value, try not to look before attempting them yourself. Once you're done, compare your answers and reasoning. Over time, this practice will help strengthen your understanding and build confidence in applying ISO 27001 in real environments.

CASE 1: THE DATA FORTRESS IN NAIROBI

The morning sun was rising over the outskirts of Nairobi when Aisha Kamau entered the gates of SecureNet Data Centre for her first week as the Lead Implementer of ISO 27001. The facility was about 35 miles from the city—a cluster of glass and concrete buildings surrounded by tall fencing and humming generators that seemed never to stop.

SecureNet managed critical systems and data for several banks, fintech startups, and logistics companies across East Africa. From the outside, it appeared to be everything it claimed—with armed guards at the entrance, biometric access doors, and hundreds of surveillance cameras quietly monitoring.

Recently, SecureNet's CEO, Mr. Otieno, decided that the company needed to align with ISO 27001. He had noticed clients requesting certification as part of their vendor risk process, and he wanted to stay ahead of the competition. That's how Aisha, a young but energetic information security professional, was brought in as the Lead Implementer.

Her first few days were a mix of excitement and concern. On paper, SecureNet looked impressive—CCTV coverage, biometric gates, and strict visitor controls. But as she explored further, the flaws began to surface.

Her first tour of the Data Hall was impressive, but when she asked the IT team to show her the network configuration records, James, the IT Head, hesitated. "They're all in the system," he said vaguely. "We don't really maintain them separately."

The Operations team, led by Grace, proudly showed her their visitor logbook—handwritten, smudged, and missing entire weeks of data. Evelyn, the HR Manager, had neat onboarding forms for new employees but smiled nervously when asked about access removal after someone left. "We usually handle that through IT... unless they forget."

Aisha nodded thoughtfully and took notes.

Later that afternoon, she met with the CEO, Mr. Otieno, who clearly stated that certification was a business objective, not just a technical goal. "Our clients are asking for ISO 27001," he said. "You have my full support—but we need results in six months."

Aisha understood the pressure. She decided her first step would be to conduct a Gap Analysis to compare SecureNet's current practices with ISO 27001 requirements. She explained this to the management team during her kickoff meeting. "Conducting a gap analysis," she told them confidently, "is one of the requirements of ISO 27001. It's the best way to start." The team nodded in agreement, happy to see her taking charge.

She started arranging one-on-one meetings with each department head. During her discussion with Evelyn from HR, their conversation became lively.

"How do you classify sensitive employee information?" Aisha asked.

"Mostly by department—we keep HR files in a locked cabinet," Evelyn replied.

"And digital records?"

"They're saved on a shared folder. I think IT manages permissions."

Aisha observed everything. She wasn't just watching—she was learning the culture. People were cooperative but not accustomed to being questioned about processes.

Within a week, she had filled pages with observations. Some were straightforward process weaknesses; others were more serious. She organized her notes into Documentation Gaps, Process Gaps, and Control Gaps to streamline the follow-up work.

To keep her project on track, she created a Gantt Chart that listed every task: Gap Analysis, risk assessment, policy writing, training sessions, and internal audit preparations. She mostly put the chart together herself to keep things moving and only shared it with the team once it was complete. "It's better to move fast," she thought. "We can make adjustments later."

By the end of her second week, her office whiteboard was covered with timelines, post-it notes, and a long list of action items. She was making progress—but she also realized that implementing ISO 27001 wasn't just about structure and deadlines. It was about people, communication, and clarity.

SecureNet had the potential to set a standard for security excellence—if Aisha could balance her focus on results with teamwork and precision. The real challenge was just starting.

Case Discussion—Test Your Understanding

1. **What was the main purpose Aisha aimed to achieve by conducting a Gap Analysis before implementing ISO 27001?**

   A. To identify the gaps between the organization's existing practices and the requirements of ISO 27001
   B. To finalize the information security policy
   C. To prepare for the certification body's Stage 1 audit
   D. To assess staff satisfaction with current controls

2. **Aisha mentioned to the management team that conducting a Gap Analysis is a requirement of ISO 27001. Is her statement correct?**

   A. True
   B. False

3. **Which of the following tools best supports Aisha in tracking implementation activities and milestones?**

   A. Strengths, Weaknesses, Opportunities, and Threats (SWOT) Analysis
   B. Risk Matrix
   C. Control Checklist
   D. Gantt Chart

4. What could Aisha have done better while preparing her implementation plan?

A. Exclude technical teams from planning to save time
B. Submit the plan directly to the certification body for approval
C. Seek input from key departments before finalizing timelines
D. Focus only on IT and HR departments during planning

5. During her meetings with department heads like James, Grace, Evelyn, and Patrick, what should have been Aisha's main focus to ensure a strong start to the ISMS implementation?

A. Checking employee attendance records and overtime logs
B. Identifying each department's key processes, information assets, and existing controls
C. Reviewing only IT-related system configurations and server data
D. Preparing draft documents for the upcoming certification audit

6. When Aisha met with CEO Mr. Otieno and discussed the 6-month certification goal, why was top management involvement so critical at that stage?

A. It helped her schedule the certification audit earlier with the chosen certification body
B. It allowed the CEO to delegate all ISMS responsibilities to Aisha and her team
C. It reduced the amount of evidence auditors would later review during certification
D. It ensured leadership commitment, resource allocation, and alignment between ISMS goals and business priorities

Chapter 8

Clause 4—Understand your world before you secure it

Mapping context, interested parties, and scope for a strong ISMS foundation

INTRODUCTION

Welcome to the build phase, or the Plan phase of the PDCA framework, in your ISO 27001 journey. From this point forward, we'll work through each clause, turning understanding into action. To keep things clear and practical, I'll break down each requirement into four parts:

1. **Summary of the Clause Requirements:** A brief, high-level overview of what the clause requests. This won't replace the actual standard, so if you need the precise wording, always refer to your own copy of ISO 27001.
2. **Explanation with Real-World Examples:** Here, I'll translate the requirement into plain language and connect it with practical, real-world scenarios. This helps you see how the standard applies beyond theory.
3. **Implementation Guidance:** Step by step, I'll show you how to implement the clause. We'll discuss recommended actions, related documentation, and practical tips to keep your ISMS effective and manageable.
4. **Toolkits and Resources:** To streamline the process, I'll share templates, checklists, and tools you can customize for your organization. Each comes with simple instructions and sample entries to guide you, but the examples are broad intentionally. They're meant as starting points, not final solutions, so you'll need to adapt them to your specific situation. Remember, the tools I provide are generic—not comprehensive. Your own context will add more detail. A word of caution: Don't just copy and paste them. Continually review and modify to fit your specific business needs.

With this approach, each clause becomes manageable and actionable, not just words on paper, but a clear path to building a strong ISMS.

From this point, we'll begin applying this four-part approach and steadily work through Clauses 4–10. My advice is simple: follow each step carefully. This sequence is deliberate and helps build a strong ISMS foundation. If you've already made progress on specific clauses, that's great—use these chapters to double-check, refine, and strengthen your earlier work.

We'll start with Clause 4 because it truly sets the stage for everything that follows. Here, you'll establish your organization's context, identify the interested parties, and define the scope of your ISMS. Think of this as laying the foundation before building the walls. When you get this part right, every other step becomes more focused, efficient, and much easier to manage.

DOI: 10.1201/9781003744139-9

Author's Note: From now on, I'll frequently suggest creating documentation, even for clauses where the standard doesn't explicitly require it. Why? Because of two key truths in ISO 27001:

- **Clause 7.5.1(b)** says you must have documented information that *you* determine is necessary for the effectiveness of your ISMS.
- **Clause 8.1** says documented information should be available to the extent necessary to give confidence that processes have been carried out as planned.

Here's the catch: If you decide not to document something simply because the specific clause doesn't require it, you may later struggle to show evidence during an audit. The auditor's natural question will be, *"How do you prove you actually did this?"* If you can't produce something tangible—meeting notes, awareness program—it becomes a matter of opinion, and opinions rarely win in audits.

⚠ **Caution:** While I encourage you to document wisely, don't fall into the trap of over-documenting. ISO 27001 focuses on securing information and improving your system—not drowning in paperwork. If you spend all your energy creating documents instead of implementing real, adequate controls, you'll miss the point entirely. The goal is evidence and effectiveness, not endless files and forms.

My advice: Document whenever it improves clarity, enhances traceability, or provides proof that your processes are effective and occurred as planned, but always stay focused on what truly matters.

Remember: *Document enough to prove it, but not so much that you never get around to doing it.*

GUIDING PRINCIPLES FOR EVERY CLAUSE

Before moving on to Clause 4, there's something we need to clarify. The way you approach implementation here will set the tone for the rest of the clauses. Think of what follows as your guide, a principle to keep you on track throughout the build. Consider it your guiding principle.

Effective implementation starts with people. Make sure you have a capable team in place and involve them from the beginning. Don't try to handle this alone. Conduct brainstorming sessions, include diverse perspectives, and ensure department heads and key staff contribute. The goal is to gather a range of ideas and feedback, giving you enough options to choose from based on your organization's needs and business situation.

Equally important is engaging the right voices at the right moments. For example, if you analyze external issues but neglect to include your procurement team, you'll miss valuable insights about suppliers. Or if you design a risk control without consulting the department that will use it daily, don't be surprised if it fails in practice. People who feel left out of decisions rarely support them; in fact, they may find creative ways to bypass them.

Motivation also significantly affects success. Be open with your team about why you're implementing ISO 27001. Don't send mixed signals. Suppose the main reason is to secure that key customer; state it clearly. If it's about improving internal processes, explain that as well. People work best when they know the actual goal. Setting clear objectives keeps the team engaged, collaborative, and focused.

Delegation is another powerful tool. Whenever possible, delegate responsibilities purposefully—not just to lighten your workload, but to develop your future managers. When delegation is intentional and clear, it motivates people to take initiative, fosters ownership, and supports continuity planning. Just remember, delegation without context can feel like dumping work. Delegation with vision builds leaders.

Here's the key rule: Involve, motivate, and delegate purposefully. Whether you're defining context, setting goals, or putting controls in place, success depends on engaging those closest to the issue and giving them a reason to take ownership of the outcome.

WHY CONTEXT MATTERS IN ISO 27001

Every organization is unique, not just in what it does, but in how and where it operates. Even two IT service companies sharing the same building could have very different realities. One might work with government agencies bound by strict compliance rules, while the other supports fast-moving startups that prioritize speed and innovation above all else. Their risks, priorities, and security measures will naturally differ significantly.

The same applies within a single organization. Consider two data centers operated by the same company—one in a high-security industrial zone and the other in a flood-prone suburban area. Although they are part of the same business, the risks, legal requirements, and operational challenges at each location will vary greatly.

Context encompasses more than just location or infrastructure. It includes your legal and regulatory environment, organizational culture, technology maturity, financial standing, stakeholder expectations, and even internal politics.

That's why Clause 4 of ISO 27001 starts with understanding the organization's context. Before implementing controls, purchasing security tools, or even drafting your first ISMS policy, you should step back and ask:

- Who are we as an organization?
- What external pressures and internal priorities shape our decisions?
- Which risks are genuinely relevant to our situation?

When you understand your context, you can:

- Align your ISMS with actual business needs, not generic templates.
- Avoid wasting resources on controls that don't address your real risks.
- Clearly communicate your security priorities to leaders, staff, and stakeholders.
- Keep your ISMS adaptable so it can evolve as your organization changes.

In short, context is your guide. It keeps your ISMS directed correctly—relevant, resilient, and firmly rooted in your organization's actual environment.

CLAUSE 4.1: UNDERSTANDING THE ORGANIZATION AND ITS CONTEXT

Summary of the Clause Requirements: Clause 4.1 requires an organization to understand its operating environment, both internally and externally. The aim is to identify issues relevant to the organization's purpose and that could impact its ability to achieve the desired outcomes of its ISMS.

This isn't a one-time exercise. As context changes over time, understanding must be kept current and updated as circumstances shift. The insights gained here will lay the groundwork for defining the ISMS scope, evaluating risks, and choosing controls that truly support the organization's objectives.

Basically, Clause 4.1 makes sure you understand your world before securing it, keeping your ISMS focused, flexible, and practical.

Explanation with Real-World Examples: Clause 4.1 is all about stepping back and asking, *"What kind of world are we operating in, and how does that world affect our information security?"*

This isn't just a box-ticking exercise. It's a continuous habit of examining both external and internal factors that could influence the effectiveness of your ISMS. These insights assist in three key ways:

- **Defining the ISMS Scope:** Knowing precisely what's in and out of your information security boundaries.
- **Identifying Risks and Opportunities:** Spotting where you need to strengthen controls or seize opportunities.
- **Keeping the ISMS Relevant:** Adjusting when your environment changes.

External issues are factors outside your direct control—the broader environment in which you operate. They can be:

- Social and cultural trends
- Political, legal, and regulatory changes
- Economic or financial conditions
- Technological developments
- Natural or environmental factors
- Competitive pressures

Even organizations in the same sector or location can face very different external realities. For example, imagine you are an IT service provider in the Kingdom of Saudi Arabia with offices in Jeddah and Dammam. In Jeddah, flooding might be a significant natural risk, while in Dammam, frequent sandstorms could be the bigger concern. Same country, same type of business, but very different external contexts to consider.

Consider another IT service provider with offices in Bangalore, India, and Manama, Bahrain. Bangalore's talent pool makes it easier to find skilled IT staff quickly. However, in Manama, you might encounter local market shortages, leading to dependence on expatriate hires and potentially longer project timelines. These external factors directly influence how you plan, resource, and secure your operations.

Internal issues are within your control—they're about the way your organization works from the inside. These can include:

- Organizational culture
- Policies, objectives, and strategies
- Governance, structure, and roles
- Adopted standards, guidelines, and models
- Contractual obligations that influence your ISMS
- Established processes and procedures
- Resource and competency levels (people, systems, technology, budget, and time)
- Infrastructure and working environment
- Information systems, information flows, and decision-making processes
- Insights from previous audits and risk assessments

For example, even if you have a strong external hiring market, internal gaps in staff skills or knowledge can slow down ISMS implementation. A team lacking awareness of security best practices may unintentionally weaken your controls, making training and capability development a crucial internal issue.

In short, understanding both the external environment and your organization's internal reality provides a solid foundation for effectively building, managing, and adapting your ISMS.

Implementation Guidance: As we discussed in the Guiding Principles, implementation begins with people. For Clause 4.1, gather a competent, cross-functional team. Please avoid skipping any function; every department provides valuable insights, and excluding someone will likely create blind spots later.

The key question to guide the process is simple:

How does a certain category of issues affect our information security objectives?

Here's how I usually approach it when I'm working with an organization:

- **Kick-off Workshop:** Gather everyone together and clarify the clause in plain language. Walk them through what it requires, share a few examples of common issues (both internal and external), and explain how these issues can influence the ISMS. Then, open the floor. Ask the team to brainstorm all the possible internal and external issues that could impact your ISMS. Record everything without filtering.
- **After the Workshop: Reflection Time:** Share the compiled list with everyone and give them about a week. Ask them to reflect, consult with their colleagues, and add anything that might have been overlooked. The goal is to cast the widest possible net.
- **Second Workshop: Refine and Finalize:** In the follow-up session, gather all the additional inputs. Review them one by one, clear up any confusion, and reach a consensus. By the end, you should have a clear draft list of issues that everyone agrees on and supports. Please share this with department heads for their final review and approval.

Once you have the finalized list, record the process and results. Keep this as documented information—not only because ISO requires it but also because it ensures your ISMS remains transparent and defensible during audits.

Finally, don't treat this as a one-time task. Internal and external issues change over time. Market shifts, new regulations, technological advancements, or even internal reorganizations can all alter your ISMS context. That's why you need to review and update the list regularly.

By doing this from day one, you achieve two things:

1. Everyone understands what you're doing and why.
2. You build ownership across the organization, which means better engagement and more substantial support when it comes time to put controls in place.

Toolkit and Resources: Below is a general list of internal and external issues to help you get started with Clause 4.1. These examples are intentionally broad so you can adapt them to your own circumstances—whether you're running a multinational corporation, a government agency, a startup, or a nonprofit organization. Whenever relevant, I've included tips on customizing the tools to reflect your specific business model, regulatory environment, or strategic priorities. Remember, these examples are general and not comprehensive. Your unique situation will continue to evolve, so expand and refine it to highlight what truly matters in your organization.

Internal Issues and Their Impact on the ISMS:

- **Structure of the Organization:** A complex or unclear structure can slow decision-making and weaken accountability for information security.
- **Roles within the Organization:** Poorly defined roles may create gaps or overlaps in ISMS responsibilities, leading to non-compliance.
- **Availability of a Reliable, Qualified, and Competent Workforce:** Without skilled staff, security controls may be poorly implemented or maintained.
- **Stability of Workforce:** Frequent staff changes can disrupt consistency in applying security measures.
- **Staff Retention:** High turnover increases the risk of knowledge loss and potential insider threats.
- **Impact of Unionization:** Labor disputes or negotiations may affect operational stability and access to sensitive systems.
- **Staff Training and Awareness Levels:** Insufficient training leaves employees unaware of security responsibilities, making them easy targets for attacks.
- **Contractual Arrangements with Customers:** Poorly worded contracts may expose the organization to liability for security breaches.
- **Payment Terms from Customers:** Delays in payments may reduce available funds for maintaining or upgrading security systems.
- **Expansion of Customer Base:** Rapid growth can stretch resources and introduce new security risks if not properly managed.
- **Overall Strength of Business to Support Funding Needs:** Weak financial health can limit investment in necessary ISMS controls.
- **Opportunities to Improve Technology:** Leveraging new technology can strengthen the ISMS, but may also bring integration risks.
- **Power Consumption:** High dependency on electricity increases vulnerability to outages, affecting critical security operations.
- **Data Center Capacity:** Limited or poorly managed capacity can result in downtime or loss of data integrity.
- **Resilience of Infrastructure:** Weak infrastructure increases susceptibility to failures, affecting system availability and security.
- **Relationship with Investors:** Poor investor confidence may affect funding for ISMS improvements or continuity planning.
- **Credit Terms Available:** Limited credit may constrain the organization's ability to respond quickly to emerging security needs.
- **Service Level Agreements with Customers:** Weak Service Level Agreements (SLAs) may leave the organization exposed to disputes in the event of security incidents.
- **Culture within the Organization:** A culture that ignores security awareness undermines ISMS effectiveness at every level.
- **Processes and Procedures:** Poorly defined or inconsistent processes can create security loopholes and make incident handling unreliable.

- **Physical Infrastructure and Environment:** Vulnerable buildings, insecure facilities, or poor environmental controls expose the ISMS to physical risks like theft, fire, or outages.
- **Previous Audits and Previous Risk Assessment Results:** Ignoring audit findings or repeating the same risks erodes ISMS credibility and exposes the organization to recurring threats.
- **Lack of Leadership Commitment:** Without visible top management support, the ISMS will likely be underfunded, under-prioritized, and ineffective.

External Issues and Their Impact on the ISMS:

- **Political, Economic, Social, Technological, Legal, and Regulatory Factors:** Government changes, geopolitical instability, or new laws can force rapid ISMS adaptation.
- **Environmental Factors (e.g., Recycling, Disposal of Equipment):** Regulations or shortages can disrupt IT operations and security of assets.
- **Overall Economic Performance in the Country:** Poor conditions may limit budgets for information security, reducing ISMS maturity.
- **The Nature and Impact of the Economy on the Hosting Market:** Cloud/hosting instability or pricing shifts can impact service reliability.
- **Customer Demographics:** Diverse customer groups drive different levels of security expectations (e.g., stricter corporate demands).
- **General Levels of Consumer Confidence:** Reduced trust increases reputational risks, highlighting the need for a robust ISMS.
- **Growth of Outsourcing Business:** Heavy reliance on vendors increases exposure if suppliers lack adequate ISMS practices.
- **Competitive Environment (Low Cost of Entry into the Market):** New players may undercut on price, leading organizations to deprioritize security spending.
- **Customer Expectations:** Increasing demands for privacy, transparency, and speed mean ISMS controls must keep evolving.
- **Standardization and Certification within the Industry:** Industry certifications become benchmarks, making non-compliance risky.
- **Fuel Prices (International/Domestic Pressures, Taxation Regimes, etc.):** Rising costs can strain infrastructure budgets, especially for data centers.
- **Regulation within the Industry:** Sector-specific laws (finance, healthcare, telecom) impose extra ISMS requirements.
- **Licensing Requirements in Respect of Software:** Failure to comply exposes organizations to legal action and operational risks.
- **Trade Associations and Lobbying Powers:** Industry groups may shape standards that influence ISMS design.
- **Impact on Neighbors:** Local protests, disputes, or community risks may affect infrastructure critical to the ISMS.
- **Cybercrime and Threat Landscape:** Evolving attacks (phishing, ransomware, nation-state threats) require constant ISMS updates.
- **Supply Chain Dependencies:** Security failures at suppliers or partners can directly compromise an organization's ISMS.
- **International Data Transfer Restrictions (e.g., GDPR, Cross-Border Rules):** Laws on data movement may limit hosting options and demand stronger ISMS controls.

- **Natural Disasters and Climate Risks:** Floods, earthquakes, or extreme weather can damage physical assets and disrupt ISMS operations.
- **Global Pandemics and Public Health Emergencies:** Sudden shifts to remote work or workforce disruption strain ISMS capabilities.
- **Technological Disruption (AI, IoT, Blockchain, Quantum Computing):** Emerging tech may bring both new opportunities and vulnerabilities.
- **Reputation and Brand Image in the Global Market:** Negative publicity around data breaches elsewhere in the industry may drive stricter customer expectations for ISMS.
- **Insurance and Liability Frameworks:** Rising cyber insurance costs and stricter policy requirements may force ISMS enhancements.

Author's Note: Make sure to identify all relevant internal and external issues for your organization based on its business context. It is equally important to review these issues periodically or whenever there is a significant change in your operating environment. From my experience, I have seen organizations overlook issues that later caused serious challenges for their ISMS. For example, during an internal audit of a commercial bank in West Africa, I found they had not considered frequent power supply disruptions as a critical issue. Even more surprising, they had not recognized the impact of currency volatility, where the US dollar was steadily rising against their local currency. At first, they couldn't understand how exchange rates could affect their ISMS. I explained that since most of their hardware and software licenses were purchased from Western countries, any fluctuation in the dollar would directly impact their IT security budget. This, in turn, could affect their ability to maintain or upgrade systems, which is a clear ISMS concern.

Implementation Task #3: Determine Internal and External Issues

It's time to put this into action. Close this book for a moment and take a fresh look at your organization. Write down all the internal and external issues you think could impact your ISMS. Don't worry about making it perfect on the first try—this is your starting point.

Once you have listed them, come back and compare your notes with the examples I've shared in this chapter. Use my list as a reference, not a strict checklist. If you find gaps, add them to your own version. If you identify something unique to your business that I haven't mentioned, that's even better—you're already customizing the ISMS to fit your needs.

Author's Note: The actual value of this exercise is in your list, not mine. The more your issues mirror your real situation, the more solid your ISMS foundation will be.

CLAUSE 4.2: UNDERSTANDING THE NEEDS AND EXPECTATIONS OF INTERESTED PARTIES

Summary of the Clause Requirements: Clause 4.2 requires your organization to adopt a structured approach to identifying and managing the needs of people and entities interested in your ISMS. Specifically, you need to:

- **Identify the interested parties** that are relevant to your ISMS (for example, customers, regulators, suppliers, employees, shareholders).

- **Understand their requirements** related to information security (such as legal obligations, regulatory demands, or contractual terms).
- **Decide which of those requirements** you will address and integrate into your ISMS.

These requirements may include laws, regulations, standards, contracts, or even customer expectations. In short, the clause ensures your ISMS doesn't operate in isolation but remains aligned with the essential obligations and expectations that influence your business.

Explanation with Real-World Examples: Interested parties are defined as *persons or organizations that can affect, be affected by, or perceive themselves to be affected by a decision or activity of the organization.*

Now, it's usually easy to identify the first two categories—those who affect you and those who are affected by you. Where I often see organizations fall short is in recognizing the third category: Those who perceive themselves to be affected. Ignoring this group can create blind spots in your ISMS.

Interested parties exist both inside and outside your organization, each with their own needs, expectations, or requirements related to information security.

External interested parties might include:

- regulators and legislators
- shareholders, owners, and investors
- suppliers, subcontractors, consultants, and outsourcing partners
- industry associations
- competitors
- customers and consumers
- activist groups

Internal interested parties might include:

- top management and decision-makers
- process owners, system owners, and information owners
- support functions like IT or HR
- employees and end-users
- information security professionals

Now, let's stretch our thinking with some real-world angles:

You're probably agreeing that employees are internal interested parties. But what about their family members or dependents? Consider this: When you collect, store, and process large amounts of employee-related information, you also hold sensitive data about their families. Many organizations provide health insurance covering not just the employee but also spouses, children, and parents. If that information is ever leaked, stolen, or mishandled, the family members—though not directly involved in your business—are still impacted. That makes them relevant external interested parties.

Many organizations overlook the media's influence on information security. But if a data breach happens, don't you think local, national, or even international media outlets will want to know the details? Their reporting can shape public perception, customer trust, and even regulatory scrutiny. That's why the media should also be seen as a potential interested party in your ISMS.

Another common oversight is limiting legal obligations solely to the country where the organization is headquartered. In reality, if you operate or serve customers in multiple countries, you may also be subject to their jurisdiction. For example, if your company is based in South Africa but serves a large customer base in Europe, then the EU's GDPR applies to you. Failing to recognize such obligations could put your ISMS—and your organization—at serious risk.

Here's another example that might surprise you: The general public or citizens of your country can also be external interested parties. Imagine a large IT services company headquartered in your country. You don't work there. You're not a customer. You have no direct connection. But one day, they suffer a significant data breach—and it makes international headlines. Social media explodes with memes mocking the company, and news outlets question the country's cybersecurity standards. How do you feel? Probably not great. You may even think, "*They should have done better—this reflects poorly on all of us.*" It's similar to watching a national athlete get caught in a doping scandal. You don't follow the sport, you don't know the athlete—but you still feel disappointed, even offended. You want accountability. That emotional response, that sense of shared reputation, makes you an interested party. Because when an organization's actions affect public trust, national pride, or global perception, the public becomes part of the security conversation—whether the organization realizes it or not.

These examples illustrate why taking a broad and thoughtful approach to identifying interested parties is so important. It's not just about a checklist. It's about understanding the real-world ecosystem in which your organization operates.

Implementation Guidance: Build on what you've already done in Clause 4.1. The process or method you used to identify internal and external issues—such as brainstorming, stakeholder mapping, interviews, or structured analysis—can be applied here to understand the needs and expectations of interested parties. So don't reinvent the wheel. Start with that foundation.

But Clause 4.2 introduces additional layers. This time, you're not just focusing on general concerns—you need to identify any legal, regulatory, contractual, or other obligations that could affect your ISMS. And this is where expert assistance becomes necessary. If your organization has a legal team, involve them early. Ask them to compile a list of all relevant laws, regulations, and binding requirements related to information security and privacy.

Now, if you don't have a legal department, that's okay—but you'll need to hire an outside legal firm. And if your organization operates or has business interests in more than one country or region, the scope becomes broader. You'll need to identify and understand the legal and regulatory requirements in every location where you work, have clients, vendors, or conduct data processing activities.

Once you have that list, ensure it is adequately documented. You should be able to show that:

- You have an up-to-date and comprehensive list of applicable legal, regulatory, and other obligations.
- You are adhering to all of them.
- You have a process to review and update the list regularly—because laws change, and your business might too.

This isn't just about ticking boxes. It's about demonstrating that your ISMS is based in reality and that you're genuinely committed to accountability.

✦ **Remember:** Many organizations fail audits not because they lack a list of obligations, but because they cannot demonstrate that the list is complete, current, and supported by evidence of compliance.

Author's Note: In my consulting work, I've found it very effective to use a simple Excel workbook for this task. Each sheet in the file corresponds to a specific country and includes a detailed list of all relevant legal, regulatory, and other obligations related to information security and privacy.
To make it practical:

- I include a column for the reliable source (for example, the official regulator's website or government publication) so the team knows where to verify the requirement.
- I also added a review/update date column for each requirement. This helps track when the obligation was last reviewed and ensures the ISMS team knows when it's time to check for changes.

This method simplifies how the ISMS team keeps the list current, shares updates across departments, and shows a systematic process to auditors.

Toolkit and Resources: Below is a generic list of interested parties and their potential information security needs. Please view this as a starting point and customize it to fit your organization's specific context. I recommend creating a list for your organization that identifies these interested parties and their needs, and shows which requirements will be addressed through your ISMS. This exercise will help you connect theory with practice and ensure your ISMS truly reflects your organization's realities.

External Interested Parties and Their Possible ISMS Requirements:

- **Regulators, legislators, and government bodies** expect strict compliance with laws, regulations, and reporting obligations related to information security and privacy.
- **Shareholders, business owners, and investors** want assurance that the organization is protecting its assets, avoiding security breaches, and safeguarding its reputation to protect financial returns.
- **Suppliers, subcontractors, consultants, and outsourcing partners** expect clear contracts, defined security controls, and protection of shared data throughout the supply chain.
- **Trade bodies and industry associations** require adherence to industry standards, codes of practice, or sector-specific guidelines that affect information security.
- **Competitors** while not directly engaged, they may perceive themselves as affected if poor security damages overall industry reputation or market trust.
- **Customers and consumers** demand assurance that their personal and sensitive data is protected from loss, misuse, or unauthorized access.
- **Activist groups** may expect transparency, ethical handling of data, and responsible responses to security or privacy incidents.
- **Insurers** require evidence of adequate controls and risk management to underwrite policies and reduce potential liability.
- **Emergency services** need timely and accurate information to respond effectively in case of incidents (e.g., data center fire, physical breach).
- **Employee dependents and family members** expect confidentiality of personal and health-related data submitted to the organization (e.g., for insurance or benefits).
- **Banks and financial service providers** require secure handling of financial transactions, records, and compliance with anti-fraud measures.
- **Business partners (joint ventures, alliances, collaborators)** expect mutual protection of shared intellectual property, data, and resources.

- **Neighbors (nearby businesses or residents)** expect that operations do not cause physical, environmental, or reputational risks due to security incidents.
- **Media (local, national, international)** expect timely, transparent, and accurate communication in case of a breach or incident.
- **General public and citizens of the country** expect responsible data handling, as a significant incident can impact national reputation and public trust.
- **External auditors** require access to accurate, reliable records to confirm compliance and verify security practices.
- **Certification bodies** demand conformance with ISO 27001 requirements and evidence of effective ISMS implementation.
- **Cloud service providers/IT hosting vendors (if not already captured under suppliers)** expect clear agreements on security responsibilities and incident handling.
- **Professional associations (lawyers, doctors, accountants, etc., if applicable to the sector)** may require compliance with profession-specific confidentiality rules and codes of conduct.
- **Trade unions (where applicable)** in some countries, such as India, France, and the UK, external trade unions can influence how organizations operate. They may not be formally represented within your company. However, they can still raise concerns or set expectations around how their members' personal data and privacy are protected, and how security-related policies impact staff. By contrast, an employee union formally registered within your organization can be considered an internal interested party, depending on your context.

Internal Interested Parties and Their Possible ISMS Requirements:

- **Decision-makers, including top management and owners**, expect assurance that the ISMS aligns with business goals, protects organizational assets, and demonstrates compliance with regulators and customers.
- **Process owners, system owners, and information owners** require clarity on their responsibilities, strong access controls, and mechanisms to ensure that data under their custody is protected.
- **Workers' (labor) representatives** expect staff concerns on working conditions, information handling, and workplace monitoring to be considered reasonably in ISMS policies.
- **Employees (full-time, part-time, temporary staff, and interns)** expect their personal data, payroll, performance, and work-related information to remain confidential, accurate, and used only for legitimate purposes.
- **Employee unions (where applicable)** seek fair treatment of members, protection of sensitive employee information, and involvement in policy or security practices that directly affect staff.
- **Internal audit group** requires transparent access to security policies, records, and controls to verify that the ISMS is effective and continuously improving.
- **Support functions (e.g., IT, HR, Finance, Admin)** as internal customers, they depend on secure IT systems, reliable access, and protection of sensitive departmental data.
- **All IT service users within the organization** need systems that are available, secure, and user-friendly, with safeguards that prevent data loss, misuse, or unauthorized access.
- **Information Security Professionals (if present)** expect clear policies, sufficient resources, and organizational support to design, monitor, and improve security controls.

- **Board of Directors or governing body (if applicable)** require assurance that information security risks are managed at a strategic level and that the ISMS supports reputation, compliance, and resilience.

🛠 *Implementation Task #4: Determine Needs and Expectations of Interested Parties*

Now it's your turn again. Close this book for a moment and focus on identifying all relevant interested parties for your organization's ISMS. Write down who they are—both internal and external—and what their main needs, expectations, or requirements are regarding information security and privacy.

Be as specific as possible. For example, regulators may expect legal compliance, employees may expect their personal data to be protected, and customers may demand confidentiality of sensitive business information.

Once you've compiled your list, go back to this chapter and compare it with the examples I provided. Use my list for inspiration, but don't treat it as a finished product. If you find unique interested parties or special requirements I haven't mentioned, that's a sign you're doing this exercise correctly—it means you're already aligning the ISMS with the realities of your business.

UNDERSTANDING THE CLIMATE-CHANGE AMENDMENT

In February 2024, the ISO published Amendment 1: Climate Action Changes to the ISO/IEC 27001:2022 standard. This amendment explicitly requires organisations to consider climate change as part of their ISMS. The specific changes affect Clauses 4.1 and 4.2 as follows:

- Under **Clause 4.1: Understanding the Organization and Its Context**, the text now includes: *"The organisations shall determine whether climate change is a relevant issue."*
- Under **Clause 4.2: Understanding the Needs and Expectations of Interested Parties**, a new note is added: *"NOTE 2 Relevant interested parties can have requirements related to climate change."*

The purpose of these additions is not to completely overhaul the standard but to ensure that climate-related issues are explicitly recognized as potential contextual and stakeholder factors affecting an ISMS.

Why This Amendment Matters for Your ISMS

Although the amendment's wording is brief, its implications are substantial. Climate change can affect your information security landscape in numerous ways:

- **Physical and Infrastructure Risks:** Extreme weather events, rising sea levels, floods, storms, or fires can damage data centers, impact cooling systems, disrupt power supplies, or force the relocation of services.
- **Supply Chain and Service Delivery Disruption:** Vendors or partner organizations might experience climate-related disruptions, affecting the availability, integrity, or continuity of your information assets.

- **Regulatory, Reputational, and Stakeholder Risks:** As sustainability and climate resilience become top priorities globally, regulators, customers, and investors will increasingly expect organizations to manage climate-related risks. Ignoring these risks could harm your brand or compliance status.
- **Cybersecurity and Resilience Implications:** Climate-driven disruptions (e.g., power outages, network failures, surges in remote work) can create new vulnerabilities or worsen existing ones.

In short, if climate change is relevant to your business, it must be considered within your ISMS context. If it is not relevant, you still need to provide evidence that the issue was considered and determined not relevant.

How to Address the Climate-Change Amendment in Your ISMS:

1. **Review your context (Clause 4.1): Is climate change a relevant issue?**
    - Assemble your ISMS core team and facilitate a workshop to ask: "Does climate change—either directly or indirectly— affect our ability to achieve ISMS outcomes?"
    - Consider factors such as location (e.g., flood-prone sites), infrastructure (e.g., heat sensitivity in data centers), supply chain exposure, regulatory domain (e.g., carbon-reporting laws), and business continuity issues.
    - If the answer is Yes, you should document climate change as a contextual issue.
    - If the answer is No, you should still record that you have considered climate change and concluded it is not relevant—maintaining transparency for audits.
2. **Identify stakeholder/interested-party expectations** (Clause 4.2)
    - Revisit your list of internal and external interested parties and ask if any have climate-related requirements (e.g., customers demanding sustainable IT, regulators imposing climate reporting).
    - Document any new or changed requirements in your interested parties register and assess their relevance to information security.
    - Decide which of those requirements will be addressed via your ISMS.

Author's Note: The amendment does not require creating a separate climate-management system solely for information security. Instead, you should consider climate change as a relevant factor wherever it applies. If your organization determines that climate change is not relevant, then documenting that decision is enough—the focus is on consideration, not necessarily implementing major changes. Use this amendment as an opportunity: Integrating climate resilience into your ISMS can improve your overall security, business continuity, and stakeholder trust.

CLAUSE 4.3: DETERMINING THE SCOPE OF THE ISMS

Summary of the Clause Requirements: Clause 4.3 concentrates on defining the boundaries of your ISMS. The standard requires you to clearly specify which parts of your organization are included and, equally important, which are excluded. To achieve this, you need to consider three elements: The internal and external issues identified in Clause 4.1, the needs and expectations of interested parties from Clause 4.2, and the interfaces or dependencies where your activities connect with other organizations.

Finally, this scope is not just an internal understanding—it must be documented. In simple terms, Clause 4.3 requires you to put your ISMS "fence line" in writing, so there's no confusion later about what is inside and what is outside.

Explanation with Real-World Examples: The scope of your ISMS is like creating a blueprint of what you will protect. It outlines where the ISMS applies, what it includes, and what falls outside the boundaries. This isn't a box-checking task—it's the foundation for everything that comes afterward. Risk assessments, control choices, audits, and even certifications all depend on how clearly you define these boundaries.

If the scope is vague or incomplete, you risk leaving vulnerabilities unaddressed, implementing controls that don't add value, or creating confusion about who is responsible for what. That's why Clause 4.3 emphasizes not only the areas within your scope but also the interfaces and dependencies—especially where your work connects with external parties or suppliers.

Factors That Influence Scope: When defining your scope, you'll need to look at three main elements:

- **External and Internal Issues (Clause 4.1):** For example, a fintech startup in a tightly regulated market may include compliance demands and rapid expansion as key considerations.
- **Interested Parties and Their Requirements (Clause 4.2):** A hospital must consider regulators, patients, and insurance partners who all expect secure handling of sensitive health data.
- **Interfaces and Dependencies:** If your payroll is outsourced, you must show how that vendor is covered in your ISMS (e.g., through contractual security clauses or monitoring).

You might also evaluate the readiness of business activities and support functions. For example, a retail chain might exclude a recently acquired e-commerce division until it's fully integrated. Meanwhile, a logistics company could include its warehouse access systems because they directly affect service delivery.

Real-World Scope Variations: There's no single "correct" scope—it always depends on your organization's needs, priorities, and maturity. Table 8.1 shows some real-world examples of how organizations commonly define their ISMS scope.

Each approach reflects a strategic choice: Balancing risk, resources, and where the most value exists. Just remember, once you define the scope, any future expansion or adjustments should be approached carefully, because changes will affect your risk assessments, controls, and overall conformance requirements.

Table 8.1 Real-world examples of ISMS scope variations

Scope type	*Example*
Specific process	A bank applies ISMS only to its loan approval workflow.
Specific function	A university scopes ISMS to its admissions department.
Specific service	A cloud provider covers its data hosting service.
Specific location	A multinational begins with its Singapore office before expanding globally.
Entire legal entity	A mid-sized law firm applies ISMS across all departments.
Entity plus suppliers	A government agency includes both its IT department and contracted vendors.

Author's Note: To make Clause 4.3 more practical and easier to understand, I often use a dinner analogy in my classes. Imagine you've invited me to your home. I arrive at your gate—now ask yourself: which areas am I allowed to access? That list is your ISMS scope.

If it's a hot evening, you'll probably invite me inside rather than leaving me at the Lawn. That reflects the internal and external factors influencing your decision. Will you let me use the guest bathroom? If not, consider my needs as a guest—I represent the interested parties. Since I'm dining with you, access to basic amenities becomes a reasonable expectation.

And if I'm staying overnight, the guest bedroom is included. If not, it remains outside. This simple example shows how scope, context, and stakeholder needs interact. Clause 4.3 isn't just about compliance—it's about setting thoughtful boundaries, managing expectations, and ensuring your ISMS protects what truly matters.

Implementation Guidance: Defining the scope of your ISMS isn't just paperwork—it's about setting clear boundaries for what's covered and what's not under your security. Getting this wrong can lead to overextending by protecting unnecessary things or creating gaps by missing key areas. The best way to prevent this is to involve the right people.

Start with a brainstorming session. Bring together representatives from all relevant functions—IT, HR, Finance, Operations, Procurement, Facilities, and, of course, top management. You can't decide the scope alone at your desk. Consultation and participation are your best allies here.

Here's a step-by-step way to approach it:

1. **Preliminary Scope:** Start with a small group of management representatives. Draft an initial outline—determine which business unit, location, or process should be included in scope.
2. **Refined Scope:** Review the preliminary scope with broader stakeholders, including support functions like HR, IT, and facilities. Ask whether excluding them will create too many interfaces at the boundaries. For example, if HR handles onboarding, can they be excluded without creating a security gap?
3. **Final Scope:** Share the refined version with all management within the proposed scope. This ensures buy-in and alignment and helps identify any missed dependencies. Make adjustments as needed until it accurately reflects the situation.
4. **Approval of Scope:** Document the final scope clearly and obtain formal approval from top management. This official approval grants the ISMS authority and legitimacy.

Remember to include outsourced activities or functions managed by third parties. Interfaces—whether physical (such as a data center operated by a supplier), technical (like an externally hosted payroll system), or organizational (such as a partner handling your customer data)—should all be identified and incorporated into your scope.

When you write down your scope as documented information, make sure it covers:

- **Organizational Scope:** Which units, departments, or locations are included.
- **ICT Scope:** The systems, networks, and applications covered.
- **Physical Scope:** The sites, offices, or facilities that fall inside (or outside) the boundaries.

Remember: A clear scope isn't just for auditors—it's for you. It communicates to everyone in the organization, "This is where our ISMS applies, and this is where it doesn't." When done correctly, it prevents confusion, sets clear expectations, and directs resources to where they're needed most.

Toolkit and Resources: Example ISMS Scope Statement

Example 1: Managed Hosting Service Provider
The scope of [Company Name]'s Information Security Management System (ISMS) includes providing and supporting managed hosting and network services delivered to customers from its headquarters in [Location]. It applies to all activities related to the collection, storage, processing, use, sharing, or management of employee, corporate, and client information.

The scope covers staff, processes, and information assets that directly support these services at the headquarters.

It also applies to [Company Name]'s assets and operations situated at third-party data centers, including:

- [Name and location of third-party data center]

📌 **Remember:** If your organization relies on multiple offices, cloud platforms, or outsourced providers, list them clearly. Auditors seek accuracy—avoid vague terms like "all operations" unless you truly mean every business unit and site.

Example 2: Commercial Bank
The scope of [Bank Name]'s ISMS encompasses providing retail, corporate, and digital banking services to customers from its headquarters in [City, Country] and through its branch network. It applies to all activities involving the collection, storage, processing, use, transmission, and protection of customer, employee, and corporate information.
The scope includes:

- Staff, processes, and information assets that support banking services at headquarters and branch locations.
- Core banking applications, internet banking platforms, mobile banking services, and supporting IT infrastructure hosted within the bank's data center in [Location].
- Critical third-party service providers involved in payment processing, ATM management, and cloud-based systems, with clearly defined interfaces and responsibilities.

📌 **Remember:** In a banking setting, regulators often require your scope to clearly specify digital channels, outsourced services, and customer data protection. Be as detailed as possible to prevent ambiguity during audits.

Example 3: Hospital
The scope of [Hospital Name]'s ISMS applies to providing healthcare services, including inpatient, outpatient, diagnostic, and emergency care, from its main hospital in [City, Country] and affiliated clinics. It covers all activities related to collecting, storing, processing, using, and protecting patient health records, employee information, and hospital operational data.
The scope includes:

- Clinical, administrative, and support staff, along with information assets used in delivering medical services.

- Hospital Information Systems (HIS), Electronic Health Records (EHR), Laboratory Information Systems (LIS), Radiology Information Systems (RIS), and supporting IT infrastructure located in the hospital's data center in [Location].
- Third-party service providers involved in medical transcription, diagnostic imaging storage, cloud-based health applications, and outsourced billing services, with defined interfaces and responsibilities.

📌 **Remember:** In a healthcare environment, patient data confidentiality, regulatory compliance (e.g., HIPAA in the United States, GDPR in the EU), and third-party vendors handling sensitive health information must be clearly included in the ISMS scope. This prevents gaps during regulatory audits or certification reviews.

Implementation #Task 5: Determine Your ISMS Scope

Now it's your turn again. Set this book aside for a moment and draft an ISMS scope statement for your organization. Keep it practical, clear, and specific. Your scope should answer:

- *Where* does the ISMS apply? (locations, systems, functions)
- *What* does it cover? (processes, data, services)
- *Who* is involved? (staff, departments, third parties)

Don't worry about making it perfect on the first attempt. The idea is to get your thoughts on paper.

Once you've written your draft, revisit it and compare it with the examples I've shared in this chapter—such as the scopes for an IT service provider, a commercial bank, or a hospital. Use them as reference points to improve your own work.

📌 **Remember:** Your ISMS scope will evolve as your organization changes, but this exercise provides a solid starting foundation.

CLAUSE 4.4: INFORMATION SECURITY MANAGEMENT SYSTEM

Summary of the Clause Requirements: Clause 4.4 consolidates all previous groundwork. It requires the organization to formally establish, implement, maintain, and continually improve its ISMS. This isn't just about writing policies or setting controls; it's about creating a dynamic management system that encompasses all the processes necessary to protect information security and how those processes work together.

The expectation here is clear: Your ISMS must not be a one-time project. It has to be a structured, ongoing system aligned with ISO/IEC 27001 requirements, continually evolving and improving.

In simple terms, Clause 4.4 says: *"Build the system, make it work, keep it working, and keep improving it."*

Explanation with Real-World Examples: Clause 4.4 is where your ISMS truly comes to life. So far, you've examined your context (Clause 4.1), identified your interested parties (Clause 4.2), and determined your scope (Clause 4.3). Now, it's time to integrate all that groundwork and create the actual system that will protect your information day after day.

To meet this requirement, your organization must establish, implement, maintain, and continually improve its ISMS—not as just a set of documents, but as a living, functioning

system of processes. These processes should work together like gears in a smoothly running machine.
Let me give you a few real-world illustrations:

- If you're working in a commercial bank—Don't just write a policy and call it an ISMS. You need processes for risk assessment, change management, incident reporting, and vendor oversight. These processes must communicate with each other. For example, when procurement onboards a new vendor, that process must feed into your risk management and compliance functions.
- If you're in a hospital—Your ISMS isn't only about IT. It must cover patient records, physical access to wards, staff training, and compliance with health privacy laws. Think about this: When a doctor resigns, does HR notify IT to restrict their access? And does compliance make sure their medical notes are properly archived? If yes, that's your ISMS in action.
- If you're running a small IT services company, your ISMS may be lean, but it still needs to work as a system. Even if one person wears multiple hats, you should have clear policies, regular risk assessments, incident logging, and lessons learned feeding back into continual improvement. The size of your team doesn't excuse skipping the system.

The main point? An ISMS isn't just paperwork. It's about how effectively your organization's processes work together, how consistently they are maintained, and how seriously you prioritize continual improvement.

Implementation Guidance: Clause 4.4 is the core of ISO/IEC 27001. It's brief but impactful: it directs you to establish, implement, maintain, and continually improve your ISMS. Nothing more, nothing less.

The good news is that you don't need to do anything "extra" for this clause. If you go through the rest of the standard—clause by clause, requirement by requirement—then you'll automatically satisfy Clause 4.4. In other words, this clause is considered fulfilled when the entire ISMS is built and operating as intended.

Think of it as the umbrella requirement. Every activity you do—defining scope, assessing risks, managing incidents, running audits, reviewing performance, and driving improvements—contributes to it. By fulfilling all the requirements of ISO 27001, you are, by definition, satisfying Clause 4.4.

So don't overthink this. Focus on systematically addressing each requirement in the standard, and Clause 4.4 will naturally fall into place.

💬 **Author's Note:** I often remind my students that this clause is like the "summary line" in an exam answer—it ties everything together. If you follow the ISO 27001 structure and continue improving as you go, Clause 4.4 will take care of itself.

Toolkit and Resources: No specific preparation is needed for this clause. As long as you've met the requirements of all the other clauses in ISO/IEC 27001, you'll naturally achieve conformance with Clause 4.4.

Key Takeaway—What You've Learned

- Start by understanding your environment—consider both external and internal factors before selecting controls or creating policies. Context influences everything.

- Engage the right people early—cross-functional input prevents blind spots and fosters ownership (IT, HR, Legal, Ops, Procurement, etc.).
- External issues are as important as internal ones—laws, market dynamics, suppliers, threats, environment, and geography shape your ISMS priorities.
- Internal factors are genuine risks—culture, staffing, skills, legacy systems, budgets, and past audit findings will either limit or support your security choices.
- Identify interested parties broadly—customers, regulators, suppliers, employees, media, neighbors, and even "those who feel affected" can create obligations or reputational risks.
- Don't treat the stakeholders list as just a roll call—understand their real needs and determine which requirements your ISMS will address. Record this decision.
- Set a clear, practical scope—specify what's included and what's excluded (locations, systems, processes, suppliers).
- Consider interfaces and dependencies—outsourced services, cloud platforms, and supply chain links must be visible and managed within your scope and risk assessments.
- Keep the context current—review and update your environment, stakeholder needs, and scope regularly, mainly when changes occur such as mergers, new laws, new services, or incidents.

QUIZ #7

True/False statement

Sr.	Statement	True/False
1	It is not a requirement of ISO 27001 to document internal and external issues.	
2	Technological changes are considered an external issue when assessing organizational context.	
3	Once the ISMS scope is documented, it cannot be changed.	
4	The ISMS scope must always be available as documented information.	
5	An organization must include every department and every process in the ISMS scope.	
6	Interested parties include only those who directly affect the organization.	

CASE 2: MONSOONS, MARKETS, AND MESSY CHENNAI POLITICS

When Ravi Menon arrived at the Chennai site of Coastline Cloud Services (CCS), the first thing he noticed was the smell of salt in the humid breeze. The data center was near the Bay of Bengal—convenient for cooling and fiber routes, but also a spot where the monsoon can quickly test resilience. Ravi had been hired as the Lead Implementer for ISO 27001. His goal: Get the Chennai site certified within nine months and reassure a major banking client about disaster readiness.

CCS had clear advantages. Chennai's talent market was extensive, making hiring straightforward, and local vendors and contractors were easy to find. The operations manager, Nila, guided Ravi through well-organized racks and introduced an enthusiastic team. The CTO, Arjun, emphasized resilient power feeds and recently renewed SLAs with a local backup provider. The finance head, Manoj, focused on costs—even suggesting cheaper local subcontractors where possible.

But the site had quirks Ravi would soon learn to observe. Outside the compound, the neighborhood sometimes experienced political protests. Local leaders could pressure companies for favors—from fast-tracking permits to hiring preferences—and some politicians had reputations for heavy-handed tactics. Last year, a street protest temporarily blocked the main access road; the site had no formal plan for such an event.

Ravi began his context review with workshops involving IT, Ops, HR, Legal, and Procurement. He asked teams to identify internal issues such as NOC staff turnover, aging backup generators, and many responsibilities handled by only one person, along with external issues like monsoon flooding, supply-chain dependencies, and changing telecom regulations. He recorded these in two columns and used color-coding to show their impact.

Ravi linked physical risks like flooding to business continuity needs, identified the telecom provider as a key dependency, and considered cultural factors such as local labor unions and community expectations. He believed that hiring locally would reduce supplier risk and thought that excluding certain vendors from the initial ISMS scope would help keep the project manageable. After 2 weeks, his working draft included a context register, a preliminary list of interested parties, and a scope proposal.

Ravi presented the draft list of interested parties and the scope to senior management but did not distribute it to all department heads. He scheduled the scope-approval meeting on a weekday afternoon without inviting the procurement head, who was on a site visit. During the meeting, the head of Legal objected: "Ravi had not thoroughly reviewed all contractual obligations affecting the ISMS." The CTO also protested: "We rely on vendors to manage backups and secure disposal of media."

Case Discussion: Test Your Understanding

1. **Which of these is the best example of an external issue Ravi should record in the context register?**

   A. Staff boredom in the Network Operations Center
   B. Monsoon flooding that can disrupt physical access and power
   C. An employee's personal preference for remote work
   D. The color of the server racks

2. **When identifying interested parties for the CCS ISMS, which set should Ravi be sure to consider?**

   A. Only customers and shareholders
   B. Only internal staff and the CEO
   C. Only the certification body and auditors
   D. Customers, local emergency services, regulators, community groups, and critical suppliers

3. **Ravi suggested excluding some vendors from the initial ISMS scope. Is this decision aligned with Clause 4?**

   A. Yes—local hiring eliminates supplier risk.
   B. No—suppliers and outsourced services that affect the ISMS must be considered when defining scope..
   C. Yes—scope should always be kept minimal to speed certification
   D. No—scope never includes any third parties.

4. Which of the following shows a weakness in Ravi's approach to defining the scope?

A. He documented flood risk and telecom dependency.
B. He listed internal issues like single-person responsibilities.
C. He prepared a draft scope but did not circulate it to all department heads.
D. He scheduled workshops with cross-functional teams.

5. Which action would best help Ravi demonstrate that he has identified and managed legal and contractual obligations relevant to the ISMS?

A. Verbal assurance from the procurement lead that "we'll handle it."
B. Waiting until the audit to find out which laws apply.
C. Excluding all contracts from consideration to keep the scope simple.
D. A documented register of applicable laws, contractual clauses, and a source/reference for each item, with review dates.

6. Which statement best describes a sensible scope for the Chennai ISMS at this stage?

A. Define the scope to include the Chennai site, its IT systems and staff, and any outsourced services or suppliers that interface with these systems, with clear boundary descriptions.
B. Include only the data hall and exclude any outsourced backup or network providers to reduce work.
C. Claim the ISMS covers all company operations globally to make certification more valuable.
D. Leave the scope intentionally vague so changes won't require rework.

Chapter 9

Clause 5—Leadership isn't optional

Setting direction, roles, and commitment for information security success

When it comes to ISO 27001, leadership isn't just a box you check—it's the driving force behind the entire ISMS. Top management must do more than sign policies or attend audits. They are expected to set the direction, allocate resources, and actively demonstrate commitment to information security. Without this visible ownership, an ISMS becomes merely another set of documents on a shelf. Clause 5 makes it clear: Leadership and commitment are not optional extras. They are the foundation for building credibility, engaging employees, and ensure that your ISMS delivers real results rather than just being a paper exercise.

CLAUSE 5.1: LEADERSHIP AND COMMITMENT

Summary of the Clause Requirements: Clause 5.1 clearly states that top management must actively lead the ISMS. This isn't about delegation or just paying lip service—it's about visible ownership and accountability. To comply with this clause, your leadership team needs to do the following:

- **Set the Direction:** Establish the information security policy and objectives so they align with your organization's overall strategy.
- **Integrate ISMS into Daily Business:** Information security should not sit in a silo. It must be woven into core processes and decision-making.
- **Provide Resources:** Make sure people, tools, and budgets are available to run and improve the ISMS.
- **Communicate Importance:** Regularly emphasize why information security matters and why conforming to ISMS requirements is non-negotiable.
- **Deliver Results:** Ensure the ISMS achieves its intended outcomes, not just on paper but also in practice.
- **Support and Direct People:** Encourage staff at all levels to contribute to ISMS effectiveness.
- **Promote Continual Improvement:** Show that security is never "done," but always evolving.
- **Enable other Leaders:** Back-up managers across departments so they can demonstrate leadership in their own areas.

In short, Clause 5.1 clearly assigns top management the duty to lead by example, allocate resources, and integrate information security into the organization's culture.

Explanation with Real-World Examples: Leadership and commitment are essential, not optional—they form the backbone of an effective ISMS. ISO 27000 describes top

DOI: 10.1201/9781003744139-10

management as the individuals or group at the highest level who direct and control the ISMS. This same group, responsible for setting budgets, defining strategies, and driving business priorities, also holds the ultimate responsibility for information security.

Yes, day-to-day tasks can be delegated. Yes, you can appoint a CISO or ISMS Manager to oversee operations. However, accountability for the success or failure of the ISMS remains with top management. They cannot outsource responsibility.

Who exactly counts as "top management"? That depends on your ISMS scope:

- If your ISMS covers the **entire organization**, top management might be the Board of Directors, the CEO, or the Executive Committee.
- If your ISMS scope is limited to **one department**—say, IT—then the IT Director could be the top management for that scope.
- Many organizations also form an **ISMS Steering Committee** made up of senior leaders from across functions. This group provides leadership, allocates resources, and removes roadblocks.

Top management must also demonstrate their commitment through actions: Participating in management reviews (Clause 9.3), ensuring resources are available (Clause 7.1), and actively promoting continuous improvement (Clause 10). Leadership isn't just about signing off on a policy once—it's about consistently reinforcing that information security is a business priority, not just an IT issue.

Author's Note: I once worked with a telecom operator where the ISMS scope included only the data center division. The Chief Technology Officer (CTO) served as the top management for ISMS, directing and managing all activities within that scope. At another client—a central bank—the Governor was the top management for the ISMS because information security was considered vital to national trust and financial stability.

Implementation Guidance: This clause is about more than just words on paper. It involves visible, active participation from top management. If leadership treats the ISMS as "just another compliance project," it will fail. If leadership champions it, allocates resources, and communicates its importance, the ISMS stands the best chance of success.

Here's what you should be looking for from your top management—and how to make it work in practice:

- **Set Direction and Objectives:** Leadership must ensure the **information security policy** and **objectives** exist and align with the organization's overall strategy. If the business is aiming for international expansion, for example, then data protection in multiple jurisdictions must be part of the ISMS objectives.
- **Integrate ISMS into Daily Operations:** Information security shouldn't sit in a silo. Leadership should embed ISMS requirements into everyday processes. For example, if process owners exist, they can be tasked with implementing relevant controls. Top management must also help overcome resistance to change—because let's face it, controls often mean extra effort.
- **Provide Resources:** No ISMS runs on promises. Leadership needs to commit actual resources:
  - financial budgets
  - skilled personnel
  - appropriate facilities, and
  - reliable technology and infrastructure.

The amount required will depend on your organization's size, complexity, and risks. Regular **management reviews** (Clause 9.3) should test whether resources are sufficient.

- **Communicate the Importance of Security:** Leadership must openly and frequently discuss information security—not just during audits. Using real examples can be effective: Illustrate how a breach could impact customer trust or how meeting compliance requirements can help secure new business.
- **Ensure the ISMS Delivers Results:** Leaders should request and review status updates and performance reports from audits, monitoring, or KPIs. This keeps the ISMS on track and demonstrates that it's effective, not just theoretical.
- **Guide and Support Staff:** A supportive word from the CEO or Director can be more impactful than numerous policies. Leadership should provide feedback, help staff prioritize ISMS tasks, and express appreciation for their contributions.
- **Promote Ongoing Improvement:** Security is a continuous process. Leaders should encourage enhancements, evaluate new resource needs, and support initiatives that strengthen the ISMS over time.

If your ISMS covers only a part of a larger organization, such as just the IT division of a global company, don't stop there. Seek engagement from the leadership of the wider organization as well. Their support ensures consistent direction, proper resource distribution, and alignment between the ISMS scope and the overall organization.

Author's Note: In my experience, staff can immediately sense whether leadership is truly committed or merely paying lip service. The difference is striking. When top management is active and present, the ISMS becomes part of the culture—not just a project.

Toolkit and Resources: Use Table 9.1 as a simple self-assessment to check whether top management in your organization is genuinely demonstrating leadership and commitment

Table 9.1 Leadership and commitment self-assessment checklist for ISO 27001

Area of Leadership Commitment	*Key Questions to Ask*	*Yes/No / Partial*	*Evidence Available?*
Policy and Objectives	Has top management established an information security policy and measurable objectives aligned with business strategy?		
Integration into Processes	Are ISMS requirements and controls built into day-to-day business processes (not isolated in IT or Security alone)?		
Resource Allocation	Has leadership committed sufficient financial, human, and technical resources to establish, maintain, and improve the ISMS?		
Communication	Does top management actively communicate the importance of information security across the organization (e.g., town halls, emails, strategy updates)?		
Results and Outcomes	Does leadership review ISMS performance (audit results, monitoring, KPIs) to ensure intended outcomes are achieved?		
Support and Direction	Do managers and staff feel supported by leadership in carrying out their ISMS roles and responsibilities?		
Continual Improvement	Is leadership encouraging and driving continual improvement (e.g., approving new initiatives, adapting to changes, learning from incidents)?		
Cross-Organization Engagement	If the ISMS scope is only part of the business, is wider organizational leadership also informed and engaged?		

to the ISMS. This isn't meant to be a tick-box exercise. Treat it as an honest reflection tool. If you hesitate to mark any item as "Yes," that hesitation itself is valuable—it highlights an area worth discussing, strengthening, or documenting more clearly.

💡 Tip: Maintain a folder (physical or digital) with supporting evidence for each of these areas—meeting minutes, emails, budget approvals, training schedules, management review reports, etc. This will not only strengthen your ISMS but also prepare you for external audits.

CLAUSE 5.2: POLICY

Summary of the Clause Requirements: Clause 5.2 requires you to develop the foundation of your ISMS: The Information Security Policy. This isn't merely a formality—it's the document that guides direction, establishes commitment, and communicates intent throughout the organization.
To meet this clause, you must ensure your organization has a policy that:

- Fits the **purpose of your business**—not generic words, but something relevant to what you do and how you operate.
- Either **sets information security objectives directly** or provides the framework for setting them later (see Clause 6.2).
- Shows a clear **commitment to meeting applicable requirements**, such as legal, regulatory, contractual, or customer-specific obligations.
- Includes a **commitment to continual improvement** of the ISMS.

And it doesn't stop at writing. The policy must also:

- Be kept as **documented information.**
- Be **communicated within the organization**, so staff know it exists and understand their role in supporting it.
- Be made **available to interested parties**, where appropriate (for example, customers, regulators, or partners may ask to see it).

In short, Clause 5.2 is about making sure your information security policy isn't just a poster on the wall. It's a living statement of intent, supported by leadership, that guides decisions and actions throughout the ISMS.

Explanation with Real-World Examples: Your information security policy acts as the primary foundation of your ISMS. It is not intended to be a lengthy rulebook or operational guide. Instead, think of it as a high-level statement that sets the overall tone, direction, and purpose for all your organization's information security activities. It should be straightforward enough to guide decisions, yet concise enough that people genuinely read and understand it.

A good policy answers:

- Why information security matters to your organization.
- What commitments leadership is making (compliance, continual improvement, protecting customer trust).
- How information security connects to the organization's overall purpose and strategy.

⚠ **Common Confusion:** Avoid mixing this with other detailed policies. You may (and should) include several supporting policies, such as a Clear Desk and Clear Screen Policy, an Authentication Policy, or a Data Sharing Policy. These are lower-level documents. The Information Security Policy sits at the top, providing the overall framework.

💬 **Author's Note:** Let me give you an example. While auditing a commercial bank in Africa, I was given its "policy" document. It was over 100 pages long, covering every possible rule and procedure. But that wasn't really a policy—it was a mix of manuals, guidelines, and instructions. In truth, a solid information security policy can be drafted on a single A4 page. Short, clear, and strategic.

The point is: Your policy isn't about volume; it's about clarity. A well-written one should make sense even to someone outside the IT team. It demonstrates leadership commitment, aligns with business goals, and shows your people (and your stakeholders) that information security is part of your core operations.

Implementation Guidance: If you ask me, the information security policy is like your organization's statement of intent. It's not meant to be a lengthy legal document full of technical jargon. Instead, think of it as your "north star"—a short, clear statement that provides guidance and ensures everyone knows your direction.

Here's how you should approach it:

1. **Keep It High-Level and Simple:** The policy should focus on intent and direction, not the detailed controls. Save specifics for procedures and guidelines. Aim for something everyone in the organization can read and agree with.
2. **Make It Relevant to Your Organization:** Avoid the trap of copying a template from the internet. Your policy should reflect your culture, your business context, and the issues you actually face. A bank's policy will naturally differ from a hospital's or a university's policy.
3. **Connect Everything Back to the Policy:** All your other security procedures, objectives, and controls should trace back to this policy. If the policy is the "roof," then the rest of the ISMS are the "walls" holding it up.
4. **Demonstrate Leadership Commitment:** Top management's support must be clear. The policy should include their commitment to:
    - Protecting information and meeting all applicable security requirements.
    - Supporting ongoing improvement in security activities.
    - Providing resources and leadership for the ISMS to succeed.
5. **Clarify How Objectives Will Flow:** Some organizations include security objectives directly in the policy. Others use the policy to describe who sets objectives and how they cascade across departments. Either way, the policy should point to a clear framework so everyone understands how security goals are set and tracked.
6. **Share It Broadly:** A policy kept hidden (or in a forgotten intranet folder) is useless. Please share it with all employees and make sure the language is easy to understand. For external audiences such as customers, suppliers, contractors, or regulators, you can share a simpler version—just ensure it doesn't include confidential details.

7. **Integrate It into Your Management System:** Your security policy can stand alone or sit alongside other policies (such as quality or environment). If your organization already has a standard policy template, keep the format consistent.

Author's Note: In my experience, the best information security policies are concise, impactful, and motivating. If it resembles a textbook, most employees will never read it. Keep it clear, make it meaningful, and ensure leadership takes ownership—not just IT.

⚠ ***Caution:*** *Don't Overdo It. For example, ISO 27001 requires the policy to be "available to interested parties, as appropriate." That doesn't mean you need to wallpaper your offices with framed copies! I once saw an organization print hundreds of glossy, framed copies of its policy and hang them on every wall, in every corridor, and on every office door. Impressive? Maybe. Useful? Not really. After the first day, nobody noticed them anymore. Be sensible. Make sure the policy is visible and accessible—on your intranet, included in onboarding, discussed in team meetings—but don't waste time or money turning it into wall art. The real value lies in employees' understanding and applying the policy, not in how many frames you hang up.*

Tip: More Effective Ways to Share Your Policy: You don't need fancy frames to make your policy noticeable. Instead, try these simple methods that really work:

- Add it to your intranet homepage so it's always a click away.
- Include it in onboarding packs for new employees.
- Share it in team meetings or town halls, with a quick reminder of *why it matters*.
- Print a **miniature poster version** for notice boards in common areas (canteen, reception, HR).
- Add a short reference in employee email signatures or newsletters: *"We protect information—see our policy here."*

Keep it practical, visible, and, most importantly, ensure people connect with it.

Toolkit and Resources: Information Security Policy—Commercial Bank
⚠ **Reminder:** This is only an example. When writing your organization's policy, constantly adapt it to your specific business situation, risks, and culture. Never copy-paste a sample policy.

Information Security Policy

At ***ABC Bank***, protecting our customers' trust is at the heart of everything we do. Every piece of information—whether in our systems, our records, or our conversations—must be treated with the highest level of care and confidentiality.

To ensure this, ABC Bank has adopted the ISO/IEC 27001 Information Security Management System (ISMS) to guide our efforts to protect the ***confidentiality, integrity, and availability*** of information.

ABC Bank is committed to:

- Keeping customer information safe and only accessible to those who genuinely need it.

- Meeting all legal, regulatory, and contractual requirements related to information security.
- Continually improving our ISMS to stay ahead of risks and evolving threats.
- Providing resources, training, and support so our employees can follow good security practices.
- Engaging our employees in protecting information and encouraging them to suggest improvements.

Access to customer information is strictly controlled. Only authorized employees or partners with a clear business need are allowed access. No information will be shared with external parties without the information owner's approval or as required by law.

Information security objectives will be set each year by management, reviewed regularly to track progress, and managed through the *PDCA (Plan-Do-Check-Act) cycle* to ensure they remain effective and aligned with business needs.

This policy will be:

- Communicated to all employees and relevant partners.
- Made available to customers, regulators, and other interested parties, as appropriate.
- *Reviewed annually, or earlier if required,* to ensure it stays relevant to business needs, risks, and changes in the environment.

Approved by:
Managing Director
December 20XX

Author's Note: Notice how brief and straightforward this policy is. A bank handles sensitive financial data daily, yet the message remains clear and easy to grasp. That's the goal—keep it concise, meaningful, and aligned with the organization's purpose.

Quick Checklist for Policy Creation

Use this checklist to ensure your Information Security Policy covers all the essential elements. Mark each item once you're confident it is addressed:

- **Top Management Approval:** The policy has been officially approved by senior leadership.
- **Clear Commitment:** It includes promises to safeguard information, meet requirements, and support ongoing improvement.
- **Objectives' Framework:** It explains how information security objectives are established and reviewed (e.g., through PDCA: Plan, Do, Check, Act).
- **Communication Plan:** It describes how the policy will be shared with employees and, if applicable, with interested parties such as customers, suppliers, and regulators.
- **Accessibility:** The policy is easy to locate and written in clear, understandable language.
- **Integration:** If the organization has other management systems (quality, environmental, etc.), the policy aligns well with them.
- **Review Cycle:** It indicates how often the policy will be reviewed (e.g., annually or after significant changes).

Author's Note: Don't focus too much on signatures. What matters is that top management approves and takes responsibility for the policy. Whether documented in meeting minutes, a digital workflow, or a management portal, it's equally valid in an audit.

Implementation Task #6: Draft Your Information Security Policy

It's time to turn theory into practice. Grab a notebook or open a blank document and draft the first outline of your organization's Information Security Policy. Keep it short, simple, and meaningful.

Here's a step-by-step to guide you:

1. *Write Your Opening Statement*
   - **Example:** *"At [Your Organization], protecting the trust of our customers and partners is a top priority..."*
2. ***List At Least Three Key Commitments*** your organization will make (e.g., protecting information, meeting legal requirements, and continual improvement).
3. *Define Access Principles*
   - Who gets access, and under what conditions?
4. *Set the Objective Framework*
   - How will objectives be set, reviewed, and improved (hint: use PDCA—Plan, Do, Check, Act)?
5. *Add Communication and Review*
   - Who will see the policy, and how often will it be reviewed?

Task Outcome: By the end of this exercise, you'll have a one-page draft policy that captures your organization's voice. It doesn't need to be perfect—you can refine it later with your team. The key part is that you get started.

Author's Note: Don't overthink or over-polish at this stage. The best policies are ***short, clear, and authentic.*** Get the draft out, then build on it with your team's input.

CLAUSE 5.3: ORGANIZATIONAL ROLES, RESPONSIBILITIES, AND AUTHORITIES

Summary of the Clause Requirements: Clause 5.3 emphasizes role clarity. Top management must ensure that everyone involved in information security understands precisely what they are responsible for—and that these responsibilities are clearly communicated throughout the organization.

In simple terms, management must assign someone (or sometimes a team) to:

- Ensure the ISMS actually meets the requirements of ISO/IEC 27001.
- Report regularly to top management on how well the ISMS is performing.

The standard also allows top management to share or delegate these reporting responsibilities further within the organization, as long as accountability is clear.

Explanation with Real-World Examples: Think about managing a football team. You can't just send 11 players onto the field and hope they figure out who will defend, who will score, and who will captain. Without clear roles, chaos will follow. Someone has to assign responsibilities: "You're the goalkeeper, you're the striker, and you're the captain who reports back to the coach." That's precisely what Clause 5.3 is asking for in an ISMS.

In an organization, top management acts as the coach. They must ensure that someone is responsible for establishing and operating the ISMS in accordance with ISO 27001. Additionally, someone (sometimes the same person) regularly reports to management on how the ISMS is performing—highlighting what's working well and what needs improvement.

Here's another example: Think about a flight crew. The captain pilots the plane, the first officer assists, and the cabin crew handles safety and service. Everyone knows their roles, but the captain still must report back to air traffic control on performance and progress.

Now, if roles in a bank, hospital, or IT company aren't clear, information security can easily fall into the trap of being "everyone's responsibility." That sounds good, but in reality, it often means nobody is truly accountable. Clause 5.3 addresses this by requiring top management to formally assign and communicate responsibilities, ensuring there's no confusion about who owns the ISMS and who reports on its status.

But Clause 5.3 isn't just about responsibilities; it also covers authorities—and the two are closely connected. Responsibility refers to what you are expected to do, while authority pertains to what you are permitted to decide or approve while doing it.

Take the case of spending money at work. If you ask yourself, *"Do I have the authority to spend?"* many of you will say, *"Yes."* But then comes the following question: *"How much?"* You may be responsible for buying laptops for your team, but you may only have the authority to approve spending up to ***$5,000.*** If you want to pay ***$10,000,*** you'll need additional approval. So yes, you're responsible for making sure laptops are purchased, but your authority is limited to a certain amount. That's why both must be crystal clear in an ISMS.

Here's another example I often share with delegates: Do you have children? Do they go to school? If yes, consider this. The teacher is responsible for teaching your child, but does the teacher have the authority to take your child on a school trip without your permission? Of course not. That authority belongs to you, the parent.

Notice the difference? Responsibility without authority leads to frustration. Authority without responsibility causes confusion. Both should be clearly defined and communicated. That's why Clause 5.3 requires top management to assign and communicate both responsibilities and authorities for information security. This makes sure the ISMS is not only well-organized but also practical. People understand what they need to do—and what decisions they are authorized to make.

Author's Note: In information security, it's not enough to say "You're responsible." You also need to clearly define the limits of authority. For example, your IT Manager may be responsible for granting access to systems, but not authorized to approve exceptions for the Director's laptop without higher approval.

Implementation Guidance: Clause 5.3 focuses on making sure that individuals understand their responsibilities regarding information security—and that they have the proper level of authority to perform their duties.

Top management doesn't need to handle every small responsibility personally, but they must ensure that key roles and authorities are clearly approved and properly delegated. The important part is that nobody is left wondering, *"Am I responsible for this or not?"*

So, what kind of responsibilities and authorities should be assigned? At a minimum, you'll want to cover things like:

- Coordinating the establishment, implementation, and maintenance of the ISMS.
- Reporting on performance and recommending improvements.
- Advising on information security risk assessment and treatment.
- Designing information security processes and systems.
- Setting standards for the operation of information security controls.
- Managing information security incidents when they happen.
- Reviewing and auditing the ISMS.

Beyond these core information security roles, don't forget that information security responsibilities are also part of everyday roles across the organization. For example:

- Information owners are responsible for the data they create and use.
- Process owners must make sure their processes follow information security requirements.
- Asset owners (like application or infrastructure owners) are accountable for the systems they manage.
- Risk owners are responsible for handling specific information security risks.
- Information security coordinating functions or persons may provide support across teams.
- Project managers must factor in information security when running projects.
- Line managers need to make sure their teams follow information security practices.
- Even information users have a role—using systems responsibly and reporting suspicious issues.

A common question is whether everything needs to be documented. Clause 5.3 itself does not require a formal document, but Clause 7.5.1(b) states that you must document information as necessary for your management system's effectiveness. In practice, most organizations keep a simple responsibility and authority matrix or a short section in their ISMS manual. It doesn't need to be complicated—just clear enough to show who is responsible for what and their level of authority.

Author's Note: I always tell my delegates, *"If everyone thinks information security is someone else's job, it becomes nobody's job."* That's why Clause 5.3 is so necessary. Think of it this way—if someone asked you tomorrow, *"Who is responsible for managing information security incidents?"* or *"Who has the authority to approve exceptions?"*—could you answer without hesitation? If yes, you're in good shape. If not, that's exactly the gap this clause is meant to fix.

Toolkit and Resources: Before we jump into the template, let me quickly introduce the RACI Matrix. RACI is a straightforward tool that stands for Responsible, Accountable, Consulted, and Informed. It was first developed as a project management method to ensure everyone on a project team knew their specific role. Over time, it gained popularity in many fields—including information security—because it reduces confusion and finger-pointing.

Now, here's something important. The ISO 27001 standard does not require you to create a full RACI Matrix. Instead, it only mandates that roles, responsibilities, and authorities related to information security are clearly assigned and communicated. That's the minimum.

However, using a RACI Matrix is a good practice. It offers more detail and structure by showing not only who is responsible but also who approves, who must be consulted, and who should be informed. For larger or more complex organizations, this extra clarity can significantly make a difference.

💬 **Author's Note:** My advice? Keep it as simple as possible for your organization. If a short list of roles and responsibilities is enough, that's fine. But if you often hear people say, *"I didn't know I was supposed to do that,"* then a RACI Matrix can save you a lot of headaches.

■ **Toolkit Example: RACI Matrix**

⚠ **Reminder:** Table 9.2 is only an example. Every organization needs to tailor roles, responsibilities, and authorities to match its own structure, culture, and way of working. Please don't copy this blindly. Use it as a reference and a source of inspiration, then adapt it so it genuinely fits how your organization operates.

How to use Table 9.2:

- *Responsible (R):* The person doing the work.
- *Accountable (A):* The person who owns the outcome.
- *Consulted (C):* People who give input before a decision is made.
- *Informed (I):* People kept up to date after a decision is made.
- *Authority Level:* Specify what authority comes with the role (e.g., *can approve spending up to $5,000*, *can authorize system access but not exceptions*).

■ **Toolkit Example: Roles, Responsibilities, and Authorities—Simple Version**

⚠ **Reminder:** Table 9.3 is only an example. Every organization needs to adapt roles, responsibilities, and authorities to suit its own structure, culture, and information security needs. Use this as a starting point, not a finished solution, and shape it around how your organization actually works.

💬 **Author's Note:** Table 9.3 shows a simple format that works very well for many organizations. If a full RACI matrix feels too complicated, don't force it. What matters most is that roles, responsibilities, and authorities are clear, documented, and communicated in a way people actually understand and follow.

📌 **Remember:** Top management must ensure that responsibilities and authorities are both assigned and clearly communicated. Having responsibility does not automatically grant someone authority. For example, your Information Security Manager may be responsible for the daily operations of the ISMS but might not have the authority to approve major policy changes. Make sure the boundaries are well defined, agreed upon, and practical.

Table 9.2 Example RACI matrix for ISMS roles, responsibilities, and authorities

Activity/Role	*Responsible (R)*	*Accountable (A)*	*Consulted (C)*	*Informed (I)*	*Authority Level (Limit/Scope)*
Establishing and maintaining the ISMS	ISMS Manager	Chief Risk Officer	IT Head, HR Manager	All employees	Authority to design ISMS processes, escalate gaps to CRO
Reporting ISMS performance	ISMS Manager	Chief Risk Officer	Internal Audit	Board of Directors	Authority to submit quarterly reports to management
Information security risk assessment	Risk Team Lead	Chief Risk Officer	Business Unit Heads	ISMS Manager, Board	Authority to approve risk ratings up to the medium level
Information security risk treatment	Risk Team Lead	Chief Risk Officer	IT Head, Compliance Officer	Business Units	Authority to recommend treatment; high risks need CRO approval
Designing ISMS processes and controls	IT Security Architect	CIO	ISMS Manager, Risk Team	Process Owners	Authority to design and propose controls; approval by CIO
Managing information security incidents	Incident Response Lead	CIO	Legal, HR, Risk Team	Top Management, Affected Units	Authority to contain and report; major incidents need CIO approval
Approving access rights	IT Security Admin	CIO	HR, Line Managers	ISMS Manager	Authority to grant/revoke access based on HR validation
Reviewing/auditing the ISMS	Internal Audit	Audit Committee Chair	ISMS Manager, CRO	Board of Directors	Authority to request records and conduct audits
Setting information security objectives	ISMS Manager	Chief Risk Officer	CIO, HR Manager, Business Heads	All Staff	Authority to draft objectives; final approval by CRO
Approving exceptions	CIO	Chief Risk Officer	ISMS Manager, Process Owner	Board of Directors (if critical)	Authority to approve exceptions up to defined thresholds

Table 9.3 Simplified roles, responsibilities, and authorities for the ISMS

Role	*Responsibilities*	*Authority (Limit/Scope)*
Chief Risk Officer (CRO)	Overall accountability for ISMS; approve information security objectives; review ISMS performance	Authority to approve exceptions, allocate resources, and escalate to the Board
ISMS Manager	Coordinate establishment, implementation, maintenance, and improvement of ISMS; report performance to CRO.	Authority to design ISMS processes and recommend improvements
IT Security Architect	Design and configure information security controls and processes	Authority to propose new controls; requires CIO approval for implementation
Incident Response Lead	Manage information security incidents, coordinate response, and ensure lessons learned.	Authority to contain incidents; escalate major incidents to the CIO
Risk Team Lead	Conduct information security risk assessment and treatment planning	Authority to approve risk ratings up to medium; escalate high risks to CRO
Internal Audit	Review and audit the ISMS for effectiveness and compliance	Authority to request ISMS records and conduct audits
Line Managers	Ensure their teams follow information security requirements	Authority to enforce compliance within their teams
Employees / Information Users	Use systems responsibly and report information security incidents	Authority limited to their job role; no approval authority

🛠 *Implementation Task #7: Organizational Roles, Responsibilities, and Authorities*

It's time to put theory into practice. Grab your notebook (or open a new document) and start drafting the roles, responsibilities, and authorities for information security in your organization. Keep it simple and meaningful. You can use the RACI matrix from the toolkit, the simpler structure we discussed earlier, or create something that better fits your organization's way of working.

💬 **Author's Note:** Don't overcomplicate this exercise. Start small, focus on the essential roles, and improve as you go. The goal isn't to create a perfect chart on day one, but to ensure everyone understands their responsibilities—and what decisions they are actually allowed to make.

Key Takeaway—What You've Learned

- Leadership propels ISMS success—top management must visibly own, direct, and be accountable for the ISMS, not just sign off on documents.
- Commitment is active, not passive—attendance at meetings isn't enough; leaders must provide direction, remove obstacles, and support ISMS priorities with action.
- Policy = guiding principle—a concise, relevant Information Security Policy (one page is enough) should state intent, commitments (such as compliance and continual improvement), and how objectives are established.
- Connect policy to strategy—objectives should derive from the policy and align with business goals so security supports, not obstructs, what the organization seeks to achieve.

- Resources must be genuine—budgets, personnel, tools, and time are essential; "we'll do it later" is a recipe for audit issues and missed controls.
- Integration exceeds isolation—embed ISMS requirements into daily processes (HR, procurement, IT, projects) so security becomes part of how work is done, not an additional task.
- Clear roles + authority—assign responsibilities and grant corresponding authority. Responsibility without authority (or vice versa) leads to delays and confusion.
- Communicate frequently and effectively—leadership should regularly remind staff why security matters, share results, and celebrate achievements—transparency fosters culture.
- Never outsource ultimate accountability—while tasks can be delegated, top management remains responsible for ISMS performance and results.
- Leadership shapes culture—genuine executive engagement transforms the ISMS from "a compliance file" into business value: resilience, trust, and competitive edge.

QUIZ #8

True/False statement

Sr.	*Statement*	*True/False*
1	Ensure that responsibilities and authorities for relevant roles are assigned and communicated within the organization.	
2	Ensure the integration of the ISMS requirements into the organization's business processes.	
3	Establish an ISMS policy that provides a framework for setting ISMS objectives.	
4	Ensure that staff are aware of the regulator's requirements.	
5	Ensure that the ISMS scope and boundaries are established.	
6	Ensure the ISMS policy includes a commitment to continual improvement.	
7	Ensure the ISMS system achieves its intended outcome(s).	
8	Ensure that the resources needed for the ISMS are available.	
9	Top management must assign responsibility for reporting on the ISMS's performance to them.	
10	The ISO/IEC 27001 standard requires that the information security policy be signed by top management.	

CASE 3: LEADERSHIP ON THE LINE—ABU DHABI

When Farah Al-Khatib entered the marble-floored lobby of Gulf Trust Bank, she paused briefly. The bank's head office overlooks the Corniche in Abu Dhabi—a symbol of strength and stability. With branches across all seven Emirates and three data centers (in Abu Dhabi, Sharjah, and Ras Al Khaimah), Gulf Trust has built its reputation on reliability. But now, facing increasing regulatory pressure and regional cybersecurity directives, the Board has decided it's time to implement ISO 27001.

Farah, recently named Lead Implementer, was prepared for the challenge. She had years of compliance experience, although this was her first full ISO 27001 project. She anticipated strong support from the leadership team, especially from the CEO, Mr. Hassan Rahman, a respected banker known for his efficiency and precision.

At her initial steering meeting, Mr. Rahman leaned back in his chair and said, "This ISO certification is an IT issue. Let the IT team handle it." The Chief Information Officer, Kareem Al-Nuaimi, nodded but appeared uneasy. "We'll do our best," he said quietly.

Farah attempted to clarify. "Sir, ISO 27001 requires top management involvement and leadership commitment—"

Mr. Rahman smiled politely. "Yes, yes, we'll sign whatever documents are needed. Just make sure the audit goes smoothly."

Farah started work. She assembled a small ISMS core team including members from IT, HR, Operations, and Risk. She began drafting the Information Security Policy and prepared an initial Roles and Responsibilities Matrix. During a team meeting, she said confidently, "We'll need to document every role because ISO 27001 requires it."

Resources were not an issue at Gulf Trust. The bank had modern systems, a generous IT budget, and access to top cybersecurity tools. What it lacked was personnel. Everyone was busy managing core banking projects or regulatory initiatives. When Farah asked for two dedicated staff members to help with ISMS implementation, HR replied, "We can assign them part-time, maybe two hours a week."

Kareem attempted to assist by reallocating an IT analyst to her team, but progress stayed slow. Farah worked late into the evenings mapping out processes and drafting policies herself.

Farah met with the Risk Department Director, Ms. Haya—a young, energetic management graduate from Zayed University—to align the ISMS risk methodology with the bank's enterprise-risk framework. Along with the CIO and other department heads, they worked to ensure ISMS requirements were incorporated into new projects. Farah also suggested that any existing project changes or updates include an information security risk assessment before implementation, so security was considered early and consistently. She later persuaded the CIO to include a security awareness segment in the next town hall, where she spoke briefly about protecting customer data and the role every employee plays in safeguarding information.

The CEO, however, never brought up the ISMS in management meetings, nor did he review progress or performance reports. When auditors visited for a pre-assessment, they asked for evidence of leadership involvement. Farah responded, "The CEO has signed our Information Security Policy."

Case Discussion: Test Your Understanding

1. **Which of the following best demonstrates true leadership commitment under ISO 27001?**

   A. Signing the Information Security Policy once and delegating everything to IT.
   B. Approving budgets but staying uninvolved in implementation.
   C. Participating in management reviews, ensuring resources, and communicating the importance of information security.
   D. Waiting for auditors to confirm compliance before taking interest.

2. **When the CEO stated that the ISMS was an IT issue, what leadership gap was revealed?**

   A. He failed to delegate tasks efficiently.
   B. He misunderstood that accountability for the ISMS rests with top management, not IT alone.

C. He wanted faster implementation.
D. He was focused on cost-saving measures.

3. **Farah said it is an ISO requirement to document every role and responsibility. Is this accurate?**

A. Yes—roles must be listed in the Information Security Policy.
B. No—ISO 27001 does not mention roles at all.
C. Yes—every ISO 27001 role must be formally documented.
D. No—the standard requires roles and authorities to be clearly assigned and communicated, not necessarily documented.

4. **Which resource challenge is most evident in Gulf Trust Bank's ISMS implementation?**

A. Lack of financial resources.
B. Shortage of technical tools.
C. Absence of external consultants.
D. Limited availability of skilled human resources.

5. **Which action by Farah best demonstrated Clause 5.1's requirement to integrate ISMS into the bank's business processes?**

A. Ensuring that ISMS requirements were embedded into new projects and that existing projects conducted information security risk assessments during updates.
B. Preparing a list of controls before defining the ISMS scope.
C. Assigning one IT analyst part-time to the implementation team.
D. Drafting a generic information security policy copied from another bank.

6. **Which of the following statements best captures what Farah could do next to strengthen leadership commitment?**

A. Request that the CEO sign a few more policy documents.
B. Conduct a management review and actively involve top management to discuss ISMS performance and resources.
C. Delegate all leadership functions to the CIO.
D. Delay implementation until after certification auditors visit.

Chapter 10

Clause 6—Plan your risks, control your future

Mastering risk management and the statement of applicability

By now, you already know ISO 27001 is based on risk-based thinking. Clause 6 takes that concept and turns it into action. This is where you go from just recognizing risks to actually deciding what to do about them. It's the planning stage where you make deliberate choices: Which risks are worth addressing? Which opportunities could strengthen your ISMS? And how do you ensure the effort you invest today pays off in the future?

Something I always tell my delegates in class is this: the best practice is to be prepared. The scout motto, "Be Prepared," emphasizes being in a constant state of readiness—physically and mentally—to fulfill your duty and assist others, whether in everyday life or during unexpected emergencies. In the context of an ISMS, this doesn't mean just being ready if something happens, but being prepared for when it happens. Because in information security, it's not a question of "if" threats or incidents occur—it's only a matter of time.

Think of it this way: spotting risks is like seeing dark clouds on the horizon. Clause 6 is where you decide whether to carry an umbrella, change your route, or reschedule the trip. Similarly, for your organization, this clause is about developing practical responses—whether that's reducing, avoiding, transferring, or accepting risks—and ensuring opportunities aren't overlooked along the way.

Author's Note: Clause 6 is where "what could go wrong" meets "what we're going to do about it." It acts as the bridge between theory and action and prepares the foundation for creating your Statement of Applicability (SoA) later.

BEYOND THIS CHAPTER: WHERE TO LEARN MORE ABOUT RISK

In this chapter, I'll walk you through the key risks and opportunities for your ISMS. My aim is to make the concepts clear, practical, and easy to apply for your ISO 27001 implementation. I'll emphasize risk planning related to building and maintaining your ISMS—enough to boost your confidence without overwhelming you with theory.

However, risk management is a broad field in its own right, with many methods, tools, and approaches available. If you want to explore the subject further—either out of curiosity or because your role requires more expertise—here are some excellent standards you can examine:

- **ISO 31073:2022** [22]**—Risk Management: Vocabulary:** A valuable reference for risk-related terms and definitions, so everyone in your organization speaks the same language.

DOI: 10.1201/9781003744139-11

- **ISO 31000:2018—Risk Management: Guidelines:** The global gold standard for risk management principles and framework. It goes beyond information security and applies to all kinds of organizational risk.
- **IEC 31010:2019** [23]**—Risk Management: Risk Assessment Techniques:** A catalog of techniques, from simple to advanced, to identify and analyze risks.
- **ISO/IEC 27005—Risk Management Guide:** Specifically tailored for information security. This one zooms in on information security risks and gives guidance on where to focus your efforts and apply controls most effectively.

Author's Note: You don't need to master all these standards to achieve ISO 27001 certification. However, if you want to delve deeper, particularly into advanced risk assessment methods, these serve as excellent references.

A QUICK REFRESHER: RISK MANAGEMENT

Before we move on to Clause 6.1, let's take a quick pause. If you're already familiar with the risk management process, feel free to skip ahead. But if this is new to you or if you'd like a brief refresher, this section will give you a solid foundation to build upon.

Key Terms You Need to Know

Hazard: A hazard is any source of potential damage. Imagine a candle burning in your living room. The candle itself isn't bad, but left unattended near the curtains, it becomes a hazard.

Threat: A threat is anything that might exploit a weakness. Think of a burglar eyeing your house. The burglar is the threat, actively looking for an opportunity.

Vulnerability: A vulnerability is a weakness that can be exploited. Leaving your front door unlocked is a vulnerability. It doesn't cause harm on its own, but it gives the burglar an easy way in.

Risk: Risk is the effect of uncertainty on objectives. In simple terms, it's the chance that something unwanted will happen and affect your goals. For example, the risk of the burglar (threat) using your unlocked door (vulnerability) to steal your valuables, resulting in financial loss and stress.

Asset: In the context of an ISMS, we focus mainly on ***information assets***—the things that hold value because they support your organization's information and operations. These can be tangible or intangible. For example, your customer database, your HR records, your core banking application, your laptops and servers, or even your employees' knowledge and skills are all assets. Each has value, and if compromised, the organization could face financial loss, reputational damage, or legal consequences.

Author's Note: Hazards, threats, vulnerabilities, and risks are like puzzle pieces. A hazard creates the potential, a threat tries to act, a vulnerability makes it possible, and the risk is the impact when all of them come together.

Explaining the Interconnection

Figure 10.1 shows a powerful truth: ***not every threat is a risk, not every vulnerability is a risk, and not every asset is at risk.*** A risk only exists where all three overlap:

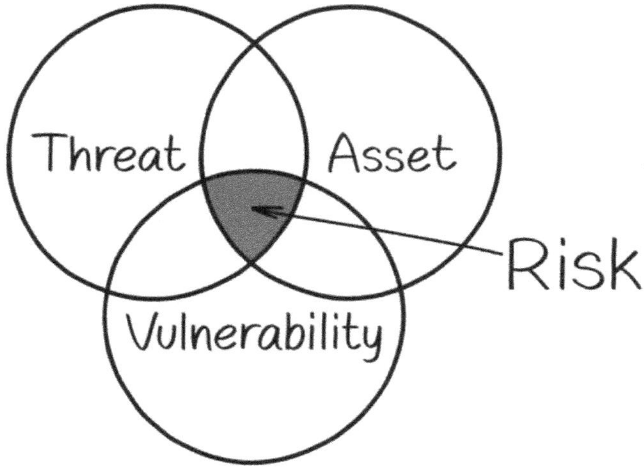

Figure 10.1 Where risks really live: The overlap of threats, vulnerabilities, and assets.

- You have an ***Asset*** (something valuable, like customer data).
- That asset has a ***Vulnerability*** (like weak passwords).
- And there is a ***Threat*** that can exploit it (like a hacker using brute force).

When all three conditions meet, you have a ***risk***.
Practical Examples:

- If you own a ***building (asset)*** and there's a ***flood in the city (threat)*** but your building is on a hilltop with no water exposure, then there's no ***risk*** to you.
- If you have a ***server (asset)*** with a ***software bug (vulnerability),*** but it's not connected to the internet, many external ***threats*** may not apply; there is no risk.
- If a hacker is scanning for open ports (***threat***) and you have no exposed servers (***no asset in that context***), there is no risk.

Author's Note: I always remind my delegates: risk lives only where assets, vulnerabilities, and threats overlap. That's why ISO 27001 emphasizes the importance of understanding context. Don't waste effort trying to fix every vulnerability or worry about every threat. Concentrate on the ones that impact your information assets.

Risk Management Process

In an ISMS, the risk management process isn't just a one-time task that you forget afterward. It's a continuous part of everyday information security management. Each decision you make about protecting data, granting system access, or adopting new technology already involves risk management.

Think of it less like a fire extinguisher on the wall and more like a seatbelt you wear every day. It's not just for "just in case." It's how you operate—embedded in your processes, decisions, and culture.

The process applies at different levels:

- **Strategic:** Deciding whether to move customer data to the cloud.
- **Operational:** Managing how employees use email securely.
- **Project-Based:** Launching a new mobile banking app with secure coding practices.

Because information security risks constantly evolve—including new malware, attack techniques, and regulations—the process remains dynamic and iterative. You don't complete it once; instead, you revisit it as your environment and threats change.

Risk Assessment: The Heart of It All

Risk assessment is the foundation. It includes three steps: ***risk identification, risk analysis, and risk evaluation.***

1. **Risk Identification:** This is asking: *"Where could information security fail?"*

   You need to consider:

   - Information assets (customer databases, HR records, applications, laptops)
   - Threats (hackers, phishing attacks, insider misuse, natural disasters)
   - Vulnerabilities (weak passwords, outdated software, misconfigured firewalls)
   - Context changes (new compliance laws, staff turnover, third-party dependencies)
   - Emerging risks (cloud misconfigurations, AI-driven attacks, deepfakes)

💡 **Example:** A bank identifies that employees clicking on phishing emails could expose customer login credentials.

No single method is mandatory, but if you want a catalog of techniques, ***ISO 31010*** provides detailed options.

2. **Risk Analysis:** Once you've identified the risks, you ask: *"How serious are they?"*

   Here you look at:

- How likely is it to happen? (e.g., phishing emails are highly probable)
- What's the potential impact? (e.g., compromised accounts could cause significant financial loss)
- What controls are already in place? (e.g., multi-factor authentication (MFA) reduces the likelihood of account takeover)
- How confident are we in this judgment?

💡 **Example:** The likelihood of ransomware hitting the organization may be moderate, but the impact could be severe if backups are not tested regularly.

3. **Risk Evaluation:** Now it's decision time: which risks are worth treating, and which can you accept?

You compare the risk levels against your organization's criteria and decide:

- Do we need stronger controls?
- Can we accept the risk as it is?
- Do we need more information before deciding?

Example: A bank might accept the risk of a non-critical internal system, such as a meeting room reservation system, being temporarily unavailable, but it cannot accept the risk of unencrypted cardholder data being stolen.

Risk Treatment: Taking Action

Once you've identified and assessed your information security risks, the next step is to decide how to address them. ISO 27001 doesn't specify a single method—rather, it offers flexibility. Here are the main options:

- **Reduce:** Apply controls to lower the likelihood or impact of a risk.
  Example: If weak passwords are a risk, introduce MFA to reduce the chance of compromise.
- **Avoid***:* Stop the risky activity altogether.
  Example: If storing sensitive data on USB drives is too risky, stop the practice entirely and use secure cloud storage instead.
- **Transfer:** Shift the risk to another party.
  Example: Buy cyber insurance, or outsource hosting to a certified provider that assumes part of the responsibility.
- **Accept:**Formally agree to live with the risk.
  Example: A bank may accept the risk of a meeting room reservation system being temporarily unavailable, as the business impact is low and the cost of additional controls may outweigh the benefit.

Author's Note: When I explain the four classic risk treatment options (accept, avoid, transfer, reduce), I like to keep it light. In class, I sometimes ask a delegate (usually someone I already know is married—I always check during introductions or over coffee), *"Do you consider marriage a risky proposition?"*
Some laugh, some say yes, and that's when the fun begins:

- **Acceptance:** You know the risks, but you still go ahead. You got married—that's risk acceptance!
- **Avoidance:** Some friends never marry at all. That's risk avoidance.
- **Transfer:** In India, many of us don't choose our own partners—our parents do. If things don't go well, you can always say, *"You picked the partner, why blame me?"* That's risk transfer.
- **Reduction (Mitigation):** Some couples sign a pre-nuptial agreement before marriage. That's risk reduction —limiting the potential damage.

I always caution delegates not to take this example out of context—but it works because everyone remembers it. Whether in life or in information security, your options come down to the same four: accept, avoid, transfer, or reduce.

Exploit: The Forgotten Fifth Option

This might seem unconventional, but sometimes the smartest move isn't to reduce or avoid risk—it's to embrace and leverage it. Risk isn't always negative; it can also offer opportunities.

- **Exploit:** Take or increase the risk to pursue an opportunity.

Example: A bank decides to launch mobile-only onboarding for new customers. Yes, it increases the risk of online fraud. Still, by implementing strong identity verification controls, the bank can safely assume the risk—and gain thousands of new customers faster than its competitors.

Author's Note: I often tell my delegates that exploiting risk is not recklessness. It's about understanding the risk so well that you can turn it into an advantage. In information security, this might mean confidently adopting cloud services, AI-driven analytics, or biometric authentication—areas where risks exist. Still, the potential benefits are too significant to ignore.

CLAUSE 6.1: ACTIONS TO ADDRESS RISKS AND OPPORTUNITIES

Summary of the Clause Requirements: Clause 6.1 focuses on moving from good intentions to structured action. You've already examined your issues (Clause 4.1) and requirements of interested parties (Clause 4.2). Now, it's time to use that knowledge to identify the risks and opportunities you need to address to keep your ISMS effective.
In plain words, this clause says:

- Identify the risks and opportunities that could affect your ISMS.
- Make sure you're doing enough to achieve your intended outcomes.
- Prevent or reduce problems before they happen.
- And, as always, keep improving.

Once you've identified them, the standard expects you to:

- Plan specific actions to deal with those risks and opportunities.
- Integrate those actions into your existing ISMS processes (not as a bolt-on extra).
- And finally, check whether those actions actually worked.

Author's Note: I see Clause 6.1 as "the bridge." On one side, you have your context (Clause 4) and leadership (Clause 5). On the other side, there's your detailed risk assessment and treatment. Clause 6.1 connects these, making sure risks and opportunities don't just stay on paper—they're acted upon, integrated into your ISMS, and measured for effectiveness.

Explanation with Real-World Examples: Clause 6.1 is all about being proactive. It's not enough to say, *"Yes, risks exist."* You need to plan how you'll handle them and identify opportunities where your ISMS can add value.
Let's break it down with some real-life flavor:

- **Risks to the ISMS Itself:** Imagine a bank where top management is only half-engaged with the ISMS. Budgets are small, roles are unclear, and staff see information security as "just IT's job." That's a risk to the ISMS outcome. If leadership doesn't commit, the system will never achieve its intended results.
- **Risks in Day-to-Day Information Security:** A hospital using outdated operating systems for medical equipment may be vulnerable to ransomware. That's a risk to confidentiality, integrity, and availability—the very things ISO 27001 protects.
- **Opportunities for Improvement:** A software company introduces a cloud-based ISMS dashboard that allows managers to track incidents in real time. Not only does it improve efficiency, it also shows customers that the company takes security seriously—turning compliance into a competitive advantage.
- **Opportunities Through Business Growth:** An airline expanding into new regions sees an opportunity to use its ISMS as proof of trustworthiness. Having ISO 27001 certification becomes a powerful marketing tool, helping win contracts with regulators and corporate customers.

In every case, Clause 6.1 expects you to do two things:

1. **Plan Actions:** For the bank, that might mean assigning an ISMS manager and running awareness workshops. For the hospital, it could mean patching systems or segmenting networks.
2. **Integrate and Evaluate:** Whatever actions you choose, they should be built into your ISMS processes and reviewed regularly. Did the awareness training reduce phishing clicks? Did the cloud dashboard actually speed up incident response? If yes, great. If not, adjust.

Author's Note: I often remind my delegates that opportunities are just as important as risks. ISO 27001 isn't about creating barriers; it's about building more innovative organizations. If you only focus on risks, you'll always play defense. But by seizing opportunities, your ISMS can also become a tool for growth, efficiency, and trust.

Implementation Guidance: Clause 6.1 focuses on moving from good intentions to concrete action. You've already examined your issues (Clause 4.1) and requirements of interested parties (Clause 4.2). Now, you need to use that information to identify the risks and opportunities that could impact your ISMS—and decide how to address them.

Here's how to approach it in practice:

1. **Start with Your Context and Stakeholders:** Look at the issues you identified earlier (e.g., dependence on third-party IT providers, strict banking regulations, or customer concerns about privacy). These are the building blocks for spotting risks and opportunities.

   Example: In a hospital, patient safety is the top priority. The use of outdated medical devices is both a ***risk*** (vulnerability to malware) and an ***opportunity*** (upgrade to modern, secure equipment).
2. **List Out Risks and Opportunities Clearly:** Don't just think about hackers and malware. Risks can also come from weak management support, unclear roles, or poor staff awareness. Opportunities could include faster reporting through automation or building customer trust by publishing a strong ISMS policy.

Example: A bank realized that unclear incident reporting channels were a risk (staff didn't know whom to call during a phishing attack). The opportunity was to introduce a simple "Report Phishing" button in their email system.

3. **Plan Actions at Different Levels:** Clause 6.1 allows you to act at the strategic, tactical, or operational level. Not every risk needs a boardroom solution. Some need a training session, others a technical fix.

Example:

- **Strategic:** Leadership approves funding for a new security operations center.
- **Tactical:** IT updates access controls and strengthens backup policies.
- **Operational:** Frontline staff receive quarterly phishing simulations and awareness training.

4. **Integrate Actions into Existing Processes:** Don't reinvent the wheel. If you already have business planning cycles or compliance reviews, weave your ISMS actions into them. This avoids duplication and ensures security becomes part of the business fabric, not an add-on.

Example: An airline with an existing safety management system integrated ISMS checks into its regular safety audits—saving time and making both processes stronger.

5. **Evaluate Effectiveness:** Planning actions is one thing, but verifying if they worked is equally important. Did the phishing button decrease incident response time? Did new supplier contracts actually lower third-party risks? If not, make adjustments and enhance them.

Example: An IT firm introduced mandatory encryption on laptops. A year later, they measured incidents of lost laptops. Result: data was no longer being compromised. That's effectiveness in action.

Author's Note: A common question I hear is, "Do we really need to document all this?" The truth is, Clause 6.1 itself doesn't require a formal document. But remember that Clause 7.5.1(b) states you need to keep documented information as necessary for the effectiveness of your ISMS.

In real life, most organizations keep it simple—a short "Risks and Opportunities Tracker" or an action plan. Nothing fancy. Just the essentials: the risk or opportunity you identify, the action you plan to take, who owns it, and how you'll measure success. That's it.

Remember, Clause 6.1 isn't just about paperwork. It's about being practical and proactive. Risks and opportunities will keep changing as your business, technology, and environment evolve. The smartest move is to keep your ISMS active by identifying those changes early, responding to them, and using opportunities to strengthen and secure your organization.

Toolkit and Resources: ***Clause 6.1 Action Planner***

Use this planner (see Table 10.1) to map your risks and opportunities, decide what actions to take, and then check whether those actions worked. Keep it short and simple. The goal isn't to create more paperwork, but to make sure risks are addressed and improvements are real, visible, and effective.

Author's Note: This tool isn't about creating a huge spreadsheet that nobody reads. It's about capturing the essentials—the risk or opportunity you've identified, the action you plan to take, who's responsible, and how you'll measure success—as laid out in Table 10.1.

Table 10.1 Action planner for addressing ISMS risks and opportunities

Risk/Opportunity	*Level (Strategic/ Tactical/Operational)*	*Planned Action*	*Who Owns It*	*How to Measure Effectiveness*
Risk: Staff not reporting phishing emails	Operational	Add "Report Phishing" button in email	IT Manager	Number of phishing reports before vs. after
Opportunity: Use ISMS as a marketing advantage	Strategic	Highlight ISO 27001 certification in client bids	Sales Director	Number of deals won citing certification
Risk: Third-party IT vendor not following controls	Tactical	Update contracts to include ISMS requirements	Procurement Head	Vendor compliance score in audits
Opportunity: Automate access reviews	Tactical	Introduce an access management tool	ISMS Manager	Time saved in quarterly access reviews
Risk: Poor management commitment	Strategic	Quarterly ISMS updates in Board meetings	CEO	Documented minutes of meetings and actions

Keep it practical, keep it usable, and review it regularly so it actually drives improvement rather than just filling a folder.

🛠 *Implementation Task #8: Actions to Address Risks and Opportunities*

Now it's your turn to create an action plan for your ISMS. Take a fresh page in your notebook and outline the key risks and opportunities you've identified. For each, decide what action you'll take, who will be responsible, and how you'll verify if it worked. Keep it short, simple, and practical—this doesn't need to be a massive spreadsheet nobody will ever use.

📌 **Remember:** Many organizations focus solely on risks and overlook opportunities altogether. Don't make that mistake. Opportunities are where your ISMS can truly stand out—whether it's improving processes, cutting costs, or using your ISO 27001 certification as a trust-building asset with clients.

💬 **Author's Note:** If you only pursue risks, you'll always be on the defensive. Opportunities allow you to take the offensive too. Ensure your plan includes both aspects.

CLAUSE 6.1.2: INFORMATION SECURITY RISK ASSESSMENT

Summary of the Clause Requirements: Clause 6.1.2 specifies how your organization will assess information security risks. It's not about guessing or improvising. The standard mandates a consistent, structured approach to identify, analyze, and evaluate risks in the same way each time.

Here's what it asks you to do:

- **Set Your Criteria Upfront:** Define your rules of the game. What counts as an acceptable risk? What method will you use for assessments? These become your risk criteria.

- **Be Consistent:** If you repeat the assessment next year (or even next month), you should get comparable results. That way, you can track progress and spot trends instead of reinventing the wheel.
- **Identify Risks:** Apply your assessment process to find risks to the confidentiality, integrity, and availability of information in your ISMS scope. And don't forget: assign each risk to a clear ***risk owner***. Someone has to be accountable.
- **Analyze Risks:** For each identified risk, ask:

  1. What would the consequences be if it actually happened?
  2. How likely is it to happen in real life?
  3. Based on these, what's the overall level of risk?

- **Evaluate Risks:** Compare the results of your analysis against your risk criteria. Then prioritize: which risks need immediate treatment, and which can wait or be accepted?

Finally, you must keep documentation of your risk assessment process. The standard doesn't specify a specific format—it can be a policy, a procedure, or even a simple documented workflow—but it needs to be clear enough that your process is repeatable and effective.

Author's Note: Clause 6.1.2 addresses discipline. If two different teams evaluate the same risk, you want consistent results. By creating clear criteria, assigning owners, and maintaining consistent priorities, you ensure your ISMS is built on a stable foundation rather than relying on gut feelings.

Explanation with Real-World Examples: Clause 6.1.2 is where we put theory into action and evaluate risks. The standard states: don't just discuss risk—establish a process, follow it, and ensure it works reliably over time.

Let's break it down in plain English, with some examples along the way.

Step 1: Set Your Criteria: Before you start assessing risks, you need some rules. Otherwise, two teams looking at the same risk will give you completely different answers.

- *Risk acceptance criteria:* How much risk is your organization willing to live with?
- *Assessment criteria:* How do you measure likelihood and impact? Are you using numbers (quantitative), words like "high/medium/low" (qualitative), or a mix of both?

Example: A bank might say: "Any risk with more than a 10% chance of impacting customer transactions is unacceptable." A hospital might say: "Any risk that could threaten patient safety is critical, no matter how unlikely."

Step 2: Identify Risks: Here, you list risks to the ***confidentiality, integrity, and availability*** of information. And you assign each risk to a ***risk owner***—someone who is responsible for managing it.

Example:

- *Risk:* Phishing emails trick staff into revealing customer account details.
- *Risk Owner:* Head of IT Security.

- *Risk:* Cloud provider outage disrupts online services.
- **Risk Owner:** Head of IT Operations.

Without risk owners, risks quickly turn into "somebody else's problem."

Step 3: Analyze Risks: Now you dig into the details. For each risk:

1. What are the potential consequences if it happens? (Money, reputation, compliance fines, even safety issues.)
2. How likely is it to happen? (Based on data, history, or expert judgment.)
3. What's the overall risk level (a mix of likelihood and consequence)?

Example:

- A retailer finds that ransomware could stop its online sales for days. Consequence = huge revenue loss + reputation hit. Likelihood = moderate, based on recent attack patterns. Risk level = high.
- The same retailer also notes that its Wi-Fi could drop for 5 minutes occasionally. Consequence = minor. Likelihood = high. Risk level = low.

This shows why risk analysis matters: not every problem deserves the same attention.

Step 4: Evaluate Risks: Here, you compare your results with the acceptance criteria you set in Step 1. Anything above your threshold is "unacceptable" and must be addressed. You also prioritize the risks: which ones need urgent attention and which can wait?

Example: A telecom company might decide that the risk of SIM swap fraud is "high priority" (requires immediate action). In contrast, the risk of temporary printer downtime is "low priority" (acceptable).

Step 5: Keep It Consistent and Documented: ISO expects your process to be repeatable. If you assess the same risk next year, you should be able to see whether it's improving, worsening, or staying the same. That means documenting your method and results—not a lengthy report, just enough so you and your auditors can understand the logic.

Author's Note: I often tell my delegates that a risk assessment is similar to a medical check-up. If you visit two different doctors with the same symptoms, you should receive similar results. Otherwise, how can you trust the diagnosis? That's why criteria, consistency, and clear ownership are so important.

Implementation Guidance: Clause 6.1.2 contains a lot of details, and trying to address it all at once can feel overwhelming. To make it simpler, I'll break it down into smaller parts—6.1.2(a), 6.1.2(b), and so on—and guide you through each requirement step by step. This way, instead of tackling the entire clause at once, you'll understand each part clearly: setting risk criteria, identifying risks, analyzing them, and then evaluating them. Think of it like eating a big meal—much easier when you take it one bite at a time.

Setting Risk Criteria (6.1.2a): Before assessing risks, establish the rules. Risk criteria make your evaluations consistent and comparable, and they clarify what is considered "acceptable" for your ISMS. Follow these steps.

1. **Start from Context and Stakeholders:** Look back at Clause 4 outputs: internal/external issues and interested-party requirements. These shape what matters.

Example: A bank's regulators will drive low tolerance for customer data loss; a hospital will treat risks to patient safety as unacceptable.

2. **Get Top Management to State Risk Appetite:** Ask leaders how much risk we are willing to accept. Identify high-level preferences (conservative, moderate, opportunistic) and any strict limits. This is not just a formality—it guides the entire process.

Example: "Top management will not accept risks that could lead to regulatory fines over ***$100,000*** or patient-safety incidents."

3. **Define Consequence (Impact) Categories:** Determine which types of impact are important, such as financial, operational downtime, legal/regulatory, reputational, and safety. Establish levels (e.g., Negligible to Catastrophic) and assign simple values or descriptions. Use USD for financial examples to keep things concrete.

To keep things simple and consistent, use a ***1–5 scale***, where ***1 = negligible*** and ***5 = catastrophic***. This helps you assign a number to each risk and compare them later.

■ **Toolkit and Resources:** Here's an example consequence (impact) scale you can adapt to your organization, covering financial, operational, and broader business impacts, as shown in Table 10.2.

Table 10.2 Consequence (impact) categories for information security risk assessment

Rating	Impact Level	Financial Loss (USD)	Operational Downtime	Other Impacts
1	Negligible	<$5,000	<1 hour	No noticeable effect
2	Minor	$5k–$50k	1–8 hours	Small reputational impact, minor inconvenience
3	Major	$50k–$500k	1–3 days	Noticeable customer impact, moderate reputational harm
4	Severe	$500k–$5M	Several days	Significant regulatory penalty, severe reputational damage
5	Catastrophic	>$5M	Extended outage	Loss of license, safety issues, or severe harm

Example:

- For a ***bank***, losing access to online banking for two days would score at least a *4 (Severe)* —high financial loss + reputational harm.
- For a ***hospital***, even a short system outage that delays critical treatment could jump to *5 (Catastrophic)* because of patient safety.
- For a ***retail shop***, a 1-hour internet outage may only be a *2 (Minor)* if it barely affects sales.

Author's Note: Keep in mind, Table 10.2 is only a guide. Every organization should adjust the impact levels, numbers, and descriptions to fit its own situation. What feels "minor" for a global bank could easily be "severe" for a small local business. Use it as a starting point, not a rigid rulebook.

4. **Define Likelihood Categories:** Next, decide how you'll measure the likelihood of a risk occurring. You can use probability, annual frequency, or simple words. The key is to keep it straightforward, consistent, and realistic for your organization.

■ **Toolkit and Resources:** Here's an example likelihood scale using 1–5 ratings, where 1 means rare and 5 means almost certain, as shown in Table 10.3.

Table 10.3 Likelihood categories for information security risk assessment

Rating	*Likelihood Level*	*Frequency (per Year)*	*Probability*	*Example*
1	Rare	<0.1 times/year (once in 10+ years)	<1%	A significant earthquake hits your data center
2	Unlikely	0.1–1 times/year (once every 1–10 years)	1–10%	A severe insider attack in a small company
3	Possible	1–3 times/year	10–30%	Phishing attack leading to a successful click
4	Likely	3–12 times/year (monthly to quarterly)	30–70%	Malware attempts detected on endpoints
5	Almost certain	>12 times/year (monthly or more)	>70%	Spam or basic phishing emails are hitting inboxes

Examples in Practice:

- For a ***bank***, phishing attempts are ***5 (Almost Certain)*** —staff see them every week.
- For a ***hospital***, a power outage might be ***2 (Unlikely)*** if backup systems are reliable.
- For a ***cloud-based SaaS provider***, DDoS attempts could be ***4 (Likely)*** —not guaranteed monthly, but frequent enough to prepare for.

Author's Note: Don't overthink the math. Whether you use percentages or just plain words, what matters most is that your team can consistently apply these scales. If two people score the same risk, they should arrive at similar numbers.

5. **Choose How You'll Combine Consequence and Likelihood:** Now that you have both your consequence (impact) and likelihood scales, it's time to combine them. The most common method is using a 5 × 5 risk matrix. Think of it as multiplying two numbers:

Risk Score = Consequence × Likelihood
This gives you a number between 1 and 25. Then you map the number into a simple category:

- ***1–4 = Low*** (acceptable, monitor)
- ***5–9 = Medium*** (needs attention, maybe treat)
- ***10–15 = High*** (requires treatment and tracking)
- ***16–25 = Critical*** (urgent, must escalate to management)

Example: If you score a risk as Consequence = Major (4) and Likelihood = Likely (4), then:
4 × 4 = 16 → falls into the ***Critical*** zone. That means it's not something you can accept—it demands urgent treatment and management attention.

Toolkit and Resources: Table 10.4 provides an example of a 5 × 5 risk matrix, illustrating how likelihood and consequence are combined to determine overall risk levels.
How to read the Matrix in Table 10.4:

- A ***"3 × 2" risk*** (Major consequence, Unlikely likelihood) = score 6 → ***Medium*** risk.
- A ***"5 × 4" risk*** (Catastrophic consequence, Likely likelihood) = score 20 → ***Critical*** risk.
- A ***"2 × 1" risk*** (Minor consequence, Rare likelihood) = score 2 → ***Low*** risk.

Table 10.4 Example 5 × 5 risk matrix combining likelihood and consequence

Likelihood ↓ / Consequence →	*1 Negligible*	*2 Minor*	*3 Major*	*4 Severe*	*5 Catastrophic*
5 Almost Certain	5 (Medium)	10 (High)	15 (High)	20 (Critical)	25 (Critical)
4 Likely	4 (Low)	8 (Medium)	12 (High)	16 (Critical)	20 (Critical)
3 Possible	3 (Low)	6 (Medium)	9 (Medium)	12 (High)	15 (High)
2 Unlikely	2 (Low)	4 (Low)	6 (Medium)	8 (Medium)	10 (High)
1 Rare	1 (Low)	2 (Low)	3 (Low)	4 (Low)	5 (Medium)

Author's Note: Don't get lost in the numbers. The matrix given in Table 10.4 is simply a tool to keep discussions consistent and fair. What really matters is the conversation it triggers: "Is this risk acceptable, or do we need to do something about it?" If your team can agree on that, you're already using the matrix exactly as it was intended.

Define what scores or outcomes are acceptable, which require treatment, and which must be escalated to management/board. Use simple decision rules.

- **Examples:**
  - Accept if Risk Score ≤ 4 or expected annual loss < ***$5,000.***
  - Treat if Risk Score 5–15 or expected annual loss between ***$5,000 and $100,000.***
  - Escalate to top management for Risk Score > 15 or expected annual loss > ***$100,000***, or if regulatory impact exists.

Make treatment decisions sensible: compare the cost of controls versus the expected reduction in loss. A simple Annualized Loss Expectancy (ALE) check helps.

• **Example:** Mitigation costs ***$20,000*** and reduces expected annual loss from ***$120,000*** to ***$10,000*** → do it.

6. **Involve the Right People and Document the Method:** Invite risk owners, process owners, IT, legal, and business stakeholders to agree on the criteria. Document your criteria, matrix, and procedures (using your preferred format), then obtain approval from top management.
7. **Communicate, Apply, and Review Regularly:** Publish the criteria to assessors and risk owners. Apply them consistently. Review them at least once a year and whenever there's a significant change, such as new technology, an incident, or a regulatory update. If two assessments give very different results, revisit the criteria or the training.

Quick Practical Examples:

- **Bank—Phishing Risk:** Consequence = Catastrophic (customer account compromise → ***$500k*** potential loss). Likelihood = Likely (phishing attempted weekly). Risk score → Critical → treatment mandatory.

- **Hospital—Legacy Device:** Consequence = Severe (patient safety risk). Likelihood = Possible. Risk → High → urgent patch/isolation plan required.
- **SaaS Company—Short Downtime:** Consequence = Minor (customer inconvenience), Likelihood = Rare. Risk → Low → may accept or schedule low-cost fixes.

Mini-Checklist (Before You Finish):

- Context and stakeholder needs reviewed
- Top management risk appetite recorded and approved
- Consequence levels defined (with examples and USD where relevant)
- Likelihood categories defined (frequencies or probabilities)
- Combination method chosen (matrix/formula)
- Risk acceptance thresholds set and decision rules written
- Documentation prepared and approved by management
- Communication plan and review frequency set

💬 **Author's Note:** Keep these criteria clear and simple. The goal is consistency and repeatability, not perfect academic writing. If your team can explain the requirements in plain language and use them to decide whether to address a risk, you're already doing well. Start small, demonstrate that it works, then improve.

🛠 *Implementation Task #9: Risk Assessment Criteria*

Let's put this into action. Open your notebook and begin drafting risk assessment criteria for your ISMS. The goal isn't to build a perfect system right away—it's to create a simple, practical scale that your team can actually use.
Think about it in three parts:

1. **Probability (Likelihood):** Decide on a scale that works for you. Some organizations use ***1–3 (Low, Medium, High)***, others prefer ***1–5 (Rare, Unlikely, Possible, Likely, Almost Certain)***. Choose what fits your size and context.
2. **Consequence (Impact):** Again, set a scale. On a 1–5, ***1 might mean negligible (e.g., <$5,000 loss or less than an hour downtime)***, while ***five could mean catastrophic (e.g., >$5M loss, significant regulatory fine, or loss of license)***. Adjust the thresholds to match your business reality.
3. **Risk Acceptance Criteria:** Draw a clear line: at what score is a risk "acceptable," and at what score must it be treated? For example:

    - Risk Score 1–4 = Acceptable (monitor only)
    - Risk Score 5–9 = Needs treatment (medium priority)
    - Risk Score 10–25 = Must be treated immediately (high priority)

💡 **Tip:** Start with simple steps. You can always improve your scales later. The most important thing is that everyone in your organization can use the same "yardstick" to measure risks consistently.

Ensuring Consistent, Valid, and Comparable Results (6.1.2b): Once you've established your risk criteria, the next step is to ensure your risk assessments are consistent. This means that if two different people evaluate the same risk, or if you repeat the assessment next year, the results should not vary significantly.

Think of it like a blood test. If you send the same sample to two labs, the results should be similar. If one says "perfectly healthy" and the other says "critical condition," you'd start questioning the method. Risk assessment is no different.
Here's what consistency looks like in practice:

- **Cover All Risks at the Right Level of Detail:** Don't just look at the obvious ones. Dig into confidentiality, integrity, and availability risks across systems, processes, and people.
  Example: If you're assessing your HR system, don't only check for data leaks. Also consider unauthorized changes (integrity) and system downtime (availability).
- **Make Results Reproducible:** Someone else should be able to follow your method and come to the same conclusion. This is why clear criteria (likelihood and consequence scales) matter.
  Example: If your scale says "downtime of 1–8 hours = Minor," then no matter who does the assessment, they should categorize it as Minor.
- **Track Changes over Time:** When you redo the assessment, you should be able to see whether risks have increased, decreased, or stayed the same. That way, you're not just filling out forms—you're showing real progress.
  Example: If phishing risk was scored "Critical" last year but, after training and better email filters, it drops to "Medium," that's proof your actions worked.

⚠ **Caution:** If two people receive the same risk score but it varies significantly or if the results fluctuate randomly upon reassessment, it indicates your method is too vague. Refine your criteria until the results become consistent and meaningful.

Identifying Information Security Risks (6.1.2c): Risk identification is really the art of asking: "What could go wrong with our information?" It's not about predicting the future perfectly, but about creating a clear, practical list of risks that could prevent your ISMS from reaching its goals. Think of it as shining a flashlight into every corner of your organization—from processes to technology to people—to find where weaknesses might be hiding.

Begin by examining your internal and external issues (Clause 4.1) and the needs and expectations of interested parties (Clause 4.2). For instance, in a bank's online portal, customers (an interested party) expect their personal and financial data to stay confidential, accurate, and accessible around the clock. This means the portal itself becomes an information asset that you need to protect. From there, you can ask: what vulnerabilities are present, what threats might exploit them, and what risks could result?
Always keep the CIA triad in mind:

- **Confidentiality**—could information be exposed to the wrong person?
- **Integrity**—could data be corrupted, altered, or tampered with?
- **Availability**—could systems or information be unavailable when needed?

There are two main approaches you can use:

1. **Event-Based Approach**
   - Look at possible events that could occur, based on past incidents or expert judgment.
   - Some may have already happened (phishing emails, accidental leaks). Others are future possibilities (AI-driven attacks, tighter privacy laws).

Example: A bank reviews past fraud attempts (a **confidentiality** risk) and also anticipates new payment fraud schemes that could disrupt the **availability** of its online services.

2. **Asset–Vulnerability–Threat approach**

    - Start with your information assets (databases, applications, laptops, cloud systems).
    - Identify their vulnerabilities (weak passwords, unpatched software, poor staff awareness).
    - Link them to threats that could exploit them (hackers, insiders, or even natural disasters).

    Example: Hospital patient records (asset) stored on an outdated server (vulnerability) could be encrypted by ransomware (threat), risking both **availability** (records locked) and **integrity** (records corrupted).

Both approaches are effective—and many organizations combine them. The key is to create a practical, prioritized list of risks you can address, not just a theoretical catalog that remains untouched.

And don't forget: every risk needs a risk owner. This person is responsible for monitoring that risk and making sure the right actions are taken. Without owners, risks quickly become "somebody else's problem"—which, in practice, means nobody's problem.

⚠ **Caution:** Don't overcomplicate your first attempt. I've seen organizations start with hundreds of risks and get lost in spreadsheets. A simple, high-level list that highlights your key confidentiality, integrity, and availability risks is much more effective than an overwhelming inventory that no one manages.

Toolkit and Resources: Table 10.5 shows a practical example of risk identification, demonstrating how context, assets, threats, and consequences come together in real-world scenarios.

How to Use Table 10.5:

1. Begin with the **issues and expectations** from your context (Clauses 4.1 and 4.2).
2. Identify the **information asset** linked to those expectations.
3. Add the ***vulnerability*** that makes it weak.
4. Link it to the ***threat*** that could exploit it.
5. Note the ***possible consequence*** if it happens.
6. Identify which part of the ***CIA triad*** is at risk (Confidentiality, Integrity, Availability).
7. Assign a ***risk owner*** who is accountable for monitoring and managing that risk.

Author's Note: Assigning risk owners isn't just a formality. It makes the difference between knowing who's responsible and everyone assuming "someone else will take care of it." Clear ownership ensures risks don't slip through the cracks.

Table 10.5 Example risk identification table linking context, assets, threats, and consequences

Internal/External Issues and Interested Parties' Requirements	*Information Asset*	*Vulnerability*	*Threat*	*Possible Consequence*	*CIA triad*	*Risk Owner*
Customers expect 24/7 secure access to online banking services (Interested party: customers; External issue: growing phishing scams)	Online Banking Portal	Staff not trained to spot phishing emails	Phishing attack	Customer accounts compromised, financial loss, reputational damage	Confidentiality	Head of IT Security
Regulators require patient safety and confidentiality (Interested party: health authority; External issue: cybercrime trend targeting healthcare)	Hospital Patient Record System	Outdated, unpatched server	Ransomware	Loss of patient records, disruption of care, and regulatory fines	Availability, Integrity	CIO
Employees expect privacy of personal data; labor laws require protection of HR records (Interested party: employees; Internal issue: weak access governance)	HR Database	Excessive access rights, no role-based restrictions	Insider misuse	Leakage of employee data, loss of trust, and legal penalties	Confidentiality	HR Director
Customers expect reliable transactions; business depends on online payments (Interested party: customers; External issue: unstable power supply in the region)	Payment Gateway	No backup power line	Power outage	Transaction failures, financial loss, and unhappy customers	Availability	IT Operations Manager
Staff frequently travel; business continuity depends on secure mobile working (Internal issue: BYOD culture; External issue: malware in public Wi-Fi networks)	Corporate Laptops	Weak antivirus and no USB restrictions	Malware infection	Data theft, downtime, productivity loss	Confidentiality, Availability	IT Security Lead

🛠 *Implementation Task #10: Identification of Information Security Risks*

It's time to turn your ideas into action. Grab a new page in your notebook and jot down some information security risks in your organization. Look at it through the lens of the CIA triad:

- *Confidentiality:* What risks could lead to unauthorized disclosure of sensitive information?
- *Integrity:* What risks could allow data to be altered, corrupted, or tampered with?
- *Availability:* What risks could make critical information or systems unavailable when needed?

💡 **Tip:** Don't worry about creating a perfect list. Begin with something simple—even 3–5 examples are a solid start. The goal is to make you think about real risks that matter in your situation.

Analyzing Information Security Risks (6.1.2d): Once you've identified your risks, the next step is to analyze them. In simple words, this means answering two big questions for each risk:

1. ***What would happen if this risk materialized?*** (the consequence)
2. ***How likely is it to happen?*** (the likelihood)

Together, these determine your ***risk level.***

Let's make it practical. Say your online banking portal is vulnerable to phishing.

- *Consequence:* If exploited, customer accounts could be compromised, leading to financial loss and reputational damage.
- *Likelihood:* Based on past incidents and training levels, phishing attempts are "likely."
- *Risk level:* Combining consequence (major) and likelihood (likely) may give you a ***high or critical risk score.***

There are different ways to calculate this:

- *Qualitative:* Using words like *low, medium, and high.*
- *Quantitative:* Using numbers, like "probability of 0.3 per year" or "expected loss = $500,000."
- *Semi-quantitative:* A blend—words with numbers attached (e.g., High = 4 on a 1–5 scale).

Most organizations use a ***semi-quantitative 5 × 5 risk matrix*** (like the one we built earlier). It's simple, consistent, and works well for discussions with both technical and non-technical teams.

💡 **Example:** Imagine a hospital's outdated server storing patient records.

- *Consequence:* Severe—if ransomware hits, patient care could be disrupted, and fines may follow.

- *Likelihood:* Possible—because the server is unpatched.
- *Risk level:* Severe × Possible = ***High risk*** → needs urgent attention.

⚠ **Caution:** Don't handle this alone. Risk analysis is most effective when a team with the right experts—IT, business, compliance, HR, and legal—collaborates. Otherwise, you risk misjudging the situation based on one person's viewpoint.

Evaluating Information Security Risks (6.1.2e): Now that you've analyzed your risks, the next step is to evaluate them. This is where you stop asking "how bad" and "how likely" — and start asking: "So what do we do about it?"
Evaluation is all about ***comparing the risk levels*** (from your analysis) against the ***risk acceptance criteria*** you defined earlier in 6.1.2(a). In plain words, you're checking:

- Does this risk fall within what we agreed is acceptable?
- Or is it too high, meaning it needs further action?

For example, if your acceptance criteria says "anything above a medium risk score must be treated," and your analysis shows ransomware on an old server scored high, it's clear: you need to take action.

But evaluation is not just about deciding whether to accept or treat. It's also about assigning priorities. Some risks might be high but less urgent, while others are critical and require immediate action. Think of it like triage in a hospital—you don't treat everyone at once; you treat based on urgency and impact.

💡 **Example:**

- A phishing risk might be high, but you already have awareness training rolling out next month.
- Meanwhile, an exposed cloud storage bucket with sensitive customer data might also be high risk, but it's live right now—that's urgent.

By the end of this step, you should have a clear, prioritized list of risks that will feed into your Risk Treatment Plan.

⚠ **Caution:** Remember the context. Two risks with the same score might not need the same level of attention. For example, a potential $50,000 loss at a big bank might be acceptable, but the same loss at a small startup could be disastrous. Numbers help, but judgment is important too.

💬 **Author's Note:** I always remind my delegates—risk evaluation is where analysis intersects with decision-making. It's the point where the "math" of likelihood times consequence meets the "reality" of your business context. Without this step, you only have numbers. With it, you have a plan.

📄 **Toolkit and Resources:** Table 10.6 provides an example of how risks can be analyzed and evaluated by combining consequence, likelihood, and overall risk level, leading to clear treatment decisions

💡 ***How to Read Table 10.6***:

- The ***score*** (Consequence × Likelihood) gives you the level of risk.

Table 10.6 Example risk analysis and evaluation template for ISO 27001

Risk Description	*Asset*	*Consequence (1–5)*	*Likelihood (1–5)*	*Risk Level (Score)*	*CIA Impact*	*Risk Owner*	*Accept/ Treat?*	*Priority*
Phishing attack via employee emails	Online Banking Portal	4 (Severe)	4 (Likely)	16 (Critical)	Confidentiality	Head of IT Security	Treat	1—Immediate
Ransomware on an unpatched server	Hospital Patient Record System	5 (Catastrophic)	3 (Possible)	15 (High)	Availability, Integrity	CIO	Treat	2—High
Excessive access rights in the HR system	HR Database	3 (Major)	3 (Possible)	9 (Medium)	Confidentiality	HR Director	Treat	3—Medium
Power outage in the data center	Payment Gateway	4 (Severe)	1 (Rare)	4 (Low)	Availability	IT Operations Manager	Accept	4—Low
Malware via USB drives	Corporate Laptops	3 (Major)	4 (Likely)	12 (High)	Confidentiality, Availability	IT Security Lead	Treat	2—High

- Compare it against your ***risk acceptance criteria***—anything above the threshold goes into treatment.
- Add a ***priority*** column, so you know which risks demand urgent action and which can wait.

Author's Note: Notice how Table 10.6 combines risk analysis (consequence, likelihood, and scoring) with risk evaluation (accept or treat decisions and prioritization). This gives you a single, practical tool. You don't need separate documents for each step, just one living table that you update as your risks and context evolve.

Implementation Task #11: Analysis and Evaluation of Information Security Risks

Time to turn your lists into decisions. Using the risk criteria you prepared earlier (Implementation Task #9) and the risk list you created in Implementation Task #10, analyze and evaluate each risk so you can move directly into treatment planning. Don't rush this—the outputs here will drive your ISMS actions.

Step by Step (Keep It Practical):

1. *Gather What You Need:*
   - Open your risk criteria (consequence and likelihood scales, acceptance rules).
   - Open your risk list from Task #10.
   - Bring the risk owners and one or two subject-matter people into the room (IT, process owner, compliance).
2. ***For Each Risk, Complete the Analysis Table*** (one row per risk):
   - ***Asset | Vulnerability | Threat | CIA Impact***
   - ***Consequence (1–5)***—give the score and short reason (e.g., "3—major reputational and regulatory impact").
   - ***Likelihood (1–5)***—score and short reason (e.g., "3—possible phishing attempts monthly").
   - ***Risk Score (C × L)*** and ***Risk Level*** (map to Low/Medium/High/Critical per your criteria).
   - ***Risk Owner*** (must be a named person or job title).
3. ***Evaluate Against Your Acceptance Criteria***
   - Compare each risk level against your pre-defined acceptance thresholds and then prioritize the risks that need treatment based on urgency and impact.

Author's Note: If you ask me, do this carefully rather than quickly. Good analysis now prevents firefighting later. Keep entries concise, evidence-based, and action-oriented. Your risk register should be a tool you actively use, not just a report you file away.

CLAUSE 6.1.3: INFORMATION SECURITY RISK TREATMENT

Summary of the Clause Requirements: Clause 6.1.3 marks the point where your risk analysis and evaluation become specific actions. Once you identify which risks require attention, the standard directs you to follow a structured treatment process:

- *Select Treatment Options:* Decide how you'll deal with each risk (reduce, avoid, transfer, accept, or even exploit in some cases). The choice should be based directly on your risk assessment results.
- *Determine Controls:* Identify which controls are needed to implement your chosen options. These can be designed by you or taken from recognized sources.
- *Cross-Check With Annex A:* Make sure no crucial controls are missed. Annex A provides a comprehensive list of potential controls, but it's not exhaustive—you can add more if your situation requires it.
- *Create the SoA:* This key document lists all the controls you've chosen, justifies why they're included, notes whether they're implemented or not, and explains why any Annex A controls were excluded.
- *Prepare a Risk Treatment Plan:* Document how each risk will be treated, by whom, and in what timeframe.
- *Get Approvals:* Risk owners must approve the treatment plan and formally accept the residual risks that remain after treatment.

Finally, all of this must be documented. The SoA and treatment plan are not just "nice-to-have"—they are crucial evidence for your ISMS and a key part of ISO 27001 certification.

Explanation with Real-World Examples: By now, you've identified your risks, analyzed them, and decided which ones need attention. Clause 6.1.3 is where you turn those decisions into practical measures that reduce risk in your organization.

Think of it like seeing a doctor. The diagnosis (your risk assessment) explains what's wrong. The prescription (your risk treatment) shows you what to do—medicine, surgery, lifestyle changes, or sometimes just monitoring.

Here's how it works in practice:

1. *Choose the Treatment Option That Fits Your Situation:* For example, if your HR database has excessive access rights, the solution could be to reduce the risk by implementing role-based access controls. Another risk—like a power outage in your data center—might be accepted if you already have a manual fallback process and your business can handle short disruptions.
2. *Decide on the Proper Controls:* Controls can come from anywhere—ISO doesn't limit your creativity. I often joke in class, "If you think installing a ballistic missile will secure your data, feel free!" Of course, it's about practical, proportionate measures. For the HR database, a least-privilege policy and regular access reviews would be appropriate, with concrete controls in place.
3. *Cross-Check with Annex A:* Even if you've selected your controls, don't forget to compare them against Annex A. Think of Annex A as your safety net—not a shopping list, but a way to ensure you haven't missed anything important. For the HR database, Annex A matches the access management controls (5.18 Access rights).
4. *Create the SoA:* The SoA is one of the most critical documents in your ISMS. It states which controls you've included, why you chose them, whether they're implemented yet, and why you've excluded others.

Example: For the HR database, you might record: "Included—excessive access rights identified, role-based access controls required."

5. *Develop a Risk Treatment Plan:* Once you know your controls, you need a clear plan to implement them: who will do it, by when, and how success will be measured. ISO 27002 provides detailed guidance for each Annex A Control, which can be very helpful.

6. ***Obtain Approvals and Accept Residual Risk:*** Lastly, the risk owner must approve the plan and accept any remaining risk. If they believe the residual risk is still too high, they may request additional controls until it's acceptable. For example, the HR Director, as the risk owner, might approve the plan while formally acknowledging that a small risk of human error will always exist.

⚠ **Caution:** Risk treatment isn't about eliminating all risk. That's impossible. It's about making informed decisions, documenting them, and ensuring the right people take responsibility for what remains.

Author's Note: I always remind my delegates—your SoA and Risk Treatment Plan are the *heart* of your ISMS. Auditors love them because they show the logic of how you turned risks into action. But don't just write them for the auditor. Write them so your team actually understands and uses them. That's when ISO 27001 stops being paperwork and starts being absolute protection.

Implementation Guidance: Clause 6.1.3 has several components, and addressing them all at once can feel daunting. Just like with Clause 6.1.2, we'll divide this into smaller steps—6.1.3(a), 6.1.3(b), and so on. This approach allows you to focus on one part at a time—such as selecting treatment options, identifying controls, and building your SoA—rather than trying to tackle the entire thing at once.

Choosing Risk Treatment Options (6.1.3a): Once you've identified and assessed your risks, the next natural question is: "*So what are we going to do about them*?" That's precisely what Clause 6.1.3(a) addresses—selecting the appropriate treatment options for each risk. The choice you make will always depend on your organization's context, business objectives, and risk tolerance.
Here are the common approaches, explained:

- ***Avoid the Risk:*** If something is too risky, you may decide not to do it at all.

Example: A company with limited resources decides not to launch an online payment portal because it can't manage the cyber risks right now.

- ***Modify the Risk:*** This is the most common option. You reduce the likelihood, the consequence, or both.

Example: If phishing emails are a concern, you can reduce the likelihood by training staff and adding email filters, and reduce the consequences by limiting account privileges.

- ***Transfer the Risk:*** You pass part of the risk to others through contracts, outsourcing, or insurance.

Example: A hospital outsources its data center operations to a specialist cloud provider with stronger security measures, or buys insurance to cover ransomware-related costs.

- ***Retain (Accept) the Risk***—Sometimes, the best option is to live with the risk. The key is making an informed decision.

Example: A bank may keep its ATM network operational even though skimming attacks are possible, because the residual risk is within acceptable limits and controls are already in place.

- ***Exploit or Take the Risk:*** Sometimes you take on more risk because it creates an opportunity.

Example: Opening that same online portal may increase exposure to cyberattacks, but it also opens a vast new revenue stream. If management is prepared and resourced, they may take the risk to grow the business.

Each risk doesn't need to fit perfectly into a single category. In practice, you might combine them. For example, you could reduce the risk of phishing through training and filters while accepting the small residual risk that remains.

Author's Note: I often remind my delegates that risk treatment is about finding the right balance. You don't have to eliminate every risk (which is impossible). Instead, you need a well-thought-out, documented decision that aligns with your business goals and keeps risks at a level you're comfortable with.

Determining Necessary Controls (6.1.3b): Once you've chosen how to address a risk, the next step is to decide what controls are necessary to implement that treatment effectively. This is often where many organizations stumble. If your risk assessment was weak, your choice of controls will also be weak—like building a house on shaky foundations.
The key is balance:

- *Include all necessary controls* so risks are covered.
- *Avoid unnecessary controls* that eat up resources without a tangible benefit.

Example: If phishing is your primary concern, the proper controls might include staff training, email filters, and MFA. Adding a biometric gate at the office entrance won't help here—it's a waste of time and money.

Sometimes a single control isn't sufficient. You might need a combination to handle detection, response, and recovery.

Example: If you're concerned about ransomware, you shouldn't only install anti-malware software (prevention). You also need to implement monitoring (detection) and perform regular backups (recovery). Collectively, these measures provide complete protection.

Don't forget about suppliers and partners. If a cloud provider hosts your data, you need to include controls in your contract, such as security requirements, reporting obligations, or even the right to audit. And if the supplier implements those controls, you can still include them in your ISMS to show how risks are being managed.

⚠ Poorly chosen controls can be either ineffective (they don't solve the problem) or inefficient (they cost too much for the benefit they bring). That's why every control you select should directly relate to the risks you identified.

Author's Note: I always advise my delegates—don't select controls just because they "look good" or because another company uses them. Select them because they clearly address your risks. That's the only way your ISMS will remain effective and practical.

Cross-Checking with Annex A (6.1.3c): By now, you've selected the controls that suit your risks. The next step is simple but crucial: compare them with Annex A. Think of Annex A as your safety net—it ensures you haven't missed anything obvious.

Annex A is a catalogue of 93 controls across various areas of information security. It's not a shopping list where you must select every item, nor is it a "one size fits all" solution. Instead, you use it as a reference point:

- ***Include*** the Annex A controls that directly address your risks.
- ***Exclude*** the ones that don't apply, but write down why you excluded them (this will form part of your SoA later).
- ***Add Extra Controls*** if your risks demand something outside Annex A. ISO won't stop you from going beyond the list.

Example: Suppose you've already decided to address the risk of excessive access rights in your HR database by implementing role-based access. Comparing this to Annex A reveals a relevant control: 5.18, "Access rights." A perfect match. However, you might also notice 5.15, "Access control," which could provide additional value. That's the advantage of cross-checking: it helps ensure you're not overlooking anything important.

Author's Note: Don't treat Annex A as just a box-ticking task. If you try to implement every control without thinking, you'll waste effort and make it harder to manage your ISMS. Use it wisely—as a reference and safety net. I often compare Annex A to a travel packing list. You don't pack everything on the list for every trip, but you do look through it to ensure you haven't forgotten the essentials—like your passport before an international flight.

Implementation Task #12: Not Every Control Fits: Justify Your Exclusions

Now it's your turn to test out this concept. Annex A provides a list of controls, but remember—you don't have to use all of them. The main point is to justify your selections.

Here's the task:

1. Review the list of Annex A controls.
2. Pick one or two controls that your organization (or an example organization of your choice) could reasonably exclude.
3. Write down a clear justification for why they are not applicable in that context.

This exercise will help you understand Annex A—it is a helpful safety net, not a strict checklist. The exclusions you document should be relevant to your context and always defensible during an audit.

SoA Clause (6.1.3d): The SoA is one of the most vital documents in your ISMS. Think of it as the link between your risk assessment and your selected controls. It's more than just paperwork—it's your clear record of why you chose specific controls, whether they're implemented, and why others were left out.

Here's what your SoA should include for each control:

- A list of all controls you need (from your risk assessment and treatment plan).
- Justification for including them (what risk they address).
- Whether the control is implemented, in progress, or not yet started.
- Justification for excluding any Annex A Control (if you decided it doesn't apply).

Practical Example: Suppose you run a mid-size bank. You include ***Annex A Control 5.15—Access Control*** because your HR system had excessive access rights. Your justification: *"Needed to reduce the risk of unauthorized access to employee data."* Status: *"In progress—role-based access controls being implemented."*

On the other hand, if your organization does not develop software, you can exclude Annex A's secure coding control (*8.28*). Your justification: "*Not applicable—no in-house software development.*"

Most organizations prepare their SoA as a table listing all 93 Annex A controls in rows. But remember—93 is the minimum. You can certainly add extra controls if your situation requires it. For example, a payment processor might add PCI-DSS controls, while a bank in the UAE might include specific requirements from NCEMA (National Emergency Crisis and Disasters Management Authority). Adding these extra controls strengthens your SoA and demonstrates that you are aligning with both ISO 27001 and your industry or regulatory standards.

Typical columns in an SoA can include:

- **Control Reference or Source (e.g., Annex A, PCI-DSS, NCEMA, internal control)**
- **Name of the Control**
- **Included/Excluded**
- **Justification for Inclusion or Exclusion**
- **Implementation Status (e.g., Implemented, In Progress, Not Started)**

You can also add extra columns for your own use, such as:

- ***Responsible Person*** (who owns the control)
- ***Reference*** (to policies, procedures, or documents that show the control is in place)

⚠ **Caution:** The SoA isn't just for auditors. It should be a practical tool for your team. If it only makes sense to the consultant who wrote it, you're doing it wrong. Write it in a way that your managers and staff can actually use and understand.

Toolkit and Resources: Table 10.7 provides an example of a SoA, showing how controls are selected, justified as included or excluded, and tracked for implementation status.

Table 10.7 Example SoA for ISO 27001 controls

Control Reference	*Name of the Control*	*Included/Excluded*	*Justification*	*Implementation Status*
5.18	Access Rights	*Included*	Risk assessment identified excessive access rights in the HR system; controls are required to reduce the risk of unauthorized access.	In progress
8.23	Secure Coding	*Excluded*	Not applicable—no in-house software development. All software is sourced from third-party vendors.	N/A
PCI-DSS 10.6	Daily Log Reviews	*Included (extra control)*	Regulatory requirement for payment card data protection; supports monitoring obligations.	Fully implemented

Tip for Readers: Don't restrict yourself to Annex A's 93 controls. If your regulator, industry standards (e.g., PCI-DSS), or national authority (e.g., NCEMA in the UAE) require additional controls, include them here. This demonstrates your SoA is practical, tailored to the context, and compliant with all obligations.

🛠 *Implementation Task #13: Statement of Applicability*

It's time to bring everything together. You've already identified your risks, analyzed and evaluated them—now let's link those results to your controls.
Your task is to ***prepare an SoA***. Here's how to go about it:

1. Review all 93 Annex A controls.
2. For each, decide whether it should be ***included or excluded.***
3. Write a clear justification for your decision. If you're including a control, your justification should often point back to your risk assessment results (e.g., "Access control included because HR database showed excessive access rights").
4. Note the current ***Implementation Status***—is it already in place, in progress, or not started yet?
5. Don't stop at Annex A. Add any ***extra controls*** you plan to implement. These might come from other regulatory or industry-specific requirements.

📌 **Reminder:** Your SoA is a living document. Keep it updated as risks, controls, and your organization's context change.

Formulating a Risk Treatment Plan Clause (6.1.3e): Once you've selected your treatment options and identified the appropriate controls, the next step is to compile them into a clear Risk Treatment Plan. Think of this as your "to-do list" for managing risks. It's not meant to be a lengthy document—just a practical plan that outlines what needs to be done, who will do it, and by when.

It's important to note that ISO 27001 does not specify how controls should be implemented. For detailed guidance on implementation, you can refer to ISO/IEC 27002:2022, which is designed for organizations of all types and sizes. ISO 27002 serves as a reference for selecting and applying controls for risk treatment and can also help organizations adopt widely accepted information security practices.

In this book, I won't walk you through every control from Annex A—there are 93 of them, and covering each one here would make this book massive and distract from our practical roadmap. Instead, I'll provide detailed implementation guidance for one control as a quick reference, so you can see how the process works in practice. For all the other controls, I highly recommend referring to ISO/IEC 27002, which offers comprehensive explanations and guidance you can adapt to your own context.
At a minimum, your plan should cover each treated risk:

- The ***treatment option(s)*** you selected (avoid, reduce, transfer, accept, or exploit).
- The ***controls*** you'll use.
- The ***implementation status*** (e.g., not started, in progress, implemented).

It's also helpful to add:

- The ***risk owner*** (who's accountable).
- The ***expected residual risk*** once the controls are in place.
- Responsibilities and deadlines for each action.

A simple table format works best here. For each risk, list the controls you choose, who owns them, when they will be implemented, and how progress will be tracked. This makes your plan more than just a document—it's a practical guide your team can use daily.

❢ **Example:** Suppose your risk assessment points out mobile phones as a vulnerability. Employees might misplace devices that hold sensitive customer or business information.

- To reduce the risk of loss, you could implement a Mobile Device Policy requiring staff to take care of devices and report issues immediately.
- To lessen the impact of a lost phone, you could adopt Mobile Device Management (MDM) tools that allow you to wipe data and ensure regular backups are in place remotely. This directly relates to Annex A Control 8.1—User endpoint devices, which covers safeguards for laptops, mobiles, and tablets.
- To enhance access control, you might enforce PINs, strong passwords, or biometrics. This aligns with Annex A Control 5.1—Policies for information security, which mandates establishing policies to guide secure access and usage.

Each of these measures would be documented in your Risk Treatment Plan, linked to the risks they address and the appropriate Annex A controls. Later, when you prepare your SoA, you would list 8.1 and 5.1 as "included controls," with justifications like:

- *"Included—needed to address the risk of mobile device loss and unauthorized access."*

This way, your SoA, Risk Treatment Plan, and policies all tell a consistent story—one risk, paired with clear controls, responsibilities, and timelines.

⚠ **Caution:** Don't confuse the treatment plan with the SoA. The SoA lists the controls you've selected and explains why. The treatment plan describes how you'll implement those controls in your organization. They are two sides of the same coin, and auditors will expect to see both.

💬 **Author's Note:** I always remind my delegates that a good treatment plan resembles a project plan. If you can't identify who's responsible for what and by when, it's not truly a plan; it's just a list. Keep it actionable.

Understanding Themes and Attributes

Before we review treatment plans, let's pause and understand two key concepts from ISO/IEC 27002: themes and attributes. These help you interpret Annex A controls and implement them systematically.

Themes: Every Annex A Control belongs to one of four themes:

- ***People*** → controls that deal with individuals (e.g., training, awareness).
- ***Physical*** → controls that protect physical objects (e.g., locks, CCTV).
- ***Technological*** → controls that use technology (e.g., firewalls, encryption).
- ***Organizational*** → everything else that sets the direction or structure (e.g., policies, governance).

❢ *Think of themes as the "main buckets" into which controls fall. If you're explaining security to your CEO, themes help simplify the conversation: Are we dealing with people, processes, tech, or the physical world?*

Attributes: While themes give you the big picture, attributes allow you to focus in. Each control in ISO/IEC 27002 has attributes—essentially "tags" —that help you view and organize controls in different ways based on your audience or needs.
Here's a quick rundown of the five key attributes:

1. ***Control Type:*** When does the control act?
    - *Preventive* (stops incidents before they happen, e.g., encryption)
    - *Detective* (spots incidents in action, e.g., log monitoring)
    - *Corrective* (fixes things after the fact, e.g., backups)
2. ***Information Security Properties:*** Which part of the CIA triad does it protect?
    - Confidentiality, Integrity, Availability
3. ***Cybersecurity Concepts****—How the control lines up with the broader cybersecurity framework described in ISO/IEC TS 27110:2021* [30].
    - *Identify:* Spot what needs to be protected (e.g., assets, risks, vulnerabilities).
    - *Protect:* Put safeguards in place to reduce risk (e.g., firewalls, training, encryption).
    - *Detect:* Notice when something goes wrong (e.g., monitoring, intrusion detection).
    - *Respond:* Act quickly to contain and fix an incident (e.g., incident response process).
    - *Recover:* Restore normal operations and learn lessons (e.g., backups, continuity planning).
4. ***Operational Capabilities:*** The practitioner's view: what capability does the control strengthen?
    - **Examples:** Governance, Asset Management, Application Security, Identity and Access Management, Continuity, Supplier Security, Legal and Compliance, and more.
5. ***Security Domains*** A higher-level grouping of where the control fits:
    - Governance and Ecosystem, Protection, Defense, Resilience

Author's Note: You might wonder, "*Why should I care about all these attributes?*" Here's the thing—when you're creating your SoA or developing a Risk Treatment Plan, attributes help you tell a clear story. They not only show what control you selected but also explain why you chose it and how it contributes.

For example, imagine you've added disk encryption to laptops. Instead of just saying, "because ISO says so," you can frame it like this:

- ***Control Type***: Preventive
- ***Information Property***: Confidentiality
- ***Cybersecurity Concept***: Protect
- ***Operational Capability***: Endpoint security

Now, if an auditor or your management team asks, you're not just referencing a requirement. You're demonstrating how the control lowers the risk of data leakage if a laptop is lost or stolen. That's a much stronger, business-oriented explanation—and one your team can also understand.

Think of attributes like filters on an online shopping site. They allow you to sort and narrow down controls based on what you want to see: "Show me all preventive controls that protect confidentiality," or "Show me all resilience-related controls for continuity planning." You don't need to memorize all of them—ISO/IEC 27002 has the complete mapping. But having this framework in your head makes your ISMS controls easier to explain, defend, and actually use.

Toolkit and Resources: Risk Treatment Plan: Annex A Control 8.1—User end point Devices

When creating your Risk Treatment Plan, there isn't a single "right" method. Some organizations prefer a narrative style, outlining steps like a mini-project plan with examples and clear actions. Others favor a table format, presenting everything in rows and columns for quick reference. Both approaches are valid and accepted during audits—what matters is that your plan is practical, comprehensive, and actually used by your team. In this book, I'll demonstrate both styles side by side. You can then choose which feels more natural for your organization—or even combine them. The main goal isn't to impress auditors with formatting but to ensure your plan works effectively in real life.

Let me show you a practical example. The following box contains a sample Risk Treatment Plan for Annex A Control 8.1 (User Endpoint Devices), written in plain language so you can see how risks are addressed and treated in real life.

Sample Risk Treatment Plan—Annex A Control 8.1 (User Endpoint Devices)

Table 10.8 forms part of this template and helps you capture the attribute categories for Annex A Control 8.1 (User endpoint devices) in a clear, structured way.

Table 10.8 Attribute categories for Annex A Control 8.1 (user endpoint devices)

Control Type	*Information Security Properties*	*Cybersecurity Concepts*	*Operational Capabilities*	*Security Domains*
#Preventive	#Confidentiality #Integrity #Availability	#Protect	#Asset_management #Information_ protection	#Protection

Objective: Protect information stored on, processed by, or accessed through user endpoint devices from risks such as malware, unauthorized access, data leakage, and physical theft.

Step 1: Define the Scope of Endpoint Usage: Start by listing all types of endpoint devices your organization uses—laptops, desktops, tablets, and smartphones. Then map the kind of information they handle. Classify that data (public, internal, confidential, restricted) and decide which devices are allowed to process or store each category.

Example: Sales laptops may handle customer contact details (internal), while finance laptops may store payroll data (restricted). That's two very different risk profiles, so the controls applied should reflect the sensitivity.

Step 2: Establish a Topic-Specific Policy: Develop and communicate a clear policy for secure configuration and usage of endpoint devices. Your policy should include:

- ***Device Registration:*** Maintain an up-to-date inventory of all authorized devices.
- ***Physical Protection:*** Use cable locks, secure storage, and rules for safe transport.
- ***Software Controls:*** Restrict installation rights, enforce updates, and deploy endpoint protection.
- ***Network Rules:*** Mandate VPNs, personal firewalls, and turn off insecure protocols.
- ***Access Controls:*** Strong authentication, session timeouts, and automatic log-off.
- ***Encryption:*** Enable full-disk encryption, including removable media.
- ***Remote Actions:*** Enable remote wipe, disable, or lock functions.
- ***Backups:*** Ensure endpoint data is backed up, even when off the corporate network.
- ***Web Usage:*** Control risky web apps and enforce security on cloud services.
- ***Removable Media:*** Disable USB ports if possible, or require encryption and logging.
- ***Partitioning:*** Use secure containers or virtual partitions to separate business and personal data.

Step 3: Define User Responsibilities: Even the best technology fails if users don't play their part. Train and remind staff to:

- Log off and terminate sessions when not in use
- Never leave devices unattended in public places
- Use privacy screens in shared spaces
- Secure devices during travel
- Report theft or loss immediately

Example: I often tell users in training, *"Would you leave your wallet unattended in a café? Then why your laptop, which could hold far more valuable information?"*

Step 4: Address BYOD (Bring Your Own Device)
If your organization allows personal devices:

- Separate business and personal data with secure containers
- Require staff to sign BYOD agreements allowing remote wipe
- Clarify ownership of business data and intellectual property
- Check legal limitations on device access and licensing

Example: A consultant using their personal iPad must agree to remote wipe rights if the device is lost. This prevents business data from falling into the wrong hands.

Step 5: Secure Wireless Connections
Endpoints connect everywhere—office Wi-Fi, airports, hotels. Define clear rules:

- Disable outdated protocols (e.g., WEP)
- Enforce VPN or secure tunneling for remote connections
- Reserve enough bandwidth for backups and updates

Example: Remote staff should never connect to cloud services without an active VPN session.

Step 6: Tailor Controls by Location
Controls don't always need to be identical everywhere. Differentiate:

- *Inside Secured Premises:* Rely on physical access controls and internal firewalls.
- *Outside the Office:* Stronger protections like enforced encryption, auto-lock, and remote monitoring.

Example: A field engineer's laptop must auto-lock after 5 minutes and use encrypted storage because it's often carried between sites.

Step 7: Document and Monitor
Finally, create clear procedures for:

- Device onboarding and offboarding
- Handling incidents such as theft or loss
- Meeting legal, regulatory, and contractual requirements
- Conducting regular audits and monitoring usage behavior

Final Note: Automate whenever possible. Enforce policies using configuration management tools (e.g., MDM, Group Policy). The less you depend on manual user actions, the more dependable your controls will be.

Now, let's look at the same Risk Treatment Plan for Annex A Control 8.1, this time presented in a table format for quick reference.

Risk Treatment Plan—Annex A Control 8.1: User Endpoint Devices (Table Format)

Here, the same attribute category structure from Table 10.8 is intentionally reused in a table-driven format. You can include this table in whichever form layout you choose. Table 10.8 forms part of this template and helps you capture the attribute categories for Annex A Control 8.1 (User endpoint devices) in a clear, structured way.

Table 10.8 Attribute categories for Annex A Control 8.1 (user endpoint devices)

Control Type	*Information Security Properties*	*Cybersecurity Concepts*	*Operational Capabilities*	*Security Domains*
#Preventive	#Confidentiality #Integrity #Availability	#Protect	#Asset_management #Information_protection	#Protection

Control Reference: Annex A, Control 8.1
Control Name: User Endpoint Devices
Purpose: To protect information against the risks introduced by laptops, phones, tablets, and other endpoint devices.
How to Use This Plan: Use Table 10.9 as a working guide to build and maintain your Risk Treatment Plan for user endpoint devices. As you go through it, keep the following points in mind:

- ***Start Simple:*** Pick the main risks for endpoints (loss/theft, malware, BYOD, Wi-Fi).
- ***Tie Each Risk to a Control:*** Controls can come from Annex A (8.1, 5.1) or custom sources like MDM solutions.
- ***Keep It Actionable:*** Name who is responsible, what they'll do, and by when.
- ***Get Approval:*** Always ensure the residual risk is reviewed and signed off by the risk owner.

Table 10.9 Example Risk Treatment Plan for Annex A Control 8.1 (user endpoint devices)

Risk Description	*Treatment Option*	*Selected Controls*	*Responsible Person*	*Implementation Steps*	*Timeline*	*Residual Risk and Owner Approval*
Loss or theft of a company laptop leading to a data breach	Reduce the likelihood and consequences	- Mobile Device Policy - Full-disk encryption-Remote wipe via MDM (8.1) - PIN/biometric login (5.1 Access Control)	IT Security Lead	Draft and approve mobile device policy, deploy MDM, enforce encryption, and mandate PIN/biometric login.	Q2	Residual risk: Low. Approved by CIO
Malware infection via USB drives	Reduce likelihood	- Block/turn off USB ports - Approved removable media policy - Endpoint protection software	IT Operations Manager	Configure group policies to disable USB, whitelist approved devices, and install AV/EDR	Q3	Residual risk: Low. Accepted by the IT Risk Committee
Unauthorized use of personal devices (BYOD)	Transfer/reduce	- BYOD policy - Partitioning - User acceptance of remote wipe	HR and IT Security	Update policies, require user agreement, and deploy MDM containerization	Q2	Residual risk: Low. Approved by HR Director
Data leakage via unsecured Wi-Fi connections	Reduce likelihood	- Enforce VPN - Block insecure protocols - User awareness training	Network Security Manager	Configure VPN as mandatory, disable WEP/TLS1.0, run awareness campaign	Ongoing	Residual risk: Low. Approved by CISO

Getting Risk Owners' Approval Clause (6.1.3f): Once your Risk Treatment Plan is prepared, you can't just put it aside—it must be approved by the risk owners. Why? Because they are ultimately responsible for the asset or process connected to that risk. If they don't agree with the plan or feel uncomfortable with the residual risk (the risk remaining after controls are implemented), then the plan isn't finished.

Think of it like a medical treatment: the doctor (ISMS team) recommends surgery, but the patient (risk owner) must agree and sign off before it proceeds. Without that consent, the treatment plan can't move forward.

Here's how this works in practice:

- ***Document the Residual Risk:*** What's left even after controls are in place.
- ***Record the Risk Owner's Approval:*** Usually by updating the Risk Treatment Plan with a column for residual risk and approval.
- ***Use Clear Language:*** The risk owner should understand what they're agreeing to. If they don't, you'll need to explain the risk in business terms, not technical jargon.

Example: Suppose your HR Director is the risk owner for the HR database. Your treatment plan reduces unauthorized access risk with role-based access controls, but a small residual risk still exists—for example, the chance of human error during quarterly access reviews. The HR Director must decide: "Am I comfortable with this level of residual risk?" If yes, they approve the plan. If not, they may request stronger measures, such as automated access review tools.

⚠ **Caution:** Never skip this step. If risks lack an owner's approval, they'll remain in a gray zone of "unofficial acceptance." That's risky—and auditors will spot it quickly.

Toolkit and Resources: Table 10.10 provides a comprehensive structure that covers both Clause 6.1.2 (Information Security Risk Assessment) and Clause 6.1.3 (Information Security Risk Treatment). Instead of managing separate documents, you can use this single tracker to follow the entire risk management journey—from identifying issues and risks, through likelihood and impact analysis, to selecting Annex A controls and recording residual risk and approvals. It keeps everything connected and practical, allowing your risk assessment to flow naturally into your risk treatment without duplication. Think of Table 10.10 as your ISMS risk dashboard—one place where the whole story comes together clearly and logically.

Implementation Task #14: Comprehensive ISMS Risk and Treatment Tracker

Now it's your turn to put everything together. Using the Comprehensive ISMS Risk and Treatment Tracker provided, complete the entire cycle:

1. ***Start with Risk Assessment:*** List the information security risks you've identified. Capture the issue, risk cause, how it affects CIA, and rate the likelihood and impact.
2. ***Choose Your Treatment:*** Decide whether you will accept, avoid, transfer, or treat each risk. Select suitable Annex A (or other framework) controls that best fit your treatment plan.
3. ***Update with Control Implementation:*** Record the status of controls (implemented, in progress, or not started).
4. ***Calculate Residual Risk:*** Once controls are in place, re-assess likelihood and impact to determine the residual risk.
5. ***Get Risk Owner Approval:*** Finally, have the risk owner review and approve, confirming they accept the residual risk.

Table 10.10 Comprehensive ISMS risk and treatment tracker

Comprehensive ISMS Risk and Treatment Tracker: A single table format to record your risk assessment results, chosen treatments, residual risks, and approvals—all in one place.

#	*Issues*	*Risks*	*Dept*	*Risk Cause (How It Will Occur)*	*CIA Triad*	*Existing Controls*	*Likelihood*	*Impact*	*Risk Priority Number (RPN)*	*Proposed Risk Treatment*	*Annex A Control Reference*	*Implementation Status*	*Residual Likelihood*	*Residual Impact*	*Residual RPN*	*Risk Owner Approval*
1	Loss or theft of employee laptops/smartphones	Unauthorized access to sensitive company data	IT Security	Employees may lose devices during travel; stolen devices could expose business emails, client data, or payroll information	Confidentiality, integrity, availability	Basic anti-virus installed; password logins enabled	3	4	12	Treat—introduce Mobile Device Policy, enforce full-disk encryption, implement MDM for remote wipe, enforce PIN/biometric logins, and enable backups	8.1 User Endpoint Devices 5.1 Access Control	Policy drafted, MDM rollout in progress; training sessions scheduled	1	3	3	IT Security Lead—15-02-20XX

📌 **Remember:** This single tracker is created to cover both Clause 6.1.2 (Risk Assessment) and Clause 6.1.3 (Risk Treatment). By centralizing everything, you avoid duplication, make audits more efficient, and provide management with a clear view from risk identification to residual risk acceptance.

CLAUSE 6.2: INFORMATION SECURITY OBJECTIVES AND PLANNING TO ACHIEVE THEM

Summary of the Clause Requirements: Clause 6.2 focuses on establishing clear information security objectives and ensuring they are actually achieved rather than just written down. Think of them as the "targets" that guide your ISMS in the right direction.

Here's what ISO 27001 expects you to do:

- *Set Objectives at the Proper Levels:* Not just at the top, but across relevant functions and departments.
- *Keep Them Aligned with Your Security Policy:* Your objectives should support the promises made in your policy.
- *Make Them Measurable Where Possible:* Numbers or clear milestones work better than vague statements.
- *Base Them on Your Context:* Include legal/regulatory requirements, and the results of your risk assessment and treatment.
- *Monitor and Track Progress:* Don't set and forget; objectives should be checked regularly.
- *Communicate Them Clearly:* So people across the organization know what they're working toward.
- *Update When Needed:* If your risks, technology, or business priorities change, so should your objectives.
- *Document Them:* You must retain them as part of your ISMS records.

And when you plan to achieve these objectives, you need to be specific:

- *What* will be done
- *What* resources are required
- *Who* will be responsible
- *When* will it be completed
- *How* success will be measured

📌 In short, Clause 6.2 encourages you to transform your information security policy into concrete, actionable objectives, backed by clear plans and accountability.

Explanation with Real-World Examples: Setting information security objectives is where your ISMS transitions from broad intentions to clear, measurable goals. Your information security policy may state your commitment to confidentiality, integrity, and availability—but Clause 6.2 asks: *"How exactly will you make that happen, and how will you prove it?"*

These objectives serve as signposts. They help keep your ISMS aligned with your organization's strategy, risks, and stakeholder needs. They also provide a way to measure performance—to determine whether your controls and processes are genuinely effective.

📌 *What ISO 27001 expects from your objectives:*

- They must ***fit with your policy***.
- They should be ***measurable*** (if you can't measure it, you can't track it).
- They must be ***based on risks, treatments, and requirements***.

- They should be ***communicated and monitored.***
- And, importantly, they should be ***kept up to date*** as your business and risks change.

Now, let's make this practical.

Example 1: Reducing Phishing Risk

- ***Policy Says:*** "We will protect customer data from unauthorized access."
- ***Objective:*** *IT Security, with support from HR, will reduce the percentage of staff clicking on simulated phishing emails from 20% to less than 5% by the end of this calendar year.*
- ***Plan:*** Run quarterly phishing simulations, provide targeted training for employees who fail, and track results after each campaign. Report improvements to management at the end of each quarter.

Example 2: Improving System Availability

- ***Policy Says:*** "We will ensure the availability of critical services."
- ***Objective:*** *The IT Infrastructure team will maintain at least 99.9% uptime for the online payment system during this financial year.*
- ***Plan:*** Add redundant servers and backup internet lines, monitor system uptime daily, and ensure any outage longer than 1 hour is escalated immediately to senior management.

Example 3: Strengthening Data Integrity

- ***Policy Says:*** "We will safeguard the integrity of financial records."
- ***Objective:*** *The Finance Department will ensure that 100% of financial transactions are logged, verified, and reconciled within 24 hours throughout the year.*
- ***Plan:*** Use automated transaction logging, carry out daily reconciliations, and perform monthly internal audits to confirm compliance.

What goes into planning your objectives? For each one, you'll need to be clear on:

- ***What*** will be done
- ***Who*** is responsible
- ***What*** resources are required
- ***When*** it should be completed
- ***How*** success will be measured

⚠ **Remember:** Objectives aren't a one-time setup. As risks change—whether from new regulations, emerging technologies, or threats—your objectives should adapt accordingly. For example, after a ransomware incident at a peer company, you might aim to cut backup recovery time from 24 hours to 4 hours.

💬 **Author's Note:** You might have noticed something about the examples—each objective has a clear owner, a measurable target, and a deadline. That's what makes it a SMART objective. SMART is simply a helpful way to check if your objectives are solid:

- *S*pecific—clear and focused (not vague like "improve security")
- *M*easurable—you can track progress with numbers or evidence

- *A*chievable—realistic given your resources and context
- *R*elevant—tied to your business goals and information security policy
- *T*ime-bound—has a deadline, so it doesn't drift forever

Without these ingredients, objectives look nice on paper but rarely drive real change. With SMART, you're setting goals that your team can actually understand, work toward, and deliver.

Implementation Guidance: Clause 6.2 focuses on transforming "plans on paper" into clear, measurable objectives that advance your ISMS. Many organizations see objectives only in terms of risk treatment, but that's just one source. Objectives can also stem from identified opportunities, continual improvement ideas, or recommendations from internal or external audits.

Here's a step-by-step way to make it practical:

Step 1: Gather Your Inputs: Review all the places where potential objectives can come from:

- ***Risk Treatment Plans*** → If you're treating phishing risk, your objective might be: *"Reduce click rates in phishing simulations to below 5% this year."*
- ***Opportunities*** → Maybe you see a chance to improve customer trust by getting ISO 27001 certified; your objective could be: *"Achieve certification by Q4."*
- ***Continual Improvement*** → If backup restore tests were slow last year, set an objective to: *"Reduce average restore time from 8 hours to under 2 hours by June."*
- ***Audit reports*** → If an audit found weak password resets, your objective might be: *"Implement self-service password reset with MFA by Q2."*

Step 2: Make Them SMART: Ask yourself:

- What needs to be done?
- How will success be measured?
- Is it realistic for our resources?
- Does it connect to our ISMS policy or business goals?
- When will it be achieved?

Step 3: Plan the "How": For each objective, outline:

- ***Activities*** (the actual steps)
- ***Resources*** (budget, tools, staff)
- ***Responsible owner*** (who makes sure it happens)
- ***Timeline*** (target dates or milestones)
- ***Evaluation*** (how progress will be tracked or verified)

Step 4: Document and Share: Write your objectives in a simple tracker or table. Please share them with the appropriate teams and review progress regularly. Objectives are not meant to sit in a drawer—they're intended to guide action and improvement.

Author's Note: Some of the most effective objectives don't come from significant risks but from minor improvements or opportunities. For example, one of my clients aimed to "consolidate three separate access request forms into one by the end of the year." It wasn't flashy, but it saved time, reduced errors, and made life easier for everyone—and that's precisely the spirit of continual improvement ISO 27001 is built on.

Toolkit and Resources: Table 10.11 provides a practical way to define, track, and review your information security objectives, including targets, responsibilities, timelines, and evidence of achievement.

Table 10.11 Information security objectives tracker

Objective Source	*Objective Statement*	*Responsible Person*	*Timeline*	*Resources Needed*	*Evaluation Method*	*Status*
Risk Treatment	Reduce staff phishing click rate from 18% to <5% through quarterly phishing simulations and awareness training.	HR and IT Security	12 months	Awareness platform, trainer time	Quarterly phishing test results	In Progress
Opportunity	Achieve ISO/IEC 27001 certification to strengthen customer trust and open new markets.	Compliance Manager	Q4 this year	Consultant support, certification fees	External certification audit	Planned
Continual Improvement	Reduce system restore time from 8 hours to <2 hours by upgrading the backup solution and testing monthly.	IT Operations Lead	6 months	New backup tools, staff training	Test restore times logged monthly	Ongoing
Audit Finding	Implement multi-factor authentication (MFA) for all remote access users, as recommended in the last internal audit.	IT Security Lead	3 months	MFA software, license budget	Internal audit verification	Not Started

How to Use Table 10.11:

1. Start by identifying the ***source*** of your objective (risk, opportunity, improvement, audit).
2. Write the objective in a ***SMART way*** (specific, measurable, achievable, relevant, time-bound).
3. Assign a ***responsible person*** so ownership is clear.
4. Add a ***timeline*** and ***resources*** needed.
5. Define ***how you'll measure success.***
6. Keep the ***status*** updated so you always know where things stand.

🛠 *Implementation Task #15: Information Security Objectives*

Now it's your turn. Pause and think: what are your information security goals? Write down at least three information security objectives for your organization at relevant functions and levels. Keep them simple and practical—they don't need to be grand or overly technical. The key is that they are clear, measurable, where possible, and directly linked to your risks, opportunities, or ongoing improvement goals.

CLAUSE 6.3: PLANNING OF CHANGES

Summary of the Clause Requirements: Clause 6.3 may seem brief—just one sentence—but it holds significant importance. It emphasizes that any change to your ISMS must be carried out in a controlled, planned manner, not impulsively.

Simply put, ISO 27001 requires you to think before acting. Whenever your organization decides to make a change—whether it's updating a policy, adding a new process, onboarding new technology, or restructuring teams—you must evaluate how that change might affect your ISMS.

The goal is to prevent unplanned or poorly managed changes from introducing new risks, disrupting existing controls, or causing confusion. Planning guarantees that every change supports, rather than interferes with, your ISMS.

Your change planning process should answer key questions such as:

- What exactly is changing—and why?
- Who will be affected by the change?
- How will this change impact information security risks, objectives, or controls?
- What resources, timelines, and responsibilities are involved?
- How will the change be verified and communicated once implemented?

So, while the clause may seem brief, it emphasizes one of ISO 27001's core principles—control. An ISMS is not a fixed system; it adapts as your business grows. But every change must be purposeful, documented, and risk-aware.

Basically, Clause 6.3 ensures your ISMS changes are strategic, safe, and sustainable—not quick reactions that could endanger your organization.

Explanation with Real-World Examples: Clause 6.3, Planning of Changes, might seem deceptively simple, but it adds an essential layer of discipline to your ISMS. It guarantees that any change to your ISMS is intentional, risk-aware, and thoughtfully planned—not a hurried reaction.

Now, many organizations confuse Clause 6.3 with other change-related areas of ISO 27001—particularly Clause 8.1 (*Operational planning and control*) and Annex A Control 8.32 (*Change management*). So, let's clarify how they differ.

Clause 6.3 addresses changes to the ISMS itself—including its structure, policies, scope, objectives, or even how your risk management process functions. It concerns the management system as a whole, not its daily operations.

Clause 8.1, on the other hand, addresses operational control—the execution and monitoring of processes such as risk treatment, incident response, and asset management.

Annex A Control 8.32 further specifies—it focuses on managing changes to information systems and infrastructure, including servers, applications, or configurations.

Think of it this way:

- Clause 6.3 is about strategic change—evolving your ISMS framework.
- Clause 8.1 is about operational control—keeping processes stable.
- Annex A Control 8.32 is about technical change management—ensuring IT changes don't cause chaos.

Let's make this more tangible with some real-world examples:

Example 1: Expanding Your ISMS Scope: Suppose your organization decides to add an extra office location to your ISO 27001 certification scope. That's a change to the ISMS itself—new people, new assets, new risks. Clause 6.3 requires you to plan this change carefully: review your scope document, update your risk assessments, identify new legal requirements, revise your SoA, and ensure your team is trained for the expanded coverage.

Example 2: Introducing New ISMS Objectives: Your top management decides to set a new information security goal: "Reduce phishing-related incidents by 50% over the next year." Before jumping into awareness campaigns or purchasing tools, Clause 6.3 asks you to plan the change—align it with business priorities, identify the necessary resources, evaluate any risks (such as employee fatigue from too many awareness emails), and determine how to measure success.

Example 3: Updating the Risk Assessment Methodology: If your organization decides to switch from a qualitative to a quantitative risk assessment method, this marks another ISMS-level change. It affects how risks are identified, analyzed, and managed across the organization. This shift requires careful planning—including pilot testing, training, updates to documentation, and validation steps—to ensure a smooth transition.

In all these examples, Clause 6.3 functions as your seatbelt—it doesn't prevent you from evolving, but it makes sure you do so safely and intentionally.

Author's Note: In my experience, unplanned changes are among the main reasons ISMS implementations lose consistency. I've seen teams alter risk registers, add policies, or remove controls without considering how these changes affect the entire system. Over time, the ISMS can turn into a patchwork rather than a cohesive framework. Clause 6.3 helps prevent that. Treat every ISMS change—whether big or small—as a project. Assess the impact, record the decision, inform the right people, and only then proceed. That's how you keep your ISMS stable, scalable, and ready for audits.

Implementation Guidance: Let's focus on the main idea behind Clause 6.3: changes to your ISMS shouldn't just "happen." They should be planned, thought out, and implemented in a way that keeps your system stable, compliant, and effective.

Now, "planning" doesn't have to mean bureaucracy or piles of paperwork. In simple terms, it means thinking ahead—understanding what's changing, why it's changing, who's involved, what it might affect, and how you'll ensure it works as planned.

Remember, ISO 27001 doesn't require documenting every tiny detail. It offers flexibility to plan changes that suit your organization's size, complexity, and context.

If you're a small startup with five employees, planning a change might involve discussing it in a team chat and summarizing the key points in an email. But if you're a large enterprise with thousands of employees, you might follow a formal change control process—including risk assessments, approvals, and timelines. Both methods are acceptable, as long as your approach is thoughtful and proportionate to the change's size and impact.

I offer the step-by-step guidance below for planning changes to your ISMS. Feel free to tailor these steps to your organization's context, size, and maturity.

Step 1: Identify the Need for Change: Start by asking the simple question—What's changing, and why?

Changes can arise from nearly anything—internal audits, management reviews, incidents, new risks, legal or regulatory updates, customer feedback, or strategic business moves like mergers or acquisitions. The trigger might be as minor as updating a policy or as significant as broadening your ISMS scope to include new sites, systems, or business functions.

You're already planning for changes in many parts of ISO 27001—often without realizing it. Some of the most common sources include:

- Risk assessments (6.1.2)
- Internal audits (9.2)
- Management reviews (9.3)
- Nonconformities and corrective actions (10.2)
- Feedback or requirements from interested parties (4.2)
- Continual improvement initiatives (10.1)

Here are a few real-world examples of what those changes might look like:

- Moving your IT infrastructure to the cloud.
- Adding new subsidiaries or departments to your ISMS scope.
- Outsourcing payroll or HR to an external provider.
- Updating your risk assessment methodology or control framework.
- Integrating new security models such as NIST Cybersecurity Framework or CIS Controls.

The point is—changes are constant, but planned change keeps your ISMS healthy, aligned, and under control.

Step 2: Assess the Impact: Before you implement, assess what the change might affect. Ask:

- Will this introduce new information security risks?
- Will it affect existing controls or compliance obligations?
- Does it require more resources, training, or new tools?
- Do you need to update your SoA, policies, or procedures?

Even a simple change—such as adding a new access control policy—can ripple through your ISMS. Make sure you understand those ripples before you move forward.

Step 3: Define Responsibilities and Resources: Clearly identify who is responsible for planning, approving, and implementing the change. Also, prepare the necessary resources—including time, personnel, budget, and technology. For significant changes, consider appointing a change owner or forming a small cross-functional team.

Step 4: Plan the Implementation: Now, decide how and when the change will be made. Create a simple change plan that covers:

- What needs to be done
- Who will do it
- When will it happen
- How you'll communicate the change to affected people
- What success looks like (how you'll know it worked)

For small organizations, this could be a checklist or a shared document. For larger organizations, you might use a change control form or a mini-project plan.

Step 5: Communicate and Execute the Change: Once the plan is approved, communicate it clearly to everyone involved. Don't assume people will adapt—explain the "why" and "how" of the change.

Then, execute the plan as outlined. Ensure your documentation—such as your Risk Treatment Plan, SoA, or process maps—is current and reflects the change.

Step 6: Verify and Review the Change: After implementation, assess whether the change achieved its goals. Did it enhance your ISMS? Did it introduce any new issues or risks? If so, make further adjustments.

Evidence of planning can be as simple as meeting notes, change logs, or emails showing that you thought through the change before acting. That's often all an auditor needs to see.

Author's Note: Don't make this clause more complicated than it needs to be. Clause 6.3 isn't asking for extra paperwork—it's asking for awareness. In one of my implementations, a large retail client added "Change Planning" as a small checklist in their internal audit findings tracker. Every time an auditor suggested a change, the ISMS manager quickly documented what needed to change, who would do it, and when. That simple habit kept their ISMS aligned and ready for audits all year long.

So, keep it simple—plan your changes, document your reasoning, and ensure your ISMS evolves with your organization, not against it.

Toolkit and Resources: Use Table 10.12 to document and track every proposed change—from minor policy updates to major shifts in ISMS scope or structure. This record helps demonstrate that your organization planned the change carefully, assessed its impact, implemented it responsibly, and verified its effectiveness.

Although ISO 27001 does not require documented information for Clause 6.3 (Planning of Changes), maintaining Table 10.12 as documented information adds real value and is widely regarded as good practice. It creates a clear audit trail, showing that ISMS changes were made in a planned, structured, and risk-aware manner. Auditors appreciate clear, traceable evidence of planned change, and this table provides exactly that.

How to use Table 10.12 in practice:

Step 1: Record the proposed change and explain why it's needed, including the trigger source such as an audit finding, management review output, or change in risk.

Table 10.12 Template for planning and managing changes within the ISMS

Field	*Details / Description*
Change Reference Number	Unique identifier for tracking (e.g., CHG-2025-001).
Date Raised	Date when the change was proposed.
Proposed By	Name and role of the person initiating the change.
Description of the Proposed Change	Briefly describe what is changing (e.g., updating the data retention policy, adding a new server).
Reason for Change/ Trigger Source	Mention why this change is needed (e.g., audit finding, new legal requirement, risk review, customer feedback, continual improvement).
Scope of Impact	Identify which areas are affected (people, process, technology, sites, suppliers, etc.).
Risk Assessment (Before and After)	Summarize the risk levels before and after implementation. Mention whether new risks were identified and how they were treated.
ISMS Documents or Controls Affected	List the relevant documents, controls, or records to be updated (e.g., SoA, risk register, policy document).
Implementation Plan and Timeline	Outline key steps, responsible persons, and completion deadlines.
Responsible Owner	Who will oversee and ensure the change is implemented as planned?
Approval	Signature or confirmation from the ISMS Manager / Top Management before implementation.
Verification / Effectiveness Review	After implementation, verify if the change achieved the intended result. Record any follow-up actions needed.
Status	Select from: Planned / In Progress / Completed / Closed.
Remarks / Notes	Any additional comments, lessons learned, or improvement ideas?

Step 2: Identify the scope of the change and assess potential impacts on people, processes, technology, locations, or controls.
Step 3: Perform a brief risk assessment before and after the proposed change.
Step 4: Assign ownership, obtain required approvals, and plan the implementation timeline.
Step 5: After implementation, verify effectiveness and close the record with appropriate evidence.

This keeps everything aligned with your style: simple, realistic, audit-ready, and written as if you're guiding students step by step in a classroom.

🧭 Key Takeaway—What You've Learned

- Clause 6 guides you from identifying risks to deciding precisely what to do about them.
- Start with context: every risk or opportunity should connect back to your business environment, stakeholders, and objectives.
- Clause 6.1 teaches you to be proactive—spot risks and opportunities early, plan actions, integrate them into your ISMS, and verify if they worked.
- Always plan at multiple levels: strategic (leadership priorities), tactical (team-level actions), and operational (daily practices).
- Remember, ISO 27001 emphasizes both sides—risks that can harm your ISMS and opportunities to strengthen it. Don't just play defense; play offense too.

- Your risk assessment process (Clause 6.1.2) must be structured, consistent, and repeatable—so that different people assessing the same risk reach similar results.
- Define clear risk criteria before you start: set measurable scales for likelihood, consequence, and acceptance. This ensures fairness, comparability, and credibility.
- Keep risk assessments practical—focus on real, relevant information security risks, not hypothetical ones that never occur in your context.
- Assign clear ownership for every risk. Without a risk owner, no one is accountable—and unowned risks quickly become unmanaged.
- Clause 6.1.3 turns your analysis into action—choose how you'll treat each risk: reduce, avoid, transfer, accept, or even exploit it when it presents an opportunity.
- Cross-check all selected controls with Annex A. Think of it as your safety net, ensuring no important aspect is missed.
- Your SoA bridges risk assessment and control implementation—it justifies what's included or excluded and why. Keep it current and updated.
- The Risk Treatment Plan is your action blueprint—it shows who will do what, by when, and how success will be measured. Without it, risk management remains theoretical.
- Always get approval from the risk owner for residual risks. This demonstrates accountability and informed decision-making, which auditors look for.
- Clause 6.2 emphasizes measurable information security objectives—turn your ISMS policy into concrete, SMART goals that foster continual improvement.
- Clause 6.3 reminds you that ISMS changes must be intentional—not accidental or reactive. Every change, big or small, should be planned, risk-assessed, and communicated.
- In summary: Clause 6 helps you plan for risks and control your future—not just to stay compliant, but to build a secure, resilient, and forward-looking ISMS that evolves with your organization.

QUIZ #9

True/False statement

Sr.	*Statement*	*True/False*
1	Risk assessment criteria must always be expressed in financial terms.	
2	Organizations must define both likelihood and consequence when establishing their risk assessment criteria.	
3	Risk identification is about predicting the future with precision.	
4	Assigning a risk owner is optional in ISO/IEC 27001.	
5	Risk analysis always requires a fully quantitative (numbers-only) method.	
6	The purpose of risk evaluation is to prioritize risks for treatment by comparing them with your acceptance criteria.	
7	When determining controls, organizations can only use those listed in Annex A.	
8	The Statement of Applicability (SoA) must include justification for including or excluding each Annex A Control.	
9	ISO/IEC 27001 requires organizations to use ISO/IEC 27002 for all controls, without exception.	
10	Information security objectives shall be measurable where practicable.	

CASE 4: PLANNING IN MOTION—SINGAPORE

When the partners of Ascend Advisory initially leased their co-working space on Robinson Road in Singapore, they felt unstoppable. They were eight young management graduates, all from top universities across Southeast Asia, eager to make their mark in the consulting industry. Their clients were mainly regional banks and fast-growing fintech companies, and they wanted to demonstrate that they were more than just a new firm with fresh résumés.

During a strategy meeting, one of the partners, Kelvin Lim, proposed something bold. "If we want to win contracts with major banks," he said, adjusting his laptop glasses, "we need ISO 27001 certification. It signals trust. It tells clients that we take protecting their information seriously."

Everyone agreed.

Since Kelvin was the only one with a Computer Science background—an NTU graduate who had also worked briefly in IT security—he was appointed as the Lead Implementer. Kelvin accepted the responsibility with confidence. He was technically sharp and energetic, though he lacked formal ISO 27001 training.

He started planning immediately.

Kelvin developed a straightforward risk assessment framework. It appeared clean, logical, color-coded, and easy to understand. However, when it came to defining risk criteria, he didn't set measurable values. Instead, he told the team:

"If you're unsure whether a risk is high or low, just ask me. I'll decide. We'll keep it flexible."

The team trusted him and followed his direction.

Next, Kelvin drafted the SoA. He included only the controls he believed the consultancy needed, which were the ones they planned to use. Not all 93 controls.

"We don't need to list controls that don't apply," he explained. "We'll just list the ones we chose." The team accepted this too.

Kelvin noticed how quickly the organization moved—project proposals, new client engagements, vendor onboarding—and so he created a Change Management Process that was clear, structured, and simple to understand. He explained it during a weekly meeting.

Any change that affects information, systems, or processes should go through a quick review. Not to slow us down, but to make sure nothing slips by unnoticed.

But when it was time to define Information Security Objectives, Kelvin had difficulty steering the discussion. The team brainstormed eagerly, and soon the ISMS objectives list looked like this:

1. Open four new offices within the year (Bangkok, Manila, Jakarta, Kuala Lumpur)
2. Win the firm's first million-dollar consulting contract
3. Achieve ISO 27001 certification
4. Have a year-end celebration trip in Hong Kong

Kelvin approved the objectives—partly because they reflected the team's ambition, and partly because he wanted to motivate them.

As the weeks went on, the team worked diligently. The energy in the office kept growing, and everyone felt proud of the progress they were making. Conversations often shifted from project deadlines to planning their year-end celebration in Hong Kong—a trip everyone eagerly anticipated.

Case Discussion—Test Your Understanding

1. **Which of the following was a weakness in Kelvin's approach to defining risk criteria?**

   A. He created a visual risk matrix.
   B. He required the team to consult him personally to determine risk levels.
   C. He involved all partners in identifying assets.
   D. He documented the risk owners clearly.

2. **What is the issue with Kelvin's approach to the SoA?**

   A. He included controls that were not relevant to the organization.
   B. He reviewed controls with the team before documenting them.
   C. He justified the exclusion of unnecessary controls.
   D. He included only the implemented controls rather than all Annex A controls and justifications for their exclusions.

3. **Which action taken by Kelvin demonstrates a positive practice in ISMS planning?**

   A. Leaving risk prioritization to discussions rather than criteria.
   B. Approving business growth goals as security objectives.
   C. Developing a structured and clear change management process.
   D. Delegating all ISMS planning decisions to the partners.

4. **Which of the listed objectives align with the requirements for information security objectives under ISO 27001?**

   A. Achieve ISO 27001 certification
   B. Open four new offices within the year (Bangkok, Manila, Jakarta, Kuala Lumpur)
   C. Win the firm's first million-dollar consulting contract
   D. Have a year-end celebration trip in Hong Kong

5. **Which mistake did Kelvin make when enabling the risk assessment process?**

   A. He documented the risk assessment process.
   B. He identified risk owners.
   C. He failed to ensure the process produced consistent, valid and comparable results.
   D. He used a standard risk matrix.

6. **What should Kelvin have done when planning Information Security Objectives?**

   A. Approve all proposed objectives to support team motivation.
   B. Select objectives linked to information security risk treatment and policy commitments.
   C. Avoid documenting objectives until after certification.
   D. Only include objectives directly related to sales growth.

Chapter 11

Clause 7—Empower your people, manage your info

Building competence, awareness, and communication for a strong ISMS

INTRODUCTION

This chapter focuses on supporting your ISMS so it can succeed. Support isn't just about money or technology—it begins with people. You need the right resources—skilled individuals who understand their roles, a culture of awareness throughout the organization, and clear communication channels that keep everyone on the same page. Together, these components form the foundation of a strong and sustainable ISMS.

📌 **Here's a Quick Reminder:** We already discussed the requirements for documented information (Clause 7.5) earlier in Chapter 6. If you want to review policies, procedures, and records, feel free to go back. In this chapter, we focus on the other important parts of Clause 7—making sure your team is skilled, aware, and supported with the right information at the right moment.

CLAUSE 7.1: RESOURCES

Summary of the Clause Requirements: Clause 7.1 requires the organization to identify and provide the necessary resources to establish, implement, maintain, and continually improve the ISMS. These resources can include personnel, technology, time, budget, or external expertise. The main point is clear: The ISMS must be properly supported so it can operate effectively and meet its objectives.

Explanation with Real-World Examples: An ISMS doesn't operate on good intentions alone. Like any other part of your business, it requires resources—people, money, time, tools, and information. Without these, the ISMS becomes merely a paper exercise instead of an effective system.
Think of resources in five simple buckets:

1. **People:** You need competent people to drive, operate, and monitor ISMS activities. For example, appointing an Information Security Manager or ensuring IT support staff understand their role in patch management.
2. **Time:** Projects fail when people are overloaded. Time must be allocated for tasks such as running risk assessments, conducting internal audits, or holding awareness sessions.
3. **Financial Resources:** Security controls often need a budget. Maybe it's buying a new firewall, subscribing to a security awareness platform, or hiring external consultants for a gap assessment.

DOI: 10.1201/9781003744139-12

4. **Information:** Decisions rely on the correct data. For instance, incident logs, vulnerability reports, or KPI dashboards help you evaluate performance and decide on improvements.
5. **Infrastructure and Tools:** Beyond IT equipment, this includes things like secure office space, UPS systems for continuity, or even simple items like shredders for paper-based information.

💬 **Author's Note:** I once worked with a mid-sized commercial bank that proudly launched its ISMS—only to realize their IT team was already running at full throttle. The hardworking team barely had time to breathe, let alone handle new security tasks. The solution? They brought in a part-time Information Security Officer, allocated budget for endpoint protection, and scheduled time for staff awareness training. Suddenly, the ISMS stopped being "a binder on the shelf" and started functioning effectively.

But here's the catch—resources aren't static. What worked in year one won't always be enough in year three. Expanding into cloud services? You'll need new tools and skills. Opening offices in another country? Budget and time commitments will change again. Think of resources like fuel in a car: If you don't keep refueling, don't be surprised when the ISMS engine stalls.

Implementation Guidance: Clause 7.1 is simple but powerful: Your ISMS's strength depends on the resources you allocate. Having the best policies is meaningless without the right people, tools, time, and budget, as it will turn into a mere "paper exercise."

Here's how to make it work in practice:

1. **Estimate What You Need:** Start by looking at all ISMS activities—risk assessments, awareness training, internal audits, incident response, vendor reviews—and ask: *"What do we need actually to make this happen?"* Think in terms of quantity (how many people, how much time) and quality (the right skills, the right tools).

Example: A mid-sized commercial bank realized its IT admin couldn't double as the ISMS lead forever. They hired a part-time Information Security Officer and invested in audit training for the internal QA team.

2. **Acquire the Resources:** Once you know what's missing, get management's buy-in to acquire them. This could mean hiring, training, or budgeting for new tools.

Example: A hospital needed better protection for patient records. Instead of hiring a whole team, they outsourced 24/7 monitoring to a managed SOC (Security Operations Center) provider—a cost-effective, reliable solution.

3. **Provide and Maintain:** Resources aren't a "set once and forget" exercise. Just like IT equipment needs patching, people need ongoing training, and budgets need refreshing each year.
4. **Review and Adjust:** Business grows, risks evolve, and new regulations pop up. That means your ISMS resources need a health check too. Review them regularly and adjust as needed.

Example: A bank expanding into mobile payments reviewed its ISMS resources and added specialists in mobile app security, since the old team's skills were too focused on core banking systems.

✱ **Remember:** Clause 7.1 on resources does not require you to create a mandatory separate document. The only requirement comes from 7.5.1(b)—to retain documented information as needed for your ISMS to operate effectively. That said, it's a smart move to keep a simple resource plan or tracker. Not only does it help you stay organized (who owns what, where resources are allocated), but it also proves useful during internal or external audits. A clear record shows auditors—and your own team—that resources are being identified, provided, and reviewed in a structured way.

■ **Toolkit and Resources:** Table 11.1 provides an ISMS resource planning and allocation tracker you can use to identify what resources are needed, who owns them, and how they are allocated across ISMS activities.

Table 11.1 ISMS resource planning and allocation tracker

ISMS Activity / Task	*Resources Needed (People/ Tools/Time/Budget)*	*Responsible Person/Dept.*	*Current Status*	*Notes/Example*
Risk Assessment (annual)	2 trained staff, 3 days' dedicated time, risk assessment tool	ISMS Manager, Risk Team	Partially available	External consultant used last year; plan to build in-house capability.
Staff Awareness Training	Budget for e-learning platform, 4 hours per employee per year	HR and IT Security	Planned	Training aligned with phishing awareness objective.
Incident Response	Security Information and Event Management (SIEM) tool, trained SOC team, and incident response playbooks	IT Security Lead	Outsourced	SOC vendor engaged; quarterly tests required.
Vendor Risk Reviews	1 staff day per critical vendor, supplier questionnaire	Procurement and Security	Not started	Bank's online portal vendors to be reviewed annually.
Internal Audit	2 auditors, ISO 27001 audit checklist, 2 weeks	Quality/ Compliance Team	Available	Auditors trained last year; refresh planned next quarter.
Document Control and ISMS Maintenance	ISMS software tool, 1 ISMS coordinator, 5 hrs/month	ISMS Coordinator	Ongoing	Using SharePoint for document versioning.

🛠 *Implementation Task #16: Resource Requirements*

Time to make it practical. Pause here and draft a simple resource projection for your ISMS for the next **6 months**. Think about:

- **What resources will you need?** (people, budget, tools, training, infrastructure)
- **How will you get them?** (new hires, internal allocation, external suppliers)
- **By when do you need them?** (set realistic timelines)

You can use the Resource Tracker given in Table 11.1 to make this easier. Keep it simple—a clear plan showing what you need, who owns it, and when it will be delivered is more useful than a lengthy document nobody reads.

CLAUSE 7.2: COMPETENCE

Summary of the Clause Requirements: This clause emphasizes ensuring the right people with the appropriate skills are managing your ISMS. ISO 27001 requires your system to be run by capable individuals, not just well-meaning ones. Competence isn't about fancy titles or certificates—it's about possessing the proper knowledge, skills, or experience to protect information effectively.

ISO 27001 asks organizations to:

- **Determine** what competencies are needed for anyone whose work affects information security.
- **Ensure** those people are competent—based on education, training, or experience.
- **Take action** if there's a gap—by providing training, mentoring, reassigning roles, or bringing in external experts—and check whether those actions actually worked.
- **Keep documented evidence** that proves people are competent for their roles.

Explanation with Real-World Examples: Competence really comes down to one simple question—*can people do what's needed to keep information secure?*

It's not about how many certificates hang on the wall or how impressive someone's CV looks. What matters is whether they can apply their knowledge and skills to achieve results.

Let me explain this with something relatable.

How many times have you met a professor with a shelf full of degrees—but students dread attending their classes? It's not about how much they *know*; it's about whether they can *make others understand.*

I've seen the same in IT teams. Brilliant engineers who can code like magicians or fix servers in seconds—but the moment you ask them to brief senior management, they freeze, mumble, or go completely off track. That's the difference between having knowledge and being competent.

Competence involves identifying the right skills for the right job to achieve the desired results. These results could include implementing a new access control system, conducting a phishing awareness workshop, or restoring a system during an incident. Each task requires a different type of competence.

In an ISMS, competence shows up in different forms:

- **Technical Competence:** Configuring firewalls, patching systems, managing access rights.
- **Managerial Competence:** Conducting risk assessments, writing procedures, and planning incident responses.
- **Behavioral Competence:** Being trustworthy, disciplined, attentive, and able to perform calmly under pressure.

Competence applies to everyone under the organization's control—employees, contractors, temporary staff, and even vendors. Anyone whose work can impact information security must be qualified for their role.

Here are a few practical examples to make this clear:

Example 1. The Helpdesk Technician: A helpdesk technician resets user passwords daily. If they don't know how to verify the caller's identity or spot social engineering tricks, a single phone call from a clever attacker could compromise your entire network.

Ensuring competence here means providing refresher training on phishing, social engineering, and verification protocols—not just once a year but regularly.

Example 2. The HR Assistant: An HR assistant manages job applications containing personal information. They might not be IT experts, but they must understand how to securely store confidential data, identify potential data breaches, and respect privacy—even for candidates who aren't hired.

The organization should explicitly state these expectations and make sure every HR employee meets them through training and oversight.

Example 3. The External Consultant: A small company hires a consultant to conduct their annual ISMS review. They trust that the consultant is experienced—but later realize the consultant has never worked with a company of their size or in their industry.

Always verify external competence—ask for relevant experience, references, or examples of similar projects. "Consultant" is a title; competence is evidence.

Competence isn't something you check once and forget. People change. Technology evolves. New risks emerge. So, plan for ongoing learning—whether through training, mentoring, workshops, or cross-functional projects. Even informal knowledge sharing between teams can boost your ISMS.

💬 **Author's Note:** Think of competence as the fuel that keeps your ISMS running smoothly. Without skilled, confident, and informed people, even the best-written policies won't get you very far. A certificate looks good on the wall—but someone who knows exactly what to do when things go wrong is far more valuable. And for short-term needs, bringing in external experts is perfectly fine—remember, you're still responsible for their competence. Whether it's a full-time employee or a temporary consultant, the responsibility to ensure they can do the job rests with you.

Implementation Guidance: Clause 7.2 is all about ensuring your people don't just hold a job title—they actually have the skills, knowledge, and experience to do the job well, especially when it comes to protecting information.

Let's break down how to make this work in practice, one step at a time.

Step 1. Identify Who Affects Information Security: Start by listing all roles—internal and external—that directly or indirectly impact information security.

Don't just think about IT or security staff. Think broader: Who handles sensitive data, manages systems, approves access, or writes policies?

💡 **Example Roles:**

- **IT Administrator:** Manages systems and access rights
- **HR Executive:** Handles employee records and personal data
- **Receptionist:** Controls visitor access to premises
- **Finance Officer:** Manages vendor payments and banking details
- **External Support Vendor:** Maintains servers or cloud infrastructure

Each of these roles plays a part in your organization's information security. Even minor oversights in any of them can lead to vulnerabilities.

Step 2. Define the Competence Required: For each identified role, specify what "competence" means in context—the knowledge, skills, or experience required to perform effectively and achieve the intended results.

One easy way to do this is by using a simple Competence Matrix, like the one shown in Table 11.2. It clearly links each role to the competence required and explains why it matters. Keep it practical—clarity is far more important than complexity.

Table 11.2 Example competence matrix for ISMS roles

Role	*Competence Needed*	*Why It Matters*
IT Administrator	Knowledge of access control, patch management, and backup systems	Prevent unauthorized access and data loss
HR Executive	Awareness of data privacy laws and secure file handling	Protect employee personal data
Finance Officer	Understanding of fraud risks and secure online banking	Prevent financial data theft

Step 3. Assess Current Competence: Next, determine your current position. Compare your established requirements with what your team actually knows or can do. You can evaluate this through interviews, performance reviews, training records, or even self-assessments.

Example: Your IT Administrator might have strong technical skills but no incident response training—that's a competence gap worth addressing.

Step 4. Address the Gaps: Once you've identified the gaps, plan how to close them. Actions could include:

- Providing focused training or refresher courses
- Offering mentoring or job shadowing opportunities
- Reassigning roles to better match skill sets
- Hiring or contracting external experts for specific needs

Example: If your HR team is unsure about data privacy rules, organize a brief Privacy Awareness Session focused on GDPR or an ISO 27001 Awareness Workshop. Even a two-hour session can significantly improve knowledge and confidence.

Step 5. Evaluate Effectiveness: Training or hiring alone doesn't guarantee competence—you need to verify if it genuinely worked. Assess effectiveness through follow-up tests, quizzes, or by observing changes in performance and behavior.

Example: After a phishing awareness session, conduct a simulated phishing campaign.

If the "click rate" drops from 15% to 5%, congratulations—your training has achieved tangible, measurable results.

Step 6. Keep Records: Finally, make sure you keep documented evidence of your competence. You don't need a fancy HR system or a lot of paperwork—even a simple spreadsheet or tracker will work, as long as it's backed by actual evidence of ability, like certificates, attendance sheets, or manager feedback.

Useful Records Include:

- Training attendance or completion records
- Certificates or course documentation
- Internal assessment results
- Manager or mentor feedback
- Performance review notes

📌 **Remember:** ISO 27001 doesn't specify a format, but **you must retain documented evidence** that shows people are competent in their roles.

Author's Note: Think of competence as a living muscle—it needs regular exercise to stay strong. Don't stop at "we did training last year." Incorporate competence reviews into your ISMS management cycle. Ask your managers: "Are our people still equipped to handle today's threats?" Keep it practical. A basic matrix showing roles, required skills, current capabilities, and supporting evidence is all you need—it demonstrates both compliance and confidence. It'll also make your next audit a smooth, confident conversation rather than a stressful checklist.

Toolkit and Resources: I've included two toolkit examples to help you understand how competence can be defined, assessed, and developed within an ISMS framework. These examples are meant for illustration only—not as templates to copy exactly.

Every organization operates within its own unique context, with different structures, risks, technologies, and regulatory requirements. Therefore, before using any example from this book, take time to review, customize, or even redesign it to suit your organization's specific needs and environment.

Think of these tools as your skills radar—they help you identify blind spots before they become weaknesses. The goal isn't to tick boxes, but to build full confidence and capability. Over time, these small, focused development actions will help you develop a stronger, more resilient, and audit-ready ISMS team.

Example 1#: Table 11.3 shows a sample competence requirement profile for the ISMS director, illustrating how qualifications, experience, skills, and evidence can be defined for a senior ISMS role.

Example 2# Competency Matrix—Internal Auditor (ISMS): Use Table 11.4 to identify current competence requirements for ISMS internal auditors and to plan suitable training or development actions for the coming year. This helps you spot skill gaps early and build a focused, practical development program instead of reacting after an audit highlights weakness.

Use Table 11.5 to evaluate and strengthen your ISMS team's competence, one role at a time. It gives you a clear snapshot of where you stand today and acts as a simple roadmap for where skills and capabilities need to grow over the coming period.

Here's how to use it effectively:

1. **Start with the Basics:** Fill in the basic details—name, role, department, and functional relationships. This ensures clarity on who the form applies to and which areas of the organization they interact with.
2. **Rate Each Skill:** Under *Required Skills*, use the **Score** (0–5) column to show how essential that skill is for the role (5 = critical, 0 = not applicable).

   Then, rate the individual's **Current Rating** (1–5) based on actual performance, training, and experience. Be honest—this is about improvement, not perfection.
3. **Identify Gaps:** The *Gap Identified* column helps you quickly spot where development is needed. Mark a check (✓) where the current rating is lower than the required score.
4. **Add Comments and Development Needs:** Note specific observations or recommendations—for example, "Needs more exposure to risk assessment workshops" or "Excellent in report writing; presentation skills can be improved."

Table 11.3 Sample competence requirement profile for the ISMS Director

Field	*Details*
Role	Director, ISMS
Employee Name	
Qualifications	• Bachelor's degree in Information Security, Computer Science, or related field (Master's preferred). • Recognized certifications such as ISO/IEC 27001 Lead Implementer, ISO/IEC 27001 Lead Auditor, CISSP, or CISM.
Experience	• 8–10 years of progressive experience in information security, governance, or compliance. • Minimum 3–4 years in a leadership role overseeing ISMS or cybersecurity programs. • Proven experience in implementing or managing ISO/IEC 27001 within a multi-site or global organization. • Familiarity with regulatory and data protection requirements (e.g., GDPR, NCA ECC, or similar). • Skilled in cross-functional collaboration (HR, IT, Legal, Operations) to integrate ISMS practices. • Track record as a strategic, detail-oriented, and proactive leader.
Skills	• Strong understanding of risk management, incident response, and ISO 27001/27002 control implementation. • Excellent leadership, stakeholder engagement, and decision-making skills. • Ability to translate technical issues into business language for management. • Knowledge of ISMS lifecycle: context, risk assessment, audits, and continual improvement. • Proficiency in Microsoft Office and GRC or ISMS management tools. • Strong written and verbal communication; policy and report writing skills. • Analytical, problem-solving, and organizational skills. • Capability to influence security culture and promote awareness. • Experienced in driving continual improvement initiatives.
Compliant Status	☐ Compliant ☐ Partially Compliant ☐ Non-Compliant
Proposed Trainings (if applicable)	• ISO/IEC 27001:2022 Transition or Implementation Workshop • Risk Assessment and Treatment Practical Training • Data Protection and Privacy for Executives • Leadership in Information Security Governance • GRC/ISMS Tool Familiarization and Reporting
Competency Evidence	• Bachelor's degree (attach copy) • ISO/IEC 27001 or equivalent certification(s) • Internal/external audit records showing ISMS leadership • Records of Management Review participation or improvement projects
Remarks (If any)	

5. **Plan the Development Actions:** In the *Proposed Development Actions* given in Table 11.5, turn each gap into a concrete action.

   - What training, mentoring, or project will help close the gap?
   - When should it be completed?
   - Who is responsible for ensuring it happens?

   Each action should be practical and time-bound—think of it as a mini-action plan for competence-building.

Table 11.4 Competence matrix for ISMS internal auditors

Required Skills (Cross-Reference with Core Competencies)	*Score (0–5) (5 = Most Essential, 0 = Not Applicable)*	*Current Rating (1–5)*	*Gap Identified*	*Comments/Development Needs*
Knowledge of ISO/IEC 27001:2022 Requirements	5	4	✓	Strong understanding of clauses; needs more experience mapping controls to risks.
Knowledge of ISO 19011:2018 (Auditing Guidelines)	5	3	✓	Requires additional training on audit principles, evidence gathering, and sampling.
Certified ISO 27001 Lead Auditor/Internal Auditor	5	4		Certification achieved; refresher training recommended annually.
Understanding of Risk Assessment and Treatment Methodologies	5	3	✓	Needs more practical experience in identifying risks and linking them to Annex A controls.
Understanding of ISMS Documentation and Processes	4	4		Competent; can review policies, procedures, and records effectively.
Problem Solving/Analysis	5	3	✓	Needs deeper analytical skills for audit data and root cause identification.
Communication (Written and Verbal)	4	4		Strong report writing, presentation, and interview questioning can be enhanced.
Collaboration and Teamwork	3	3		Works well in audit teams; consider exposure to cross-functional audits.
Leadership and Audit Management	4	2	✓	Needs mentoring to plan and lead end-to-end audits independently.
Results Orientation	4	4		Meets deadlines and delivers actionable reports consistently.
Accountability and Integrity	5	5		Demonstrates strong ownership of findings and ethical behavior.
Analytical and Critical Thinking	5	3	✓	Develop the ability to evaluate control effectiveness and the correlation between evidence and controls.
Understanding of IT Systems and Information Security Controls	4	3	✓	Should improve understanding of network security, access controls, and logs.
Certified Information Systems Auditor (CISA) ***(if applicable)***	3	0	✓	Recommended to pursue enhanced technical audit capability.
Planning and Organizational Skills	4	4		Effectively manages audit schedules and follow-up timelines.
Continual Improvement Mindset	4	3	✓	Encourage participation in post-audit review sessions to identify process improvements.

Table 11.5 Proposed development actions to address ISMS competency gaps

Identified Gap/ Competency Area	*Proposed Development Action*	*Target Completion Date*	*Responsible Person*
Knowledge of ISO/ IEC 27001:2022 Requirements	Assign to lead a cross-departmental audit focusing on Annex A control implementation to strengthen the control–risk mapping understanding.	Q2 2025	**ISMS Manager**
Knowledge of ISO 19011:2018 (Auditing Guidelines)	Enroll in a *Practical Internal Auditing Techniques* course or ISO 19011 refresher workshop emphasizing audit sampling and evidence verification.	Q2 2025	**HR/Training Lead**
Understanding of Risk Assessment and Treatment Methodologies	Participate in the next organization-wide risk assessment exercise alongside the Risk Manager to gain hands-on experience linking risks with controls.	Q3 2025	**Risk Manager**
Problem Solving/ Analysis	Attend an *Advanced Root Cause Analysis for Auditors* training session and apply the learning in the following internal audit cycle.	Q3 2025	**Compliance Head**
Leadership and Audit Management	Assign to co-lead a complete internal audit under the supervision of a Senior Auditor. Conduct debrief sessions post-audit to evaluate leadership readiness.	Q3 2025	**Senior Auditor/ ISMS Manager**
Analytical and Critical Thinking	Task the auditor with reviewing past audit findings and performing a trend analysis to identify recurring weaknesses or systemic issues.	Q3 2025	**ISMS Manager**
Understanding of IT Systems and Information Security Controls	Arrange a *Technical Familiarization Workshop* with IT Security to demonstrate key controls—network segregation, log monitoring, and patch management.	Q4 2025	**IT Security Lead**
Certified Information Systems Auditor (CISA) ***(if applicable)***	Encourage the auditor to pursue CISA certification or equivalent, supported by study leave or reimbursement policy.	Q1 2026	**HR/Training Lead**
Continual Improvement Mindset	Include the auditor in the *Quarterly ISMS Review Meeting* and require at least one improvement suggestion per quarter.	Q4 2025	**Compliance Head**
Prepared By:			
Signature:			
Date:			

6. **Review and Update Regularly:** This form isn't a one-time task. Review it at least once a year or after major changes (like new systems, regulations, or duties). Use it during performance reviews, training assessments, or ISMS management reviews.

🛠 *Implementation Task #17: Competency Matrix*

Now it's your turn. Put the book aside for a few minutes and think about **what competence really looks like** in your organization.

Start by drafting a **Competency Matrix** for your **Information Security Manager** (or the equivalent role in your company).

Ask yourself:

- What knowledge, skills, and experience does this person need to protect information effectively?
- Which of these competencies already exist—and where are the gaps?
- What actions can you take to close those gaps over the next 6–12 months?

You can use the **sample Competency Matrix** provided earlier as a guide. List the key skills (technical, managerial, and behavioral), rate their importance, and note your current capability levels.

📌 **Tip:** Keep it simple. You don't need a long list of skills—focus on what truly matters for your organization's ISMS success.

💬 **Author's Note:** This exercise is more than just filling out a table. It's about understanding the people behind your ISMS—their strengths, potential, and areas that need support. Once you identify those gaps, you can plan real, targeted development actions that transform your team from aware to exceptional.

CLAUSE 7.3: AWARENESS

Summary of the Clause Requirements: Clause 7.3 emphasizes ensuring that everyone under your organization's control—employees, contractors, or long-term consultants—understands what information security means to them.

It's not enough for people to know that "the company has an ISMS." They must be aware of three key things:

- **The Information Security Policy:** What it stands for and how it applies to their day-to-day work.
- **Their Individual Contribution:** How their actions help protect information and improve ISMS performance.
- **The Consequences of Non-Conformance:** What could happen (to the business and to them) if policies or procedures are ignored.

In simple terms, awareness transforms your policies into action. When people fully understand why security matters and how their role contributes to the bigger picture, they stop being passive and start actively defending information security.

Explanation with Real-World Examples: Awareness is one of the most underestimated yet powerful parts of your ISMS. It's about making sure that everyone in your organization not only understands what to do but also why it's important.

Clause 7.3 wants people who work under your organization's control to understand three things truly:

1. **The Information Security Policy:** What it means and how it applies to them.
2. **Their Personal Role:** How their everyday actions keep the organization secure.

3. **The Implications of Not Following ISMS Requirements:** What could go wrong if they don't.

Awareness isn't about just dropping policies into inboxes or putting up posters. It's about creating a culture where people see the importance of information and protect it naturally, like they would defend their own wallet or phone.

Author's Note: Let me share two stories from my consulting experience that clearly demonstrate the difference between "having awareness" and "being aware." In one of my ISMS implementation projects in West Africa, the organization had done almost everything right. They had policies, procedures, and even a central IT helpdesk number for reporting incidents.

But when I started talking to employees, here's what I heard:

- "Yes, I think there's a helpline… not sure of the number."
- "I remember getting an email about it, but I'll have to check."
- "Oh, that's for IT problems? I thought it was for password resets."

In short, the system existed, but awareness didn't. And when an incident happens, confusion costs time, and time costs information.

Now, compare that with another organization I worked with—multinational company headquartered in Saudi Arabia. They had a single customer care number—1010. Simple, memorable, and known to every employee. Whether you worked in Riyadh, Singapore, or Sittard, if something went wrong, you dialed 1010. Everyone knew it, everyone used it. That's awareness in action.

Awareness is what closes the gap between policy and practice. You don't need everyone to memorize every clause of ISO 27001—but they must understand the parts that impact their role. For example:

- HR staff should know how to handle candidate or employee personal data.
- Finance should understand how to secure vendor payment details.
- IT should know how to identify and report security incidents.
- Front-desk staff should recognize what to do if someone tries to tailgate into a secure area.

That's how awareness turns your ISMS from paperwork into protection—one informed person at a time.

Remember: People can only support what they understand. Awareness isn't a one-time email or induction slideshow—it's an ongoing conversation. Keep it fresh, keep it relevant, and make it real.

Implementation Guidance: Awareness doesn't happen by accident—it's something you plan, develop, and reinforce over time. Clause 7.3 requires you to ensure that everyone who influences information security (and that's almost everyone in your organization) understands what's expected of them and why it's important. Let's break this down into practical, manageable steps.

Step 1. Tailor the Message—One Size Doesn't Fit All: Not everyone needs the same level of awareness detail. Think about it—I have a PhD in information security and handle risk assessments and controls daily. In contrast, a new hire or your main gate security guard has a completely different level of exposure and responsibilities. You can't put both of us in the same room and run the same awareness session—it wouldn't make sense for either of us.

Awareness should be customized for the audience. Adjust the content so each group receives exactly what they need to stay informed and effective in their roles.

Here's how you can approach it:

- **Executives** need to understand the big picture—strategic risks, compliance obligations, and potential reputational damage.
- **IT staff** should focus on recognizing and responding to technical threats like phishing, patch management, and access control issues.
- **General employees** need the essentials—handling information securely, reporting incidents promptly, and spotting suspicious emails or behavior.
- **Support staff (like security guards or receptionists)** need to know physical access protocols, visitor management rules, and what to do if something seems off.

Example: When I worked with a logistics company, we created three versions of the same awareness material:

- One for **management**, focusing on business risks and leadership accountability,
- one for **technical teams**, centered on control implementation and incident handling, and
- One for **drivers and warehouse staff**, covering physical security, device handling, and safe communication.

The message was the same: Protect information assets—but each audience heard it in their own language. That's what makes awareness work.

Step 2. Make Information Security a Part of Daily Life: Awareness isn't a one-time training each year or a mandatory presentation slides you rush through before clicking "Complete." Fundamental awareness means information security is integrated into daily life—something people see, hear, and think about consistently.

Make it visible, relatable, and consistent. Place reminders where people are likely to see them—and keep the message straightforward.

Here are some practical ways to do it:

- **Posters and Visual Reminders:** Place colorful posters in cafeterias, lobbies, and near elevators. Keep messages short—"Lock your screen before you leave!" or "Think before you click!"
- **Digital Reminders:** Add tips to internal newsletters, intranet banners, or even on login screens and digital notice boards.
- **Branded Items:** Give employees T-shirts, mugs, mouse pads, or desktop wallpapers with clever security slogans like *"Your password protects us all"* or *"Stop. Think. Click."*
- **Casual Moments Count:** Bring up security during coffee breaks or team huddles. Mention a recent phishing attempt or a case where someone reported an incident correctly—small wins that reinforce the correct behavior.
- **Gamify It:** Run quick quizzes, small contests, or "Spot the Phish" challenges with fun rewards.

💬 **Author's Note:** At one organization I worked with, we took a slightly creative approach—instead of changing the screensaver once a month, we did it every week. But here's the fun part: we invited employees to send in their own funny photos to be featured with an information security message. It became an instant hit. The IT team would take a submitted photo and add a witty security-themed caption. For example, there was a picture of two colleagues sharing a cake, with the caption: *"Share the cake, not your password."* Every Monday, employees couldn't wait to see whose photo would appear next—and what the week's security message would be. It turned into a light-hearted competition, and before long, everyone was talking about information security—not because they had to, but because they genuinely enjoyed it. That's how awareness should feel—fun, engaging, and unforgettable.

📌 **Remember:** The goal isn't to lecture people—it's to make security **part of your culture.** When your employees start reminding each other to lock screens, verify senders, or report suspicious activity without being told, you've succeeded in embedding awareness into daily life.

Step 3: Plan Your Awareness Schedule: Awareness works best when it's consistent, engaging, and diverse—not a single lecture or another "mandatory" compliance session everyone fears. Develop a straightforward year-round communication calendar with focused themes for each month. For example:

- January—Phishing and social engineering awareness
- April—Backup and recovery best practices
- May—Data privacy and handling personal information
- September—Mobile and remote work security

💡 **Tip:** Align your internal awareness initiatives with global cybersecurity events—it boosts both credibility and enthusiasm for your campaigns. You can leverage or modify dates like:

- **Data Privacy Day (28 January):** Host a short awareness talk or a "Protect Your Data" booth in the cafeteria.
- **Digital Cleanup Day (Third Saturday in March):** Encourage everyone to declutter their inbox and delete unnecessary files—maybe reward the team that frees up the most space!
- **World Backup Day (31 March):** Organize a "Back Up Your Files" drive or give out fun stickers like *"I Backed It Up Today!"*
- **World Password Day (First Thursday of May):** Run a password-strength contest or host a "Change Your Password" café with coffee and cookies.
- **Cyber Resilience Awareness Day (15 October):** Conduct a tabletop cyber drill to test how teams would respond to an incident.
- **Cybersecurity Awareness Month (October):** Run a full-week campaign with games, quizzes, or simulated phishing challenges.
- **Computer Security Day (30 November):** Wrap up the year with a cybersecurity fair or poster competition.
- **Global Cyber Day:** Engage schools or families of employees for a fun "Cyber Smart Family" challenge.

Remember—awareness shouldn't feel like punishment. It should be something people look forward to. Add a touch of creativity: Themed dress-up days, small giveaways, meme contests, or digital escape rooms.

💬 **Author's Note:** In one of my projects, we organized a "Cybersecurity Carnival Week"—featuring daily mini-events like password puzzles, phishing spot-the-fake games, and coffee quizzes. People actually looked forward to the next day's challenge. That's when I realized—when you make learning enjoyable, your message spreads faster than any memo ever could.

📌 **Note:** The global awareness dates listed here are for reference only—they can vary by country, region, or year. Always verify the exact date from reliable sources before planning any campaign. You don't need to observe every international awareness day; instead, select the ones that suit your organization's culture, team, and schedule. Feel free to adapt or even create your own awareness days. The goal isn't to fill your calendar; it's to build lasting habits, spark curiosity, and create memorable, engaging experiences that naturally strengthen your organization's security culture.

Step 4. Test Understanding: Awareness isn't about attendance; it's about understanding. Find out what people actually remember, not just whether they attended the session.

Try:

- Short quizzes after sessions
- Informal Q and A in team meetings
- "Phishing simulation" emails
- Random spot checks on password or document handling practices

Example: At one client site, we gave a simple quiz immediately after awareness training—just five questions. Six months later, we repeated it without notice. The improvement rate indicated whether the message had really sunk in.

Step 5. Reinforce Good Behavior: Awareness doesn't end after a training session—it truly becomes meaningful when you identify good habits and correct bad ones in everyday life. People remember stories much longer than they recall PowerPoint slides, so make every example meaningful.

Celebrate small wins. If someone reports a phishing email before clicking it, recognize their quick thinking in your next team meeting or newsletter. You don't need trophies—even a simple "Cyber Hero of the Month" shout-out works wonders.

At the same time, use slip-ups as learning moments—with a bit of humor, not humiliation. During one of my ISMS implementations for a multinational company, I would walk around different departments to observe daily practices. If I found an unlocked laptop, I'd quietly send an email from it to the CISO, signed by the employee, saying, "Can we meet for a cup of coffee?" It never failed to generate some laughs (and a quick rush to lock screens afterward).

Here are a few other fun examples you can use:

- Someone clicked a phishing simulation link? Send them a friendly follow-up email saying, "*You've just been phished—but don't worry, this one was a friendly one!*" Include a short tip on how to spot real threats next time.
- A team consistently locks their screens before leaving? Drop off a small "Thank You for Securing Our Info" card or a candy bar. Positive reinforcement spreads faster than warnings.
- Found sensitive papers left at the printer? Take a photo (without sensitive data showing) and use it in your next awareness poster: "*Your secrets aren't waiting to be picked up—are they?*"

Author's Note: Building a strong security culture involves a mix of fun, consistency, and gentle correction. Use humor, storytelling, and recognition to make information security personal. When people start policing themselves—locking screens, reporting phishing, or reminding each other to encrypt files—that's when you know awareness has truly become a part of the culture.

Step 6: Documentation (Optional): ISO 27001 doesn't require formal documentation for awareness activities, but maintaining basic records is a smart choice—it simplifies audits and helps monitor progress. A straightforward tracker can include:

- Date and topic of awareness session
- Audience (who attended)
- Trainer or communicator
- Feedback and results (quiz scores or observations)

Remember: Clause 7.3 doesn't require any mandatory documentation for awareness, but Clause 7.5.1(b) states you need to retain documented information "to the extent necessary for effectiveness." So, keep it simple but meaningful—enough to demonstrate that your awareness program is active, relevant, and improving.

Toolkit and Resources: An awareness plan helps you turn good intentions into actual, measurable actions. It's your structured roadmap—showing who you're targeting, how you'll reach them, what message you'll deliver, and how you'll determine if it was successful.

You don't need dozens of campaigns—start small, keep it practical, and most importantly, make it *visible and memorable.*

Table 11.6 provides a sample Information Security Awareness Plan that you can use or adapt for your organization.

Template: Information Security Awareness Plan

How to Use Table 11.6:

1. **Target Audience:** Identify who needs awareness: All staff, new joiners, contractors, or specific teams (like finance or IT).
2. **How:** Choose how you'll reach them—posters, emails, training, videos, quizzes, or even short stand-up talks.
3. **When:** Set frequency. Awareness works best when it's **regular and planned,** not once a year.
4. **Who:** Assign ownership (e.g., ISMS Manager, HR, IT Security Lead).
5. **What:** Keep messages simple and relevant to their daily tasks.
6. **Resources:** Note materials, tools, or budget needed.
7. **Objective:** What change do you want to see? (e.g., more incident reporting, fewer phishing clicks).
8. **Measurement:** Always check effectiveness—awareness that can't be measured often fades away.

Implementation Task #18: Information Security Awareness Program

Now it's your turn. Pause for a moment and think about how awareness actually works in your organization. Who needs to know *what*, *when*, and *how*?

Table 11.6 Information security awareness planning template

Target Audience	*How (Method of Delivery)*	*When (Frequency/ Timing)*	*Who (Responsibility)*	*What (Message/ Topic)*	*Resource Requirements*	*Objective/Expected Outcome*	*Measurement Criteria (if any)*
All Employees	Email campaign + Posters near lifts	January (Week 2)	IT Security and HR	Phishing Awareness—"Think Before You Click"	Poster design, email templates, short quiz	Build awareness about phishing risks and safe email habits	80% of staff complete the quiz; 30% reduction in phishing clicks
New Joiners	Short awareness session during induction	Every new batch	HR and ISMS Coordinator	Introduction to ISMS Policy and Information Handling Do's and Don'ts	Awareness slides, policy handout	Ensure new staff understand their information security roles from Day 1	Post-session feedback rating ≥ 90% "useful"

Using the Information Security Awareness Plan Template provided in Table 11.6—or one of your own design—begin creating a straightforward, well-organized awareness program for your organization.

Here's what to do:

1. Identify your **target audiences:** For example, all employees, new joiners, contractors, IT teams, or management.
2. Decide **what message** each group needs (e.g., phishing awareness, password hygiene, or reporting incidents).
3. Plan **how** you'll deliver the message—emails, posters, short videos, coffee sessions, or even quizzes.
4. Assign **responsibility**—who will prepare, review, and deliver each activity.
5. Schedule **when** it will happen—monthly, quarterly, or tied to special events like *Cybersecurity Awareness Month* or *World Password Day*.
6. Define **how success will be measured**—completion rates, quiz scores, or reduced incidents.

💡 **Tip:** Keep it fun and creative. Organize competitions, share success stories, or even host a "Spot the Phish" challenge. The goal isn't to lecture—it's to raise awareness naturally and make security a regular part of daily conversations.

📌 **Remember:** Your awareness plan doesn't need to be perfect from the beginning. Start small, keep it practical, and add to it over time. The real success is when people begin talking about information security without being prompted.

CLAUSE 7.4: COMMUNICATION

Summary of the Clause Requirements: Clause 7.4 ensures the correct information reaches the right people at the right time. Communication is the lifeline of your ISMS—it links policies, people, and processes.

ISO 27001 requires your organization to plan and organize how information security communication will occur—both internally within the organization and externally with suppliers, customers, regulators, or other stakeholders.

In simple terms, you need to determine:

1. **What** needs to be communicated?
2. **When** should it be communicated?
3. **Who** should it be communicated to?
4. **How** should it be communicated?

The goal is to ensure communication is clear, timely, and consistent—so that everyone involved in protecting information understands their role and can act confidently when it matters.

Explanation with Real-World Examples: Communication is the heartbeat of your ISMS. You can have the best policies, detailed procedures, and world-class controls—but if people don't know what's expected of them, it all falls apart. Clause 7.4 ensures that **information security messages flow clearly and consistently** across the organization and to all relevant external parties.

In simple terms, communication in the ISMS is about answering four questions:

- **What** to communicate—for example, security policies, incident procedures, or audit results.
- **When** to communicate—whether it's during onboarding, monthly reviews, or after an incident.
- **Who** to communicate with—employees, vendors, regulators, customers, or partners.
- **How** to communicate—through meetings, reports, emails, dashboards, or emergency alerts.

Let's make this real with some examples.

Example 1: Internal Communication—Policy Updates That People Actually Read: At a large healthcare organization I worked at, every time the IT department updated a policy—like the password standard or clean desk rules—they sent it out as a 10-page PDF. You can guess what happened next: No one read it.

So, we changed the approach. Instead of sending long documents, we created short, **"Policy in a Minute"** videos and internal posters with key takeaways:

- "Your password must be at least 12 characters."
- "Lock your screen before you leave—even for a coffee break."
- "Patient data is private. Always."

These were shared through the internal messaging app, placed near printers and cafeteria boards, and discussed in team huddles.

Result? Engagement skyrocketed. Staff remembered the rules because they saw, heard, and discussed them often.

Example 2: External Communication—Supplier Updates: During one of my ISMS projects at a medium-sized manufacturing company, a key supplier changed its cloud hosting provider without informing the client. This caused significant confusion during a security audit.

Afterward, the company added a clause to its supplier contracts requiring vendors to notify it of any significant changes to their systems, hosting, or data management processes. They also established a shared communication channel with major suppliers to exchange updates regularly. That small step enhanced transparency and trust—a great example of structured external communication.

Example 3: Upward Communication—From Staff to Management: In another organization, the IT team used to encounter recurring password reset issues but never reported them as a pattern. When they finally began sending a monthly ISMS dashboard to management, highlighting recurring incidents and trends, leadership recognized where additional training and funding were needed. Communication isn't just top-down—it must also be bottom-up.

💬 **Author's Note:** Communication isn't just about sending information—it's about making sure the right people receive it, understand it, and act on it. In an ISMS, clarity is power. A single, well-timed phone call or short alert can often prevent an incident faster than a long, unread policy document. Remember, communication doesn't have to be formal—it can take the shape of dashboards, posters, town hall meetings, supplier calls, or even a quick chat in the hallway. The real goal is to ensure that information security messages reach the right people at the right time, in the right way—clearly, consistently, and with purpose.

Implementation Guidance: Clause 7.4 emphasizes intentional, structured, and meaningful communication within your ISMS. It's not enough to assume that people "know what to do" or that messages automatically reach the right audience. Communication must be planned, purposeful, and verifiable—clearly defining who communicates what, to whom, when, and how.

Your organization must develop processes for both internal and external communication. Within each, you should plan for routine (scheduled) communication as well as crisis (emergency-triggered) communication, especially during incidents or emergencies. Table 11.7 brings these together by outlining the four key communication categories you should consider while designing your ISMS communication approach.

Table 11.7 Key communication categories for the ISMS

Type of Communication	*Internal (Employees, Management, Contractors)*	*External (Customers, Regulators, Vendors, Media)*
Routine (Planned)	Daily ISMS communication that maintains the management system as active, transparent, and compliant. Examples include sharing policy updates, awareness reminders, audit results, and progress reports.	Regular external communication that maintains trust and fulfills contractual or regulatory requirements—such as sharing ISO certificates, responding to customer questionnaires, or submitting compliance reports.
Crisis/Incident (Triggered)	Rapid, coordinated internal communication during incidents that enables immediate containment and recovery—such as alerting IT teams, informing leadership, or issuing all-staff warnings.	Timely, accurate external communication during incidents that meets legal and contractual obligations while safeguarding the organization's reputation—such as notifying regulators, customers, or the media.

Step 1. Decide What Needs to Be Communicated: Begin by determining which information security messages fit into each of the four categories listed in Table 11.7. Your list doesn't need to be lengthy—focus on what's essential, recurring, and meaningful within your ISMS.

Common examples include:

- **Risk Management Updates and Treatment Plans:** Keeping leadership and teams informed about changing risks and mitigation efforts.
- **Information Security Objectives and Achievements:** Communicating progress, milestones, and continual improvement results.
- **Incident Reports or Breach Notifications:** Ensuring timely, coordinated reporting and escalation both internally and externally.
- **Changes in Policies or ISMS Processes:** Keeping affected stakeholders informed about updates that may impact their work.
- **Roles, Responsibilities, and Authority Updates:** Clarifying who is responsible for what, especially during incidents or audits.
- **Legal or Regulatory Communication Requirements:** Submitting required reports, disclosures, or compliance confirmations to external authorities.

Author's Note: Begin with a basic communication system. You don't need dozens of messages on day one—just the essential few that keep people informed, aligned, and prepared to act. Over time, your ISMS maturity will naturally lead you to refine and expand the list.

Step 2. Define Who Communicates: Once you understand what needs to be communicated, determine who will deliver the message. This step ensures that messages come from the right person, through the proper channel, at the right time.

Not everyone should or can speak on behalf of your organization. Without clarity, even well-meaning people can cause confusion or panic.

During a security incident at a major bank, multiple department heads began emailing clients individually with their own updates. The outcome? Conflicting messages, unnecessary worry, and a decline in customer trust.

The bank quickly learned a harsh lesson: It appointed a single communication lead—the CISO—who coordinated all updates through a single approved channel. From then on, communication was clear, consistent, and calm.

📌 Why This Matters

When communication responsibilities are unclear, two things often happen:

1. **Over-Communication:** Multiple people send overlapping or conflicting messages.
2. **Silence:** Everyone assumes someone else will communicate, and no one does.

Both are dangerous in an ISMS. The first damages credibility, the second causes chaos.

Clearly defined roles prevent both.

Communication Roles and Responsibilities: As shown in Table 11.8, it's a good practice to formally assign who is authorized to communicate different types of information. You might choose one person for routine communication and another for crisis communication, and that's perfectly fine. What matters is clarity, everyone should know who speaks, when, and in which situation.

⚠ **Social Media Awareness:** In today's world, even a single employee's social media post can cause controversy. Make it clear, through awareness training, that employees should not post or comment on any social media platform about internal incidents, outages, or breaches.

Table 11.8 Communication roles and responsibilities within the ISMS

Role/Position	*Communication Responsibility*	*Typical Context*
CISO/ISMS Manager	Oversees internal ISMS-related announcements, policy updates, awareness messages, and coordination during incidents.	Internal communication (routine and crisis)
Public Relations (PR) or Corporate Communications	Handles all public-facing and media communication. Ensures external statements are accurate, authorized, and consistent with organizational policy.	External communication (routine and crisis)
Incident Response Team Lead	Coordinates communication with customers, partners, or regulators during a confirmed incident. Works closely with Legal and PR teams to ensure compliance and accuracy.	Crisis communication (internal and external)
HR/Training Coordinator	Communicates awareness programs, training schedules, and behavioral campaigns.	Routine internal communication
Legal or Compliance Officer	Manages communication related to laws, regulations, and contractual obligations. Approves regulatory notifications or data breach reports.	External and regulatory communication
Top Management/ CEO (if designated)	Provides high-level messages of assurance, leadership, and accountability—especially in serious incidents or public disclosures.	External (strategic communication)

Instead, remind them that:

> ***If you're not the official spokesperson, you're not authorized to speak on behalf of the organization—online or offline.***

A simple sentence like that, included in your awareness sessions, can prevent severe reputation damage.

Tip: Include a brief section in your Communication Plan or Incident Response Procedure titled "Authorized Spokespersons"—list who is permitted to communicate, for what purpose, and through which channels. During audits, this demonstrates maturity and control.

Author's Note: Clarity builds confidence. When people know who is communicating, they can concentrate on what needs to be done. That's the quiet strength of structure—it keeps your ISMS stable even when the outside world feels chaotic.

Step 3. Decide When to Communicate: Knowing when to communicate is just as important as knowing what and who. Clause 7.4 requires communication to be timely, consistent, and suitable for the situation. Poor timing—whether too late or too early—can lead to confusion, noncompliance, or even financial loss.

As previously discussed, communication in an ISMS generally falls into two categories: Routine (planned) communication and crisis (triggered) communication.

Routine (Planned) Communication: As outlined in Table 11.9, these are scheduled communications that keep your ISMS healthy, visible, and aligned with organizational goals. They follow a fixed timetable and ensure stakeholders stay informed about performance, awareness activities, and ongoing improvements.

Table 11.9 Routine (planned) communication within the ISMS

Type	*Typical Frequency*	*Examples*	*Purpose*
Awareness Bulletin	Monthly	"Security Tip of the Month" posters, short awareness videos	Reinforce security culture and good practices
ISMS Review Summary	Quarterly	Summary of risk updates and audit results shared with management	Keep leadership informed of ISMS performance
Employee Training Schedule	Bi-annual	Email/portal calendar of upcoming security workshops	Ensure participation and continuous competence
Supplier Security Review	Annually	Vendor audit summary or control questionnaire	Maintain external assurance and compliance
Policy Review and Updates	Annual or as defined	Review reminder for access control, mobile device policy	Ensure continued policy relevance and awareness

Tip: Align these regular communications with your management review cycle and internal audit plan. It establishes a predictable rhythm and prevents overlaps or missed updates.

Crisis (Triggered) Communication: As shown in Table 11.10, crisis communication is activated by events such as a data breach, service disruption, or serious security incident. These communications usually come with strict legal or regulatory timelines. Missing them can lead to compliance issues, financial penalties, or reputational damage, so clarity and speed matter.

Table 11.10 Crisis (triggered) communication within the ISMS

Trigger Event	*Time Frame (Typical)*	*Audience*	*Example Message / Scenario*	*Consequences of Delay*
Personal Data Breach	Within 72 hours (as per GDPR or similar laws)	Data Protection Authority/ Regulator	Notification stating scope, impact, and mitigation	Legal noncompliance, heavy fines
Major Security Incident	Immediate (within 1–2 hours of confirmation)	Incident Response Team/Top Management	Internal alert: "Incident declared—disconnect affected systems"	Delayed containment, broader impact
Customer Impact (Service Disruption or Data Issue)	As per SLA (often within 24 hours)	Affected Customers	"We've identified a service issue affecting our account; here's what we're doing."	Breach of contract, loss of trust
Supplier Incident Affecting Your Organization	As soon as it is detected or confirmed	Procurement/Legal / Affected Business Units	"Vendor XYZ reported compromise—isolate integrations immediately."	Supply chain vulnerability
Media Leak/ Public Query	Immediate, with a pre-approved statement	PR/Corporate Communications	"We are aware of the situation and are investigating."	Reputation damage, misinformation spread

📌 **Key Points to Remember**

- **Regular communication** keeps people informed; **trigger-based communication** keeps people safe and compliant.
- Map each trigger event to its **required response timeline** (e.g., 1-hour internal escalation, 24 hours customer notice, 72 hours regulatory report).
- Clearly define **who tracks the clock**—usually the ISMS Manager or Incident Response Lead.
- Maintain a **communication log** with timestamps for audit and compliance evidence.
- Always document *when* a communication was sent, *to whom*, and *through which channel*.

💬 **Author's Note:** Timing can make or break your response. The best communication plans function like well-tuned clocks—every message has its moment, and every moment serves a purpose. Don't leave timing to chance; make it intentional.

Step 4. Choose the Right Channel: Even the most well-crafted message can lose its impact—or cause harm—if it goes through the wrong channel. Choosing the right communication medium isn't just about convenience; it's about credibility, security, and compliance.

Your communication plan must specify authorized channels for both routine and crisis situations. During a crisis, this is especially important—using unofficial or insecure platforms can cause information leaks, violations of compliance, and loss of trust.

Official communication channels ensure that:

- Messages are **recognized as authentic** and bear the proper authority.
- Information **reaches the intended audience** without distortion.
- The **confidentiality, integrity, and availability** of the information are protected.
- Communication records can be **retrieved and audited** later if required.

Table 11.11 summarizes the typical communication channels used within an ISMS and explains when each one is most effective. Use it as a practical guide to choose the right channel for the right message, whether it's routine awareness, performance updates, or urgent incident-related communication.

Table 11.11 Common ISMS communication channels and their use

Channel	*Best Used For*	*When to Use*	*Security/Compliance Considerations*
Corporate Email	Routine internal communication (policy updates, awareness messages, reminders)	Daily operations	Ensure emails use official domains and are encrypted where necessary.
Intranet or ISMS Portal	Centralized announcements, policies, and awareness materials	Routine and reference communication	Access-controlled; allows version management and traceability.
Meetings/ Dashboards/ Reports	Management reviews, risk updates, performance discussions	Scheduled or ad hoc	Keep meeting minutes and track follow-up actions for audit evidence.
Secure Collaboration Tools (e.g., Teams)	Internal coordination during incidents or projects	Routine and crisis	Ensure chat history is retained and monitored; use only approved workspaces.
Incident Response Bridge (voice or virtual)	Crisis coordination between technical and leadership teams	Crisis only	Pre-approved participants; calls recorded or logged; no external links unless authorized.
Customer Portals or Secure Ticketing Systems	Sharing updates with clients or partners	Routine and crisis (status updates)	Data encrypted; access authenticated; message templates pre-approved.
Official Letters or Encrypted Email	Formal notifications to regulators, customers, or suppliers	Regulatory or contractual communication	Must follow legal format, retain proof of delivery.
Press Releases/ Media Statements	Public announcements	External communication (routine or crisis)	Approved by senior management and Corporate Communications; maintain version control.

⚠ **Caution:** Never use personal messaging apps, personal email accounts, or social media for official communication—even to "speed things up." These channels may bypass your ISMS controls, expose confidential data, and violate regulatory obligations.

❢ **Tip:** During incident simulations or drills, test your communication channels the same way you test your technical systems. Make sure everyone knows which tool to use, whom to copy, and how to escalate.

Author's Note: Every message has a voice, but the channel gives it weight. Choose carefully, document your decisions, and ensure everyone in your organization understands the rule: "If it's not an approved channel, it's not official communication."

Step 5. Verify and Reinforce Understanding: Just because a message is sent doesn't mean it's understood. In ISO 27001 communication, effectiveness is more important than volume.

After every important announcement, policy update, or awareness campaign, take a moment to check whether people actually received the message—and whether they understood it.

Here are a few practical ways to do that:

- Add short **acknowledgment links or checkboxes** to confirm receipt.
- Use a **quick quiz** or **mini survey** to check comprehension.
- Ask team leads to **summarize key takeaways** in their next meeting.
- Observe behavioral change—are people doing what the message asked for?

❢ **Tip:** Make feedback two-way. Encourage people to ask questions or share confusion—sometimes a single "I didn't understand" comment can reveal a wider communication gap.

Step 6. Keep Evidence and Improve: ISO 27001 doesn't require a formal Communication Register, but keeping basic records is one of the easiest ways to show that your communication process is controlled and consistent. While Clause 7.4 doesn't make documentation mandatory, Clause 7.5.1(b) requires organizations to retain documented information "to the extent necessary for effectiveness." Simply put, keep only what's useful—records that demonstrate your communication process is active, relevant, and secure without becoming an administrative burden.

Keep simple evidence such as:

- Your **Communication Plan** and updates to it
- **Copies of sent messages,** newsletters, or awareness campaigns
- **Incident communication logs,** especially who was informed and when
- **Feedback or quiz results** that show engagement

These records don't have to be complicated. A basic folder or tracker suffices, as long as it's kept up to date and easy to access—especially during audits.

Toolkit and Resources: Now that we've covered the steps, let's put everything together.

You can use any of the detailed tables and examples we discussed earlier, or adapt them to suit your organization's needs.

Here's a straightforward communication plan template you can begin using immediately, shown in Table 11.12. It's designed to be practical, something you can build on as your ISMS develops and matures.

Table 11.12 ISMS communication planning template

Sr.	*Internal/ External*	*Crisis/ Routine*	*With Whom*	*What – Relevant Communication*	*How (Channel/ Method)*	*Who Is Responsible*	*When/ Frequency*	*Purpose/Outcome*	*Verification/Record*
1	Internal	Routine	Employees	The importance of ISMS, achieving objectives, and meeting ISMS requirements	Email, meetings, and intranet post	Top Management	Once per year	Reinforce awareness and leadership commitment	Attendance record, meeting notes
2	Internal	Routine	Department Heads	Risk assessment results, treatment progress, and key performance updates	Review meetings, dashboard	ISMS Manager	Quarterly	Keep leadership informed for better decisions	Management review minutes
3	Internal	Crisis	All Staff	Security incident alert and containment instructions	Emergency email, internal alert banner	Incident Response Lead	Immediate (when the incident is confirmed)	Ensure quick and coordinated action	Incident log, response record
4	External	Routine	Customers	ISMS certification status, control assurance, and compliance updates	Customer portal, official letter	Compliance/Sales Team	Annually or on request	Build trust and transparency	Communication record, sent confirmation
5	External	Crisis	Regulator/ Authority	Breach notification or legal disclosure	Encrypted email, official report form	Legal/Data Protection Officer	Within 72 hours of confirmation	Meet legal and regulatory requirements	Regulator acknowledgment, report copy
6	Internal	Routine	New Employees	ISMS policy, responsibilities, and acceptable use guidelines	Induction session, email pack	HR/ISMS Coordinator	On joining	Build awareness from day one	Induction attendance list
7	External	Routine	Suppliers/ Vendors	Security requirements and compliance expectations	Contract annex, onboarding pack	Procurement/ISMS Manager	At onboarding or renewal	Align supplier controls with ISMS	Signed contract, acknowledgment
8	Internal	Routine	All Staff	Monthly awareness topic (e.g., phishing, password hygiene)	Email poster, screensaver, LMS(Learning Management System) quiz	Awareness Coordinator	Monthly	Reinforce security behavior and awareness	Quiz results, LMS completion report
9	Internal	Crisis	Top Management	Executive briefing during a major incident	Situation report, virtual bridge	CISO/Incident Commander	Hourly or as per the IR plan	Enable fast leadership decision-making	SITREP notes, decision log
10	External	Routine	Media/Public	Approved statement or announcement about ISMS updates	Official press release	Corporate Communications	As required	Maintain transparency and control the narrative	Press release record, media log

Think of Table 11.12 as your quick reference to capture the essentials: What needs to be communicated, to whom, when, how, and by whom. You can expand it, simplify it, or even integrate it into your existing ISMS plan, whatever works best for your organization.

❢ **Tip:** Keep your plan simple and effective. Review it at least once a year or whenever there's a change in structure, regulations, or communication flow within your organization.

The goal isn't to complicate things—it's to make it work for you.

📌 **Remember:** Clause 7.4 doesn't specify a format to use. You can keep this plan in Excel, Word, or even your ISMS portal. The key is that your process remains simple, consistent, and secure—and you can provide evidence when required.

💬 **Author's Note:** Over the years, I've seen many organizations overthink communication plans—long, complex spreadsheets that nobody ever updates.

Start small.

Keep it practical.

And make sure it helps you, not burdens you.

That's how you turn a communication plan from a document into a living part of your ISMS.

🛠 *Implementation Task #19: Communication Plan*

Alright, it's time to put what you've learned into action.

Put the book aside for now, grab your notepad or open a spreadsheet, and begin drafting a Communication Plan for your organization's ISMS. Don't worry about perfection—just make it genuine.

Here's how you can get started:

1. ***List Your Key Audiences:*** Who needs to be informed? Think of employees, management, vendors, customers, and regulators.
2. ***Decide What They Need to Know:*** Policy updates, risks, incidents, achievements, or compliance reports.
3. ***Pick Your Channels:*** Which medium makes sense for each? Email, meetings, dashboards, portals, or official letters.
4. ***Assign Responsibility:*** Who will send it? CISO, HR, ISMS Manager, Legal, or Communications?
5. ***Set Timing:*** Is it routine (planned) or crisis (triggered)? How often will it happen?
6. ***Add Verification:*** *How* will you confirm it was received and understood?

CLAUSE 7.5: DOCUMENTED INFORMATION

If you've been following along from the beginning, you'll remember that we previously covered Clause 7.5—Documented Information earlier in Chapter 6. And that was very deliberate. I explained that before diving into each clause, it's smarter to first build your documentation framework—because everything in your ISMS depends on how well your documents are created, controlled, and maintained. Clause 7.5 provides that essential foundation.

So, instead of repeating the exact details here, I encourage you to revisit ***Chapter 6: What You Must Deliver and Document****—Understanding ISMS Requirements and Documentation Needs*. That's where we explored the principles of Clause 7.5 in full—including how documented information should be created, reviewed, updated, and controlled, along with practical templates and examples you can use.

If you've already finished that chapter, you're in good shape. You should now have your documentation templates, structure, and version control process in place. If not, stop here and review Chapter 6 first—it will make everything that comes next easier and more consistent.

Author's Note: Good documentation is like having your *workshop ready before you start building*. It keeps your ISMS organized, saves time, and ensures every new policy or record fits neatly into place. So, if you skipped ahead earlier, take a quick detour back to Chapter 6—it's worth it.

Key Takeaway—What You've Learned

- Provide what the ISMS truly needs—people, time, budget, tools, and information—and review these regularly as your business evolves.
- Map resources to actual ISMS activities (risk assessments, awareness, audits, incident response, vendor reviews) so effort aligns with priorities.
- Clearly define what competence means for every role impacting information security (technical, managerial, behavioral).
- Honestly identify skill gaps and address them with targeted training, mentoring, role adjustments, or external experts—then evaluate effectiveness, not just attendance.
- Keep evidence of competence (a simple matrix along with certificates, feedback, and results) to demonstrate capability, not just claim it.
- Treat awareness as part of everyday behavior, not a once-a-year lecture; tailor messages by audience, keeping them visible, simple, and memorable.
- Maintain a light awareness calendar, align activities with relevant events, and measure impact through quizzes, phishing simulations, and behavior change.
- Recognize good behaviors and use mistakes as learning opportunities—build a security culture with stories, humor, and gentle correction.
- Make communication deliberate, structured, and verifiable: decide what, who, when, and how for both internal/external and routine/crises.
- During a crisis, use only authorized channels and pre-approved messages; meet legal and contractual deadlines to avoid penalties.
- Identify authorized spokespeople, prohibit informal social-media "reporting," and document what was sent, to whom, when, and through which channel.
- For documented information (covered earlier in Chapter 6): Keep it fit for purpose—create, approve, update versions, protect, retain, and dispose of it with controls; the extent depends on your context, complexity, and competence.

QUIZ #10

True/False statement

Sr.	*Statement*	*True/False*
1	The organization shall provide financial resources to support and continually improve its ISMS.	
2	Wherever applicable, the organization must evaluate whether training or other actions have been practical.	
3	Evidence of competence must be retained as documented information.	
4	Taking action to ensure competence does not always mean formal classroom training.	
5	Training is the only way to ensure competence within the ISMS.	
6	Everyone whose work affects the ISMS must be aware of their personal contribution to its effectiveness.	
7	People working under the organization's control should understand the consequences of not following ISMS requirements.	
8	The organization must determine the need for both internal and external communications relevant to the ISMS.	
9	Every employee should receive all ISMS-related communications, regardless of relevance.	
10	Communication during an incident should only be made through authorized channels.	
11	Documented information must look the same across all organizations implementing ISO 27001.	
12	The language, format, and graphics of documented information should be appropriate to its use and audience.	
13	Every single document within the organization requires the same level of formal review and approval.	
14	Documented information required by the ISMS must be protected from loss, misuse, and unauthorized changes.	
15	All ISMS documents must be available to everyone in the organization at all times.	
16	All documents should be retained forever to ensure availability when needed.	
17	Documented information from external sources must be identified and controlled if it affects the ISMS.	
18	Competence applies not only to employees but also to contractors and external providers involved in ISMS activities.	
19	Awareness activities are a one-time exercise carried out during employee onboarding.	
20	The goal of awareness is to help people understand why information security matters, not just what the policies say.	

CASE 5: CULTURE, CALLS, AND QUIET CHANGE—HYDERABAD

When Sandeep Rao joined GlobalConnect Services, he immediately picked up on the rhythm of the place. The call center, located in HITEC City, Hyderabad, supported major American and European banks. Every shift was fast-paced. Agents handled card queries, fraud disputes, identity verifications, and sensitive financial conversations. Here, protecting customer information wasn't just important—it was part of the company's identity.

Sandeep had been appointed as the Lead Implementer for ISO 27001. Although he had experience in operational compliance, this was his first time leading an ISMS from the ground up. During his first week, he noticed how teams printed out account references and handwritten notes during calls. At the end of a shift, many of those papers were casually torn and tossed into regular office bins. A few crumpled sheets lay near the pantry door beneath a poster that read "Privacy Matters."

During onboarding discussions, the HR Manager, Asha, explained, "It's not neglect—it's pace. Calls come nonstop. People focus on keeping service levels high, and sometimes document handling isn't part of that thought process."

Sandeep also met the Facility Manager, Imtiaz—a man whose smile always seemed to arrive before he did. He entered the meeting room carrying a warm tiffin of Hyderabadi biryani and proudly declared, "Brother, if there is biryani, there is happiness."

As they discussed logistics for upcoming awareness workshops, Imtiaz leaned back in his chair and said, "I always tell managers—if they want a meeting room, bring a physical memo. That way, I get to meet them. Sometimes, they bring biryani too." He winked with cheerful confidence.

Asha joined the conversation and teased, "Imtiaz, we should move this to email approval. The future is changing."

Imtiaz raised an eyebrow. "Email? If everything goes digital, who will I meet? Where's the fun in that? And what happens to my occasional biryani?"

Sandeep chuckled softly before replying, "ISO 27001 doesn't specify a particular format. It doesn't require everything to be digital or on paper. You can choose what works—as long as it's controlled, clear, and consistent. Maybe Asha suggests email because it's easier to track and reduces delays. Feel free to explore it—no pressure."

Imtiaz nodded thoughtfully. "Hmm… modernize the process, but keep the biryani culture alive. I like this balance."

Over the following weeks, Sandeep didn't hurry with changes. Instead, he watched, listened, and gained trust.

One afternoon, while speaking with the Quality Lead, he found out that certain call types—especially those involving identity checks or financial disputes—needed more accuracy. That talk led to more discussions with HR, training teams, supervisors, and Operations. Together, they decided that specific call tasks should only be done by trained and verified agents. Short refresher tests followed, along with records of completion.

Awareness quickly became another focus. In a corridor, someone joked, "We already know security—we watch crime shows!" Another asked if awareness attendance actually needed to be tracked. Sandeep responded, "Let's treat this like any key business program—planned, shared, and recorded." Soon, posters appeared near elevators, reminders showed up on calendars, and the first workshop filled quickly—helped by Asha's subtle promotional line: "Snacks included."

Document disposal also emerged as a key area for improvement. To enhance the handling of printed materials, shredders were installed on every floor. Later, Procurement helped bring in a certified disposal vendor for sensitive waste and decommissioned electronic media.

In project meetings, supervisors noted that client instructions and external regulations were scattered across inboxes, USB drives, and outdated folders. Sandeep worked with Compliance, IT, and Operations to create a controlled central repository for all documented information required by the ISMS and deemed essential by business teams. The repository was clearly labeled, version-controlled, and access-restricted.

Gradually, small yet meaningful changes began to appear.

Agents paused before discarding paper. Supervisors reminded teams to lock screens. New joiners asked thoughtful questions about data retention. Team conversation shifted—from "Do we really need this?" to "How should we do this correctly?"

The call floor remained busy—ringing phones, tight schedules, and the occasional biryani comment—but now, beneath the noise, a new awareness was emerging—one decision, one habit, one conversation at a time.

Case Discussion—Test Your Understanding

1. **Which activity best demonstrated GlobalConnect's effort to support competence?**

   A. Assigning sensitive calls only to trained and verified agents.
   B. Printing motivational posters about privacy.
   C. Sending reminder emails to employees.
   D. Allowing all agents to handle any call for flexibility.

2. **What action contributed most to improving awareness across the organization?**

   A. Keeping informal discussions about security within the IT team.
   B. Relying solely on posters near the pantry area.
   C. Hosting planned awareness sessions with communication and attendance tracking.
   D. Assuming long-term employees already understand security expectations.

3. **Which step helped strengthen documented information control?**

   A. Allowing staff to store regulatory guidelines in emails or personal folders.
   B. Creating a central version-controlled repository for documents.
   C. Keeping old reference materials on USB drives for backup.
   D. Deleting all external documents unless requested.

4. **Placing shredders on every floor and using a secure disposal vendor primarily relates to which ISO 27001 support element?**

   A. Competence
   B. Awareness
   C. Communication
   D. Documented information retention and disposal

5. **The decision to maintain a documented register of employees who completed competence training supports which clause requirement?**

   A. Clause 7.1
   B. Clause 7.2
   C. Clause 7.3
   D. Clause 7.4

6. **During a discussion with Imtiaz, Sandeep stated: "ISO doesn't mandate any specific format. It doesn't say everything must be digital or everything must stay on paper. You can choose whatever works." Is this statement true?**

   A. True
   B. False

Chapter 12

Clause 8—Put your ISMS into action

Implementing controls and avoiding common pitfalls

INTRODUCTION

Welcome to the Do phase of your ISMS journey—this is where all the planning, preparation, and policy writing finally turn into action. Everything you've built so far—your risk assessments, objectives, communication plans, and resource structures—now comes to life.

Clause 8 focuses on fulfilling commitments in a controlled, consistent, and evidence-based manner. This is where your ISMS shifts from theory to practice. The organization must plan, implement, and monitor the processes necessary to meet its information security requirements and achieve its objectives.

It's not enough to act—you also need to prove that actions were implemented as planned. That's why Clause 8 requires keeping documented information as proof of operational activities, decisions, and results. This proof provides management, auditors, and even you with confidence that your ISMS isn't just on paper—it's functioning effectively in practice.

You also need to ensure that planned changes are managed, unexpected changes are reviewed, and any outsourced processes are clearly identified and adequately controlled. In short, Clause 8 provides that daily activities align with what was planned in your ISMS framework—no surprises, no guesswork.

💬 **Author's Note:** Think of Clause 8 as the engine room of your ISMS. Everything you planned earlier—from risk treatment to awareness—now powers up here. The policies and objectives are your navigation charts, but Clause 8 is where the ship actually sails. And just like any good captain, you'll need logs, reports, and evidence to prove that the journey followed the map.

CLAUSE 8.1: OPERATIONAL PLANNING AND CONTROL

Summary of the Clause Requirements: Clause 8.1 marks the transition from planning to real-world implementation. It requires your organization to plan, execute, and manage the daily processes needed to meet your information security requirements and to carry out the actions outlined earlier in Clause 6, particularly your risk treatment plans and ISMS objectives.

In simple terms, this clause makes sure that your ISMS doesn't rely on assumptions—it depends on clear criteria, consistent controls, and visible evidence. You need to specify how each process should operate, what standards or criteria it must follow, and how you'll verify it's being done correctly.

DOI: 10.1201/9781003744139-13

You must also keep documented records—proof that these processes have been completed as planned. This can include documentation of implemented controls, system logs, meeting minutes, vendor reports, or activity records. The purpose is to have enough confidence (and evidence) that the ISMS functions as intended.

Clause 8.1 also requires you to handle changes—both planned and unplanned. When implementing a planned change, such as deploying a new cloud service or adjusting an existing control, do so in a controlled manner. And when an unintended change occurs—such as a system failure or a process deviation—you need to assess its impact, correct what went wrong, and take steps to prevent it from happening again.

Finally, the clause reminds you that outsourced or externally provided processes are still your responsibility. If a vendor, cloud provider, or partner performs a function that affects your ISMS, you must ensure that the processes involved are correctly identified, defined, and controlled. Outsourcing doesn't transfer accountability.

Explanation with Real-World Examples: Clause 8.1 is where your ISMS truly comes to life—where all the careful planning, policies, and procedures turn into tangible actions that protect your organization every day. This clause is about managing your ISMS like a well-run operation: Planned, controlled, and supported by evidence.

You already completed your planning work in Clause 6—identifying risks, defining treatments, and setting objectives. Clause 8.1 now implements those plans. It asks a simple but powerful question: "*Are you actually doing what you said you would do—and can you prove it?*"

That involves defining your operational processes, implementing them, and making sure they are adequately controlled. These processes typically include:

- ***ISMS processes*** such as internal audits, management reviews, incident management, and awareness programs.
- ***Risk treatment processes***—implementing and monitoring specific controls you identified earlier to reduce or mitigate risks.

Once these processes are in place, they must be continuously monitored and managed to ensure they produce the intended results. Like any operation, changes are inevitable—some planned, some unplanned. Planned changes may include upgrading a security monitoring tool or updating an access control procedure. Unintended changes could be sudden system failures, vendor process deviations, or staff reorganizations. In either case, Clause 8.1 requires you to assess the impact, act promptly to address any adverse effects, and document what was done and why.

Let's make this practical with a few real-world examples.

Example 1: The Law Firm's Privacy Risk Treatment in Action

A law firm handling sensitive client data identified "unauthorized disclosure of personal information" as a key privacy risk. To address this, they implemented controls aligned with *Annex A Control 5.34—Privacy and Protection of Personally Identifiable Information (PII).*

As part of their risk management plan, the firm established a Privacy Management Process to ensure compliance with data protection laws and client confidentiality agreements. They implemented data classification and access control measures, guaranteeing that only authorized personnel could access PII, and adopted multi-factor authentication (MFA) for systems containing client data.

Under Clause 8.1, they documented every step of the process: Defining access criteria, configuring MFA, training staff on privacy obligations, and testing access controls. They also retained documented evidence, including access logs, MFA enrollment records, and privacy policy acknowledgments signed by employees.

When auditors later reviewed the ISMS, these records clearly showed that the organization had not only planned the privacy controls but also implemented and verified them effectively, meeting both the operational control requirements given in Clause 8.1 and the privacy protection expectations given in Annex A Control 5.34.

Author's Note: Privacy protection isn't just a checkbox; it's a core part of your ISMS. When you treat privacy risks as operational tasks supported by documented control evidence, you shift from mere compliance to proper accountability.

Example 2: The Hospital's Vendor Management Process

A large private hospital outsourced its patient billing system to a trusted third-party service provider. Everything seemed to operate smoothly—until an external audit revealed that the vendor hadn't updated its antivirus software for several months, potentially exposing patient data to malware.

That discovery served as a wake-up call. The hospital quickly understood that even though the billing system was outsourced, the responsibility for its security still fell on them under Clause 8.1—Operational Planning and Control. Outsourcing did not eliminate accountability.

To address the gap, the hospital strengthened its oversight of supplier performance by applying *Annex A Control 5.22—Monitoring, Review, and Change Management of Supplier Services*. This control requires organizations to regularly *monitor, review, evaluate, and manage changes* in their suppliers' information security practices and service delivery.

In response, the hospital introduced a structured *Vendor Security Review Process*, including:

- A ***Vendor Security Checklist*** covering patching, antivirus, encryption, and access control practices.
- ***Quarterly performance reports*** from the vendor confirming compliance with agreed security requirements.
- A ***change notification procedure***, requiring the vendor to inform the hospital before making any change that could affect information security or privacy.
- Periodic ***supplier review meetings*** involving the ISMS Manager, Procurement Lead, and IT Security Officer.

This simple but effective step ensured that supplier systems handling patient billing data were consistently monitored and aligned with the hospital's ISMS controls.

When auditors revisited the site, they found clear documented evidence — checklists, review records, and change logs — demonstrating that supplier services were being regularly evaluated and managed in accordance with Annex A Control 5.22.

Author's Note: Outsourcing doesn't eliminate risk—the organization remains accountable for managing it. By applying Control 5.22, you create a safety net that ensures your suppliers' practices evolve alongside your own ISMS. Regular monitoring, review, and change management turn "vendor trust" into verified assurance—a hallmark of a mature, well-managed security program.

Example 3: The Manufacturing Firm's Change Control

A manufacturing company implemented ISO 27001 to protect its production data and ensure continuous operations. One afternoon, a well-meaning technician quickly updated the configuration of the production monitoring system—without informing the ISMS Manager or obtaining approval.

Within minutes, the update caused a brief network outage and disrupted data synchronization between the production system and the central database. Production reports were delayed, and some transactions had to be re-entered manually. Although the issue was resolved quickly, the incident exposed a serious gap—there was no formal process to review or control system changes before implementation.

To fix this, the organization introduced a structured *Change Control Procedure* under *Clause 8.1—Operational Planning and Control*, aligning it with *Annex A Control 8.32—Change Management*. This control requires that all changes to information processing facilities and systems be subject to clearly defined change management procedures.

Here's what the company did next:

- Created a ***Change Request Form*** that must be completed and reviewed before any update, patch, or system modification.
- Required a ***risk assessment and approval*** by the ISMS manager and system owner before implementation.
- Maintained ***records of all changes***, including who approved them, when they were implemented, and how testing was performed.
- Introduced a ***post-change review step*** to confirm that no new risks or failures were introduced into the environment.

This small but crucial step established structure and oversight for what was previously an informal process. Now, each change—even a minor software adjustment—follows a controlled workflow, minimizing disruptions and enabling actions to be traced, reviewed, and documented during audits.

When auditors later examined the ISMS, they found clear documentation showing that changes were systematically planned, assessed, approved, and verified—fully complying with the purpose of Annex A Control 8.32.

💬 **Author's Note:** Uncontrolled changes are a common cause of system downtime and data problems. By implementing Control 8.32, you add discipline to your operations—making sure every change is considered, approved, and documented. It's not bureaucracy; it's intelligent control that keeps your ISMS stable, predictable, and ready for audits.

The last part of Clause 8.1 focuses on documented evidence. It's not about bureaucracy—it's about trust and assurance. Keeping records of what was done, when, and by whom helps ensure that the ISMS processes are not only running but also performing as expected. These records will also serve as inputs for performance evaluation and ongoing improvement later (in Clause 9).

💬 **Author's Note:** Clause 8.1 is like moving from "planning on paper" to "running in reality." It's the difference between drawing a road map and actually driving the car. You plan the route, watch for obstacles, and adjust when things change—all while keeping a record of the journey. That's how you build confidence, control, and credibility in your ISMS.

Implementation Guidance: By now, you've laid the groundwork in your ISMS—you've identified your risks, chosen your controls, and planned your actions in Clause 6. Clause 8.1 is where all that planning becomes actual work. This is where you shift from thinking to doing.

In simple terms, Clause 8.1 requires you to plan, implement, and control your ISMS processes so that everything occurs as planned—with proper records to verify it. This includes not only running processes but also managing changes, handling exceptions, and monitoring outsourced activities.

Here's how to bring this clause to life step-by-step.

1. Implement and Operate Your Planned Processes

Begin by implementing the processes you previously outlined in your ISMS planning. These encompass both core ISMS processes and the risk treatment controls you selected after your risk assessment.

Some of the essential processes you'll manage include:

- ***Risk Management:*** Regularly review risks, update your risk register, and track treatment progress.
- ***Incident Management:*** Define how incidents are reported, logged, analyzed, and closed.
- ***Business Continuity Management:*** Ensure continuity plans are tested for information security continuity during any disruptions, updated, and aligned with information security goals.
- ***Internal Audits and Management Reviews:*** Schedule, conduct, and record these systematically to evaluate ISMS performance.

You should also define transparent ***reporting and meeting structures***:

- What reports will be produced (e.g., incident logs, KPI dashboards, and risk summaries)?
- How often will they be shared?
- Who is responsible for creating and reviewing them?
- What meetings are held (frequency, purpose, and participants)?

Author's Note: I've seen ISMS teams hold excellent meetings—but no records, no minutes, no follow-up. Remember, if it's not documented, it didn't happen. Keep it practical—even brief notes or summaries count as valid records.

2. Manage Planned Changes Systematically

Change is inevitable—new systems, tools, or processes will always emerge. What matters is how you manage those changes. When you plan a change, treat it like a mini-project with clear accountability. You should:

- ***Define the change*** and its purpose (why it's needed).
- ***Assign responsibilities***, deadlines, and resources.
- ***Assess risks*** to information security before implementation.
- ***Implement the change*** according to the approved plan.
- ***Monitor results*** to ensure it works as intended.
- ***Retain evidence***—approvals, communications, test results, and post-change reviews.

This aligns perfectly with ***Annex A Control 8.32—Change Management***, which ensures that all changes to information processing facilities and systems follow formal procedures.

Tip: Even a minor configuration change can cause ripple effects. Keep your change process straightforward but consistent—a short form, a quick risk review, and explicit approval make a big difference.

3. Handle Unintended Changes Quickly and Calmly
Not all changes are planned—some happen unexpectedly. A system update might run overnight, a configuration could be accidentally altered, or a third-party patch might introduce unforeseen behavior.
When such unintended changes occur:

- ***Identify and document*** what happened.
- ***Review the consequences***—what was affected, and how?
- ***Evaluate the risks***—are there any confidentiality, integrity, or availability impacts?
- ***Take corrective action*** to mitigate adverse effects and ensure it doesn't happen again.
- ***Record everything***—including your findings and mitigation steps.

This not only keeps your ISMS operationally strong but also provides valuable lessons for improving your change control process.

4. Control Outsourced Processes
Outsourcing can be efficient—but it doesn't eliminate your accountability. Under ISO 27001, the organization remains responsible for outsourced processes that affect the ISMS.
To maintain control:

- ***Identify all outsourced processes*** related to your ISMS (e.g., IT hosting, payroll, managed Security Operations Center (SOC)).
- ***Define clear interfaces***—ascertain who contacts whom, how incidents are reported, and what data is shared.
- ***Include information security clauses*** in all supplier contracts (aligned with Annex A controls such as 5.19 to 5.23 as applicable).
- ***Monitor and review*** supplier performance through reports, meetings, or audits.
- ***Manage supplier-related changes*** just as you would internal ones.

Author's Note: Outsourcing doesn't transfer responsibility; it simply changes who runs the process. Always verify that your suppliers deliver securely—don't assume, confirm.

5. Maintain Documented Evidence
Clause 8.1 also reminds us to ***document information to ensure*** that processes are operating as planned. This means retaining:

- Risk assessment and treatment records
- Incident logs and reports
- Change requests and approval forms
- Supplier monitoring records
- Meeting minutes and review summaries

These documents not only demonstrate compliance but also provide insight into how well your ISMS is functioning in practice.

Tip: Create a simple "Evidence Tracker"—a spreadsheet that lists each Clause 8.1 process and the type of documented proof you keep for it. It's a lifesaver during audits.

Author's Note: Think of Clause 8.1 as the "heartbeat" of your ISMS—steady, predictable, and always in motion. Planning and doing aren't separate worlds anymore; they're part of one continuous rhythm that keeps your information secure, day after day.

Toolkit and Resources: Clause 8.1 requires you to demonstrate that your ISMS functions as intended. This involves maintaining documented information—not excessive paperwork, but clear, practical evidence that your processes are effective, changes are managed, and suppliers are overseen.

To make things easier, I've included Table 12.1, an ISMS operational evidence-tracking template you can use to record and organize proof for each ISMS operational activity. Think of it as your "audit-ready snapshot" of what's been done, when it was done, and who was responsible. Used consistently, this one table can save you a lot of time during audits and reviews, because your evidence is already structured and easy to explain.

How to Use This Template

1. **List Your Core ISMS Processes:** Begin by listing all operational processes included in Clause 8.1—like risk assessment, change control, supplier management, incident response, internal audit, and management review.

   Tip: You can also include any other recurring activity that supports your ISMS—for example, awareness sessions, patch updates, or access reviews.

2. **Define the Frequency:** Specify how often each activity occurs—daily, monthly, quarterly, or annually. This helps you plan reviews and quickly identify missed tasks.
3. **Describe the Type of Evidence:** Note what evidence exists to prove the activity happened. Examples:
   - Risk assessment → updated risk register
   - Change control → approval form and testing records
   - Supplier monitoring → vendor review checklist
   - Incident response → incident log and corrective actions
4. **Specify the Storage Location:** Mention exactly where the evidence is stored—shared drive, ISMS portal, document control folder, or a specific repository.
5. **Assign Ownership:** Clearly name the responsible person or department. Ownership drives accountability—if everyone's responsible, no one really is.
6. **Record Completion Dates:** Update this tracker each time the process is performed. This shows your ISMS is *alive* and being maintained as planned.
7. **Add Remarks or Status:** Use this column to flag pending actions, improvement ideas, or findings from reviews. Over time, these remarks tell the story of continual improvement in action.

Table 12.1 ISMS operational evidence tracking template

Sr. No.	*ISMS Process/ Activity*	*Planned Frequency*	*Type of Evidence/ Record*	*Location (Where Stored)*	*Responsible Person/ Dept.*	*Last Completed (Date)*	*Remarks /Status*
1	Risk Assessment and Treatment Review	Annual	Risk register, risk treatment plan, approval records	ISMS SharePoint → Folder: Risk Management	ISMS Manager	10 July 2025	Completed; next due July 2026
2	Supplier Performance Monitoring	Quarterly	Vendor review checklist, meeting minutes, risk reassessment	Procurement Portal → Folder: Vendor Reviews	Procurement Head / ISMS Coordinator	01 Oct 2025	Completed; vendor “XXXX” flagged for follow-up
3	Incident Management	Ongoing	Incident log, root cause analysis, corrective action report	ISMS Incident Tracker	SOC Lead / ISMS Manager	03 Oct 2025	Two incidents closed; lessons logged

⚒ *Implementation Task #20: Evidence Tracker*

Alright, take a quick break. Close the book, open a spreadsheet, and create an Evidence Tracker for your organization. Please keep it simple. The goal is to clearly and quickly demonstrate that your Clause 8.1 processes are occurring as planned.

What To Do:

1. ***List your core activities*** under Clause 8.1: Risk reviews, change management, incident handling, supplier monitoring, management review, continuity tests, awareness runs, and access reviews.
2. ***Set the cadence*** for each (daily/monthly/quarterly/annually/as needed).
3. ***Name the evidence*** you'll keep (log, minutes, approval, test results, and reports).
4. ***Say where it lives*** (exact path or system location—no guessing).
5. ***Assign an owner*** (one name or role per row).
6. ***Add "Last completed"*** (date) and update it each time.
7. ***Add a remarks column*** for findings, delays, or follow-ups.
8. ***Populate at least 6–8 rows today***—don't aim for perfect; aim for real.
9. ***Share it*** with owners; confirm they can locate and update their evidence.
10. ***Schedule a monthly 10-minute check*** to keep it current.

Tips

- Use ***live links*** in the Location column (one click to evidence).
- Color-code "Last completed" (green = on time, amber = due soon, red = overdue).
- Add a ***"Next Due"*** helper column if that keeps you organized.

CLAUSE 8.2: INFORMATION SECURITY RISK ASSESSMENT

Summary of the Clause Requirements: Clause 8.2 marks the implementation of your risk assessment plan from earlier (Clause 6.1.2). After all the planning, defining criteria, and identifying methods, it's now time to conduct your information security risk assessments.

In simple terms, ISO 27001 asks you to do three key things under this clause:

1. ***Carry out risk assessments at defined intervals***—not just once a year, but also whenever significant changes occur in your environment. These changes might be technical (e.g., a new cloud system), organizational (e.g., a merger), or external (e.g., a new regulation).

   Think of It This Way: If something new could change your information security risk landscape, it's time to reassess.

2. ***Follow the criteria you defined earlier (in Clause 6.1.2)***—Your process must be consistent. That means using the same approach each time: How you identify, analyze, evaluate, and decide whether risks are acceptable.

   This ensures your results are reliable and comparable over time—not random opinions that vary from one person to another.

3. ***Keep evidence of the results***—ISO 27001 doesn't just require you to complete the assessment; it also requires you to demonstrate that you have done it. You must keep documented information, such as your risk register, assessment reports, or summary logs, which show how risks were identified, evaluated, and prioritized.

Explanation with Real-World Examples: This is the stage where your ISMS begins to "do" rather than just "plan." Clause 8.2 doesn't require creating anything new—it simply asks you to follow through on what you said you would do in Clause 6.1.2. You've already defined how you'll assess risks, when you'll do it, and what criteria you'll use. Now, in Clause 8.2, you carry out that plan.

Conduct the assessments according to your established process, record the results, and retain them as documented evidence. That evidence demonstrates that your risk management process is active, consistent, and effective.

In short, Clause 6.1.2 provides the blueprint for your house. Clause 8.2 is where you build the house. You don't add extra work—you bring your plan to life. Each scheduled assessment you perform strengthens your ISMS and demonstrates that it's not just designed—it's working in practice.

In simple terms, this clause makes sure your risk management process is active, used, and documented. You're not just stating how risks should be assessed—you're actually assessing them.

Risk assessments under Clause 8.2 happen in two situations:

1. ***At planned intervals***—for example, once or twice a year, depending on your organization's size, risk exposure, or industry expectations.
2. ***When significant changes occur***—such as system upgrades, mergers, regulatory updates, or security incidents. These moments often shift your risk landscape, so reassessment helps you stay in control.

Each time you conduct an assessment, you must keep documented information—your risk register, analysis results, and any scoring or ranking you've used. This documentation demonstrates that your process (defined in Clause 6.1.2) is not just theoretical but is actively implemented and maintained.

Author's Note: Clause 8.2 is where your planning finally turns into proof. It's the action stage of everything you defined back in Clause 6.1.2—your risk assessment process, criteria, and methodology. So, think of Clause 8.2 as your ISMS "reality check." It's where you stop assuming and start proving—proving that you understand your risks, that you're paying attention to change, and that you have the evidence to show it. This is where theory becomes action, and action becomes assurance.

In my classes, I often draw a simple whiteboard equation to make the connection clear:

Clause 6.1.2 (Risk Assessment Process) + Execution (Putting the Process into Action) = Clause 8.2 (Risk Assessment Results)

It resonates immediately with participants—they understand that Clause 6.1.2 focuses on planning risk assessments, while Clause 8.2 is about executing them and maintaining evidence to prove it. These clauses aren't separate—they are parts of the same cycle: Plan and perform, design and deliver, think and act.

Implementation Guidance: Here's the good news—Clause 8.2 doesn't add anything new or complex. You're not creating new procedures or reinventing your ISMS. You're simply carrying out the risk assessment process you already outlined earlier in Clause 6.1.2.

Think of this as the "action phase" of your risk management cycle. All you need to do is follow the same steps you documented before—identify, analyze, evaluate, and record your risks—exactly as described in your organization's risk assessment procedure.

For quick reference, I suggest revisiting Chapter 10. That's where we established your risk assessment foundation—the method, criteria, and toolkit you'll now use. Now it's time to put that plan into action.

How to Execute Clause 8.2 in Practice

1. **Follow Your Established Plan:** Stick to the risk assessment methodology outlined in your ISMS documentation—don't alter the process halfway through. If you've committed to assessing risks annually, quarterly, or after any significant change, then that's precisely what you should do.
2. **Schedule Regular Assessments:** Conduct a comprehensive risk assessment across the organization at least annually. This keeps you up to date with evolving threats and business developments.

   Tip: Align your annual assessment with your management review cycle—it keeps your ISMS decisions timely and data-driven.
3. **Reassess When Changes Happen:** ISO 27001 expects you to perform *additional or triggered assessments* when something significant changes, such as:

   - A new system, vendor, or process is introduced.
   - A significant incident or breach occurs.
   - There's a change in regulation or compliance requirement.
   - The organization undergoes restructuring or mergers.

   In such cases, you should determine:

   a. ***Which changes require reassessment***, and
   b. ***How those assessments will be triggered*** (e.g., through your change management process or incident review).
4. **Refine Your Detail Over Time:** Your initial risk assessment can be broad and high-level—that's completely okay. As your ISMS develops, you'll naturally improve your risk identification method, adding more detail, clarity, and precision in later iterations. This continual refinement demonstrates ongoing progress, not extra effort.
5. **Keep Evidence of the Results:** Once you've performed the assessment, don't forget to ***retain documented information***—this is your Clause 8.2 evidence. Examples include:

   - The updated risk register or tracker.
   - Risk scoring results and evaluation notes.
   - Meeting minutes or approvals related to risk reviews.
   - Screenshots, reports, or communications confirming updates.

This evidence shows that your risk assessments are conducted as planned and that your ISMS is functioning effectively.

Author's Note: Clause 8.2 isn't about doing extra work—it's about fulfilling what you already committed to in Clause 6.1.2. Think of it as hitting "play" on your risk management process. You're simply running the movie you already planned—and keeping a copy of the performance as evidence.

Go back to Chapter 10, open your Risk Assessment Toolkit, follow your steps, document your findings, and organize the results neatly. That's Clause 8.2 completed—straightforward, structured, and precisely as ISO 27001 intended.

Toolkit and Resources: There's nothing new to prepare for in this clause—Clause 8.2 is simply about executing the plan you already created in Clause 6.1.2.

So, review your Risk Assessment Toolkit from Chapter 10, Clause 6. Use the same templates, criteria, and methods you established earlier.

All you need to do here is perform the assessment, record the results, and keep the evidence—that's your compliance with Clause 8.2.

CLAUSE 8.3: INFORMATION SECURITY RISK TREATMENT

Summary of the Clause Requirements: Clause 8.3 is brief, but it truly tests whether your ISMS functions in practice. After you identify and assess your risks (per Clauses 6.1.2 and 8.2), you address them by implementing your chosen controls and actions.
In simple terms, ISO 27001 expects you to do two things under this clause:

1. **Implement Your Risk Treatment Plan:** You previously developed this plan earlier in Clause 6.1.3—where you chose controls, accepted residual risks, and assigned responsibilities. Clause 8.3 now requires you to implement that plan. This may involve applying technical measures (such as access controls or encryption), management actions (such as policy updates or training), or controls related to suppliers.
2. **Keep Evidence of What You've Done:** Every action taken to manage a risk—from applying a patch to implementing a new policy—must be supported by documented information. These records demonstrate that your treatment plan wasn't just written; it was put into action and is now functioning as intended.

In short, Clause 8.3 concerns action and proof—doing what you promised and keeping evidence that it has been completed.

Explanation with Real-World Examples: Clause 8.3 marks the point where your ISMS begins to produce results. After identifying your risks in Clause 8.2, it's time to take action by implementing the treatment steps you outlined earlier in Clause 6.1.3.

In practice, this means you're now carrying out your risk treatment plan—putting the chosen controls into action, assigning responsibilities, and ensuring each step is completed and verified.

Whenever a new risk assessment is conducted (e.g., due to a system upgrade or a new vendor), you may identify new risks or changes in existing ones. At that point, you update your risk treatment plan and redo the treatment process. The cycle continues—assess, treat, record, and improve.

Keep documentation of your treatment activities, like reports, access lists, training records, procedures, or agreements. These records prove that the plan was put in place and that risks were managed properly.

Let's make this more relatable with a few examples.

Example 1: The Accounting Firm's Data Encryption Project
An accounting firm identified the risk of "unauthorized access to financial data on laptops." In Clause 6.1.3, they decided that encrypting all company laptops was the best course of action. Under Clause 8.3, they implemented full-disk encryption on all devices, documented the plan, kept the vendor's configuration report, and trained staff on how to use encrypted drives safely.

When auditors later reviewed their ISMS, those encryption reports and training records offered solid proof that the control was implemented exactly as planned.

Example 2: The University's Awareness Reinforcement Plan
A university identified through its risk assessment that phishing attacks were the leading cause of student data breaches. The risk treatment plan included a "phishing simulation and

awareness program." Under Clause 8.3, the IT team carried this out by running simulated phishing campaigns, tracking click rates, and holding short awareness sessions afterward.

The results—lower click rates and training attendance records—were documented as evidence. They didn't just plan awareness; they proved it worked.

Example 3: The Logistics Company's Supplier Control Update
A logistics company discovered that one of its third-party tracking system vendors did not meet its ISMS security standards. The risk treatment plan called for updating supplier contracts to include data protection clauses and regular security reports. Under Clause 8.3, the procurement team collaborated with legal and ISMS to update the contracts and introduced a quarterly vendor performance review.

Those signed contracts and review reports serve as clear evidence that risk treatment was both executed and maintained.

Author's Note: Clause 8.3 is straightforward—it's the "DO IT" phase of your ISMS. You've already evaluated your risks (Clause 6.1.2), decided how to handle them (Clause 6.1.3), and reviewed them regularly (Clause 8.2). Now, you get ready to implement those decisions. In my classes, I often say this is the "we said it, we did it, and here's the proof" part of your ISMS. You're not creating anything new—you're living your plan. And when an auditor arrives, those records of implementation—screenshots, reports, meeting notes, and sign-offs—become the voice of your ISMS, confidently saying, "Yes, we did what we said we would."

Implementation Guidance: Clause 8.3 is about ***execution***—doing what you already said you would do.

This clause is not about creating anything new.

No new processes.

No new procedures.

No new forms or templates.

While working on Clause 6.1.3, you identified your information security risks, decided how to address them, chose controls from Annex A (or others), and documented your plan—detailing who will do what, by when, and how success will be measured.

Now, in Clause 8.3, you *put that plan into action.*

1. **Do What You Planned in Clause 6.1.3:** Every action you agreed to earlier—whether it's implementing new access controls, running awareness training, or updating supplier contracts—now needs to be carried out.

   You're not creating new controls here; you're implementing the ones you've already agreed upon. Think of it like this: Clause 6.1.3 is your "promise." Clause 8.3 is where you fulfil that promise.

   Example: If your treatment plan in Clause 6.1.3 states you will "implement multi-factor authentication (MFA) for all remote users," then Clause 8.3 covers when you actually deploy MFA, communicate the change, and keep the configuration reports as proof.

2. **Monitor and Verify That It's Done:** Once you begin implementing your risk treatment plan, ensure it is executed as intended. Assign responsible parties, monitor progress, and confirm completion.

You can do this through:

- Regular ISMS review meetings

- Simple tracking sheets or dashboards
- Progress updates from control owners

This ongoing monitoring ensures that your treatment actions don't stop at good intentions—they become tangible, measurable, and auditable results.

❢ **Tip:** Review your treatment plan at least quarterly to ensure actions are completed on time and remain relevant. If you've finished an action, mark it with evidence. If something is delayed, record why and when it will be resolved.

3. **Capture Evidence—This Is What Auditors Will Look For:** Clause 8.3 explicitly requires you to keep documented records of the results. This serves as proof that the information security risk treatment plan has been carried out and is functioning correctly.

Evidence could include:

- Screenshots or system reports showing controls applied
- Training attendance records
- Updated contracts or supplier review reports
- Change control logs
- Meeting minutes confirming risk treatment completion

If you've done the work, ensure you have the record. Without it, even the best control stays invisible during an audit.

4. **Keep Improving When Things Don't Go as Planned:** Sometimes, your treatment plan might not go perfectly. Maybe a control failed, or the risk evolved faster than expected. That's okay—ISO 27001 expects learning, not perfection.

If something doesn't work:

- Record what went wrong
- Adjust your plan
- Implement a corrective action
- Keep evidence of your response

This shows maturity—that you don't just execute mindlessly but adapt thoughtfully.

Author's Note: Clause 8.3 is where your ISMS shifts from words to action. You're no longer just writing policies or planning frameworks—you're demonstrating that everything you promised in Clause 6.1.3 has been accomplished. In my classes, I often illustrate this with a simple whiteboard equation to make the connection clear:

Clause 6.1.2 (Risk Treatment Process) + Execution (Putting the Process into Action) = Clause 8.2 (Risk Treatment Results)

Don't overthink it. You don't need a new process—follow your plan, complete your actions, and keep the evidence. That's all ISO 27001 expects, and it's what makes your ISMS a living, trusted system that genuinely works.

Toolkit and Resources: There's nothing new to create or design for this clause—Clause 8.3 is simply about executing what you already planned in Clause 6.1.3: Risk Treatment.

You've already created your treatment plan, identified the risks to address, chosen appropriate controls (from Annex A or other sources), and defined who will do what, by when, and how you'll measure success. Now it's time to implement that plan and gather evidence that each control or action has been carried out as intended.

Revisit your Risk Treatment Toolkit from Chapter 10, Clause 6. Use the same templates, methods, and criteria you established earlier. You don't need any new tools or documents. You just need to:

- Implement the actions you already agreed upon.
- Monitor progress and completion.
- Retain clear evidence that every planned treatment was carried out.

That's the simple secret of Clause 8.3: *No new templates, just disciplined execution and visible results.*

Key Takeaway—What You've Learned

- Clause 8 is the Do phase: Execute the processes you previously defined to meet your information security requirements and objectives.
- Specify how each ISMS process should operate (inputs, steps, outputs, success criteria) and manage it accordingly.
- Keep documented evidence that shows activities were completed as planned (logs, minutes, approvals, reports).
- Manage planned changes, review unintentional ones, reduce adverse effects, and record both.
- Identify externally supplied processes and oversee them (monitor, review, and handle supplier changes)—you remain responsible.
- In 8.2, you don't introduce anything new; you follow the risk assessment method established in 6.1.2—on schedule and when significant changes happen—and keep the results.
- In 8.3, you also do not add anything new; you carry out the risk treatment plan from 6.1.3, check that it's finished, and keep proof of the actions.
- Avoid unnecessary paperwork—keep enough records to demonstrate control, consistency, and effective operation of the ISMS.
- Clause 8 reflects your credibility: You said it, you did it, and here is the evidence.

QUIZ #11

True/False statement

Sr.	*Statement*	*True/False*
1	Clause 8 is the "Do" phase where the organization operates the ISMS processes it already planned.	
2	Under Clause 8.1, keeping documented evidence of operational activities is optional if processes are well understood.	
3	Unintended changes must be reviewed for consequences and mitigated as necessary.	
4	If a process is outsourced, accountability for information security shifts to the supplier.	
5	Clause 8.2 introduces a new risk assessment process different from Clause 6.1.2.	
6	Under Clause 8.3, creating new procedures is mandatory before executing risk treatment actions.	

CASE 6: RISK, ROLLOUTS, AND REALITY—LAGOS

The morning started with ringing phones.

At Zenith Coastal Bank in Lagos, the IT Command Center screens were usually calm, displaying routine operational logs and quiet system status messages. But today, every dashboard turned red. Thousands of customers across Nigeria couldn't log into the banking app. Transfers weren't processing. ATMs functioned, but balances wouldn't update.

By 9:15 a.m., the call center floor was swamped. Agents kept repeating the same line:

"We are aware of the issue. Our team is working to resolve it."

Meanwhile, on the 7th floor, Adewale "Ade" Ajayi — the newly appointed Lead Implementer for ISO 27001 — entered the incident war room. The Operations Manager, Thomas, looked worn out. "We applied a patch last night," he said, rubbing his forehead. "It was supposed to fix a security flaw and support a new authentication feature."

Ade paused. "Was the change logged? Tested? Approved?"

Thomas hesitated. "We followed the vendor guidance. It was a quick change."

The CISO raised an eyebrow. "Quick changes should still follow the change process."

Ade didn't blame anyone. Instead, he opened the risk treatment register stored in SecureMetrics, the bank's commercial governance and risk platform—the same tool used for risk assessment, treatment tracking, and compliance reporting. The issue was already recorded as a medium operational and privacy risk earlier. Risk controls were assigned—including "change approval," "rollback preparation," and "customer impact testing."

Some had status: Pending.

By noon, a technical rollback was in progress. The incident team recorded every action—timestamps, system logs, impacted services, and temporary workarounds for high-priority accounts. By 2:40 p.m., the services were restored. Customers gradually logged back in. Complaints decreased.

Later that week, Ade led the scheduled Operations Information Security Review meeting. Attendees included representatives from IT, operations, risk, legal, procurement, internal audit, and digital banking. Ade presented the incident timeline and findings.

"Let's review", he said calmly:

- Change was implemented.
- Testing was incomplete.
- No formal approval or communication plan existed.
- Risk treatment controls were only partially implemented.

Silence filled the room until the Head of Digital Banking spoke: "We rushed. We treated change like routine maintenance instead of a planned update."

Ade nodded and then added, "Clause 8 of ISO 27001 is not just about doing the work—it's about operating processes consistently, tracking planned changes, acting on unintended changes, and learning from them."

They agreed on the following steps:

- A structured change approval workflow.
- Mandatory rollback plans for critical updates.
- Communication triggers for business, customer service, and suppliers.
- Evidence tracking in SecureMetrics.

Procurement then raised an additional challenge: Outsourced data analytics teams had also been impacted during the downtime because no notification had been sent to external vendors. Ade added supplier notification to the revised operational workflow.

Two weeks later, at another meeting, Thomas smiled and said, "We rolled out a new update last night."

Ade raised an eyebrow.

Thomas kept his grin and said: "Documented. Tested. Approved. Implemented at 2:05 a.m.—Zero disruption."

The room laughed—but with relief.

Operational discipline wasn't just improving.

It was becoming normal.

Case Discussion—Test Your Understanding

1. **Which action best aligns with ISO 27001 Clause 8 requirements for planned changes?**

   A. Informal approval through verbal confirmation
   B. Implementing changes directly based on urgency
   C. Logging change details, testing, approval, and documenting results
   D. Applying patches only during non-business hours

2. **The risk register and treatment plan stored in the SecureMetrics software are:**

   A. Non-compliant because ISO requires physical documents
   B. Invalid unless printed and signed
   C. Optional and not required
   D. Acceptable, as ISO allows any format and media

3. **What failure most contributed to the customer disruption?**

   A. Lack of an outsourced vendor
   B. Patch was applied outside business hours
   C. Lack of formal change control and testing
   D. Using commercial security tools

4. **After the unintended service outage, what activity aligns with Clause 8 actions for unintended changes?**

   A. Ignoring it if systems recover
   B. Blaming the operations team
   C. Reviewing consequences and taking action to mitigate any adverse effects, as necessary
   D. Marking the change as a normal deployment

5. **Why was notifying the outsourced analytics supplier important?**

   A. ISO requires suppliers be notified of all emails.
   B. Supplier services must be monitored and integrated into operations.
   C. It was optional but polite.
   D. Because Risk asked for it.

6. **Which statement reflects the purpose of operational meetings under Clause 8?**

   A. To approve employee promotions
   B. To evaluate operational security activities and ensure coordinated ISMS actions
   C. To schedule company social events
   D. To track attendance for awareness training

Chapter 13

Clause 9—Is it working? Evaluate and improve

Measuring performance, auditing, and management review

Welcome to the Check phase of your ISMS journey—the moment when you pause to think instead of just doing. You've built the system, planned your actions (Clauses 4–7), and put them into motion (Clause 8). Now, step back and ask the big question: Is our ISMS really working the way we intended?

Clause 9, Performance Evaluation, is where you measure, monitor, analyze, and assess the effectiveness of everything you've implemented. Think of it as a routine health check for your management system: you're not just verifying whether processes exist—you're determining whether they are healthy, effective, and aligned with your goals.

This isn't just about monitoring risk controls. Performance evaluation applies throughout your entire ISMS: how well you understand your context in Clause 4, how effectively you're meeting your objectives in Clause 6, how consistently operations run under Clause 8, and more. Organizations often stumble here—not because they didn't work hard, but because they didn't define what to monitor, how to measure it, or how to learn from the results.

In this chapter, we'll turn on the headlights and closely examine how your ISMS performs. You'll learn what to monitor, how to measure, and how to interpret the results—so the Check phase becomes more than just a compliance task. It becomes a practical tool for learning, improvement, and demonstrating that your ISMS functions effectively in the real world. Grab your metaphorical microscope; it's time to zoom in and see what's really happening inside your ISMS engine.

CLAUSE 9.1 MONITORING, MEASUREMENT, ANALYSIS, AND EVALUATION

Summary of the Clause Requirements: Clause 9.1 is where you verify whether your ISMS is performing as intended. It encourages your organization to adopt a structured approach to monitoring and measurement—not just collecting data, but transforming it into insights.

Here, ISO 27001 expects you to decide a few key things clearly:

- What needs to be monitored and measured—this includes both your ISMS processes (like communication or awareness programs) and your controls (like access management or encryption).
- How you will monitor and measure—the methods must be consistent, reliable, and capable of producing valid results that can be compared over time.
- When monitoring and measurement will take place—this could be daily, monthly, quarterly, or annually, depending on the activity.

DOI: 10.1201/9781003744139-14

- Who is responsible for monitoring, measuring, analyzing, and evaluating the results—clear ownership ensures accountability and consistency.
- When and how the results will be analyzed and evaluated—it's not enough to collect data; someone must interpret it and decide what it means for your ISMS.

You also need to record your monitoring and measurement results as evidence. These records show that your ISMS performance is regularly reviewed and that decisions are based on actual data rather than guesswork.

Finally, Clause 9.1 highlights that your organization must assess both the performance of your ISMS and the effectiveness of its controls. Essentially, this clause ensures your ISMS isn't operating automatically—it's actively monitored, measured, and improved based on actual results.

Explanation with Real-World Examples: Clause 9.1 is where you stop guessing and start knowing. This is where you discover whether all those ISMS activities you've been planning and executing are delivering the results you expected. It's not just about collecting numbers or ticking boxes; it's about understanding what those numbers tell you.

Monitoring involves keeping an eye on something to understand its status—for example, tracking how often incidents happen or how many people finish awareness training. Measurement, however, assigns a value to that monitoring—for instance, "five incidents this quarter" or "98% of staff completed training." When you track these measurements over time, you start to see trends—and that's when real insights occur.

In practice, organizations need to define:

- What will be monitored and measured (for example, incident trends, system uptime, training completion rates).
- Who will do it and when (maybe IT tracks uptime weekly, HR tracks training quarterly, and the ISMS Manager compiles an overall performance report monthly).
- How they'll ensure the data is valid, consistent, and comparable—because meaningless data can be worse than no data at all.

Once you've collected the data, the next step is to analyze and evaluate it. This is where you interpret what the numbers signify. There are two main types of evaluation:

1. **Performance Evaluation:**Are you doing things as planned? Are the processes and activities working as intended?
2. **Effectiveness Evaluation:** Are you doing the right things? Are you achieving your information security objectives?

Let's look at a few real-world examples:

Example 1: The "Tick-the-Box" Awareness Program: A large organization proudly announced that it had achieved 100% completion of its annual awareness training. Impressive, right? But during a simulated phishing campaign, 35% of employees still clicked on fake links. That's when they realized they were tracking training completion but not its effectiveness. The numbers looked good, but the results did not. Afterward, they introduced new metrics—such as phishing test results and incident reports caused by user error—to accurately measure awareness effectiveness.

Example 2: The Quietly Failing Backup System: An IT department assumed its backups were working correctly because the software showed "Successful" every night. However, during a minor incident, they attempted to restore data and found that half the files were corrupt—backups hadn't been verified in months. They had been monitoring completion, not validity. Afterward, they started conducting weekly restoration tests and recording verification reports as part of their ISMS evidence.

Example 3: The Security Control That Looked Good on Paper: A financial firm implemented multi-factor authentication (MFA) and marked it as "Implemented." However, during an internal review months later, they discovered that only 60% of users had actually enrolled in MFA. The control was in place but not effective. By monitoring MFA adoption rates and reviewing results monthly, they achieved full compliance and significantly decreased login-related incidents.

These examples demonstrate why monitoring and measurement are more than just technical tasks—they are management tools. They help you determine if your ISMS is truly protecting what it should.

When done correctly, Clause 9.1 transforms data into awareness, awareness into insight, and insight into improvement. You're not generating more paperwork—you're giving your ISMS a voice that reveals what's truly working and what needs attention.

💬 **Author's Note:** I can't emphasize this enough—Clause 9.1 is one of the most essential parts of your ISMS. I've seen many organizations proudly say, "We've implemented the control, and we haven't had any incidents, so everything must be fine." But that's not enough. Just because nothing seems wrong doesn't mean everything is correct.

Monitoring and measurement aren't just about proving that controls are working—they're about learning, improving, and helping the system evolve. Without measurement, you'll never know if your efforts are truly effective or just comfortable routines.

Let me share a true story from one of my audits. I once asked an HR manager if they had evaluated the effectiveness of their awareness program. She smiled and enthusiastically told me about the one-day session they held at a five-star hotel. Everyone had a great time, she said—it was a big success. When I asked how many people attended, she confidently replied, "100."

Now, "100" is one of those numbers that sounds nice and round—usually what people say when they don't know the exact figure. So, I asked to see the attendance sheet. After checking, we found that only 46 people had attended. More than half the staff missed the program, yet it was still declared a success. They booked and paid for dinner for 100 people, but only 46 learned something that day. Was that really an effective use of resources?

The lesson here is straightforward: if you don't measure, you can't improve. Monitoring and measurement distinguish activity from achievement. They reveal what's working, what's not, and where your focus needs to be. Without them, even the most well-meaning ISMS can silently drift off course—looking busy but not necessarily effective.

Implementation Guidance: Let's be honest—most organizations either measure too little or measure way too much. Some gather no data at all and say, "Everything's fine." Others drown in endless spreadsheets and colorful dashboards that no one ever reads or understands. Clause 9.1 encourages you to find the middle ground—measure what truly matters and use that information to make meaningful, informed decisions.

Monitoring, measurement, analysis, and evaluation are not just routine tasks—they are the heartbeat of a successful ISMS. Without them, you're essentially flying blind, doing things without knowing if they're effective. ISO 27001 clearly states that organizations must assess the effectiveness of what they do, not just confirm that they've completed tasks.

You'll see this requirement appear in several clauses throughout the standard. Clause 6.1.1(e) asks you to integrate and implement actions into your ISMS processes, then evaluate their effectiveness. Clause 7.2(c) requires you to take actions to build or acquire the necessary competence—and again, to *determine how effective those actions were*. Finally, Clause 10.2(d) reminds you to *review the effectiveness* of any corrective actions you take to address nonconformities.

These examples demonstrate that effectiveness evaluation isn't optional or confined to a single clause—it's integrated throughout the entire ISO 27001 framework. Whether you're managing risks, training staff, or correcting mistakes, you need to ensure your actions achieve the desired results. That's exactly what Clause 9.1 helps you do—add structure, consistency, and evidence to how you measure and demonstrate that your ISMS is truly effective, not just active.

So, effectiveness isn't just about ticking boxes—it's about demonstrating that what you've implemented truly works. That's why Clause 9.1 is essential: it provides structure to your monitoring and ensures you're measuring for real improvement, not just for compliance.

The easiest way to start is by defining what information you need. Simply ask yourself: "What do I truly want to learn about my ISMS?"

An information need could sound like:

- "Are our security incidents reducing over time?"
- "Are the controls we implemented for data protection actually working?"
- "Are employees more aware of security now than they were six months ago?"

Once you know what you want to learn, it becomes easier to decide what to monitor and measure. You're not just collecting numbers randomly—you're gathering information that helps you assess performance and make improvements.

Here's a quick caution: tracking too many things can backfire. When you try to monitor everything, you end up learning nothing. Focus on a few key metrics that truly reflect your ISMS. Prioritize quality over quantity.

There are two main types of measurement that you'll typically use:

1. **Performance Measurement:** These are about *doing the work right*. They tell you how well you are following your plan or completing your activities. Examples include:
   - Number of incidents reported versus resolved
   - Percentage of staff who completed security training
   - Timeliness of applying patches or updates
   - Completion of planned internal audits or management reviews
2. **Effectiveness Measurement:** These go deeper and ask, *Is the work making a difference?* They connect actions to outcomes. For example:
   - Did the number of phishing clicks drop after awareness training?
   - Did response times improve after introducing the new incident management tool?
   - Are risk levels actually reducing as a result of the controls we implemented?

Each of these provides a different perspective: performance indicates activity, effectiveness demonstrates impact. You need both to honestly assess your ISMS.

When setting up your monitoring and measurement system, make sure to define clearly:

- ***What*** you'll monitor or measure (e.g., incidents, risks, training completion)
- ***How*** you'll measure it (e.g., reports, surveys, logs, dashboards)
- ***When*** it will happen (e.g., weekly, quarterly, annually)
- ***Who*** is responsible for measuring, analyzing, and evaluating the results

Don't assign everything to one person—that's a common mistake. Different people bring different strengths:

- IT may collect the data (incident logs, system uptime).
- HR may measure awareness training participation.
- The ISMS Manager may analyze results and report findings.

Separating roles avoids bias and improves accuracy.

Also, remember—monitoring and measurement don't stop at controls. You can assess how well your entire ISMS operates—from how effectively your context (Clause 4) was defined to how well your objectives (Clause 6) are being met.

And if you want to explore further, ISO/IEC 27004 provides detailed guidance on establishing meaningful ISMS measurements—including templates, examples, and role definitions. But start simple: one question, one measure, one improvement.

The golden rule is this—if you can't explain why you're measuring something or what decision it helps you make, don't measure it. Your ISMS doesn't need more data. It requires more insight.

■ **Toolkit and Resources:** We've reached the core of Clause 9.1—where you stop guessing and start knowing. Monitoring and measurement are how you determine if your ISMS is performing as expected, if your actions are making a difference, and where improvements are needed.

This isn't about gathering fancy statistics or getting lost in dashboards. It's about asking the right questions, tracking what's important, and turning your results into clear insights.

To help you get started, I've included Table 13.1, a monitoring and measurement tracking template you can use to evaluate ISMS performance in a structured way. It is inspired by the guidance in ISO 27004, which focuses on how to measure the effectiveness of an ISMS in practical terms. You can apply this template to any process, control, or activity—awareness training, risk treatment actions, incident response, supplier monitoring, or anything else that matters in your environment.

Use it as-is or adapt it to suit your organization's context. The goal is not perfection, but consistency, clarity, and evidence you can confidently explain during reviews and audits.

How to Use the Template:

This template works best when you understand why each field exists and how it supports meaningful, auditable measurement. In Table 13.1, every row has a purpose—not to create paperwork, but to help you show that monitoring and measurement are planned, consistent, and actually used for decision-making. So let's walk through it together, step by step, the same way we would in a classroom.

Step 1. Identify the Clause or Control Number: Begin by identifying the specific clause, control, or process you are monitoring—for example, Clause 7.3 (Awareness) or Annex A Control 8.32 (Change Management). This helps ensure your measurements stay aligned with particular ISMS requirements and simplifies cross-referencing during audits.

Table 13.1 Monitoring and measurement tracking template for the ISMS

Field	*Description*
Clause or control number	7.3
Clause details	Information security awareness
Measure ID	XXX
Information need	Assess the status of compliance with the organization's security awareness policy among relevant personnel.
Measure	Progress to date / current status Percentage of personnel who pass during an unannounced spot audit
Formula/scoring	a) Derive the "progress to date" by adding the status for all personnel who have signed and are planned to be completed to date b) Derive "progress to date with signing" by dividing personnel having signed to date by personnel planned for signing to date c) [divide progress to date by (personnel planned to date times 100)] and progress to date with signing d) Compare status with previous statuses [Number of employees successfully qualified during the spot audit/total number of employees audited] * 100
Target	a) Resulting ratios should fall between 0.9 and 1.0 to conclude the achievement of the control objective, and no action is required. b) Trend should be upward or stable
Implementation evidence	1.1. Count the number of personnel scheduled to have signed and completed the training to date 1.2. Ask the responsible individual for the percentage of personnel who have completed the training and signed 2.1. Count the number of personnel scheduled to have signed by this date 2.2. Count the number of personnel who have signed user agreements 2.3. Internal Audit results on the same
Frequency	Collect: Quarterly Analysis: Quarterly Report: Quarterly Measurement Revision: Review annually Period of Measurement: Annual
Responsible parties	Information owner: Information security officer and Training manager Information collector: Training management—Human resource department Measurement client: Managers responsible for an ISMS Training
Data source	1.1. Information security awareness training plan/schedule: Personnel identified in plan 1.2 Personnel who have completed or are in progress with the training: Personnel status regarding the training 2.1. Plan for signing user agreements/schedule: Personnel identified in plan for signing 2.2. Personnel having signed agreements: Personnel status regarding the signing of the agreement 2.3 Internal Audit results
Reporting format	Bar graph with bars color-coded based on the target. A summary of what the measure means and the possible management actions should be attached to the bar chart.
Remarks	Add any applicable remarks here.

Step 2. Assign a Measure ID: Give each measure a short ID, such as *ISMS-M01* or *TRAIN-02*. This makes your register searchable and helps you organize results neatly across multiple controls or departments.

Step 3. Define the Information Need: Ask yourself: What am I trying to learn or confirm? For example, "Are employees aware of their information security responsibilities?" Or "Are incident responses completed within target timeframes?" If you can't explain why you're measuring something, it's probably not worth measuring.

Step 4. Define the Measure Itself: Describe precisely what you'll measure. It could be a percentage, a count, or a ratio—anything that provides an objective view of performance. Example: "Percentage of staff who completed awareness training in the last quarter."

Step 5. Write the Formula or Scoring Method: Explain how you'll calculate the result. Keep it simple—use basic math or percentages so anyone can easily repeat the measure. Example: (Number of employees trained / Total number of employees planned) × 100.

Step 6. Set a Target or Threshold: Define what success looks like. For example, you might set a goal of 95% awareness or aim for fewer than 2% of incidents to be overdue per quarter. Targets give purpose to your data—without them, you're just collecting numbers.

Step 7. Identify Implementation Evidence: List the specific documents or records that demonstrate a measurement has been completed. Examples include attendance lists, Learning Management System (LMS) completion reports, audit checklists, or system logs. This is what auditors and management will review when assessing effectiveness.

Step 8. Define Frequency and Timing: Decide how often you'll collect, analyze, and report your data. Example: Collect quarterly, analyze quarterly, report quarterly, review annually. Consistency matters more than frequency—don't measure daily if quarterly is sufficient.

Step 9. Assign Responsible Parties: Define who owns, collects, and uses the information:

- **Information Owner:** the process or control owner (e.g., ISMS Officer)
- **Information Collector:** the person gathering data (e.g., HR or IT Team)
- **Measurement Client:** the person or role using the data for decisions (e.g., Management Representative)

You can also add any other roles if needed.

Step 10. List Data Sources: Clearly specify the source of your data—whether it's a learning management system, incident tracker, or vendor report. This enhances traceability and boosts confidence in the validity of your results.

Step 11. Choose a Reporting Format: Visuals make data easier to interpret. You can use a bar chart, trend line, or pie chart—just be sure to include a summary explaining what the data means and what actions may be needed.

Step 12. Add Remarks or Observations: Use this section for insights or follow-ups—things you noticed while analyzing results. For example: "Attendance dropped this quarter due to shift changes—rescheduling planned for next month."

A Quick Reminder: Monitoring and measurement aren't optional extras—they're at the core of an effective ISMS. Several clauses in ISO 27001 explicitly require you to *evaluate effectiveness* (see 6.1.1(e), 7.2(c), and 10.2(d)). So don't treat this as a paperwork exercise.

When done right, this template becomes your ISMS dashboard—showing what's working, what needs attention, and how your organization is improving over time.

It's not about proving compliance; it's about proving progress.

🛠 *Implementation Task #21: Monitoring and Measurement Plan*

Alright, it's your turn now. Please take a short break, grab your notes, and let's make this real.

It's time to create a *Monitoring and Measurement Plan* for any control or clause of your choice. You can pick something simple to start with—maybe your training program (Clause 7.2), or your screening process (Control 6.1), or even Labelling of information (Control 5.13). The goal isn't to make it perfect—it's to make it practical.

Use the template provided in the toolkit and fill it out step by step. Carefully review each field, consider what information you need, and think about how to measure it effectively.

Don't overdo it. Start small. Focus on one or two key areas that are easy to monitor. Once you understand how each part works—from defining your information need to identifying your evidence and setting a realistic goal—you can add more controls later.

The key is to make your monitoring and measurement plan realistic, measurable, and valuable—something that provides you with real insight, not just data.

CLAUSE 9.2 INTERNAL AUDIT

Summary of the Clause Requirements: Clause 9.2 is where your ISMS honestly examines itself. It requires you to perform internal audits at scheduled intervals to verify whether your management system is both compliant and effective. In other words, you're checking that your ISMS meets your own specified requirements and the ISO 27001 standard—and that it functions as intended.

In simple terms, the internal audit helps you answer three key questions:

1. Are we following our own ISMS processes and procedures?
2. Are we complying with the ISO 27001 requirements?
3. Are our ISMS working as intended and being properly maintained?

To do this, your organization needs to establish and maintain a well-structured internal audit program. This program outlines how often audits will be conducted, which methods will be employed, who will perform them, and how the results will be communicated.

When planning your audit program, consider the significance of the processes being audited and review the results of previous audits; areas that had issues before may require more frequent monitoring.

Each audit should have a clearly defined audit objective (why the audit is being conducted), audit scope (which locations, functions, or processes will be audited), and audit criteria (the standards, policies, or requirements against which it will be evaluated). Auditors must be objective and impartial, meaning they should not audit their own work or areas where they have direct responsibility.

Finally, the results of the audits must be communicated to relevant management for review and action. Additionally, as with ISO 27001, you must maintain documented information—evidence that your audit program is being followed and that audit results have been recorded, reviewed, and acted upon.

In short, Clause 9.2 ensures your ISMS remains healthy through regular, structured, and unbiased internal reviews—a self-check system that keeps your organization aware, aligned, and conforming to ISO 27001 requirements, while supporting continual improvement.

Explanation with Real-World Examples: Clause 9.2 is where your ISMS pauses to assess itself honestly—not based on assumptions, but through structured internal audits. Think of it as your organization's built-in health check that verifies whether your ISMS is working as intended, meeting both ISO 27001 and your internal requirements, and continues to improve over time.

Internal audits aren't just about checking boxes. They are guided by key principles outlined in ISO 19011 (Guidelines for auditing management systems)—integrity, fair presentation, professional care, confidentiality, independence, and an evidence-based approach. In simple terms, this means your audit process must be honest, factual, and unbiased.

When you conduct an internal audit, you're checking two main things:

1. Whether your ISMS conforms to what you've committed to in your own policies, objectives, and procedures—for example, your information security policy, control framework, or risk treatment plans.
2. Whether it conforms to the ISO 27001 standard itself—meaning your system meets the standard's structure and intent, not just its wording.

An audit program provides the big picture—indicating which areas will be audited, when, and by whom. It serves as your overall plan for ISMS audits over the course of a year (or more). In contrast, each audit plan concentrates on a single audit, specifying its scope, criteria, and schedule.

Audit criteria are the standards or rules you check against—for example, your own procedures, ISO clauses, or legal, regulatory, and contractual requirements. The auditor compares objective evidence (records, interviews, observations) to these criteria to determine conformance.

Internal audits often uncover nonconformities but also identify risks, opportunities, and areas for improvement. Nonconformities are addressed in your corrective action process (Clause 10.2), while risks and opportunities should be evaluated under Clauses 4.1 and 6.1.

In short, Clause 9.2 transforms your ISMS into a self-aware system—one that doesn't wait for an external auditor to identify weaknesses but regularly checks, questions, and improves itself from within.

And yes, ISO 27001 clearly requires that you retain documented evidence of both your audit program and your audit results. These records demonstrate that your internal audits were planned correctly, conducted, and reviewed.

Along with these mandatory records, it's also wise to keep supporting materials like audit plans, checklists, and lessons learned. The standard doesn't strictly require these, but they help you improve your approach over time—turning each audit into a chance to enhance your overall audit process continually.

Author's Note: Many people ask me, "How often should we conduct internal audits—every month, every quarter, or once a year?" The truth is, ISO 27001 doesn't specify a fixed frequency. It simply says you must plan your audit program based on your organization's context, risks, priorities, and previous audit results.

If frequent audits help your ISMS by catching issues early, building discipline, or adapting to rapid changes, then go for it. Conversely, if your operations are steady and risks are low, you can opt for fewer audits, as long as they're practical and well-planned. The main point is that your audit program should make sense for you.

The same flexibility applies to who conducts the audits. The standard doesn't require a full-time internal auditor. You can certainly appoint one if your organization is large enough. However, many organizations successfully assign the internal audit role as an additional duty—as long as there's no conflict of interest. The essential rule is simple: auditors must not audit their own work.

I've worked with organizations that adopt an innovative, collaborative approach—they train two or three employees from different departments as internal auditors. These qualified individuals then audit each other's areas, ensuring independence and new perspectives. Others prefer to outsource their internal audits to outside professionals like me. That way, they gain objectivity, expertise, and flexibility without maintaining a dedicated internal audit team.

Whichever approach you choose, the goal stays the same—to have a fair, factual, and value-adding internal audit process that keeps your ISMS strong, relevant, and continually improving.

Implementation Guidance: Let's keep this simple. Clause 9.2 is where you put on your "ISMS detective hat" to verify what's working and what you're conforming to. The standard clearly states that internal audits are conducted to determine whether the ISMS complies, so start with that mindset. Your goal isn't to hunt for mistakes; it's to confirm conformance and collect facts. If, while verifying conformance, you find something that doesn't meet a requirement, record a nonconformity and assist the team in fixing it. But don't turn the audit into a fault-finding mission. Audits that chase defects just for the sake of finding them don't strengthen the system; audits that verify conformance, identify gaps respectfully, and promote improvement do.

Step 1. Build a Risk-Based Audit Program: Start by designing your audit program with risk at the forefront. You're creating the master plan for the year (or cycle), but you're doing it by asking: where would a failure cause the most harm?

1. Decide what matters most
   - Identify processes or departments where a miss could cause real impact: sensitive data handling, customer-facing systems, high-availability services, regulatory hot spots.
   - Allocate more time and auditor attention there; cover lower-risk areas less frequently, but still within your cycle.

To simplify this concept, let me share how I explain it in class. I ask participants to imagine they have two children in school, and I've just moved into their city and offered to help them study in the evenings. Naturally, I ask, "Which child should I focus on first?" Usually, someone says, "The one who's weak in math or science." That's precisely how you decide your initial audit priorities—focus more on areas that have higher risks or weaknesses.

Now, 6 months later, let's say the weaker child has improved significantly, but the other one has fallen behind in a subject. What would you do? Every delegate immediately says, "Shift focus to the one struggling now." That's precisely what a good audit program does. You adjust your focus based on your audit results—spend more time on the processes or departments that performed poorly or showed weaknesses in the last audit.

That's how your audit program should develop: begin with high-risk areas; after the initial round, refocus based on audit findings and emerging risks.

2. Plan with care so audits help, not hinder
    - Schedule smartly to avoid peak periods (month-end finance, go-live windows, clinical rush hours).
    - Think about audit side effects: auditors in sterile rooms or prod environments can create their own risks. Plan to minimize disruption.
3. Set the structure clearly
   Your program should show:
    - What will be audited and when (clauses, processes, sites)
    - Who will audit (competent, independent auditors)
    - How you'll audit (interviews, sampling, observation, document review)
    - How findings, reports, and follow-ups will be handled
4. Right-size the detail
   Keep the plan proportionate to complexity and risk. A simple departmental audit needs a light plan; a multi-site or combined audit needs more structure.
5. Do a pre-flight check before you lock it in
    - Do we have the right mix of auditor competence and independence?
    - Are sampling methods appropriate and efficient?
    - Can we run this with minimal disruption to operations?
    - What's the risk of not achieving the audit objectives, and have we mitigated it?
6. Review and tune after each cycle
   After your first round, look at the results. Keep the focus on critical areas, and allocate more time to any department or process that performed poorly. Your program should evolve with your ISMS and your reality.

Bottom line: don't create a generic calendar; develop a risk-aware, dynamic audit program that concentrates where it counts, adapts to evidence, and continuously enhances your ISMS with each cycle.

Step 2. Define Audit Scope, Criteria, and Objectives: Before beginning any audit, take a moment to identify three essential elements: scope, criteria, and objectives. These keep your audit organized, fair, and relevant.

Audit Scope—Where You're Auditing: Think of the audit scope as your boundary line. It clearly defines where the audit will take place. Don't confuse this with your ISMS scope that you outlined earlier in Clause 4.3—that's the overall boundary of your management system. The audit scope might cover the entire ISMS or just a part of it.

For example:

- You may decide that in January, you'll audit only two departments—those two become your audit scope for that audit.
- Or, your audit scope could be one specific data center and all its operations. Even if your organization has multiple data centers, this audit would focus only on the one you've selected.
  Therefore, your audit scope could cover a single department, an entire building, a single location, or even a specific process spanning multiple teams. The key is—you decide the scope based on what you want to audit and why.

Audit Criteria—What You're Auditing Against: Your audit criteria are the requirements you'll compare your evidence against. In simple terms, these are the "rules of the game." Generally, audit criteria can include any of the following five areas:

1. Legal requirements (national or international laws relevant to your business context)
2. Regulatory requirements
3. Contractual requirements
4. ISO 27001 or any other standard requirements
5. Your own internal policies, procedures, and controls

For example, you might set your audit criteria as "all clauses of ISO 27001," or you could narrow it down to a specific clause—like Clause 7.2 (Competence)—depending on your focus.

Audit Objectives—Why You're Auditing: Your audit objective defines why you are conducting the audit and what you want to achieve.

It could be to:

- Verify whether controls are effective
- Check conformance against specific ISO clause requirements
- Assess whether policies and processes are being followed as intended
- Identify improvement opportunities or weaknesses

So, before any audit begins, ask yourself three simple questions:

1. ***Where am I auditing?*** → That's your *scope.*
2. ***What am I auditing against?*** → That's your *criteria.*
3. ***Why am I auditing?*** → That's your *objective.*

Once these three are clearly defined, your audit becomes targeted, efficient, and meaningful—not just a random checklist exercise, but also a purposeful review that strengthens your ISMS with each cycle.

Step 3. Select and Prepare the Right Audit Team: Now that you've planned what to audit and when, it's time to decide who will conduct the audit—and this is a crucial part of your internal audit program. The success of your audit relies heavily on the competence, objectivity, and preparation of your auditors.

Begin by identifying the skills necessary for each audit. Consider the knowledge or experience needed to achieve your audit goals within the defined scope. For example, auditing IT operations may require someone with a strong technical background, while auditing HR processes may require familiarity with privacy and access control practices.

When you form your audit team, make sure that collectively, the auditors have the right balance of knowledge, skill, and perspective. Here's how to do it:

1. **Identify the Competence Needed:** Define what kind of expertise the audit requires—technical, process-based, managerial, or domain-specific.
2. **Select Auditors Accordingly:** Choose auditors whose experience matches the audit's complexity and focus. The team should have:
   - Knowledge of ISO 27001 and ISMS requirements
   - Experience in auditing methods and techniques
   - Familiarity with your organization's operations and context
3. **Ensure Objectivity and Independence:** Auditors must be impartial—they should never audit their own work or areas over which they have direct responsibility. Independence maintains credibility and fairness.

4. **Balance the Team:** Consider factors such as audit scope, complexity, and method (onsite, remote, or hybrid). If the audit is highly technical, bring in a technical expert to support the auditors. Technical experts aren't auditors themselves, but they provide specialized insight to help the audit team understand complex systems, configurations, or processes.
5. **Adapt to Your Organization's Size**
    - If you're a small organization, train a few employees from different departments as internal auditors. Rotate them across audits so that no one reviews their own department.
    - If you have limited resources or want an external perspective, hire professional auditors or consultants to perform the audits. This ensures independence and brings in seasoned expertise.
6. **Mind the Practicalities:** Keep language, culture, and communication in mind—especially if audits span multiple regions or sites. A good auditor isn't just technically competent; they can communicate findings respectfully and clearly.
7. **Prepare and Brief the Team:** Before the audit begins, share the audit plan, scope, and objectives. If you're assigning an audit leader, they should coordinate responsibilities and ensure everyone understands their roles.

And remember—audit teams aren't fixed forever. If a conflict of interest or competence gap is found during the audit, modify the team accordingly. It's always better to make a change early than to compromise audit integrity.

In short, select auditors who are competent, objective, and curious—individuals who understand the system, ask the right questions, and can turn their findings into meaningful improvements. The right team doesn't just identify issues; they strengthen your ISMS with each audit.

Step 4. Plan the Audit: Now comes the exciting part—planning the audit. Think of this as mapping your route before you start driving. You already have your audit program—your yearly roadmap. Now, from that program, pick one upcoming audit and develop a detailed plan for it.

For example, if your audit program states that January is designated for the Data Centre audit, this is where the real work begins. You'll now create an audit plan specifically for that audit—detailing precisely what you'll review in the data center, who you'll meet, what you'll check, and when everything will take place.

A solid audit plan provides guidance, sets clear expectations, and ensures everyone is aligned. However, keep in mind—it's not set in stone. An effective audit plan is adaptable enough to change as the audit unfolds. You may find new areas to explore or realize you need more time in certain sections—and that's completely fine. Flexibility is a key part of good auditing.

Start with the basics. Your audit plan should clearly spell out:

- **Objectives:** What do you want to achieve? For example, are you checking control effectiveness, process conformity, or ISMS maturity?
- **Scope:** Which departments, sites, or processes are you auditing this time? Remember, audit scope isn't the same as your ISMS scope. You might focus only on your HR process this quarter or a specific data center next month.
- **Criteria:** What are you auditing against? This could be ISO 27001 requirements, your internal policies, legal or contractual obligations, or even customer-specific requirements.

- **Schedule and Locations:** When and where will the audit happen? Include physical and virtual sites, expected duration, and who needs to be available.
- **Timetable:** Create a detailed timetable for the audit day(s). For example, 9:00 a.m. opening meeting with the CISO, 10:00 a.m. site walkthrough, 11:00 a.m. documentation review, 12:00 p.m. meeting with ISMS Manager, and so on. If you have multiple auditors, make sure each auditor's time and assignments are included so everyone's efforts are coordinated and resources are fully utilized.
- **Audit Methods:** How will you gather evidence? Through interviews, observation, sampling, or record review?
- **Roles and Responsibilities:** Who's leading the audit, who's assisting, and who's the department contact person? Clarity avoids confusion later.
- **Resources and Logistics:** Identify logistical needs such as meeting rooms, projectors for presentations, internet access, or any special equipment. Make sure everything is ready before the audit day.
- **Observers or Trainee Auditors:** If you have observers or auditors-in-training attending, include them in your plan. Define their role so they can learn without disrupting the audit process.
- **Risks and Constraints:** Note any potential challenges, such as limited staff availability, security restrictions, or data confidentiality issues that might affect your audit.

Here's a little secret most new auditors overlook—effective audit planning relies as much on coordination as on expertise. Think about potential cultural or communication issues, especially if your audit involves teams from different departments or regions. If you're auditing a secure area like a data center, arrange access permissions beforehand—you don't want to waste your audit time waiting outside the gate.

Also, don't forget to review the results of past audits and any open nonconformities. These are your clues—they show where extra attention may be needed and help you track improvements over time.

Finally, always share your audit plan with the relevant department well in advance. No one likes a surprise audit (well, except the auditor sometimes). Sharing the plan fosters trust and ensures the team has the right people, documents, and records in place, leading to smoother discussions and more substantial evidence.

In short, your audit plan should inspire confidence—clear, practical, and adaptable. It's not about scripting every moment; it's about knowing your destination, understanding why you're going there, and being prepared to adjust if the path changes.

Step 5. Conduct the Audit: Now it's time to roll up your sleeves and get into the real action—this is where the audit happens. You've planned it, scheduled it, and now you're in the field (or on the screen) to see how things really work.

Stick to your audit plan, but stay flexible if something unexpected comes up. During the audit, your main goal is to collect objective, verifiable evidence—the kind that proves whether your ISMS is truly being implemented and working as intended.

You can use any or all of these three methods to collect evidence:

1. **Interview Key People:** Talk to employees, managers, or anyone responsible for ISMS processes. Ask open-ended questions, such as "How do you handle this?" rather than "Do you follow the procedure?" You'll often uncover how things really work, not just how they're supposed to.
2. **Review Relevant Documented Information:** Check policies, records, reports, and logs. But don't stop there. If someone shows you a document right away, set it aside for a

moment and ask, "Can you explain how this process works in practice?" That one question often reveals the real story.
3. **Observe the Process Yourself:** Watch people perform their tasks. Sometimes, what you see speaks louder than what's written down.

Remember, every piece of evidence you collect should be objective and verifiable. If you can't recheck it or trace it back later, it's not solid evidence.

Now, let's discuss sampling—because no auditor has the time or need to review every document or interview every employee. Sampling allows you to focus your efforts where they matter most. Use a consistent sampling method throughout the audit—whether it's random, judgmental, or risk-based—and apply it consistently.

Here's a small reminder I often share with my delegates: An audit isn't a destination; it's a journey. Don't rush to gather every document or check every box. Instead, follow the trail. If someone proudly hands you a procedure, accept it and thank them, but first ask: "Please walk me through how you actually do this." You'll often find out if that procedure is genuinely practiced or just well-documented.

Documentation is important, yes—but what truly matters is how people use it in everyday life. Today, anyone can download templates or ready-made toolkits from the Internet, but only those who understand and practice their processes daily make the system work.

Keep your audit fact-based, fair, and focused on reality. Remember, the goal isn't to catch people doing something wrong—it's to understand how the system works, confirm what's effective, and identify where it can improve.

Step 6. Record Findings and Prepare the Audit Report: Now that the audit is finished, it's time to bring everything together—the evidence you collected, the observations you made, and the insights you uncovered. This is where the evidence-based approach truly comes into play. Your work now becomes concrete: clear, factual, and useful audit findings grounded in what you actually saw, heard, and verified.

Start by evaluating all the evidence you collected against your audit criteria—the "rules of the game" you set in your audit plan. Every finding should be backed by verifiable evidence, not opinions or assumptions. Remember, good auditors don't just think something's wrong—they can prove it.

Your audit findings will usually fall into five categories:

- **Conformities:** Areas where things are working as they should. Always recognize what's being done well—it reinforces good practices and motivates people.
- **Good Practices:** Exceptional ideas, innovative methods, or controls worth sharing across departments.
- **Opportunities for Improvement (OFIs):** Areas that aren't nonconforming but could be done better or more efficiently.
- **Observations:** Matters noted during the audit that may warrant attention or monitoring. While they do not constitute a nonconformity at present, they may indicate a potential issue or weakness that could develop into a nonconformity if not addressed.
- **Nonconformities:** Where the requirements of ISO 27001, company policy, or other applicable criteria are not being met.

When documenting nonconformities, always include supporting evidence—what you observed, heard, or read. Nonconformities can also be graded based on their importance. Some organizations use minor and major categories, while others use a numerical scale (such as 1–5). Choose the method that works best for your situation, but stay consistent.

Before finalizing your findings, review them with the relevant department head or process owner. Make sure they understand the evidence, agree on the facts, and acknowledge the issue. This prevents confusion later and ensures everyone is on the same page about what actually happened. If there's a disagreement you can't resolve, state it clearly in your report—transparency is important.

Once findings are agreed upon, the audit team should meet to consolidate results and form *audit conclusions*. These should address questions such as:

- How well does the ISMS conform to the audit criteria?
- Are the ISMS processes and controls effective and achieving their intended outcomes?
- Is the management system being maintained and improved over time?
- Are there patterns or trends across different audits that need attention?

Now, let's talk about the *audit report*—your final product. It should be *clear, factual, and to the point*, providing a complete picture of what was audited, what was found, and what it means.

Your audit report should include:

- Audit objectives, scope, and criteria
- Dates, locations, and people involved
- A summary of audit methods used
- Key findings—conformities, good practices, observations, OFIs, and nonconformities
- Evidence supporting each finding
- Audit conclusions and overall evaluation of the ISMS
- Any unresolved issues or disagreements
- A note that audits are sampling exercises—evidence reviewed may not represent the entire system

If needed, you can also add:

- Obstacles faced during the audit
- Confirmation that audit objectives were achieved
- Areas that couldn't be covered and why
- Follow-up or action plan, if agreed
- A confidentiality statement, especially for sensitive findings

And don't forget about the logistics—submit the report within the agreed timeframe. If there's a delay, explain the reason. Once finalized, share the report with the relevant management and any other stakeholders listed in your audit program. Always treat audit reports as confidential documents.

Author's Note: An audit report isn't about pointing fingers or bragging about your findings. It's a snapshot of how the organization is doing—what's strong, what's weak, and where improvements can boost the system. Your audit report should tell a story—not a dramatic one, but an honest, helpful story of your ISMS. It should assist management in making informed choices, support ongoing improvement, and show that your organization is committed to getting better, not just achieving certification.

Step 7. Agree on Corrective Action and Follow Up: We've reached the final stretch—this is where your audit truly pays off. You've identified what works, spotted what doesn't, and now it's time to turn those findings into real improvements.

Every audit should conclude with a clear, mutually agreed-upon action plan. For each nonconformity or improvement opportunity, collaborate with the responsible department or process owner to develop a Corrective Action Plan.

Always agree on realistic timelines. Nothing hinders progress faster than a plan that appears perfect on paper but is impossible to execute in reality. Once all corrective actions are agreed upon, document them—along with their deadlines and responsible parties—so progress can be tracked and monitored.

Now comes the follow-up—the part most organizations forget (and auditors always check). Once corrective actions are implemented, an auditor must verify that they have been completed and are effective. Did the fix solve the problem, or just cover it up?

Verification can be done through:

- Reviewing updated documents or records
- Interviewing responsible staff
- Observing the new or revised process in action

If everything checks out, you can safely close the issue. If not, it remains open until the corrective action reaches its goal.

Remember, this isn't just paperwork—it's central to ongoing improvement. An unresolved issue today could turn into tomorrow's audit finding, so make sure to tie up loose ends.

Step 8. Keep Documented Evidence: ISO 27001 requires you to keep documented information as proof of your audit program and audit results. Additionally, it's beneficial to save your audit plans, checklists, notes, and lessons learned. These will help you improve your audit process and make it more effective each cycle.

Toolkit and Resources: Now that you know how to plan and carry out internal audits, it's time to apply that knowledge. This toolkit includes three ready-to-use templates: the Internal Audit Program, the Audit Plan, and the Audit Report.

These examples are here to guide you, not to be copied word-for-word. Every organization is different—your processes, structure, and risks will influence how your audit program looks. So, take these as a starting point, adapt them to your own context, and make them truly yours.

As you review each template, consider your organization's size, the type of data it manages, and its ISMS maturity level. The aim isn't to create perfect documents; it's to develop practical, useful tools that genuinely help you plan, execute, and enhance your internal audits.

Let's begin with Table 13.2, an example of an ISMS internal audit program. From there, we'll move on to a sample audit plan and a sample audit report. Together, these pieces show how the individual parts connect to form a complete, practical internal audit cycle—not as separate documents.

How to Use Table 13.2:

1. **Start with Your Risk Priorities:** Focus on processes that handle sensitive data or are essential for your business continuity.
2. **Spread Audits Logically:** Avoid bunching too many audits in one month—plan them evenly across the year.

Table 13.2 ISMS internal audit program template

Department/Process	*Jan*	*Feb*	*Mar*	*Apr*	*May*	*Jun*	*Jul*	*Aug*	*Sep*	*Oct*	*Nov*	*Dec*
1. Data Center Operations	✓						✓					
2. IT Infrastructure and Network Security		✓						✓				
3. Access Control and User Management			✓						✓			
4. Information Security Risk Assessment and Treatment				✓							✓	
5. HR and Employee Awareness			✓							✓		
6. Physical and Environmental Security				✓							✓	
7. Legal and Regulatory Compliance						✓						✓
8. Incident Management and Response					✓				✓			
9. Vendor and Third-Party Management								✓				
10. Asset Management	✓									✓		
11. Internal Audit Function Review												✓

3. **Use Follow-Ups Wisely:** Schedule short follow-up audits two or three months after high-risk or problematic areas.
4. **Keep Flexibility:** If a department undergoes significant changes, new risks, or incidents, adjust the program—it's not fixed in stone.
5. **Include a Final Review:** End the year with an internal audit process review—reflect on lessons learned and how to improve your next year's plan.

Sample Audit Plan

Table 13.3 provides a sample ISMS internal audit plan for ready reference. Use it as a guide to understand how an audit is planned in advance—what will be audited, when, by whom, and against which criteria. Adapt the structure to match your organization's size, scope, and audit approach.

Logistics and Support

Table 13.4 outlines the logistics and support arrangements for the audit. This section ensures everyone knows the practical details in advance—audit location, facilities, access requirements, and any support needed. Getting this right avoids last-minute confusion and helps the audit run smoothly and professionally.

Audit Plan Approval

Table 13.5 records who prepared and who approved the audit plan. This may look like a small detail, but it's an important one. It shows ownership, accountability, and formal authorization.

Sample Audit Report—ISO/IEC 27001:2022

Client: Kolkata Data Centre Pvt. Ltd.
Report Author: Dr. Swapan Purkait
Date of Report: 16th January 2025
Report Reference: KDC/INT/001/2025

Table 13.3 Sample ISMS internal audit plan

Ref. No.	*KDC/INT/001/2025*
Audit Plan Date	2nd January 2025
Audit Dates	14th–15th January 2025
Organization	Kolkata Data Centre Pvt. Ltd.
Registered Office	Ballygunge Circular Road, Kolkata 700019, West Bengal, India
Management Standard	ISO/IEC 27001:2022
Site Audited	Data Centre and Head Office, Ballygunge Circular Road, Kolkata
Audit Scope	The internal audit of the ISMS of Kolkata Data Centre Pvt. Ltd. covers data center operations, IT infrastructure management, network services, HR, finance, planning, and physical site security, including outsourced support services where applicable. The audit covers approximately 180 staff across the Kolkata facilities.
Audit Criteria	ISO/IEC 27001:2022; Kolkata Data Centre's ISMS Policies and Procedures; Legal, regulatory, and contractual requirements applicable to data center operations and client services.
Audit Objectives	1) Verify that the ISMS conforms to the organization's own requirements and to ISO/IEC 27001:2022. 2) Evaluate the effectiveness of implemented information security controls and related processes. 3) Assess readiness for certification audits.
Audit Team Leader	Dr. Swapan Purkait
Audit Team Member(s)	Mr. Bala Subramanian
Client Representative	Mr. Sabyasachi Sen, ISMS Manager
Audit Language	English
Opening Meeting (Date/Time)	14/01/2025—09:00 AM
Closing Meeting (Date/Time)	15/01/2025—04:30 PM

Date	*Time*	*Auditor*	*Area/ Process*	*Clause(s)*	*Auditor*	*Area/Process*	*Clause(s)*
14-Jan	09:00	Dr. Swapan Purkait	Opening Meeting	—	Bala Subramanian	Opening Meeting	—
	09:30	Dr. Swapan Purkait	Review of Context, Scope, and Interested Parties	4.1, 4.2, 4.3	Bala Subramanian	Legal and Regulatory Compliance	4.2, 4.3

	11:00	Dr. Swapan Purkait	Leadership and ISMS Objectives	5.1, 6.2	Bala Subramanian	Physical and Environmental Security	8.1, Annex A relevant controls
	12:15	Dr. Swapan Purkait	Documented Information Control	7.5	Bala Subramanian	Human Resource Security and Awareness	7.2, 7.3
	13:00	Working Lunch					
	14:00	Dr. Swapan Purkait	Risk Assessment and Treatment	6.1.2, 6.1.3	Bala Subramanian	Data Centre Operations	8.1, 8.2, 8.3
	16:30	Team Discussion/Interim Review					
15-Jan	09:00	Dr. Swapan Purkait	IT Infrastructure and Network Controls	Annex A: 5–8 (as applicable)	Bala Subramanian	Access Control and User Management	Annex A: 5–8 (as applicable)
	11:00	Dr. Swapan Purkait	Monitoring, Measurement & Evaluation	9.1	Bala Subramanian	Internal Audit Process	9.2
	11:45	Dr. Swapan Purkait	Incident Reporting and Corrective Action	10.2	Bala Subramanian	Management Review	9.3
	13:00	Working Lunch					
	14:00	Joint	Continual Improvement Activities	10.1	Joint	Review of Outstanding Nonconformities	—
	15:30	Team Meeting	—	—	—	—	—
	16:30	Closing Meeting	—	—	—	—	—

Table 13.4 Audit logistics and support details

Requirement	*Details*
Meeting Room	Conference Room—Data Centre, 3rd Floor
Presentation Equipment	Projector, screen, internet access
Special Notes	Pre-arrange access to secure areas and systems; ensure all relevant records are available per schedule.

Table 13.5 Audit plan preparation and approval record

Prepared by	*Dr. Swapan Purkait*	*Approved by*	*Mr. Sabyasachi Sen*
Date	5th January 2025	Date	5th January 2025
Signature		Signature	

1. Introduction

We want to extend our sincere thanks to all participants at Kolkata Data Centre Pvt. Ltd. for their cooperation and support during the internal audit. Their timely assistance and open communication helped the audit run efficiently and on schedule.

This report summarizes the internal audit conducted as part of Kolkata Data Centre's ISMS in accordance with ISO/IEC 27001:2022.

Table 13.6 captures the essential background of the audit—the reference, type, duration, dates, scope, and locations covered. This information sets the context for everything that follows in the audit report. It helps readers, management, and auditors quickly understand what was audited, where, and under which standard, before diving into findings and conclusions.

Table 13.6 Audit overview and scope details

Visit Ref/Type/Duration	*KDC/INT/001/2025/Internal Audit/2 Days*
Audit Dates	14th–15th January 2025
Number of Employees Covered	Approximately 180
Audit Standard	ISO/IEC 27001:2022
Site Audited	Data Centre and Head Office
Registered Office	Ballygunge Circular Road, Kolkata 700019, India

2. Audit Objective

The objective of this audit was to:

- Verify that the ISMS conforms to the organization's own requirements and to ISO/IEC 27001:2022.
- Evaluate the effectiveness of implemented information security controls and related processes.
- Assess readiness for certification audits.

3. Audit Scope

The internal audit of the ISMS of Kolkata Data Centre Pvt. Ltd. covers data center operations, IT infrastructure management, network services, HR, finance, planning, and physical site security, including outsourced support services where applicable. The audit covers approximately 180 staff across the Kolkata facilities.

4. Audit Criteria

- ISO/IEC 27001:2022;
- Kolkata Data Centre's ISMS Policies and Procedures;
- legal, regulatory, and contractual requirements applicable to data center operations and client services.

5. Audit Team

Table 13.7 lists the members of the audit team and their respective roles. This confirms who conducted the audit and in what capacity, and it provides transparency around auditor competence and independence—something both management and external auditors will expect to see in a well-prepared audit report.

Table 13.7 Audit team composition and roles

Name	*Role*
Dr. Swapan Purkait	Lead Auditor
Mr. Bala Subramanian	Auditor

6. Audit Participants (on behalf of Kolkata Data Centre Pvt. Ltd.)

Table 13.8 records the key auditee participants who took part in the audit. This shows who represented the organization during interviews, walkthroughs, and evidence reviews. Including this information adds transparency and helps demonstrate that the audit involved the right roles and process owners across the ISMS scope.

Table 13.8 List of auditee participants involved in the audit

Name	*Position*
Mr. Sabyasachi Sen	ISMS Manager
Ms. Rupa Das	HR Manager
Mr. Arindam Ghosh	IT and Network Manager
Mr. Aniket Roy	Operations Manager
Mr. Sujit Paul	Finance Manager
Ms. Tanima Dutta	Data Centre Security Lead
Mr. Abhijit Mitra	Compliance Officer

7. Audit Summary

The audit was conducted in accordance with the approved audit plan (Ref: KDC/INT/001/2025). The team used a combination of interviews, document reviews, and process observations to gather objective evidence. Sampling methods were used to verify implementation across departments and sites.

8. Conformities

Kolkata Data Centre Pvt. Ltd. has demonstrated a strong commitment to implementing and maintaining its ISMS. The following strengths were noted:

- Comprehensive ISMS documentation aligned with ISO/IEC 27001:2022.
- Top management commitment is evident through defined objectives, policies, and periodic management reviews.
- Structured processes for access control, incident management, and change management.
- Regular awareness sessions for employees and contractors.

9. Nonconformities

Table 13.9 provides a sample nonconformity report from the audit. It shows how audit findings are formally recorded, including the requirement reference, objective evidence, and classification.

Table 13.9 Sample nonconformity report from an ISMS audit

NONCONFORMITY REPORT Incident Number: *NC01*

Area under Review: ISMS Documentation **ISO/IEC 27001:2022 Clause:** 5.2
Category: () MAJOR (✓) MINOR
Description of the nonconformity: During the ISMS documentation review, it was observed that the organization's Information Security Policy does not include a stated commitment to continual improvement as required by ISO/IEC 27001:2022.
Evidence: Organization's Information Security Policy, v.2, dated 21st January 2025
Requirements: ISO/IEC 27001:2022 Clause: 5.2 Top management shall establish an information security policy that: d) includes a commitment to continual improvement of the information security management system.
Auditor: Dr. Swapan Purkait **Auditee:** ISMS Manager

10. Observations and OFIs

Table 13.10 captures observations and OFIs identified during the audit. These are not nonconformities, but areas where processes can be strengthened, clarified, or made more effective to improve the overall performance of the ISMS.

Table 13.10 Sample observations and opportunities for improvement (OFI) report

Ref.	*Area*	*Observation/Opportunity for Improvement*
OFI-001	HR Security	Awareness training sessions can include scenario-based exercises for better employee engagement.
OFI-002	Incident Response	The incident log format can include response time and closure verification for better tracking.

11. Audit Conclusion

The audit confirmed that Kolkata Data Centre Pvt. Ltd. has effectively implemented its ISMS in line with ISO/IEC 27001:2022. However, particular areas require attention to ensure full conformity and continual improvement.

Given the identified nonconformities, it is recommended that corrective actions be planned and implemented within the agreed timelines. Verification of effectiveness should be carried out during the next internal audit or, if applicable, earlier.

12. Corrective Action Plan and Follow-Up

The ISMS Manager is requested to:

1. Submit a corrective action plan addressing all nonconformities by 31st January 2025.
2. Include root cause analysis, proposed actions, responsibilities, and target dates.

A follow-up verification audit will be conducted approximately 21 days after submission of the corrective action plan.

Table 13.11 documents the preparation, review, and approval of the audit report, ensuring accountability and formal sign-off of audit results.

Table 13.11 Audit report preparation and approval record

Prepared by	*Reviewed and Approved by*
Dr. Swapan Purkait Lead Auditor Date: 16th January 2025	Mr. Sabyasachi Sen, ISMS Manager Client Representative Date: 17th January 2025

🛠 *Implementation Task #22: Audit Program*

Alright, it's your turn now. Take a moment, grab your notebook (or open a spreadsheet), and begin constructing your Internal Audit Program.

This is where you plan when and what you'll audit throughout the year. Think of it as your audit roadmap—it keeps you organized, focused, and ensures you're not leaving any part of your ISMS unchecked for too long.

When creating your audit program, keep these points in mind:

1. **Start with a Risk-Based Approach:** Ask yourself: Which processes or departments carry the highest risks? Which ones could cause the most significant impact if something went wrong? These are the ones that deserve your early or more frequent attention.
2. **Consider Importance and Business Impact:** Some processes, even if not high-risk, might be mission-critical for your organization—like HR, finance, or IT operations. Include them in your program and decide how often they should be reviewed.
3. **Look Back Before You Move Forward:** If you've conducted audits before, revisit those results. Departments or processes that had significant or recurring findings last time should get more focus in this cycle.

4. **Spread It Out Wisely:** Don't overload one month. Spread your audits evenly across the year so that they're manageable and productive.
5. **Stay Flexible:** Remember, an audit program isn't carved in stone. You can constantly adjust it if priorities shift, new risks emerge, or significant changes occur.

Use the example template in the toolkit as your guide—but make it your own. Replace the sample departments and processes with those from your organization, adjust the months, and create a schedule that suits your needs.

The goal isn't perfection; it's practicality. Build something you can use. Once finished, you'll have your first Audit Program—a living plan that keeps your ISMS healthy, active, and continually improving.

CLAUSE 9.3 MANAGEMENT REVIEW

Summary of the Clause Requirements: Clause 9.3 is where top management gets involved to see the bigger picture. It requires your organization's leadership to review the ISMS at scheduled intervals—not just to tick a box, but to make sure the system stays suitable, adequate, and effective as your business and risks evolve.

In simple terms, management review is the ISMS "boardroom health check." It's about stepping back, assessing everything that's been done, and asking: Is our ISMS still functioning as intended? Are we making progress? Are we aligned with our goals and risks?

Here's what ISO 27001 expects you to cover in a management review:

1. **Status of Previous Actions:** Review whether the actions decided in the last management review have been completed and if they have achieved their purpose.
2. **Changes in Context:** Consider any new internal or external issues that could affect your ISMS, such as new regulations, technologies, mergers, or business changes.
3. **Interested Parties:** Check if the needs or expectations of customers, regulators, or partners have changed since the last review.
4. **Performance Feedback:** Look at key data and trends, including:
    a. Nonconformities and corrective actions
    b. Monitoring and measurement results
    c. Internal audit findings
    d. Achievement of information security objectives
5. **Feedback from Stakeholders:** Review inputs from employees, customers, or suppliers related to information security.
6. **Risk Management Results:** Evaluate the latest risk assessment results and see if the risk treatment plan is effective and up to date.
7. **Continual Improvement Opportunities:** Identify areas where the ISMS can be enhanced.

Finally, management reviews should result in concrete decisions—not just discussions. These decisions may involve actions such as improving, allocating resources, updating policies, or modifying the ISMS itself.

And yes, as with everything in ISO 27001, documented evidence of the management review results must be kept. This record not only proves that the review occurred but also shows that leadership is actively involved in the ISMS and promoting continual improvement.

Explanation with Real-World Examples: The management review is the point where your ISMS comes full circle. Think of it as a strategic pause—the moment when top management steps back, reviews the dashboard, and determines whether the ISMS is still heading in the right direction.

The goal is simple: to make sure your ISMS remains suitable, adequate, and effective.

- ***Suitable*** means your ISMS still aligns with your business goals and direction. For example, if your organization began offering cloud-based services this year, your ISMS must adapt to address new risks, compliance requirements, and customer expectations.
- ***Adequate*** means your ISMS is designed well—it covers what it should and has enough resources, roles, and structure to function correctly.
- ***Effective*** means it's not just existing on paper—it's working in practice and achieving its intended results.

In most organizations, management review doesn't occur only once a year in a boardroom. It's an ongoing activity that can happen through team meetings, department reviews, or operational discussions. The key is that top management takes ownership—they're the ones who ultimately ensure the ISMS stays strong and relevant.

Let's clear up a common misunderstanding right away—ISO 27001 doesn't specify how often you must conduct a management review. There's no hidden rule that says it has to be once a year, twice a year, or quarterly. The standard states that it should be done at planned intervals.

Now, the phrase "planned intervals" is essential. It means you choose the timing, but you need to be able to justify it.

So, if you say, "We'll conduct our management review once a year," that's perfectly fine—but be prepared to explain why once a year makes sense for your organization. Maybe your business environment is stable, or your operations don't change much. In that case, once a year could be reasonable.

But what if your organization is expanding rapidly, adopting new technologies, or regularly undergoing customer audits? In that case, you might need to do it twice a year—or even quarterly—to stay on top of changes.

The main point is that there's no universal answer. How often you review depends on your organization's situation, rate of change, and the risks involved. Just ensure your review is intentional, well-planned, and documented.

And here's something many organizations overlook—management review is not just an ISMS team meeting. It's not a task you delegate to your ISMS Manager or department heads. ISO 27001 clearly states that top management must lead the management review. Why? Because leadership sets the direction for the system. When top management actively participates, reviews performance, and allocates resources, the ISMS becomes stronger, smarter, and more aligned with business goals.

💬 **Author's Note:** I've seen organizations transform their ISMS simply because top management took the time to review it regularly. When leadership begins asking questions, showing interest, and providing direction, the system improves much like a well-tuned engine. However, I've also observed the opposite—companies where management thinks, "Oh, that's the IT team's problem." In those cases, the ISMS gradually loses its way. Controls weaken, enthusiasm diminishes, audits become more difficult, and eventually, the certificate disappears.

So, my advice is straightforward—don't treat management review as a mere formality. Consider it as your ISMS's steering wheel. The more frequently leadership conducts it, the smoother and more secure your information security journey will be.

Implementation Guidance: Management review isn't just a scheduled event; it's an ongoing process where top management actively assesses how well the ISMS is performing and whether it continues to align with the organization's goals and context. It provides a structured way for leadership to stay informed, evaluate performance, and guide continual improvement.

Top management should regularly review reports, measurements, updates, or summaries of ISMS performance. This can be done in many ways—through reports, dashboards, electronic communication, or periodic updates—as long as it helps leadership clearly understand how the system is functioning.

Think of management review as your organization's control center for information security—a process where evidence and insights flow upward, and decisions, directions, and improvements flow back down. It keeps the ISMS aligned, effective, and evolving with your business.

Step 1. Decide the Format and Frequency of Management Review: Here's an important point—management review doesn't have to be a meeting. Over time, many organizations have turned it into a formal session with minutes, attendance sheets, and presentations because that's what auditors often request. However, if you look closely, the ISO 27001 standard never states it must be a "meeting." What it truly requires is that top management reviews the ISMS at planned intervals—the method is up to you.

You can design your management review process in any format that aligns with your organization's culture and operations. For example, some organizations have an online portal where department heads regularly upload reports—covering performance, risks, incidents, and improvements. Top management can log in anytime, review updates, comment on findings, ask for clarification, and record decisions or action items directly on the portal. Others prefer structured monthly or quarterly summaries shared via email or dashboards that highlight key metrics.

What matters is that your chosen method ensures two things:

1. Top management is actively reviewing ISMS performance.
2. There's clear evidence of decisions and follow-up actions.

Now, about the frequency—ISO 27001 doesn't specify how often you must do this. The standard states it should occur at planned intervals, and you need to be able to explain why you selected that interval.

- For a newly implemented ISMS, quarterly reviews might be more effective.
- For a stable, mature ISMS, once or twice a year may be sufficient.

The key is to make it meaningful, not mechanical. Whether your review takes place in a meeting, through a portal, or via an automated dashboard, it should serve its true purpose: keeping your ISMS alive, aligned, and improving.

Author's Note: If your organization is preparing for ISO 27001 certification, keep this in mind. Certification bodies perform annual surveillance audits and expect evidence that your ISMS has completed a full cycle—covering Clauses 4–10—within that year.

This means they will look for proof that you've performed both an internal audit and a management review at least once a year. Although the standard doesn't explicitly state "once a year," in practice, this has become the minimum expectation for certified organizations.

So, even if your internal rhythm is comfortable with longer intervals, remember that certification auditors will want to see that your ISMS has been actively reviewed and updated within the past 12 months. Doing so not only keeps you compliant but also ensures your management system remains sharp and responsive to change.

Step 2. Gather Inputs and Prepare the Review Agenda: This is the core of your management review process—gathering the right inputs and organizing them so top management can make meaningful, evidence-based decisions. ISO 27001 Clause 9.3.2 clearly states what must be included in every management review, and omitting any of these items can easily lead to a nonconformity during an audit.

Your management review must include consideration of the following:

1. Status of actions from previous management reviews.
2. Changes in external and internal issues relevant to the ISMS.
3. Changes in the needs and expectations of interested parties.
4. Feedback on information security performance, including trends in:
   a. Nonconformities and corrective actions.
   b. Monitoring and measurement results.
   c. Audit results.
   d. Fulfillment of information security objectives.
5. Feedback from interested parties.
6. Results of risk assessment and the status of the risk treatment plan.
7. Opportunities for continual improvement.

These are the basic requirements. You're always welcome to add other relevant topics for your organization—such as major project updates, emerging threats, or resource constraints. The aim is to make the review meaningful and aligned with your business reality, not just a box-checking task.

Once you've gathered all the inputs, organize them into a simple, structured format—often called a management review pack. This can include reports, dashboards, summaries, or key metrics that help leadership understand the current state of your ISMS without getting lost in details.

Now, ensure your top management—not just ISMS or departmental heads—participates in the review process. ISO 27001 clearly states that top management must review the ISMS, so their active involvement is essential. If you're using a digital platform or portal, upload the agenda and reports there so leaders can review them at their convenience and comment directly. If you prefer to circulate the agenda beforehand, that works too—make sure they have enough time to review the material and come prepared.

Remember—a well-prepared and clearly communicated agenda is key to keeping the management review process running smoothly. It helps leadership stay informed, engaged, and ready to make decisions that strengthen your ISMS, not just review it on paper.

Step 3. Conduct and Record the Results of the Management Review: Now comes the most critical part—conducting the management review and documenting its results. Remember, this is not about flashy slides or colorful presentations. I've seen many management reviews where the ISMS manager presents a polished PowerPoint, and everyone politely listens—but there's no discussion, no questioning, and no genuine input from top management. That's not a review; that's just a presentation.

A proper management review is an ongoing process of evaluation and decision-making. It's where top management thoroughly reviews the ISMS performance, analyzes the data, and determines the next steps.

You can conduct your management review in multiple stages or formats—there's no need for it to be just one meeting. For instance, you might review risk results in one session, audit outcomes in another, and monitor performance trends through your dashboard over time. As long as you address all the required inputs from Clause 9.3.2 and make clear, documented decisions, you've fulfilled the standard's intent.

Here's how to make the process effective and meaningful:

1. **Review All the Inputs with Your Top Management:** Go through each input—previous actions, context changes, risk assessments, performance data, and feedback—and discuss what they mean for your organization. Don't rush. The value lies in understanding the trends, not just listing the numbers.
2. **Encourage Honest Discussion and Challenge:** Ask questions like: Are our controls still effective? Are residual risks acceptable? Do we have enough resources? Where are we struggling? Let your leadership reflect, question, and recommend improvements.
3. **Make Decisions, Not Just Observations:** The outcome of your review must include clear decisions related to:
   - Opportunities for continual improvement.
   - Changes required in ISMS scope, policies, or objectives.
   - Updates to risk assessment or risk treatment plans.
   - Adjustments in resources, budgets, or responsibilities.
   - Actions to enhance monitoring, measurement, or communication.
4. **Record Everything—Decisions, Evidence, and Actions:** ISO 27001 requires documented evidence of management review results. This doesn't mean long reports; even concise records that show what was reviewed, what was decided, and who's responsible for each action are perfectly fine. The key is traceability.
5. **Communicate and Follow Through:** Once your management review results are finalized and approved, share them with the relevant people responsible for implementation. Make sure action plans are tracked, progress is monitored, and updates are reflected in your next review cycle.

Think of this step as closing the loop—you've looked back to assess, and now you're looking ahead to improve. A management review that results in clear, actionable decisions is one of the strongest signs of a mature, well-functioning ISMS.

■ **Toolkit and Resources:** The following template is a practical example you can use to record and document your management review process. You are free to use it as is or customize it to fit your organization's structure and style. The key is to ensure your review covers all the required inputs and outputs listed in ISO 27001, Clause 9.3. These include everything from reviewing previous actions and risk assessments to recording improvement decisions and resource needs.

Whether you conduct your management review through meetings, online collaboration, or a mix of both, this template will help you structure the process, capture key discussions, and document evidence of the review effectively. Remember—the goal isn't to fill out forms; it's to ensure your ISMS remains suitable, adequate, and effective in supporting your business goals.

Management Review Report template

The purpose of this review is to ensure the continued suitability, adequacy, and effectiveness of ISMS.

Table 13.12 Management review report template for the ISMS

Date:		
Reference number:		
List of Attendees:		
Sr.	Name of the Attendee	Job title
Agenda		Comments / Actions item
The status of actions from previous management reviews		
Changes in external and internal issues that are relevant to the ISMS		
Any requirement for variations or changes to the scope of the ISMS		
Requirement for any modification of procedures and controls to respond to internal or external issues that may impact the ISMS		
How the effectiveness of controls will be measured;		
Information on ISMS performance, including trends in: • nonconformities and corrective actions; • monitoring and measurement evaluation results; • audit results;		
The need for changes to the ISMS, including the policy and objectives;		
Procedures and resources that could be used in the organization to improve the ISMS's performance and effectiveness		
Information from the risk assessment and risk treatment results		
Output from the evaluation of information security documentation and capabilities		
Risks or issues not adequately addressed in any previous risk assessment		
Opportunities for continual improvement		
Customer satisfaction survey results and other feedback from customers and interested parties		
Adherence to and suitability of the ISMS policy and other policies and procedures required by ISMS		
Performance of the ISMS against the set policy, plan, and objectives		
Post-implementation reviews of changes that can affect the ISMS		
Any other item related to ISMS as deemed fit.		

The above minutes of the ISMS Management Review held on the date mentioned above are confirmed as a true and accurate representation of the discussion and decisions made by those in attendance (Table 13.12). The information detailed in this report relates to the management review of the ISMS, which was undertaken objectively in accordance with approved company procedures. The action item in this report and the activities discussed during the management review remain confidential to the company. Further, the actions referenced above shall be undertaken in accordance with the ISMS Policies and Procedures and the requirements of ISO/IEC 27001:2022.

Approval of the Report

Table 13.13 Management review report approval and sign-off record

Role	*Name*	*Title*	*Date*	*Signature*
Prepared by				
Reviewed by				
Approved by				

Table 13.13 records the formal approval and sign-off of the ISMS Management Review Report by authorized management, confirming acceptance of the conclusions, decisions, and action items arising from the review.

Key Takeaways—What You've Learned

- Clause 9 is the "Check" phase—stop, look, and learn: assess whether your ISMS is achieving what you planned.
- Decide what to monitor and measure, how to measure it, when to do it, and how results will be analyzed.
- Focus on valid, comparable, and reproducible methods—consistency outweighs quantity. A few good metrics are better than a mountain of useless data.
- Measure two aspects: performance (are we doing the work?) and effectiveness (is the work making a difference?).
- Keep documented evidence of results—logs, reports, dashboards—so decisions are based on proof, not opinions.
- Use a risk-based mindset for monitoring: higher-risk areas need closer, more frequent attention.
- Internal audits are honest self-checks. Plan audits, keep them objective and impartial, report results, and use findings to improve—not to catch faults.
- The audit program should be risk-aware, regularly reviewed, and adjusted based on previous findings and changing circumstances.
- Select competent auditors and involve technical experts when needed; auditors must not audit their own work.
- Keep documented evidence of the audit program and audit results.
- Management review is leadership's opportunity to evaluate ISMS suitability, adequacy, and effectiveness—it must be planned, evidence-based, and lead to decisions.
- Management review inputs must include previous actions, changes in context, interested-party needs, performance trends, audit results, risk assessments and treatment status, and OFIs.
- Document management review outputs (decisions, resource needs, changes to policy/objectives, and actions) and follow up accordingly.

QUIZ #12

True/False statement

Sr.	*Statement*	*True/False*
1	Clause 9.1 requires you to decide what needs to be monitored and measured.	
2	Methods for monitoring and measurement should produce comparable and reproducible results.	
3	ISO 27001 prescribes exact frequencies (e.g., monthly) for monitoring activities.	
4	The organization must record documented information as evidence of monitoring and measurement results.	
5	Monitoring is limited only to technical controls (systems and networks).	
6	Internal audits are intended to check both conformance and effectiveness of the ISMS.	
7	Auditors can audit their own work as long as they are experienced.	
8	The internal audit program must consider the importance of processes and previous audit results when scheduling audits.	
9	Nonconformities identified during internal audits are not relevant to the management review.	
10	Management review must include consideration of the status of actions from previous management reviews.	
11	Management review frequency is fixed by ISO 27001 (one per year).	
12	Management review outputs can include changes to ISMS policy, resources, and risk acceptance criteria.	
13	ISO/IEC 27004 provides guidance on monitoring and measurement for ISO 27001.	
14	Top management can delegate the responsibility for conducting the management review to the ISMS Manager or department heads.	
15	The management review must be conducted as a formal meeting with minutes and attendance sheets.	

CASE 7: WHEELS, AUDITS, AND WAKE-UP CALLS—KIGALI

Kigali BodaShare had become a well-known name throughout Rwanda. Their mobile bike-sharing app connected riders and customers with just a tap. Fast, affordable, and proudly local, they promoted themselves as "Mobility for Everyone."

The company received ISO 27001 certification four years ago and has maintained a consistent routine since then. Every October, without fail, each department is audited once. Finance, HR, Operations, Customer Support, IT, and Procurement—one audit for each department annually, checked off like items on a checklist.

Internal audits were carried out by employees trained when the system was first put into place. Most of them now lead major projects, so they often squeezed audit time between product releases, sprint reviews, and meetings with investors. Departments often joked: "If it's audit season, bring coffee—because the auditor is already tired before they arrive."

Audit reports from the past three years showed a consistent pattern: most nonconformities originated from the Application Development Team. Issues such as:

- Insufficient monitoring of log activities
- Delayed control review cycles
- Inconsistent tracking of secure coding practices

However, the audit program remained the same. Each department was audited once a year—no more, no less.

Things changed when a new ISMS Manager, Jean-Luc Munyaneza, joined the company.

Jean-Luc had previously worked at a telecom company in Nairobi, where internal audits were dynamic, risk-focused, and adaptable. When he reviewed BodaShare's audit history, one question immediately came to mind:

"If one area consistently shows more issues, why are we auditing everything at the same frequency?"

During his first audit review meeting, he spoke calmly:

"Internal audit exists to help us understand effectiveness—not just compliance. We're not just checking if controls exist; we're checking if they work."

The room went quiet—not defensive, just reflective.

Jean-Luc proposed adjustments:

- Increase audit frequency for the Application Development Team based on audit results.
- Rotate audit themes (e.g., incident response, secure development, supplier management).
- Use cross-functional auditors to boost independence and minimize blind spots.
- Provide additional training so more employees can audit objectively and confidently.

At first, there were puzzled looks. One developer asked, "Are we being punished?"

Jean-Luc shook his head softly and said:

> "Not at all. This isn't about blame. ISO 27001 requires us to adjust audit frequency when previous results reveal ongoing gaps. Since the development team is crucial to our business success, improving this area isn't a punishment. It's where better controls will have the most positive impact."

He also rephrased messaging about the audit program. During a team meeting, he said, "Audit shouldn't feel like a search for mistakes. It should help us answer a simple question: Is our ISMS truly working as intended?"

Reactions gradually softened. A senior auditor from the HR team said, "It feels more purposeful this way."

Before finalizing the new audit program, Jean-Luc shared a chart outlining risks, control maturity, and audit frequency. The team could clearly see why certain areas needed more attention than others.

When the updated program was approved, it didn't feel like a disruption—it felt like evolution.

Audit season arrived again—but this time, something was different.

People were prepared because they understood why.

Departments asked more thoughtful questions.

The Application Development Team even requested a pre-audit briefing.

And when the first new-cycle audit was completed, the feedback wasn't nervous or defensive. It was hopeful.

Because now, the audit wasn't just a routine.

It was a tool.

Case Discussion—Test Your Understanding

1. Which statement best reflects Jean-Luc's approach to redesigning the audit program?

A. All departments must be audited only once a year.
B. The audit program should remain fixed for consistency.
C. Audit frequency should reflect the importance of the process, and past audit results.
D. Only top management should decide audit frequency.

2. Why was the Application Development Team prioritized in the revised audit plan?

A. Because they requested fewer audits.
B. Because previous audit results showed repeated nonconformities.
C. Because they were a new department.
D. Because auditing them less was more efficient.

3. Which statement best aligns with ISO 27001 requirements for internal auditor competence and independence?

A. Only IT staff should perform all audits.
B. Auditors must always audit their own department.
C. External auditors must conduct every internal audit.
D. Using trained auditors from functions independent of the area being audited helps maintain objectivity and impartiality.

4. Which purpose of internal audits did Jean-Luc emphasize?

A. To identify errors and assign blame
B. To verify if controls are effective and aligned with ISMS requirements
C. To eliminate documentation altogether
D. To reduce operational workloads during the year

5. Which element should the audit program include under ISO 27001?

A. Audit scope, criteria, methods, frequency, and schedule
B. A list of public holidays
C. Only names of IT staff
D. Policies without evidence requirements

6. What improvement action aligns with ISO expectations after repeated NC findings?

A. Continue auditing in the same cycle without changes
B. Increase audit focus in areas with higher risk or repeated nonconformities
C. Eliminate the audit requirement
D. Only report the findings without corrective action

Chapter 14

Clause 10—Get better, stay better

Handling nonconformities, corrective actions, and continual improvement

Welcome to the Improvement clause, the Act phase of your ISO 27001 journey. By the time you reach this point, you have already built your ISMS (Clauses 4–7), operated it in practice (Clause 8), and evaluated its performance (Clause 9). Clause 10 is where all of that learning comes together. This is the stage where you act on what you have discovered, strengthening your ISMS, correcting weaknesses, and making it more resilient, responsive, and effective over time.

This phase ensures that your ISMS does not remain static. Instead, it evolves with your organization, adapts to change, and grows stronger through structured improvement and learning.

This clause reminds us that no system—no matter how mature—is ever "done." Threats evolve, technology changes, people move, and businesses grow. Your ISMS must evolve with them. Clause 10 ensures that your organization not only maintains compliance but also continually enhances its ability to protect information, adapt to change, and recover from setbacks.

Improvement in ISO 27001 isn't just about fixing what went wrong—it's about identifying opportunities to enhance performance. It's where you turn nonconformities into insights, incidents into lessons, and feedback into action. Think of it as the pulse that keeps your ISMS active and adaptable.

So yes, Clause 10 may be the final clause of the standard, but in essence, it marks the start of your next cycle—the fuel that keeps your ISMS moving forward, one improvement at a time.

CLAUSE 10.1 CONTINUAL IMPROVEMENT

Summary of the Clause Requirements: Clause 10.1 might seem deceptively brief—just one sentence in the ISO 27001 standard—but don't be misled by its simplicity. That single line conveys one of the most powerful messages in the entire ISMS framework: your organization must continually improve the suitability, adequacy, and effectiveness of its information security management system (ISMS).

But here's the thing—continual improvement (CI) isn't a once-a-year event or something you do after audit season. It's not a "final step" in your ISMS journey; it's a mindset that should permeate every stage of your management system. Clause 10.1 gives it a name and a place, but the idea of CI has been quietly guiding your ISMS from the very beginning.

In fact, the ISO 27001 standard has been addressing CI since Clause 4, integrating it into various requirements throughout. Let's take a quick look at where else it appears:

DOI: 10.1201/9781003744139-15

- **Clause 4.4:** When you first establish your ISMS, you're asked to establish, implement, maintain, and continually improve it. Improvement begins here, not at the end.
- **Clause 5.1 (g):** Top management must promote CI, showing leadership through example.
- **Clause 5.2 (d):** Your information security policy must include a commitment to CI.
- **Clause 6.1.1 (c):** When planning your ISMS, you're asked to address risks and opportunities that help achieve CI.
- **Clause 7.1:** You must provide resources for CI — because improvement requires investment, not just intent.
- **Clause 7.3 (b):** People working under your control should understand how their actions contribute to CI.
- **Clause 9.3.2 (g):** Management reviews must include opportunities for CI.
- **Clause 9.3.3:** Management review results must lead to decisions that drive CI.

So while Clause 10.1 shines the spotlight on CI, it's really been part of your ISMS story all along—quietly pushing you to learn, adapt, and evolve.

In short, CI isn't a destination you reach at Clause 10—it's the journey you've been on since Clause 4. It's the thread that ties your entire ISMS together, ensuring it never stands still, never grows stale, and always keeps getting better.

Explanation with Real-World Examples: Let's be honest—no ISMS ever reaches a point where you can say, "We're done." Business environments change, technology evolves, people move, and new threats emerge every day. Clause 10.1 reminds us that your ISMS must keep evolving.

Continual improvement is more than just a statement—it's a culture. It begins with leadership, influences every policy and process, and ultimately shapes how people think and act throughout the organization.

When top management demonstrates genuine commitment to CI, it sets the tone for everyone else. It's not enough to say "we believe in improvement"; leadership must provide resources, recognize contributions, and reward progress. The ISMS policy itself should explicitly include a commitment to continual improvement. This way, improvement isn't just an expectation—it's a firm promise to customers, employees, and regulators.

And let's not forget the people. Everyone in the organization should understand how their work contributes to the ISMS and how small improvements in their area can make a significant impact on overall security. When staff members see that better performance is appreciated—and that their ideas for improvement are encouraged—they naturally become more engaged and proactive.

Think of CI as keeping your ISMS "fit and healthy." You don't just fix it when it breaks—you strengthen it every day through learning, measuring, and adapting.

Author's Note: I've often seen organizations treat CI as a "nice-to-have"—something they'll get to after everything else is done. But that's a mistake. CI isn't a box to tick at the end of your ISMS cycle; it's the mindset that keeps the system alive.

In one of my implementation projects, we created an Improvement Program that encouraged individuals and teams to suggest practical ideas to strengthen the ISMS. It could be anything—simplifying a process, automating a report, improving documentation, or reducing incident response time.

We then introduced two awards: one for the Best Individual Improvement and another for the Best Team Contribution. Every year, top management reviewed all suggestions, selected the winners, and recognized them during the annual event. What amazed me most wasn't just the ideas—it was how quickly the culture changed. People started thinking creatively, challenging the old "this is how we've always done it" mindset, and actively looking for ways to make things better.

That's what CI truly looks like—small, steady, and intentional changes that enhance your ISMS's effectiveness, efficiency, and alignment with your goals. It's not about reaching perfection—it's about making progress, one step at a time, every single day.

Implementation Guidance: CI isn't a single project or a checkbox—it's a way of thinking. It involves developing a mindset where your ISMS is never considered "done." It evolves with your organization, adjusts to new challenges, and becomes more effective over time.

Here's how you can transform CI from a vague idea into a practical, repeatable process that truly works.

Step 1. Start by looking at the Big Picture: Before improving your ISMS, you must first understand your current position. Start with a structured assessment that examines your system from three different perspectives:

- **Suitability:** Does your ISMS still align with your business goals, context, and the expectations of interested parties (Clauses 4.1 and 4.2)? For instance, if your organization recently expanded into cloud-based operations, are your controls still relevant to that new environment?
- **Adequacy:** Are your ISMS processes and controls still appropriate and sufficient for your current operations? Maybe your risk management process worked well when you had 50 employees, but with 500, is it too manual and slow?
- **Effectiveness:** Is your ISMS achieving its intended results? Are risks managed, incidents reduced, and objectives met? Look at your monitoring data, audit results, and management review outcomes (Clause 9) to judge real-world performance, not assumptions.

This step gives you clarity—what's working, what's lagging, and what's missing.

Step 2. Identify Opportunities for Improvement: Improvement ideas can come from anywhere—inside or outside your organization. The goal is to actively look for them instead of waiting for them to appear. Start by contacting the relevant parties—employees, customers, partners, regulators, and even suppliers—and asking for their feedback. Sometimes, the most valuable insights come from those who view your systems differently.

Examine customer feedback and complaints closely—they're not only issues to resolve but also opportunities to strengthen your processes and improve your services. Likewise, investigate industry best practices and compare yourself to other organizations of similar size and complexity. If there's no suitable example within your country, look at global leaders in your field. Discover what they're doing differently and see how their practices could inspire improvements in your ISMS.

Improvement opportunities can also come from many other sources:

- **Performance Evaluations (Clause 9):** Trends and data often reveal what's working and what isn't.
- **Nonconformities and Corrective Actions:** Every issue teaches you something that can prevent future problems.
- **Internal and External Audits:** Auditors often spot inefficiencies, outdated methods, or missing links between policy and practice.

- **Management Reviews:** these discussions frequently uncover new technologies, regulatory changes, or shifts in business priorities that signal areas for improvement.
- **Employee Feedback:** Frontline staff often know exactly where friction exists and how to fix it, if only someone asks.

Remember, any source is valuable—whether it's a new idea from your own team, a trend you read about in an industry report, or an observation from a customer. The key is to gather and record every improvement opportunity, so nothing gets overlooked. Treat each idea as a potential seed—some will grow quickly, some more slowly, but all have the potential to strengthen your ISMS over time.

Step 3. Evaluate and Prioritize Improvements: Not every idea is worth pursuing right away. Once you've identified potential improvements, evaluate them just like you would assess risks:

- **Impact:** How much benefit will it bring?
- **Effort and Cost:** What resources and time will it take?
- **Feasibility:** Can it be implemented with current systems and processes?
- **Alignment:** Does it support your ISMS objectives and organizational goals?

Sometimes, small improvements can make a big difference—like automating a log review or streamlining an approval process. Choose wisely and focus on enhancements that strengthen your ISMS in meaningful ways.

Step 4. Plan and Implement the Changes: Once you've decided which improvements to pursue, treat them like any other planned change. Define:

- **What exactly will change** (e.g., a new tool, an updated procedure, a new KPI).
- **Who's responsible** for implementing it?
- **When and how** it will be rolled out.
- **How you'll measure success.**

Remember to clearly communicate the change to everyone involved. People support what they understand—especially when they see how the change improves their work or makes it more effective.

Step 5. Evaluate the Effectiveness of Your Actions: Improvement doesn't end after making a change. You should verify if it was effective. Did the improvement achieve the desired results? Did it fix the problem or introduce new challenges?

Use measurable indicators whenever possible—such as time saved, fewer incidents, better compliance rates, improved audit results, or increased user satisfaction.

If the results aren't what you expected, don't see it as failure—see it as feedback. CI is a cycle of learning.

Step 6. Celebrate and Share Success: Improvement flourishes in a culture that values effort. Celebrate successes, no matter how minor. Share stories across teams so others can learn and emulate good ideas.

Author's Note: In one of my implementation projects, we introduced a simple yet powerful feature—an "Improvement Wall" on the company intranet. Anyone could post their ideas there, regardless of size—from adjusting a report format to automating a repetitive task. What started as a quiet corner soon became one of the organization's most active areas. People started sharing, collaborating, and celebrating practical improvements that genuinely made their work easier and strengthened the ISMS.

That's the real magic of CI—it doesn't have to be grand or complex. Small, consistent actions build momentum and gradually turn improvement from a formal requirement into a living habit within the organization.

Clause 10.1 isn't about reinventing everything; it's about refining what already exists—making every process a little smoother, every control a little sharper, and every team a little more aware. It ties together everything you've built—leadership commitment, risk management, audits, and reviews—into one continuous cycle of learning and improvement betterment.

So, don't wait for the next audit or review to discuss improvement. Make it part of your daily ISMS routine—talked about in meetings, encouraged in teams, and celebrated across departments. The more you foster this culture, the more resilient, efficient, and forward-thinking your organization will become. CI isn't the final step of your ISMS journey—it's what keeps the journey moving.

Toolkit and Resources: You can use or adapt the following tools and templates to create a structured process for identifying, evaluating, and tracking improvement opportunities in your organization. Remember, these are examples—customize them based on your own context, size, and maturity level. What matters is not how the form looks, but that you genuinely use it to capture ideas, take action, and keep improving.

Template 1: CI Log

Use Table 14.1 to capture and track improvement ideas from across the organization. This log allows you to record inputs from audits, feedback, incidents, and even practical suggestions from your own team, ensuring that improvement opportunities are not lost and are followed through systematically.

Template 2: Improvement Evaluation Sheet

Before implementing a new improvement, it's useful to pause and evaluate its value and potential impact. Table 14.2 helps you assess proposed improvements in a structured way, so you can prioritize changes that deliver real benefit and avoid investing effort in ideas with limited return.

Template 3: Post-Implementation Review Form

Once an improvement has been implemented, it's important to review whether it worked. Table 14.3 helps you assess effectiveness, confirm whether the original problem was resolved, and record lessons learned or any further actions required.

CLAUSE 10.2 NONCONFORMITY And Corrective Action

Summary of the Clause Requirements: Clause 10.2 shows how your ISMS can learn from mistakes, not just fix them. It focuses on making sure that when something goes wrong, you don't just patch the issue but also understand why it happened, how it happened, and how to prevent it in the future.

Whenever a nonconformity occurs—whether identified through audits, incidents, complaints, or routine monitoring—your organization must adopt a structured, evidence-based approach to corrective action. ISO 27001 expects you to:

Table 14.1 Continual improvement log for the ISMS

Sr. No.	*Source of Idea (Audit, Feedback, Risk, etc.)*	*Description of Improvement Opportunity*	*Department/ Process*	*Owner/ Responsible Person*	*Priority (High/ Medium/Low)*	*Planned Action*	*Target Date*	*Status*	*Verification/ Evidence*	*Remarks*
1	Internal Audit	Automate the access review process to reduce manual effort	IT Security	Rajesh Sharma	High	Evaluate automation tools and pilot	30 Nov 2025	In Progress	Minutes of audit follow-up meeting	Awaiting budget approval
2	Employee Suggestion	Create short awareness videos for new joiners	HR / ISMS	Priya Das	Medium	Develop three pilot videos	15 Dec 2025	Planned	N/A	To be reviewed by the ISMS Manager

Table 14.2 Improvement evaluation sheet for the ISMS

Field	*Details*
Improvement Reference No.	CI-2025-04
Proposed By	ISMS Team
Description of Proposed Improvement	Introduce an automated patch management tool for critical systems.
Business/Security Need	Reduce time and risk associated with delayed patching.
Expected Benefits	Faster deployment, reduced vulnerabilities, improved compliance
Estimated Effort/Resources	$ 50,000 software license, 2 weeks of IT configuration time
Risks or Side Effects	Initial downtime during setup
Evaluation Result	High value, manageable risk
Decision	Approved
Approver Name/Date	CIO / 15 Oct 20xx

Table 14.3 Post-implementation review form for ISMS improvements

Field	Details
Improvement Reference No.	CI-2025-04
Description of Improvement	Automated patch management tool implemented across servers
Implementation Date	1 Dec 2025
Key Results/Outcomes	70% reduction in patching time, zero missed updates since deployment
Stakeholder Feedback	Positive response from IT operations and audit team
Lessons Learned	Early testing minimized downtime, and the communication plan worked well.
Further Action Required	Extend tool coverage to backup systems by Q2 2026
Verified By	ISMS Manager
Date of Verification	15 Jan 2026

1. **React to the Nonconformity:** Take immediate action to control and correct the issue and address any consequences. For example, if an access control failure is detected, immediately restrict access and secure the system before investigating further.
2. **Evaluate the Need for Deeper Action:** Look beyond the surface problem. Review the nonconformity, identify its root cause, and check if similar issues exist elsewhere or could occur in the future.
3. **Implement the Corrective Actions:** Once you understand the cause, take appropriate action to eliminate it and prevent recurrence. The action taken should be proportional to the seriousness and impact of the issue.
4. **Review the Effectiveness:** After implementation, confirm whether the corrective action actually worked. Did it fix the problem without introducing new ones? Has the issue stopped recurring?
5. **Update the ISMS If Necessary:** If the investigation reveals weaknesses in your system, policies, or controls, update them. This could mean revising a procedure, tightening access rights, or changing responsibilities.

And yes, as with everything in ISO 27001, documented information is mandatory. You must keep records showing:

- The nature of the nonconformity and what actions were taken.
- The results of any corrective action and how effectiveness was verified.

The idea is straightforward but impactful: each mistake is an opportunity to strengthen your ISMS. Clause 10.2 guarantees that your organization doesn't just respond but learns, adapts, and improves, transforming failures into valuable lessons that foster long-term resilience.

Explanation with Real-World Examples: Let's be honest—no matter how mature or well-designed your ISMS is, things will go wrong. Systems fail, people make mistakes, controls break, and sometimes incidents slip through even the best defenses. Clause 10.2 is your safety net. It's where ISO 27001 tells you, "Don't just fix it—learn from it."

When a nonconformity occurs, most organizations rush to correct it—they take quick action to stop the problem. But that's only the first step. The true strength of this clause lies in what happens afterward: understanding why it happened and how to prevent it from happening again.

Think of it this way—if your car gets a flat tire, replacing the tire is the correction. But investigating what caused it (a nail on the road, low pressure, worn-out rubber) and taking steps to prevent it from happening again—that's your corrective action.

Now, here's where many organizations stumble. In my career, I've reported most of my nonconformities in this very section. Why? Because many teams stop after making corrections. They fix the issue, send an email saying "closed," and move on. But they never look for the root cause.

Let me share a real example. During one of my audits, a company reported that one of its critical servers went down due to a hard drive failure. The IT team quickly replaced the disk, restored the backup, and declared victory—problem solved. But that's not a corrective action; that's a correction.

When I asked them, "What caused the hard disk failure?" there was silence. Nobody had checked. The same type of disk had failed in another server just 2 months earlier. No one had looked at temperature logs, power stability, or even disk age. The root cause wasn't the disk itself—it was poor preventive maintenance. The result? Another nonconformity in the next audit cycle.

Another interesting case came from a bank I audited in Africa. The IT manager had assigned a task to an employee without verifying if the person was truly qualified for the job. The task failed, causing a minor disruption. The manager's response was quick—he sent the employee for extra training and closed the nonconformity. Problem solved, right?

Not quite. The true question is—was the lack of training really the root cause? Or was the real problem the absence of a procedure that required the manager to verify competency before assigning any critical task?

If that underlying weakness isn't addressed, the same problem will recur—perhaps not with the same person or task, but certainly in another form elsewhere in the organization. That's the difference between treating a symptom and fixing the system-level cause.

That's the key lesson of Clause 10.2—don't just focus on what went wrong, dig deeper into why it didn't go well. Keep asking "Why?" until you can't ask anymore. Often, the first answer you find is only a symptom, not the root cause.

Here's another way to look at it—corrections prevent pain; corrective actions heal the root cause.

When properly implemented, this clause makes your ISMS smarter with each mistake. It's how your organization learns, adapts, and strengthens over time.

The process is simple but powerful:

1. Identify what went wrong.
2. Fix the immediate problem (correction).

3. Investigate the root cause.
4. Take action to prevent recurrence (corrective action).
5. Verify that your action worked.

And yes, document everything—what happened, what was done, what caused it, and what changed. Those records are proof that you're not just reacting but making improvements.

Clause 10.2 isn't about assigning blame. It's about growing. Every nonconformity is an opportunity, a mirror revealing where your ISMS needs improvement. The more you focus on it, the fewer surprises you'll encounter in the future.

So, next time you see a nonconformity, don't rush to close it. Take your time, ask why, and address the root cause. Because real improvement doesn't come from avoiding mistakes—it comes from learning from them.

Implementation Guidance: Let's face it—no system works perfectly forever. People make mistakes, processes drift, suppliers miss steps, and sometimes technology refuses to cooperate. That's life in any organization. Clause 10.2 explains what you do when that happens—how you respond, correct it, and most importantly, make sure it doesn't happen again.

A nonconformity means something didn't meet a requirement. That requirement could originate from anywhere—a clause of ISO 27001, your own policy or procedure, a customer contract, or a legal or regulatory obligation. Nonconformities appear in many forms: missed steps, controls that don't work, suppliers who fail to deliver, people not following procedures, or processes that produce the wrong outcome. In short, it is anything that strays from what should have happened.

The goal here isn't to assign blame or write long explanations—it's to understand why something went wrong and improve your ISMS because of it. Every nonconformity is a learning opportunity, a small alert that something in your system needs attention.

Here's how to develop a practical, structured approach to managing nonconformities and corrective actions so your ISMS not only recovers but also improves.

Step 1: Spot and Record the Nonconformity: Nonconformities can originate from anywhere—internal audits, external audits, monitoring results, incidents, customer complaints, even a casual chat in the corridor. If something doesn't align with your plans, documentation, or commitments, it's a nonconformity.

The moment you notice one, record it. Write down what occurred, when it happened, who discovered it, and which part of the ISMS it impacts. This forms the basis for your corrective action process.

Tip: Some organizations keep a straightforward Nonconformity and Corrective Action Register—a single document or digital tracker that records all issues, actions, owners, and statuses. It makes follow-up and trend analysis much easier later.

Step 2: React to the Nonconformity: First things first—control the damage. Contain the problem, limit its impact, and stop it from spreading. This is what ISO calls a correction.

Examples include restoring a failed system, revoking compromised access, or notifying affected parties. Corrections are immediate, practical steps—they prevent the problem from worsening.

But don't confuse this with taking corrective action. You're putting out the fire, not yet figuring out why it started.

⚠ **Caution:** Always monitor your quick fixes to ensure they don't cause new risks or side effects. For example, deactivating a user account might prevent an incident, but it could also disrupt essential business services if done without proper coordination.

Step 3: Find the Root Cause (This Is Where the Magic Happens): Once the fire is out, it's time to put on your detective hat and investigate the "why." Ask yourself—what caused this nonconformity? Was it a process failure, a human error, a system limitation, or something environmental?

But before you even start, remember this—the quality of your root cause analysis (RCA) relies entirely on the competence of those involved. If the wrong people lead the study, the whole process can quickly turn into a guessing game rather than a learning opportunity. I've seen this many times—people with only a surface understanding of the issue sit down to analyze it, and what follows are discussions full of assumptions, not facts.

Let me share an example from one of my classroom sessions. I usually start by asking the participants, "How many of you spend time in your kitchen? Do you cook?" Typically, a good number of hands go up, and that's when I smile and ask the following question: "Alright then, how long does it take to make an omelet?" Almost everyone answers confidently, "Five minutes!" That's perfectly fine—it's what I expect. But then I ask, "How long does it take to make a Spanish omelet?" and that's where things get interesting.

At this point, a few people confidently say, "Five to ten minutes." And that's when I know—they've never actually made a Spanish omelet in their life! Because if you check online or try it yourself, you'll see that a proper Spanish omelet—the *Tortilla Española*—takes about 35–45 minutes to prepare.

Now, imagine asking someone who believes an omelet and a Spanish omelet are the same thing to analyze why the Spanish omelet didn't turn out right. Would that make sense? Of course not. They might have a general idea of cooking, but they lack the deep knowledge needed to figure out what went wrong.

The same applies to your ISMS. If someone doesn't understand what a firewall, iptables, or nftables do, then there's no point in asking them to perform an RCA on a firewall problem. It's like asking someone who can fry an egg to critique the texture of a soufflé—they'll offer an opinion, not a solution.

When performing an RCA , ensure that the people involved truly grasp the subject. Include the right combination of subject matter experts, process owners, and implementers—individuals who can examine the issue from multiple perspectives and have a solid understanding. Otherwise, your analysis will only skim the surface and won't uncover the true cause.

Now, once you have the right team in place, select a method that matches your organization's context and skill level. There's no single correct way to do it—different problems require different tools. Some of the most common ones include:

- **5 Whys Technique:** Keep asking "Why?" until you reach the real cause. Simple, but powerful.
- **Fishbone (Ishikawa) Diagram:** Great for visualizing all possible causes — people, process, technology, materials, and environment.
- **Pareto Chart (80/20 Rule):** Helps identify which few causes are responsible for most of your problems.
- **Histogram:** Useful for spotting trends and recurring patterns in issues.
- **Nominal Group Technique (NGT):** Excellent for collecting ideas from a group and ranking the most probable causes.

💬 **Author's Note:** Always keep your RCA practical and meaningful. Don't overcomplicate it or let it become just paperwork. The real goal is to understand why something went wrong and how to prevent it—not to create six pages of flowcharts and diagrams. A good RCA focuses more on insight than on formality.

Step 4: Evaluate and Plan Corrective Actions: Once you identify the root cause, it's time to take action. Decide which changes will eliminate that cause, and make sure those actions are appropriate to the risk and impact.

For example:

- If the issue was a missing backup, create and test a new backup procedure.
- If the problem was caused by poor awareness, update your training content and frequency.
- If it were a system flaw, change the configuration and validate it before rollout.

Assign responsibilities, establish deadlines, and ensure accountability. If multiple issues share the same cause, address them together instead of individually—it saves time and promotes consistency.

A simple action tracker or "Corrective Action Plan" template can help you record who's responsible, what's being done, when it's due, and how success will be verified.

Step 5: Verify Effectiveness: Never assume your fix worked—verify it. After implementing corrective actions, assess their effectiveness through follow-up audits, monitoring reports, or user feedback.

Ask these questions:

- Did the nonconformity reappear?
- Did the corrective action introduce new risks?
- Are we now meeting the intended outcome?

Only when you can confidently answer yes to "It worked" and no to "It caused new issues" should you close the nonconformity.

Step 6: Learn, Share, and Improve: Every nonconformity teaches you something about your system. Don't waste that lesson. Share the findings with teams. Maybe what happened in one department could help prevent similar issues elsewhere.

Use data from your nonconformity register to identify recurring patterns. Are most issues linked to a specific process, control, or supplier? That's where your next improvement project starts.

Author's Note: RCA is where your ISMS learns to think. It's not a blame game; it's a learning game. In one organization, we held short "Root Cause Clinics"—15-minute weekly sessions where teams shared one issue they solved and how. Within months, people became naturally curious about prevention, not just firefighting.

And remember, Clause 10.2 is not about perfection. It's about persistence—finding one small cause at a time and fixing it properly. Every well-handled nonconformity moves your ISMS a little closer to excellence.

Toolkit and Resources: For managing nonconformities and corrective actions, feel free to use any of the tools we discussed earlier—whichever best suits your organization's size, culture, and competence. In this section, I've included two ready-to-use templates for your reference.

1. **Nonconformity and Corrective Action Report Template:** To record and analyze each nonconformity (see Table 14.4).
2. **Nonconformity and Corrective Action Report Tracker Template:** To monitor progress, responsibilities, and closure status (see Table 14.5).

Table 14.4 Nonconformity and corrective action report template

<table>
<tr><td colspan="5">NONCONFORMITY and CORRECTIVE ACTION REPORT</td></tr>
<tr><td rowspan="9">TO BE COMPLETED BY AUDITOR</td><td>DATE</td><td colspan="2">Department/Area/Process Audited:</td><td>Ref No.</td></tr>
<tr><td>xx/xx/20xx</td><td colspan="2"></td><td></td></tr>
<tr><td colspan="2">NON CONFORMITY Requirement Reference (ex., ISO clause/ Law ref./ Contact ref)</td><td colspan="2"></td></tr>
<tr><td colspan="4">NON CONFORMITY Details</td></tr>
<tr><td colspan="4"></td></tr>
<tr><td colspan="4">NON CONFORMITY – DESCRIPTION OF OBJECTIVE EVIDENCE:</td></tr>
<tr><td colspan="4"></td></tr>
<tr><td>GRADE (MINOR/MAJOR)</td><td>LEAD Auditor</td><td>Auditor (if any)</td><td>FUNCTION REP.</td></tr>
<tr><td></td><td></td><td></td><td></td></tr>
<tr><td rowspan="9">TO BE COMPLETED BY THE DEPARTMENT/PROCESS LEAD</td><td colspan="4">ROOT CAUSE ANALYSIS</td></tr>
<tr><td colspan="4"></td></tr>
<tr><td colspan="4">Investigated by:</td></tr>
<tr><td colspan="4">Date:</td></tr>
<tr><td colspan="4">CORRECTIVE ACTION & CORRECTION PLAN (Also include evaluation and review plan of the proposed action, proposed Changes to ISMS and related services, and proposed update to risks and opportunities)</td></tr>
<tr><td colspan="4"></td></tr>
<tr><td colspan="4">Proposed by:</td></tr>
<tr><td colspan="4">Proposed date:</td></tr>
<tr><td colspan="4">Agreed completion date:</td></tr>
<tr><td></td><td colspan="4">FOLLOW–UP</td></tr>
<tr><td rowspan="3"></td><td rowspan="2">VERIFICATION OF CORRECTIVE ACTIONS</td><td>DATE</td><td colspan="2">STATUS (Closed)</td></tr>
<tr><td>xx/xx/20xx</td><td colspan="2">YES / NO</td></tr>
<tr><td>AUDITOR COMMENTS</td><td colspan="3"></td></tr>
<tr><td></td><td>AUDITOR'S NAME AND SIGNATURE</td><td colspan="3"></td></tr>
</table>

Use these templates as starting points, adapt them to your organization's context, and make them your own. The real goal is to create a simple, effective system that ensures every issue becomes an opportunity for improvement.

How to Use Table 14.5:

Table 14.5 Nonconformity and corrective action report tracker template

Nonconformity and Corrective Action Report Tracker Template

NC Reference	*Source of NC (Audit/ Incident/ Complaint/ Other)*	*Date Identified*	*Description of Non-conformity*	*ISO Clause / Internal Reference*	*Immediate Correction Taken*	*Root Cause Identified*	*Corrective Action Proposed*	*Responsibility*	*Due Date*	*Status of Action Taken & Changes to ISMS (if any)*	*Verification / Effectiveness Review*	*Verified By*	*Date Verified*	*NC Closed (Yes/ No)*	*Remarks / Follow-up Notes*
NC-001	Internal Audit	10-04-25	Context of the organization not defined, including activities and scope.	ISO 27001:2022 Clause 4	Discussed with management; agreed to define ISMS scope and activities.	ISMS team unaware of requirement.	ISO Lead Auditor and Lead Implementer training proposed for ISMS team. External expert engaged for scope definition.	ISMS Manager	20-04-25	Training completed. External resource assisted in defining context. Document approved.	Scope and context reviewed during management review — effective.	Dr. Swapan Purkait	25-04-25	Yes	Awareness program planned for other teams.

1. **Keep it Live:** Update it immediately when new nonconformities are identified.
2. **Assign Accountability:** Ensure each corrective action has a clear owner and deadline.
3. **Link to Evidence:** Wherever possible, attach supporting records (training reports, screenshots, review notes).
4. **Verify Before Closing:** Only close the NC after confirming that the corrective action eliminated the root cause.
5. **Review Trends:** Periodically analyze your NC log for recurring issues or systemic weaknesses.

🛠 *Implementation Task #23: Nonconformity and Corrective Action Process*

It's time to bring this clause to life in your organization!

Your task is to develop a straightforward, organized process for managing nonconformities and corrective actions—one that aligns with your culture, size, and methods.

Start by identifying how you currently deal with issues when something goes wrong. Ask yourself:

- What happens when a procedure isn't followed?
- Who investigates when a control fails?
- How do we ensure it doesn't happen again?

Now, build your own process step-by-step:

Step 1. Define what a nonconformity means for your organization: Write a simple definition that everyone can understand. Include examples such as policy violations, missed controls, failed audits, or customer complaints.

Step 2. Decide how to record and track them: Use a simple log or the Nonconformity and Corrective Action Tracker Template provided in the Toolkit. Each nonconformity should have a unique ID, a description, the person responsible, and a due date.

Step 3. Plan how you'll identify and verify the root cause: Choose the tools that work best for you—5 Whys, Fishbone Diagram, or even a quick team brainstorming session. The goal is to identify the true cause, not just the obvious one.

Step 4. Define your corrective action process: Write clear steps for how actions will be approved, implemented, and verified. Remember to specify who will review whether the action was successful and when the issue can be officially closed.

Step 5. Build the feedback loop: Make sure each closed nonconformity is reviewed in your next management review or internal audit follow-up—this allows the organization to learn and continually improve.

💡 **Tip:** Don't turn this into a heavy, bureaucratic process. Keep it simple, clear, and fair—one that encourages learning, not fearing mistakes.

🧭 Key Takeaways—What You've Learned

- Treat improvement as a daily habit, not an annual chore—continually enhance the suitability, adequacy, and effectiveness of the ISMS.
- Record every issue and idea in simple logs: one Nonconformity and Corrective Action Register and one CI log—keep them visible and actively used.
- Differentiate correction from corrective action: fix (address the issue now), then investigate (find the root cause), and finally implement corrective action (prevent recurrence).

- Require owners, deadlines, verification steps, and proof for every corrective action; do not close items until effectiveness is confirmed.
- Document what has changed in the ISMS (risk register, SoA, policies, objectives) whenever corrective actions lead to system-wide updates.
- Prioritize improvements like risks: evaluate impact, effort, feasibility, and alignment with ISMS goals before allocating resources.
- Track all KPIs (time to contain, time to close, repeat nonconformities, CI ideas implemented) and display trends in management reviews.
- Foster a no-blame learning culture—encourage staff to report issues and propose improvements; reward practical contributions and share success stories.
- Incorporate lessons into training, awareness programs, supplier reviews, and future risk assessments so the ISMS learns from experience.
- Ensure management visibly sponsors improvement: allocate resources, review outcomes, and celebrate measurable progress—leadership transforms fixes into sustained resilience.

QUIZ #13

True/False statement

Sr.	*Statement*	*True/False*
1	Continual improvement in ISO 27001 is only required once the ISMS has been fully implemented.	
2	Clause 10.1 requires organizations to continually improve the suitability, adequacy, and effectiveness of their ISMS.	
3	The main purpose of corrective action is to fix the immediate issue, not to find or eliminate its cause.	
4	Nonconformities should be reviewed to determine if similar issues exist or could occur elsewhere.	
5	According to ISO 27001 – Documented information must be retained for continual improvement.	
6	Documented information must be retained to show both the nature of the nonconformities and the results of any corrective actions.	
7	Clause 10 applies only to major nonconformities and not to minor ones.	
8	Continual improvement should be driven by data and lessons learned from audits, incidents, and management reviews.	

CASE 8: A LOOP OF FIXES—LONDON

Sterling Shield Insurance operated from a glass-fronted office overlooking Canary Wharf. With over 1,800 employees across the UK and millions of customer records processed each quarter, the company had built its reputation on trust. Their business model depended heavily on stable operations, secure handling of customer data, and regulatory compliance.

They had been ISO 27001-certified for three years. Each surveillance audit was passed—not always easily, but always with results they could "patch."

The most common audit finding?

A common issue: Unauthorized modifications to policy templates and customer communication forms.

Sometimes the wrong disclaimer appeared. Sometimes an incorrect revision was used. Sometimes teams relied on an older copy stored on a shared drive instead of the correct one from the compliance portal.

The root cause? No one had actually asked.

Before every audit, the Compliance Manager, Mark, reassured the team:

"Don't worry. We trained everyone. If they use the wrong version again, we'll retrain them. Job done."

And each year, the nonconformity came back—just with a slightly different form, and a different department name attached.

Then came Amelia Carter—the newly appointed ISMS Manager.

She arrived with a calm demeanor and an analytical approach. During her initial review of corrective action records, she noticed the pattern immediately.:

- Same issue appearing yearly
- Same corrective action: training completed
- No reference to RCA
- No follow-up effectiveness checks

During a meeting with Operations, she asked politely, "Why do we think this keeps happening?"

The room was quiet.

Finally, someone said, "People forget."

Someone else added, "Maybe they don't take it seriously."

Another joked, "Or maybe it's Monday every day."

Amelia smiled lightly but continued:

"Training can be part of the solution, but repeating the same error across different teams usually indicates a deeper issue. We need to differentiate between correction and corrective action."

Mark raised an eyebrow. "Isn't training the corrective action?"

Amelia paused before responding.

"Training can help when a mistake occurs because someone lacked the right knowledge or skill," she said calmly. "But when the same issue keeps happening, it might mean we haven't understood the real cause yet. Correcting the incident fixes what happened that day — but finding and addressing the root cause is what prevents it from happening again."

She walked to the whiteboard and wrote:

- Correction = Fix now
- Corrective Action = Prevent recurrence

Then she asked again, "Why do we think this keeps happening?"

Silence in the room.

Amelia led the team through a structured RCA. Together, they used the 5 Whys technique, questioning each step until assumptions and surface explanations were removed. To confirm their findings, they mapped contributing factors with a fishbone (Ishikawa) diagram, examining people, processes, technology, and governance.

After a careful review, the true cause became clear:

Anyone with access to the shared folder could change the templates. There was no approval process, no ownership assignment, and no access controls—meaning errors weren't just possible, but guaranteed. Training wasn't the issue. The process was.

With leadership approval, Amelia:

- Introduced a controlled access workflow in the document management system
- Required competency validation before assigning document owners
- Added version control checks in change management
- Implemented periodic effectiveness reviews

Later, during an ISMS steering committee meeting, the COO commented:

"This is the first time in years that the corrective action felt... final."

Amelia nodded professionally.

"Nonconformities are not just mistakes — they are chances to make the system better. Solving the problem is crucial. Stopping it from happening again is leadership."

And this time, the audit report looked different.

There was no recurring nonconformity.

At the end of the report, the auditor had added a simple comment:

"Improvement noted."

Case Discussion: Test Your Understanding

1. **What mistake was repeatedly made by Sterling Shield before Amelia joined?**

   A. Performing risk assessments too frequently
   B. Using external auditors for internal audits
   C. Creating too many documented procedures
   D. Applying only corrections without corrective actions

2. **Why did the nonconformity continue appearing each year?**

   A. Too many people performed audits
   B. Only training was used as the response instead of addressing root causes
   C. There were no documented policies
   D. The audit scope was incorrect

3. **Which of the following best describes a proper corrective action?**

   A. Fix the issue quickly and move on
   B. Replace the template and inform staff verbally
   C. Identify the underlying cause and implement process improvements to prevent recurrence
   D. Store multiple versions of documents for redundancy

4. **Which statement aligns with ISO requirements discussed in the case?**

   A. Training alone is always a complete corrective action
   B. Corrective actions are optional if corrections are performed quickly
   C. Corrective actions should be proportional, documented, and based on RCA
   D. Only IT teams are responsible for corrective actions

5. **Which statement from Operations indicated a misunderstanding of corrective action?**

   A. "We have trained the staff, so the nonconformity is closed."
   B. "We should review access control and workflow."
   C. "Let's perform a root cause analysis before responding."
   D. "We should restrict ownership to competent roles."

6. **Which improvement introduced by Amelia best demonstrates preventing recurrence rather than fixing symptoms?**

   A. Reminding staff verbally to use the correct document templates
   B. Updating the wrong template when discovered
   C. Filing completed training records in the personnel folders
   D. Implementing controlled access, approval workflow, and version control

Chapter 15

Preparing for ISO 27001 certification

What auditors want and how to pass with confidence

Congratulation—you made it!

If you've reached this chapter, it means you've stayed the course, followed the plan, and built your ISMS step by step. That's a significant accomplishment. Most people talk about implementing ISO 27001; only a few reach this point. So, take a moment to recognize what you've achieved—you've laid the foundation of a secure, structured, and resilient organization.

Now comes the exciting part—preparing for ISO 27001 certification. This is where your ISMS will be independently reviewed by an accredited certification body to confirm that it meets the requirements of ISO/IEC 27001:2022. Getting certified isn't just about hanging a framed certificate in your office (though that's always satisfying!)—it's about showing your customers, partners, and regulators that you take information security seriously and have the discipline to support it.

But here's the truth—certification isn't mandatory. Whether you pursue it depends entirely on your organization's needs and priorities. For some, it's a regulatory or contractual requirement—a box they must check to keep doing business. For others, it's a strategic choice—a sign of credibility, a marketing edge, or a way to stand out in a competitive market.

And then, there are leaders I've worked with who pursued certification for a very different reason—not because they had to, but because they wanted to. They aimed to test their systems, gauge their progress, and bring in an independent perspective to validate their efforts. For them, certification wasn't just an audit; it was a test of truth—an opportunity to see how well their ISMS performed in the real world.

No matter where you stand on that spectrum, this chapter will get you ready. We'll cover what auditors look for, how the certification process works, what evidence you need to gather, and most importantly, how to approach your certification audit with confidence.

You've done the hard part — you've built your ISMS. Now, let's make sure you finish strong and steady—not just to get certified, but to show that your organization truly lives and breathes information security.

WHY CONSIDER ISO 27001 CERTIFICATION?

Let's clarify—depending on your organization's context, ISO 27001 certification may or may not be mandatory. For some, it's a regulatory or contractual requirement, especially when working with government clients, financial institutions, or international partners. For others, it's a strategic choice—a way to demonstrate their commitment to information security and improve their market reputation.

DOI: 10.1201/9781003744139-16

Either way, if you're considering taking that final step toward certification, let me share a few reasons it can be a powerful and rewarding choice for your organization.

Certification is more than just a badge on your website or a logo in your email signature. It's an independent proof that your organization's information security practices meet globally recognized standards. It shows your customers, partners, and even regulators that you don't just claim to prioritize security—you've demonstrated it.

Here are some of the key benefits of getting certified:

1. **Enhanced Credibility and Trust:** Certification instantly boosts your reputation. It gives customers, partners, and regulators confidence that your organization protects information responsibly and systematically. In today's world of ongoing cyber threats, trust can be a key factor.
2. **Competitive Advantage:** An ISO 27001 certificate often becomes the deciding factor when clients choose between vendors. It shows that your processes aren't just functional—they're verified, structured, and dependable. In short, it's a credibility boost that helps open doors to bigger opportunities.
3. **Access to New Markets:** Many government contracts, tenders, and multinational clients now require ISO certification as a condition for doing business. For many organizations, certification is not just a source of pride—it's a gateway to new markets and international collaborations.
4. **Better Risk Management:** The certification process encourages your organization to identify, evaluate, and manage information security risks proactively. This enhances your ISMS's resilience, lowers the risk of costly incidents, and boosts your ability to respond effectively when issues arise.
5. **Greater Operational Efficiency:** ISO 27001 helps identify inefficiencies and redundant practices. During the certification process, many organizations streamline workflows, clarify roles, and enhance coordination—all of which improve performance.
6. **Stronger Stakeholder and Investor Confidence:** When independent auditors verify your conformance with an international standard, it reassures your stakeholders—including investors, partners, and even your own employees—that the business is well-governed and secure.
7. **Improved Employee Engagement:** The certification process engages everyone, not just the IT or compliance teams. Employees understand their role in safeguarding information, feel more responsible, and take pride in being part of a certified, globally recognized organization.
8. **Continual Improvement Culture:** Certification audits don't just evaluate—they inspire growth. Each assessment provides insights into what's working and what can be improved, helping your organization grow steadily over time.

So, if you decide to pursue ISO 27001 certification, view it not as the end of your ISMS journey but as a confirmation of everything you've accomplished so far. It's your opportunity to demonstrate to the world that your commitment to information security isn't just internal—it's verified, visible, and valued.

Author's Note: In my experience, certification does more than just impress clients — it transforms how teams think. Once that certificate is displayed, there's a clear sense of pride and accountability. People begin to see security as part of their identity, not merely their job. That's the true reward of ISO 27001 certification.

CHOOSING THE RIGHT ISO 27001 CERTIFICATION BODY

Let's discuss one of the most vital—and frequently overlooked—steps in your certification journey: choosing the right certification body.

Now, I hate to say this, but there are many fly-by-night operators in this space. They'll gladly hand you a certificate — sometimes faster than you can print it yourself — and for some, the cost of the paper it's printed on might be the only real expense involved. The problem is that this kind of certificate has no value. It won't be recognized by your clients, regulators, or even your own management when it matters.

So, please take this seriously. You've invested months building your ISMS. Don't let all that effort go to waste by choosing the wrong certifying body. Do your due diligence and make sure you're working with a reputable, accredited, and internationally recognized certification organization.

Here are some key things to look for:

1. **Accreditation—The Most Crucial Factor:** Always make sure your certification body is accredited by a recognized national or international accreditation body, such as the United Kingdom Accreditation Service (UKAS), the ANSI National Accreditation Board (ANAB) in the United States, or another member of the International Accreditation Forum (IAF). You can verify their accreditation directly on the IAF website or through IAF CertSearch (Global Database of Accredited Certifications). Accreditation ensures that the auditors themselves are independently assessed and meet international standards—giving your certificate real, recognized credibility.
2. **Industry Experience and Expertise:** Choose a certification body that understands your industry. For example, auditing a data center isn't the same as auditing a hospital or a logistics company. An auditor with relevant sector experience can ask meaningful questions and offer better insights, not just tick boxes.
3. **Reputation and Track Record:** Check how long they've been in business, who their major clients are, and what others say about them. A well-established, trusted certification body adds credibility to your certificate and enhances your organization's reputation.
4. **Transparent Audit Process:** Ask about their audit process, from Stage 1 (document review) to Stage 2 (implementation assessment) and beyond. Reputable certification bodies will have a transparent, structured process and communicate timelines, requirements, and costs upfront.
5. **Cost and Value—Be Smart, Not Cheap:** Certification is an investment, not a commodity. Be cautious of quotes that seem too good to be true. Extremely low prices are a red flag—they often originate from unaccredited or low-quality organizations. Focus on value rather than just cost. Ensure you understand what's included—travel, surveillance audits, and documentation reviews should all be part of your comparison.
6. **Integrated Audit Capabilities:** If you're planning to implement multiple standards (such as ISO 27001 together with ISO 9001 or ISO 22301), choose a certification body that can conduct integrated audits. This approach will save time, lower costs, and lessen audit fatigue for your teams.
7. **Geographic Presence and Flexibility:** A certification body with a local presence can simplify scheduling audits and cut travel expenses. Plus, local auditors often understand regional business practices and regulations better.

8. **Additional Support and Services:** Some certification bodies also provide training or awareness sessions (not consultancy, but general guidance). These can be helpful if your team is new to ISO audits.

In short, selecting the right certification body is about credibility, trust, and recognition. Don't rush—research, compare, and verify. Your ISO 27001 certificate is only as strong as the organization that issues it.

💬 **Author's Note:** I've seen organizations proudly display certificates from organizations nobody has heard of—only to realize later they weren't accredited or recognized globally. It's heartbreaking to watch months of effort go to waste because of one poor decision. So, take this step seriously. A valid, accredited certification isn't just a piece of paper—it's proof that your ISMS truly meets the worldwide standard for excellence.

🌐 ***Website Reference:*** The following websites can help you verify accreditation and explore reputable certification options.

Accreditation Bodies:

🔗 International Accreditation Forum (IAF): www.iaf.nu
🔗 IAF CertSearch: www.iafcertsearch.org
🔗 United Kingdom Accreditation Service (UKAS): www.ukas.com
🔗 ANSI National Accreditation Board (ANAB): anab.ansi.org
🔗 DAkkS: www.dakks.de
🔗 JAS-ANZ: www.jasanz.org
🔗 National Accreditation Board for Certification Bodies (NABCB): nabcb.qci.org.in

Certification Bodies:

🔗 BSI Group: www.bsigroup.com
🔗 TÜV Rheinland: www.tuv.com
🔗 TÜV SÜD: www.tuvsud.com
🔗 DNV: www.dnv.com
🔗 SGS: www.sgs.com
🔗 Bureau Veritas: group.bureauveritas.com
🔗 Intertek: www.intertek.com
🔗 LRQA: www.lrqa.com
🔗 TÜV Nord: www.tuev-nord.de

⚠ **Caution:** The websites listed above are provided solely for informational purposes. Readers are strongly encouraged to conduct their own due diligence before choosing a certification body.

The inclusion of these websites in this book does not imply any recommendation, endorsement, or partnership with any accreditation or certification organization. Always verify accreditation status directly through official sources before continuing your certification process.

UNDERSTANDING THE ISO 27001 3-YEAR CERTIFICATION CYCLE

Many organizations believe ISO 27001 certification is a one-time achievement—pass the audit, obtain the certificate, and you're finished. However, in reality, certification isn't a single event to check off; it's an ongoing commitment. It's a continuous, 3-year process where you must consistently show that your ISMS stays adequate, relevant, and keeps improving.

The certification process starts much earlier than most realize. It begins when you select your certification body, communicate with their sales or client relations team, and officially agree on the audit scope, certification standards, and business terms. After this agreement, your certification body will set the date for your initial audit—and that marks the start of your 3-year certification cycle.

Think of certification as a 3-year partnership between your organization and your certification body. Once you pass your initial audit and your ISO 27001 certificate is issued, it remains valid for 3 years from the date of the certification decision—but that validity depends on how well you maintain your ISMS.

This 3-year cycle isn't about bureaucracy or paperwork; it's about building and maintaining trust. Trust that your ISMS still works as intended. Trust that your people continue to follow what's written. Trust that your controls are effective and your risks are under control.

Your certification body doesn't just verify compliance once—it stays with you throughout the entire cycle, conducting surveillance audits and a recertification audit at the end of the third year. The goal isn't to catch you out; it's to ensure your ISMS continues to grow stronger, more efficient, and better aligned with your organization's evolving needs.

The full certification lifecycle includes:

1. **Year 0—Initial Certification Audit:** Conducted in two stages—Stage 1 (documentation review) and Stage 2 (implementation audit).
2. **Year 1 and Year 2—Surveillance Audit:** Annual check-ups to confirm your system's continued effectiveness and alignment with ISO 27001.
3. **Year 3—Recertification Audit:** A complete review of your ISMS to renew your certification for another 3 years.

Year 0—The Initial Certification Audit (Stage 1 and Stage 2)

The initial certification audit always occurs in two steps: Stage 1 and Stage 2. Together, they build the foundation of your ISO 27001 certification.

Stage 1. Documentation Review—Your Readiness Checkpoint: Stage 1 of the ISO 27001 certification process is often called the "readiness review"—and that's precisely what it is. This stage helps both you and the certification body confirm that your organization is ready to proceed to the main certification audit (Stage 2).

At this stage, the auditor from the certification body reviews your documented ISMS closely—including your policies, procedures, risk assessment and treatment plans, Statement of Applicability (SoA), and other supporting documents and records. The goal isn't just to verify that you have documents, but to confirm they reflect a functioning system that aligns with ISO 27001 requirements.

Think of it as your initial checkpoint before the actual test. If any gaps or weaknesses are identified, you'll have an opportunity to address them before the Stage 2 audit.

During the Stage 1 audit, the certification body will typically aim to:

- **Review your documented ISMS**—ensuring that your policies, procedures, and records meet ISO 27001 requirements.
- **Evaluate site-specific conditions** and hold discussions with your team to gauge readiness for Stage 2.
- **Check your understanding of the standard**, including how well you've identified your key processes, objectives, and controls.
- **Review the scope of your ISMS**—confirming your covered sites, technologies, equipment, processes, and regulatory obligations.
- **Assess your preparedness** by ensuring internal audits and management reviews have been planned and conducted.
- **Confirm logistical readiness**—agreeing on the schedule, resources, and practical arrangements for the Stage 2 audit.
- **Identify potential areas of concern** so that you can strengthen them before the next step.

In simple terms, Stage 1 is like your dress rehearsal. It's where you demonstrate that your system is not just documented but also functional and understood by your team.

If the auditor concludes that your ISMS documentation and implementation are sufficiently mature, they will recommend progressing to Stage 2: The Implementation Audit. If not, don't worry—you will receive a list of observations and gaps to address before moving forward. Fix them, improve your documentation, and you'll be ready to proceed.

Author's Note: Many organizations underestimate Stage 1 and treat it as just paperwork. Don't make that mistake. A strong Stage 1 sets the tone for a smooth Stage 2. Treat it seriously, involve your key process owners, and use it as an opportunity to refine your ISMS before the big day.

Stage 2. Implementation Audit—Where the Real Test Begins: Once you finish Stage 1, it's time for the Stage 2 audit — when your ISMS is tested to its limits. This is where your documented system comes into action, and the auditor checks how effectively it works in actual practice.

Before the audit starts, the certification body will send you a formal audit plan. This plan includes all the key details—the audit scope, criteria, objectives, audit team members, departments, processes to be audited, and the proposed schedule. The plan will also specify whether the audit will be conducted onsite, remotely, or through a hybrid model.

The audit plan isn't a surprise; it's a collaborative agreement. It must be communicated to you, the client, and the dates should be set beforehand. If specific dates or times conflict with essential business activities, you can request adjustments. Certification bodies are usually flexible and willing to reschedule within reason, as long as the audit's integrity isn't affected. Don't hesitate to discuss this; auditors value proactive communication.

Now, let's discuss what actually takes place during Stage 2.

This stage focuses on assessing how well your ISMS is implemented and whether it genuinely meets the goals of ISO 27001. The audit will be conducted at your site(s), where the auditor will observe actual operations, interview staff, and review records, logs, and evidence. Essentially, they are verifying if your ISMS functions effectively in the real world, not just on paper.

Here's what the auditor typically looks for during the Stage 2 audit:

- **Conformity with ISO 27001 Requirements** Verifying that your ISMS meets every applicable clause and control.

- **Performance and Measurement:** Assessing how well you're monitoring and achieving your information security objectives.
- **Compliance with Legal, Regulatory, and Contractual Requirements:** Ensuring your ISMS covers all relevant obligations.
- **Operational Control:** Observing how your critical processes and controls are being managed day to day.
- **Internal Audits and Management Reviews:** Confirming these have been carried out effectively and used to drive improvements.
- **Leadership and Commitment:** Evaluating top management's involvement and accountability in maintaining an effective ISMS.

The auditor's role is not just to verify conformance but also to assess effectiveness—whether your ISMS is achieving the desired results, safeguarding information assets, and supporting your business objectives.

Once Stage 2 is complete, the audit team will review all the findings and evidence from both Stage 1 and Stage 2. If your system is compliant and practical, they'll recommend your organization for ISO 27001 certification.

If any nonconformities are identified, you will receive a detailed report explaining the issues and what corrective actions are needed. You will have a reasonable amount of time to address these and submit proof of resolution. Once verified, certification can proceed without issues.

Author's Note: Stage 2 can seem like a significant moment—and it is. But remember, the auditor isn't your enemy; they're an independent reviewer helping you confirm your hard work. Treat the audit plan as your guide, prepare your team, and ensure everyone knows their role. If you need to shift the schedule slightly, ask—audits are meant to be thorough, not disruptive. The aim isn't just to get through the audit; it's to show that your ISMS truly works and adds value to your organization.

Surveillance Audit—Your ISMS Annual Health Check

Once you've achieved ISO 27001 certification, your journey doesn't end—it evolves. Over the next 2 years of your 3-year certification cycle, your organization will undergo surveillance audits. These audits ensure that your ISMS continues to meet the standard's requirements and remains effective in practice.

Think of surveillance audits as your ISMS's yearly health check—verifying it's still working well, improving over time, and adapting to changes in your business and risk environment.

Surveillance audits are required and scheduled at least once each calendar year, except during the recertification year. The initial surveillance audit must occur within 12 months of your certification decision date. Missing this deadline or not showing continuous compliance can jeopardize your certification.

These audits are on-site (or hybrid) reviews, but they are not comprehensive system audits like the initial certification. Instead, they target specific parts of your ISMS to ensure it continues to work as intended.

During each surveillance audit, the certification body will typically review:

- **Internal Audits and Management Reviews:** Confirming they are being performed as planned and leading to improvements.

- **Actions Taken on Previous Nonconformities:** Ensuring that past issues have been adequately addressed and closed.
- **Handling of Complaints:** Checking how feedback or issues from clients and stakeholders are managed.
- **Effectiveness of the ISMS:** Evaluating whether the system continues to achieve its intended objectives and results.
- **Continual Improvement:** Assessing progress on actions and initiatives that strengthen your ISMS.
- **Operational Control:** Verifying that day-to-day processes remain consistent and controlled.
- **Changes in Context or Scope:** Reviewing how the ISMS has adapted to organizational or environmental changes.
- **Use of Certification Marks and References:** Ensuring that ISO 27001 certification claims and certification body logos are used correctly and in accordance with certification requirements.

While surveillance audits are smaller in scope, they hold significant importance. Certification bodies must suspend certification if your ISMS persistently or seriously fails to meet certification requirements, including the requirement to maintain an effective management system.

I've seen cases where clients underestimate their surveillance audits—postponing reviews, delaying corrective actions, or neglecting documentation. Unfortunately, that can result in suspension or even withdrawal of certification.

So, approach every surveillance audit with the same seriousness as your initial one. It's your chance to demonstrate that your ISMS is not just compliant but also active, evolving, and adaptable.

Author's Note: Many organizations see surveillance audits as routine check-ins—but they are actually much more. Think of them as your yearly chance to confirm your system's maturity and credibility. If you regularly conduct internal audits, management reviews, and improvement activities, your surveillance audit will be easy and straightforward. However, if you've been waiting for "audit season" to start preparing—it's already too late. Keep yourself audit-ready all year, and your certificate will remain secure, strong, and respected.

Recertification Audit (Year 3)—Renewing Your Commitment

As your three-year certification cycle nears its end, it's time for the recertification audit—a comprehensive review to confirm that your ISMS is still effective, improving, and aligned with your organization's goals.

Let's be clear—like your initial certification, recertification might or might not be required, depending on your organization's situation. Some organizations choose not to renew their ISO 27001 certification after the first 3 years because their business priorities or contractual needs have shifted. Others, especially those in regulated industries or with high customer expectations, see recertification as a strategic priority. The decision is entirely yours—but it's one that warrants careful consideration.

Now, if you decide to continue your certification journey, the recertification audit gives you a chance to show maturity—how your ISMS has grown, changed, and produced results over the past 3 years.

The certification body performs this audit before your current certificate expires, and it is usually as comprehensive as your original Stage 2 audit. However, it emphasizes long-term effectiveness and improvement more than initial readiness.

Before the audit begins, the certification body will review your audit history, previous surveillance findings, any unresolved nonconformities, and complaints (if any). Then they'll plan an on-site audit that examines:

- How effective your ISMS remains in light of internal and external changes.
- Whether your system continues to be relevant and aligned with your business objectives.
- Your organization's commitment to maintaining and improving the ISMS.
- How well your ISMS continues to meet its intended outcomes and achieve information security objectives.

Simply put, the auditor is verifying whether your ISMS continues to perform its purpose—protecting information, managing risk, and fostering ongoing improvement.

If any major nonconformities are identified, you will be given a specific timeline to correct them and implement corrective actions before your certification expires. These must be verified before your certificate can be renewed.

Once all recertification activities are completed, your certificate is renewed for another 3 years. The new certificate usually has the same expiry date pattern as the previous one, ensuring a smooth continuation of your certification cycle.

However, if the certification body cannot verify corrective actions before the expiration date—or if the audit isn't finished on time—recertification will not be granted. In such cases, your certificate will expire, and you will have up to 6 months to complete the remaining activities and regain certification. If that period passes, you may need to undergo another full Stage 2 audit.

Author's Note: I've seen organizations handle recertification in two very different ways. Some treat it as a box-ticking exercise—rushing to prepare documents and evidence just weeks before the audit. Others see it as an opportunity to reflect, review, and refresh their ISMS after 3 years of learning. The difference is night and day. Those who stay engaged with their ISMS throughout the cycle move through recertification with confidence.

Remember, your ISMS is a living system. Recertification isn't just about keeping your certificate current; it's about reaffirming your organization's commitment to protecting information, staying resilient, and continually improving.

And if you ever decide not to renew, that's okay too—as long as it's a deliberate, well-reasoned choice based on your business situation, not because the system was neglected.

YOUR ISO 27001 JOURNEY—THE ROAD AHEAD

If you've reached this point, take a moment to pause—and congratulate yourself. You've traveled a long way. From understanding the foundations of ISO 27001, exploring each clause in detail, building your ISMS step by step, learning how to audit, review, and improve—you've done it all.

Implementing ISO 27001 isn't just about earning certification; it's about fostering a culture of security, responsibility, and continual improvement in your organization. It's about establishing a system that safeguards what matters most—your information, your people, and your reputation.

Whether you choose to pursue certification now or later, remember this—every effort you've made to strengthen your ISMS adds genuine value to your organization. The journey itself is your greatest achievement.

Thank you for allowing me to guide you through this roadmap. I hope this book has not only simplified ISO 27001 for you but also motivated you to view it as a practical, living system—not just a checklist.

Wishing you all the best as you move forward with confidence, dedication, and clarity.

May your ISMS grow stronger each day—not just to earn a certificate, but to build lasting trust, resilience, and excellence.

🧭 Key Takeaways—What You've Learned

- Certification is validation, not magic—it proves your ISMS works in practice; decide whether you want the market-facing benefits or it's purely optional for your context.
- Choose an accredited, reputable certification body (IAF/UKAS/ANAB member)—credibility beats the cheapest quote every time.
- Treat certification as a 3-year commitment: initial (Stage 1/Stage 2) → annual surveillance → recertification. Plan resources for the entire cycle.
- Stage 1 is your readiness check—have clear, accurate documentation (scope, policy, SoA, risk register, objectives, internal audit and management review evidence).
- Stage 2 is the real test—auditors will verify that the ISMS actually works: Interviews, records, process evidence, controls in action, and performance against objectives.
- Prepare people, not just papers: train process owners and key staff to explain what they do, why, and how they prove it. Auditors ask for evidence, not rehearsed scripts.
- Keep your scope tight and accurate—auditors will check that what's in scope truly matches operations, locations, systems, and excluded areas.
- Internal audits and management reviews are your best preparation tools—run them regularly, treat findings seriously, and show follow-up during surveillance audits.
- Don't hide nonconformities—document, correct, perform root-cause analysis, implement corrective actions, and verify effectiveness. Auditors expect learning, not perfection.
- Surveillance audits are annual health checks—stay audit-ready year-round (evidence up-to-date, actions closed, internal audit cycle ongoing).
- For recertification, demonstrate evolution and maturity: trends, improvements, resolved past findings, and how the ISMS has adapted to change.
- Use certification marks correctly—follow the cert body's rules for logos and claims; misuse can lead to suspension.
- Remember the true reward: certification is valid, but the real value lies in stronger risk management, improved operations, customer trust, and an ongoing security culture.
- Celebrate your achievement—then focus on continual improvement. A certificate is a milestone, not the finish line.

Chapter 16

Practice paper

Test what you've learned

Congratulations on reaching this point. It means you've completed your ISO 27001 learning journey and are now ready to put your understanding to the test.

This Practice Paper is designed to help you assess how much you've truly absorbed from the book. It includes 100 multiple-choice and true/false questions covering all clauses, concepts, and practical scenarios discussed so far. The questions are intentionally randomized—not grouped by topic or chapter—to give you the feel of a real exam environment.

Before you begin, resist the temptation to look at the answer key at the back of the book. Allow yourself to test your understanding honestly. This is an open-book exercise, so feel free to refer back to relevant chapters or even the ISO/IEC 27001:2022 standard itself if you have a copy. The idea is not to memorize but to understand and apply what you've learned.

Here's how to get started:

1. Take a notebook or a clean sheet of paper.
2. Number it from 1 to 100.
3. For each question, select the correct option and note your answer as follows:
   - For multiple-choice questions: choose one option—A, B, C, or D.
   - For true/false questions: choose between two options—A (True) or B (False).
4. Once you've answered all 100 questions, check your responses against the answer key provided at the end of the book.

Try to complete the paper in one sitting, just as you would in an exam. This will give you a clear picture of your confidence level, comprehension, and the areas you may wish to revisit.

Remember, this isn't a memory test—it's a reflection exercise. It's meant to strengthen your grasp of ISO 27001, help you identify gaps, and build the confidence you'll need to apply these concepts in real-life implementation.

Take your time, enjoy the process, and good luck.

1. **What does the ISO/IEC 27001 standard provide?**

   A. Requirements for organizations certifying an information security management system.
   B. Requirements for an information security management system.
   C. Guidance for auditing an information security management system.
   D. Guidelines for an ISMS.

2. **How can you get an official copy of the ISO/IEC 27001 standard?**

DOI: 10.1201/9781003744139-17

A. Go to your favorite search engine and search for it.
B. Go to the ISO website at iso.org and order it.
C. Ask your security colleagues if they have a copy.
D. Download a free version from a file-sharing or community website.

3. **Which of the statements below regarding the ISMS scope is correct?**

A. Any inclusions made in the ISMS scope should be justified.
B. A key process is not considered part of organizational boundaries.
C. The ISMS scope must be available as documented information.
D. The ISMS scope can be kept confidential and not shared with auditors.

4. **Who is responsible for establishing the information security policy according to ISO/IEC 27001?**

A. The top management.
B. Internal interested parties.
C. The information security manager.
D. The external auditor during the certification audit.

5. **An organization has decided to move its information-processing facilities to a place where the risk of flooding is low. What option of risk treatment is this?**

A. Risk avoidance.
B. Risk evaluation.
C. Risk sharing.
D. Risk transfer.

6. **What is the minimum number of controls that must be listed in the SoA as per ISO/IEC 27001:2022?**

A. 93.
B. 100.
C. 114.
D. Depends on the organization's risk assessment.

7. **Insurance and outsourcing are the two main methods of:**

A. Risk modification.
B. Risk avoidance.
C. Risk transfer.
D. Risk tolerance.

8. **Why should an organization draft a Statement of Applicability?**

A. To ensure that the ISMS is aligned with the mission of the organization.
B. To document the justifications for the inclusion and exclusion of Annex A controls.
C. To ensure compliance with industry best practices.
D. To list all security incidents that occurred during the implementation phase.

9. **The risk that remains after risk treatment is known as:**

A. Inherent risk.
B. Treated risk.
C. Residual risk.
D. Accepted risk.

10. **Organizations can obtain certification against the ISO/IEC 27002 standard if they implement all its information security controls.**

    A. True.
    B. False.

11. **A third party that performs the assessment of conformity of management systems is:**

    A. An international standard.
    B. An accreditation body.
    C. A certification body.
    D. A consultancy organization.

12. **A former employee of a commercial bank has gained unauthorized access to the company's sensitive information. What does this present?**

    A. A threat that has the potential to harm the assets of the organization, such as information or systems.
    B. A vulnerability in the monitoring system of the organization that does not have corresponding threats.
    C. A security control incorrectly implemented by the organization that is not vulnerable.
    D. An acceptable risk that does not require further action.

13. **With which of the following principles does an organization comply if it ensures that only authorized users have access to their sensitive data?**

    A. Confidentiality.
    B. Integrity.
    C. Availability.
    D. Accountability.

14. **Why might an organization build an ISO 27001-compliant cybersecurity program?**

    A. Complying with ISO 27001 is a "set it and forget it" solution to improve an organization's security.
    B. Complying with ISO 27001 means your organization is protected from security incidents.
    C. Complying with ISO 27001 is a good way to ensure that your organization has built and is maintaining a strong information security program.
    D. ISO 27001 is easy for many organizations to comply with.

15. **An organization has clearly defined the security procedures and uses an access control software to avoid unauthorized access of the personnel to its confidential data. What is the function of these security controls?**

    A. To correct errors arising from a problem.
    B. To report the occurrence of a malicious act.
    C. To prevent the occurrence of incidents.
    D. To recover data after an incident.

16. **Which one of the following phrases would apply to 'plan' in relation to the PDCA cycle for a business process?**

    A. Making improvements.
    B. Identifying risks.

C. Implementing controls.
D. Reviewing performance.

17. **How can you proactively ensure that your organization has security controls in place that may not be mentioned in ISO 27001?**

A. Implementing all controls from ISO 27002.
B. Third-party security reviews and audits will identify any missing security controls.
C. This is not necessary because ISO 27001 includes all the security controls your organization should implement.
D. Supplement your ISO 27001 compliance with other security standards and frameworks like the NIST Cybersecurity Framework.

18. **Why is it important to follow a plan when building an ISO 27001-compliant information security program?**

A. It engages project managers and other people in the organization who should be involved in ISO 27001 compliance.
B. A written plan to achieve compliance is required by ISO 27001.
C. Following a plan helps make sure none of the requirements gets missed.
D. It ensures that certification auditors are not required to visit your organization multiple times.

19. **What can have an impact on the availability of information?**

A. Performance degradation.
B. Incorrect results.
C. Deliberate change of information.
D. Unauthorized disclosure of information.

20. **How can your organization get ISO 27001 certified?**

A. Any security company or auditing firm can review your ISMS and certify it as compliant.
B. Self-assessing compliance with ISO 27001 is the same as being certified.
C. Your ISMS must be audited by an accredited certification body and verified as compliant.
D. Submitting your ISMS documentation to ISO directly for approval and certification.

21. **What does ISO 27001 mean by the "context" of the organization?**

A. Relevant details about your organization like when it was established, number of employees, etc.
B. How your organization compares to competitors or other similar organizations.
C. External and internal issues related to your organization and its ability to protect information using the ISMS.
D. The organizational chart and job titles of employees involved in information security.

22. Which of these is a mandatory document to comply with ISO 27001 according to Clause 4.3?

A. Requirements of the ISMS.
B. Scope of the ISMS.
C. Components of the ISMS.
D. Context of the ISMS.

23. ISO 31000:2018 is a requirement standard.

A. True.
B. False.

24. Which of these is not required information your users must be aware of?

A. The internal audit findings.
B. The information security policy.
C. Their contribution to the effectiveness of the ISMS.
D. The implications of not conforming with ISMS requirements.

25. Why are Clauses 6 and 8 of ISO 27001 so closely related?

A. Clause 6 is the planning phase for risk management and achieving security objectives, and Clause 8 is where those plans are put into action.
B. Clauses 6 and 8 are not closely related.
C. Clause 6 requires your organization to implement information security controls and Clause 8 requires the assessment of the controls.
D. Clause 6 deals only with documentation, while Clause 8 focuses only on internal audits.

26. If top management does not have time, it is acceptable to delegate the ISMS management review to the ISMS manager.

A. True.
B. False.

27. Which methodology does ISO 27001 require you to follow when assessing information security risks?

A. ISO/IEC 27005, the official standard for Information Security Risk Management.
B. The NIST Cybersecurity Framework.
C. ISO 27001 doesn't require you to follow a specific risk assessment methodology.
D. The COBIT 2019 Governance Framework.

28. Who must do the communications relevant to the ISMS?

A. The CEO.
B. The information security leader.
C. Who is responsible for the communications related to the ISMS is defined in advance and may be different based on what is being communicated.
D. The CIO/CTO.

29. **Which of the options below represents an example of a vulnerability?**

A. Unauthorized access by persons who have left the organization.
B. Data input error by personnel.
C. A ransomware attack on the organization's servers.
D. Unencrypted data.

30. **If your organization is small and segregating duties is difficult, your organization should:**

A. Implement a system of checks and balances.
B. Ignore this requirement of ISO 27001.
C. Hire more staff to comply with this requirement.
D. Outsource all information security activities to a third party.

31. **Which of the following best describes the integrity principle?**

A. Ensuring information is available to authorized individuals.
B. Ensuring that information remains accurate, complete, and protected from unauthorized modification.
C. Making sure information is accessible whenever needed.
D. Allowing unrestricted access to information for authorized users.

32. **Users should be trained to report when the following security events happen, except when:**

A. A user is observed violating a security policy.
B. A user makes a mistake resulting in the loss of data.
C. A user is observed watching streaming media instead of working.
D. Software is malfunctioning.

33. **Why is it helpful to get an independent review of how your organization manages information security?**

A. Independent reviewers will prove to management that your organization is secure.
B. To place blame on specific individuals for inadequate security controls.
C. Independent reviewers provide an outside perspective on the state of security controls.
D. It is required only when an organization fails an internal audit.

34. **Examples of information security requirements that should be in place when employees and contractors are terminated include the following choices except:**

A. returning metro-transit pass, if issued.
B. returning access badge, if issued.
C. removing physical and logical access rights.
D. returning documents and equipment belonging to the organization.

35. **Why is control 8.32 "Change management" important?**

A. Changes to processes or systems are a common cause of system or security failures if not managed properly.
B. Changes to processes or systems can be time-consuming if not managed properly.
C. Changes to processes or systems can be expensive if not managed properly.

D. Changes to processes or systems should only be made during audits to ensure compliance.

36. ISO/IEC 27005 supports organizations in applying a structured approach to information security risk.

A. True.
B. False.

37. What is the required interval to conduct management review?

A. Before each Information Security audit.
B. At least once in a year.
C. At least once in each quarter.
D. There is no specific interval; it shall be at planned intervals.

38. Which one of the following statements is a requirement of the standard?

A. Top management shall communicate the policy to all customers, as appropriate.
B. Top management shall appoint ISMS Manager who will be responsible to ensure that the ISMS is established and maintained.
C. Top management shall establish a policy that is appropriate to the context and purpose of the organization.
D. Top management shall communicate the relevant outputs of management reviews to relevant interested parties.

39. ISO 27001 provides guidelines on how to implement, maintain, and improve an ISMS.

A. True.
B. False.

40. Which one of the following statements is incorrect?

A. Internal audit programs should take account of changes affecting the organization.
B. An audit program will stay the same regardless of the changes in audit results.
C. Internal audit nonconformities must be addressed.
D. Risk is a theme that runs through ISO 27001.

41. Clause 10.2 requires corrective action to take place in the event of a nonconformity. What do you understand by the term "corrective action"?

A. Action to eliminate a detected nonconformity.
B. Action to eliminate the cause of a nonconformity and to prevent recurrence.
C. Action to isolate a nonconformity and analyze how it originated.
D. Action to identify who caused a nonconformity and provide them with the necessary competence.

42. Regarding ISMS internal audits, which one of the following is incorrect?

A. Internal audit plan is required to be available as documented information.
B. Internal audit frequency shall take into consideration the results of previous audits.
C. Internal audits can be conducted once in 2 years.
D. The internal audit process should be independent.

43. **Which benefit can be gained from the implementation of an ISO 27001-compliant ISMS?**

A. Increased flexibility.
B. Increased access to advanced technologies.
C. Reduced documentation requirements.
D. Increased customer confidence.

44. **Organizations can obtain certification against ______________ standard.**

A. ISO 27000
B. ISO 27001
C. ISO 27002
D. ISO 27003

45. **Which statement regarding management systems is correct?**

A. The scope of a management system can only include parts of an organization.
B. A management system facilitates achievement of objectives in one or more disciplines.
C. An organization cannot have more than one management system at the same time.
D. A management system applies only to information security activities.

46. **__________ is an iterative method that helps implement, maintain, and systematically improve an ISMS.**

A. The Plan-Act-Review-Check cycle
B. The Plan-Do-Rehearse-Act cycle
C. The Prepare-Do-Evaluate-Adjust cycle
D. The Plan-Do-Check-Act cycle

47. **Who is responsible for the effectiveness of the ISMS?**

A. ISMS implementation team.
B. Information security manager.
C. Top management.
D. Internal audit team.

48. **How should the ISMS scope statement be?**

A. Confidential and easily understood.
B. General and complex.
C. Specific, clear, and appropriate to the organization's context.
D. Vague and flexible to allow future adjustments.

49. **____________ are/is imperative for the implementation of an ISMS based on ISO 27001.**

A. Top management support and approval
B. A large number of stakeholders
C. A narrow scope
D. External consultant involvement

50. **Which statement best describes the frequency of internal audits?**

A. At planned intervals or whenever significant changes are proposed or occur.
B. At planned intervals, considering the importance of processes and previous audit results.
C. As dictated by top management on the basis of management review.
D. At least twice a year and as a consequence of risk assessments.

51. **Which one of the following statements is correct?**

A. A record is not necessarily documented information, but a process shall always be documented.
B. Procedure and the process are the same type of documents.
C. A record gives information to demonstrate that a procedure has been followed.
D. A record describes a process, whereas a procedure describes the flow of activities.

52. **An information security policy shall include a commitment to continual improvement.**

A. True.
B. False.

53. **The ISO 27001 standard requires that the ISMS policy shall be:**

A. Communicated within the organization.
B. Available and distributed to all interested parties.
C. Displayed on notice boards in the organization.
D. Signed by top management.

54. **A clearly defined information security policy does not require review, control, and evaluation.**

A. True.
B. False.

55. **Information security objectives shall be:**

A. Hardly attainable.
B. General.
C. Optional, depending on organizational size.
D. Measurable (if practicable).

56. **What is of high importance in cases when the ISMS undergoes changes?**

A. The changes are approved by interested parties.
B. The changes are communicated to and approved by interested parties.
C. Consider the consequences of the changes.
D. The changes are implemented immediately to save time.

57. **Which of the following can top management delegate in relation to the management of the ISMS?**

A. All responsibilities and accountability.
B. Ensuring that the ISMS conforms to the requirements of the standard.
C. The frequency of certification audits.
D. Management review.

58. Which one of the following is incorrect related to external and internal issues?

A. They can be inputs to the determination of an ISMS scope.
B. They have to be documented.
C. Technology may be both an internal and external issue.
D. When planning for ISMS, organization shall consider the external and internal issues.

59. Which of the following statements best describes the implementation of a management system?

A. The system is built and influenced by the structure and operation of the business.
B. The quantity and extent of documentation are standard across every business.
C. Certification is a mandatory part of the implementation of the standard.
D. Every element of the business must be included in the ISMS.

60. Which of the following elements of the standard includes all required documents?

A. Internal audit results, the ISMS policy, the context of the organization.
B. Management review results, internal audit results, ISMS objectives.
C. The ISMS policy, roles and responsibilities, the ISMS scope.
D. The ISMS scope, roles and responsibilities, management review results.

61. ISO 27001 requires organizations to apply a formal risk assessment process.

A. True.
B. False.

62. Under certain circumstances it may be permissible to exclude the following activities:

A. Monitoring the performance of security activities.
B. Information security training and awareness.
C. Review of the residual risk.
D. None of the above.

63. Risk Treatment is:

A. The process of selecting and implementing actions to address identified risks.
B. The identification of information assets and calculation of risk values.
C. The establishment of vulnerabilities and threats to information assets.
D. The elimination of all risks from the organization.

64. What is an appropriate action for ensuring that people within the organization are competent for undertaking information security-related tasks?

A. Providing training.
B. Rewarding good behavior and punishing undesirable behavior.
C. Increasing salaries.
D. Hiring external auditors to monitor staff performance.

65. **An employee who is not aware of or trained in information security practices may pose a potential risk to the organization.**

A. True.
B. False.

66. **The input into the management review of the ISMS shall include which of the following?**

A. Potential risks not adequately addressed in the previous risk assessment.
B. Recommendations for improvements.
C. Feedback from interested parties.
D. All of the above

67. **Which of the following is a requirement of ISO 27001?**

A. To have a risk manager.
B. To have a process that calculates the risk annual loss expectancy related to the ISMS.
C. To retain documented information about the risk treatment result.
D. To review risks only during external audits.

68. **ISO/IEC 27001:2022 is applicable to which of the following?**

A. Information technology only.
B. E-commerce only.
C. Paper-based information only.
D. Information in all forms.

69. **ISO 27001 states that "Documented information required by the ISMS shall be controlled to ensure adequate protection from …"**

A. loss of confidentiality.
B. improper use.
C. loss of integrity.
D. all of the above.

70. **Which of the following is not an Information Security Policy requirement of ISO/IEC 27001:2022?**

A. Available as documented information.
B. Be communicated within the organization.
C. Available as a link on the corporate website.
D. Be available to interested parties, as appropriate.

71. **Which one of the following phrases would apply to 'check' in relation to the PDCA cycle for a business process?**

A. Making improvements.
B. Identifying risks.
C. Auditing processes.
D. Implementing actions.

72. **Which claim is correct regarding documented information?**

A. Documented information provides information on the effectiveness of the processes and opportunities for improvement.
B. Despite the fact that information technology (IT) has become an integral part of organizations, the way documented information is created, handled, and stored has failed to evolve.
C. Each piece of documented information does not need be standardized in terms of format.
D. Documented information is optional and only required for certification audits.

73. **The extent of documented information for an ISMS does not differ from one organization to another.**

A. True.
B. False.

74. **Which of the following is true with regard to the documents of an ISO 27001-compliant ISMS?**

A. They must be available in electronic format.
B. They can be in any form or type of medium.
C. They must be printed, signed, and stamped by top management.
D. They should be stored only on the organization's internal servers.

75. **What is the purpose of risk identification?**

A. To identify the consequences derived from potential risks.
B. To evaluate and review the strategies in place that address potential risks.
C. To eliminate all risks before they occur.
D. To find, recognize, and describe risks that might help or prevent an organization achieving its objectives.

76. **During risk identification, an organization should not include all risks but focus only on those that they can control.**

A. True.
B. False.

77. **ISO/IEC 27004 provides guidance on monitoring, measuring, analyzing, and evaluating the performance of an ISMS.**

A. True.
B. False.

78. **Which one of the following phrases would apply to 'do' in relation to the PDCA cycle for a business process?**

A. Making improvements.
B. Identifying risks.
C. Auditing processes.
D. Implementing controls.

79. **Regarding ISO 27001 Annex A, which of the following statements is correct?**

A. All controls must be implemented.
B. The implementation of the controls is the responsibility of the ISMS manager.
C. Controls that are not implemented must be justified in the Statement of Applicability.
D. Some controls can be excluded without justification if the risk assessment clearly indicates they are not needed.

80. **Which of the following are possible risk treatment options?**

A. Avoiding risks.
B. Applying appropriate controls.
C. Knowingly and objectively accepting risks.
D. All of the above.

81. **The nonfulfillment of an ISO 27001 requirement is called:**

A. A dispensation.
B. A non-conformity.
C. A corrective action.
D. A preventive measure.

82. **Which of the following is true with regard to the documents of an ISO 27001-compliant ISMS?**

A. They must be available in electronic format.
B. They must be protected and controlled.
C. They must all be kept in the ISMS manual.
D. They must be reviewed before every audit.

83. **When conducting risk assessment an organisations must:**

A. Identify information security risks.
B. Analyze information security risks.
C. Evaluate information security risks.
D. All of the above.

84. **ISMS audits can be used to:**

A. Assist in the selection of service providers.
B. Verify conformance with contractual requirements.
C. Assess the effectiveness of the ISMS.
D. All of the above.

85. **The purpose of risk evaluation is to support:**

A. Scope definition.
B. Decision-making.
C. Objective determination.
D. Control selection.

86. **The organization should conduct monitoring and measurement activities twice a year, as specifically indicated in ISO 27001.**

A. True.
B. False.

87. **The organization needs to prioritize risks in order to focus the treatment efforts on risks that have both _________ impact and _________.**

    A. moderate; time of recovery
    B. higher; likelihood
    C. high; consequences
    D. low; severity

88. **With regard to evaluating the performance of the ISMS, which of the following statements is true if the organization conforms to the requirements of ISO/IEC 27001?**

    A. Internal audits are conducted at planned intervals by competent auditors.
    B. It executes monitoring, measurement, analysis, and evaluation processes.
    C. Top management undertakes regular reviews to ensure the continuing suitability, adequacy, and effectiveness of the ISMS.
    D. All of the above.

89. **ISO 27001 specifies that management reviews must be conducted annually.**

    A. True.
    B. False.

90. **Which action should be taken to eliminate the cause of a nonconformity and prevent recurrence?**

    A. Preventive action.
    B. Corrective action.
    C. Effective action.
    D. Remedial action.

91. **What is the main activity of Stage 1 audit?**

    A. Reviewing documented information.
    B. Verifying the effectiveness of all corrections and corrective actions taken.
    C. Verify the effectiveness of the management system.
    D. Conducting on-site employee interviews.

92. **ISO performs accreditation and certification activities.**

    A. True.
    B. False.

93. **Which of the following statements is correct?**

    A. Certification bodies are certified by accreditation bodies.
    B. Certification bodies are hired by accreditation bodies.
    C. Certification bodies are accredited by accreditation bodies.
    D. Certification bodies report directly to ISO.

94. **Which of the following is an example of an audit objective?**

A. To punish employees for nonconformities found during the audit.
B. To ensure the auditor gains detailed knowledge of all business operations.
C. To determine whether the ISMS conforms to planned arrangements and ISO 27001 requirements.
D. To redesign the organization's information security controls.

95. **Which term means "knowing how much risk the organization is comfortable assuming"?**

A. Risk appetite.
B. Insurance.
C. Unexpected damage.
D. Risk exposure.

96. **Which one of the following statements is true?**

A. Excluding any requirements specified in Clauses 4–10 is acceptable when an organization claims conformity to ISO 27001.
B. Excluding any controls specified in Annex A with justification is acceptable when an organization claims conformity to ISO 27001.
C. Excluding any controls specified in Annex A with justification is not acceptable when an organization claims conformity to ISO 27001.
D. Excluding both clauses and controls is acceptable if approved by top management.

97. **Which one of the following phrases would apply to 'audit scope' in relation to an audit?**

A. Assessing conformity.
B. Documented outcomes.
C. Audit boundaries.
D. Audit sampling.

98. **Which one of the following phrases is a "criteria" in relation to an audit?**

A. Complete the audit on time.
B. Confirm the scope of the management system.
C. Legal and regulatory requirements
D. Audit plan and checklist

99. **Which one of the following phrases would apply to "act" in relation to the PDCA cycle for a business process?**

A. Making improvements.
B. Measuring objectives.
C. Identifying risks.
D. Implementing controls.

100. **ISO 19011:2018 is a requirement standard.**

A. True.
B. False.

Chapter 17

Quiz compass

⚙ Your Guide to Self-Check Answers

⚠ **Caution:** If you've landed here before completing the quizzes in the chapters, pause for a second. I know it's tempting to scroll down and get the answers early, but trust me: It won't help you in the long run.

This section is here to **support your learning**, not shortcut it. Give each quiz a fair shot, jot down your responses, think them through, and *then* come here to compare. That way, you're not just memorizing answers—you're building confidence in your understanding.

No one's grading you. This isn't a test. It's a compass—to help you reflect, recalibrate, and keep moving forward with clarity.

QUIZ #1

Sr.	*True/ False*	*Justification*
1	**False**	ISO is not an acronym. It comes from the Greek word *isos*, meaning "equal."
2	**True**	ISO published its first standard in ***1951***, which focused on industrial reference temperatures.
3	**False**	ISO 9001, the standard for quality management systems, was published in ***1987***, while ISO/IEC 27001 (for information security) was officially published much later in ***2005***.
4	**False**	ISO standards are developed through multi-stakeholder groups including industry, academia, consumers, and governments.
5	**True**	Standards reduce technical trade barriers and align global practices.
6	**True**	ISO members often adopt international standards into national regulatory frameworks.
7	**True**	ISO uses a consensus-based approach with input from over 160 member countries.
8	**True**	That's one of the core functions of ISO standards.
9	**False**	ISO/IEC 27001:2022 is a *requirement* standard, not a guideline. It contains mandatory clauses using the word ***"shall"***, which organizations must conform to if they seek certification.
10	**False**	ISO 19011:2018 is a ***guideline standard***, not a requirement standard. It provides ***recommendations*** on auditing management systems.

DOI: 10.1201/9781003744139-18

QUIZ #2

Sr.	True/ False	Justification
1	**True**	Confidentiality ensures that only authorized individuals can access information.
2	**False**	Both malicious actions and unintentional errors can compromise integrity.
3	**False**	Availability ensures access for all authorized users, not just IT staff.
4	**False**	An ISMS is a continual system, not a one-time task, and it includes both technical and organizational controls.
5	**False**	ISO/IEC 27001 defines what must be done, but not how—that's covered in ISO/ IEC 27002.
6	**True**	ISO/IEC 27002 gives practical guidance on implementing each control listed in Annex A.
7	**True**	ISO/IEC 27005 provides structured methods for identifying and managing information security risks.
8	**True**	ISO/IEC 27004 supports measuring, analyzing, and evaluating ISMS performance.
9	**False**	ISMS is scalable and applicable for organizations of all sizes—small or large.
10	**True**	ISO/IEC 27000 provides a glossary and overview for the ISMS family.
11	**True**	Confidentiality can be breached through simple human mistakes like leaving files unattended.
12	**False**	A firewall is just one control; ISO/IEC 27001 requires a broader, systematic approach.
13	**True**	Certification is optional, but adopting the standard adds credibility and maturity.
14	**False**	Information security is a shared responsibility across all roles in an organization.
15	**True**	An ISMS exists to ensure that security efforts are tied to actual risks and business goals.

QUIZ #3

Sr.	True/ False	Justification
1	**False**	Process-based thinking focuses on how workflows across functions, not within silos. It's about inputs, outputs, and interaction between processes.
2	**False**	Risk-based thinking is a continuous mindset, not limited to one phase. It guides planning, operations, audits, and improvements.
3	**False**	As per Clause 1 of ISO/IEC 27001: "Excluding any of the requirements specified in Clauses 4 to 10 is not acceptable when an organization claims conformity."
4	**True**	The harmonized approach enables organizations to align multiple standards using a common framework, making integrated systems easier to manage.
5	**True**	Understanding ISO/IEC 27001 helps because the structure and logic are similar across other ISO management system standards.

QUIZ #4

Sr.	True/ False	Justification
1	**False**	Information security includes confidentiality, integrity, and availability—not just secrecy.
2	**False**	ISO defines risk as the effect of uncertainty on objectives, not just "something bad happening."
3	**True**	This is the correct ISO definition—controls are meant to modify risk, not necessarily eliminate it.
4	**True**	A record provides objective evidence that a task, activity, or process was completed as planned.
5	**False**	Assets can be physical, digital, intellectual (like source code), or even people with knowledge—anything of value.
6	**True**	A requirement is something mandatory, defined by ISO, laws, contracts, or internal needs.
7	**True**	ISO/IEC 27000 is the foundational vocabulary document for the entire 27001 family of standards.
8	**False**	Stakeholders include both internal and external parties—anyone impacted by or influencing the ISMS.
9	**False**	ISO/IEC 27701 and ISO/IEC 29100 clearly define PII and related privacy terms.
10	**True**	Accreditation bodies give credibility to certification bodies. Certification bodies audit organizations.

QUIZ #5

Sr.	True/ False	Justification
1	**False**	ISO 27001 requires certain mandatory documents, but not every requirement needs to be in writing. Some can be implemented operationally without formal documentation.
2	**True**	ISMS requirements originate from both external (laws, regulations, contracts) and internal (business objectives, risk assessments) sources.
3	**False**	Copy-paste compliance risks producing irrelevant or incorrect documents that don't reflect actual operations.
4	**True**	Clause 7.5.2 specifies requirements for creating clear, relevant, and fit-for-purpose documents.
5	**True**	Clause 7.5.3 requires controlling documents via version control, access rights, and protection from loss or unauthorized change.
6	**False**	The template is a guide; it must be adapted to fit the organization's unique needs and operational context.
7	**True**	Documenting associated risks strengthens the connection between ISMS documents and the risk management process.
8	**True**	Core content is the main body of the document where actual operational or compliance requirements are detailed.
9	**True**	Annexes or appendices allow inclusion of reference material without cluttering the main content.
10	**True**	A structured framework ensures consistency, making documents easier to maintain, audit, and apply.

QUIZ #6

Sr.	*True/ False*	*Justification*
1	**False**	A comprehensive gap analysis should cover **all applicable clauses**, not just those requiring documentation. This ensures a full understanding of implementation gaps, including cultural, procedural, and technical aspects.
2	**True**	The maturity score is a reflection of how thoroughly and effectively a control or requirement has been implemented. It helps identify strengths and areas needing improvement.
3	**False**	A Gantt chart is valuable for both small and large projects because it helps track timelines, and dependencies.
4	**False**	While the gap analysis provides a suggested order, tasks can be reordered or run in parallel based on organizational context.
5	**True**	Gap analysis identifies strengths, weaknesses, and missing elements, replacing guesswork with facts.

QUIZ #7

Sr.	*True/ False*	*Justification*
1	**True**	Clause 4.1 doesn't explicitly mandate documenting internal and external issues, but it is strongly recommended to maintain documented information for effectiveness (per 7.5.1(b)).
2	**True**	Technological trends and changes are examples of external issues that can influence ISMS planning and risk.
3	**False**	The ISMS scope is a living document. It can and should be updated if context, requirements, or business conditions change.
4	**True**	ISO 27001 explicitly requires the ISMS scope to be available as documented information (Clause 4.3).
5	**False**	Organizations define scope strategically. It may cover only specific functions, services, or locations, not necessarily the entire organization.
6	**False**	Interested parties also include those who *perceive themselves* as affected, even if they don't directly affect operations (e.g., citizens or media).

QUIZ #8

Sr.	*True/ False*	*Justification*
1	**True**	Clause 5.3 requires roles, responsibilities, and authorities to be clearly assigned and communicated.
2	**True**	Clause 5.1 requires leadership to integrate ISMS requirements into existing business processes.
3	**True**	Clause 5.2 requires the information security policy to include a framework for setting objectives.
4	**False**	Staff awareness of regulator's requirements is not required in Clause 5; focus is on ISMS policy, objectives, and roles.
5	**False**	This falls under Clause 4.3 (Context of the Organization), not Clause 5.
6	**True**	Clause 5.2 requires continual improvement as a commitment in the policy.
7	**True**	Clause 5.1 requires leadership to ensure the ISMS achieves its intended outcomes.
8	**True**	Clause 5.1 requires leadership to provide adequate resources for the ISMS.
9	**True**	Clause 5.3 requires top management to assign responsibility and authority for reporting on the performance of the ISMS to top management
10	**False**	The standard requires the policy to be approved and communicated; a signature is not mandatory.

QUIZ #9

Sr.	*True/ False*	*Justification*
1	**False**	Risk criteria don't have to be only financial. They can include operational, legal, reputational, or safety impacts.
2	**True**	Clause 6.1.2 requires criteria for both likelihood and consequence to be defined.
3	**False**	Risk identification is about spotting possible risks, not predicting the future with precision.
4	**False**	Assigning a risk owner is mandatory; without ownership, risks are not properly managed.
5	**False**	Risk analysis can be qualitative, quantitative, or semi-quantitative. ISO leaves the choice open.
6	**True**	Risk evaluation compares risk levels to acceptance criteria and helps prioritize for treatment.
7	**False**	Annex A is a baseline, but organizations can add extra controls from frameworks like PCI-DSS, NCEMA, or internal practices.
8	**True**	The SoA must clearly justify inclusions and exclusions of Annex A controls.
9	**False**	ISO/IEC 27002 is a guidance document—helpful, but not mandatory for implementing any control.
10	**True**	Wherever possible, objectives shall be measurable so progress can be tracked.

QUIZ #10

Sr.	*True/ False*	*Justification*
1	**True**	Clause 7.1 requires organizations to determine and provide all necessary resources—including financial—to establish, implement, maintain, and continually improve the ISMS. Without budget support, implementation becomes a paper exercise.
2	**True**	Clause 7.2 requires that when training or other actions are taken to build competence, their effectiveness must be evaluated. It's not enough to train; you must check if learning actually happened.
3	**True**	Clause 7.2(d) mandates keeping documented information as evidence of competence—such as certificates or performance reviews.
4	**True**	Competence can be achieved in many ways—through mentoring, experience, workshops, on-the-job training, or external experts. Formal classroom sessions are just one option.
5	**False**	Training helps, but it's not the only method. Competence can also come from experience, qualifications, or mentoring.
6	**True**	Clause 7.3 requires that all personnel understand how their actions contribute to ISMS performance.
7	**True**	Awareness also means understanding the implications of non-conformance—such as security breaches, compliance issues, or reputational damage.
8	**True**	Clause 7.4 requires planning communication needs—what to communicate, when, to whom, and how—for both internal and external audiences.
9	**False**	Communication must be targeted and relevant. Not everyone needs every message; otherwise, important updates may get ignored or misunderstood.
10	**True**	Crisis communication must be controlled and traceable. Using unofficial channels (like personal email or social media) can cause confusion or compliance breaches.
11	**False**	The standard is generic. Each organization defines its own documentation format, style, and level of detail based on its context and complexity. There's no fixed template.
12	**True**	Clause 7.5.2(b) requires appropriate format and media—such as language, software, or visual layout—so documents are clear and usable for their readers.
13	**False**	Review and approval depend on the document's importance. Policies and procedures require formal approval; minor records may not.
14	**True**	Clause 7.5.3(b) requires adequate protection of information—including confidentiality, integrity, and availability.
15	**False**	Access should be controlled based on need-to-know. Some documents (like incident reports) may contain sensitive or confidential information.
16	**False**	Clause 7.5.3(f) requires defined retention and disposal periods. Documents must be kept only as long as they're valid or legally required.
17	**True**	Clause 7.5.3 states that external documents—such as regulations, supplier manuals, or standards—must also be identified and controlled if relevant.
18	**True**	Clause 7.2 applies to anyone whose work can impact information security—including contractors, suppliers, or consultants.
19	**False**	Awareness must be continuous. One-time induction training is not enough; ongoing reminders and activities are essential to maintain security culture.
20	**True**	Awareness is about understanding purpose and relevance—when people grasp *why* security matters, they take ownership and make better decisions.

QUIZ #11

Sr.	*True/False*	*Justification*
1	**True**	Clause 8 is the operational "Do" phase: You run what you planned to meet information security requirements and objectives.
2	**False**	Clause 8.1 expects *documented information* to demonstrate processes were carried out as planned; evidence isn't optional.
3	**True**	Clause 8.1 explicitly requires reviewing consequences of unintended changes and mitigating adverse effects where needed.
4	**False**	Outsourcing may transfer operational responsibility to a supplier, but accountability for information security remains with the organization.
5	**False**	Clause 8.2 does *not* introduce a new method; it executes the risk assessment process previously defined in *6.1.2.*
6	**False**	Clause 8.3 is about *execution,* not creating new procedures; you carry out what you already committed to in 6.1.3.

QUIZ #12

Sr.	*True/ False*	**Justification**
1	**True**	Clause 9.1 requires the organization to determine what needs to be monitored and measured.
2	**True**	Measurement methods must produce valid, comparable, and reproducible results.
3	**False**	ISO 27001 does not prescribe fixed frequencies—organizations decide based on risk and context.
4	**True**	You must retain documented information as evidence of monitoring and measurement results.
5	**False**	Monitoring covers all ISMS processes and controls—not just technical ones.
6	**True**	Internal audits check both conformance and effectiveness of the ISMS.
7	**False**	Auditors must remain objective and impartial—they cannot audit their own work.
8	**True**	The audit program must consider process importance and previous audit results.
9	**False**	Nonconformities from internal audits are key inputs to management review.
10	**True**	Status of previous management review actions is a mandatory input under Clause 9.3.2.
11	**False**	Frequency is not fixed—reviews must occur at planned, justified intervals.
12	**True**	Management review outputs can include changes to policy, objectives, or resource allocation.
13	**True**	ISO/IEC 27004 offers practical guidance on monitoring and measurement methods for ISMS.
14	**False**	ISO 27001 clearly states that top management shall review the ISMS. Leadership ownership is essential.
15	**False**	The standard never mandates that the management review must be a meeting. The review can be done through reports, dashboards, online portals, or ongoing review processes—as long as it is effective, documented, and includes all required inputs and outputs.

QUIZ #13

Sr.	*True/ False*	*Justification*
1	**False**	Continual improvement is not a one-time activity or something to start after implementation. It's embedded throughout the ISMS, from Clause 4 onwards—beginning the moment you plan your system.
2	**True**	Clause 10.1 clearly states that the organization shall continually improve the suitability, adequacy, and effectiveness of the ISMS.
3	**False**	That's only correction. Corrective action goes beyond fixing—it identifies and eliminates the root cause to prevent recurrence.
4	**True**	ISO 27001 requires reviewing nonconformities to see if similar ones exist or could happen elsewhere, ensuring systemic improvement.
5	**False**	ISO 27001 doesn't mandate to keep documented information for continual improvement
6	**True**	The standard explicitly requires documented information showing both the nature of nonconformities and the results of corrective actions.
7	**False**	Clause 10 applies to all nonconformities, regardless of their size or impact—what changes is the proportion of response.
8	**True**	Continual improvement relies on insights from audits, incidents, performance data, and management reviews to make the ISMS more effective and resilient.

Chapter 18

Case answer key and reflections

This section contains the answers and justifications for all case-based quiz questions throughout the book. Each response is explained briefly so you can understand not just what the correct answer is, but why it matters in an ISO 27001 context. If you haven't already completed the case activities, pause and return to them first. Reviewing the answers before attempting the questions will reduce the value of the exercise. Once you've finished, come back here, compare your responses, and reflect on how your reasoning aligns with the expected approach.

Case 1: Answers

Sr.	*Answer*	*Reason/Explanation*
1	A	A gap analysis helps determine where existing processes fall short of ISO 27001 requirements, allowing the organization to prepare a practical implementation plan.
2	B	Conducting a gap analysis is a recommended best practice, not a formal requirement of ISO 27001. It's a preparatory step used to understand the organization's current maturity level.
3	D	A Gantt chart is a project management tool that helps visualize tasks, dependencies, and progress over time, ensuring accountability and timely execution.
4	C	Engaging stakeholders early ensures realistic timelines, shared ownership, and smoother coordination during ISMS implementation.
5	B	Understanding how each department operates and what information assets they handle helps define the ISMS scope and risk assessment foundation. This ensures the implementation plan reflects real business activities.
6	D	Top management involvement provides direction, visibility, and necessary support. Their commitment ensures that ISMS objectives align with organizational goals and that adequate resources are made available from the start.

DOI: 10.1201/9781003744139-19

Case 2: Answers

Sr.	*Answer*	*Reason/Explanation*
1	B	External environmental risks like monsoon flooding directly affect availability and information security continuity—they must be determined.
2	D	Interested parties include anyone who affects or is affected by the ISMS.
3	B	Excluding vendors without assessing contractual and operational impact can leave critical dependencies unprotected.
4	C	Not involving key stakeholders risks blind spots and missed obligations.
5	D	Documented, sourced lists with review cadence provide evidence of due diligence and a process for keeping obligations current.
6	A	A practical scope includes locations, systems, people, and relevant third-party interfaces—stated clearly so responsibilities and controls are unambiguous.

Case 3: Answers

Sr.	*Answer*	*Reason/Explanation*
1	C	Clause 5.1 requires top management to lead by example—review performance, provide resources, and communicate the importance of information security.
2	B	ISO 27001 makes top management ultimately accountable for the ISMS. IT can manage operations, but accountability cannot be delegated.
3	D	Clause 5.3 requires clarity and communication of roles and authorities; documentation is not a mandatory requirement.
4	D	Although budgets and systems were strong, insufficient dedicated manpower slowed implementation—a leadership issue in resource allocation.
5	A	Clause 5.1 requires top management to integrate ISMS requirements into organizational processes. By embedding ISMS considerations into new and existing projects, Farah ensured that information security became part of the bank's regular business operations, not a separate activity
6	B	Active engagement of top management through management reviews demonstrates real commitment and aligns leadership with ISMS progress.

Case 4: Answers

Sr.	*Answer*	*Reason/Explanation*
1	B	Risk criteria must allow consistent and repeatable assessments. Relying on personal judgment reduces consistency and makes risk assessment subjective.
2	D	The Statement of Applicability must consider all Annex A controls, provide justification for inclusion or exclusion, and indicate implementation status.
3	C	A defined change management process supports planned, controlled updates to the ISMS and aligns with Clause 6.3.
4	A	Objectives should relate to information security performance, align with the information security policy, and be measurable.
5	C	The standard requires risk assessment to be repeatable and consistent. Decisions based on personal judgment prevent this.
6	B	Objectives must align with the policy, consider risk results, be measurable where possible, and support continual improvement in information security.

Case 5: Answers

Sr.	*Answer*	*Reason/Explanation*
1	A	Assigning tasks based on demonstrated capability shows role-based competence aligned with ISO 27001 expectations.
2	C	Awareness sessions that are scheduled, communicated, and recorded help ensure staff understand their role in the ISMS.
3	B	A controlled repository ensures information is accurate, current, and accessible to authorized users—supporting Clause 7.5.3.
4	D	These actions support secure handling, retention, and disposal of sensitive documented information as required under Clause 7.5.3
5	B	Clause 7.2 requires the organization to retain documented information as evidence that individuals performing security-related tasks are competent.
6	A	ISO 27001 (clause 7.5.2) does not prescribe any specific format for documented information. It allows organizations to maintain documents in any format or media, including paper or digital, as long as they are controlled and suitable for use.

Case 6: Answers

Sr.	*Answer*	*Reason/Explanation*
1	C	Planned changes require structured implementation, testing, approvals, and documented results to ensure they are executed properly.
2	D	ISO 27001 does not mandate a specific format; digital tools are acceptable if information is controlled and maintained.
3	C	The incident occurred because the rollout bypassed formal planning, testing, and approval processes required for operational changes.
4	C	Clause 8 requires reviewing unintended changes, assessing adverse effects, and documenting corrective actions.
5	B	Clause 8 requires managing outsourced processes and ensuring supplier dependencies are considered in operational activities.
6	B	Meetings should support coordination, review of controls, risks, and ensure security processes are functioning effectively.

Case 7: Answers

Sr.	*Answer*	*Reason/Explanation*
1	C	ISO 27001 requires a risk-based audit program that adjusts frequency based on importance of the process, and previous audit results.
2	B	Persistent findings indicate increased risk and require more frequent audit focus.
3	D	ISO requires competence and impartiality; cross-functional trained internal auditors help achieve this.
4	B	Clause 9.2 requires internal audits to evaluate the effectiveness of the ISMS, not merely detect faults.
5	A	The audit program must define criteria, scope, methods, responsibilities, schedule, and documentation requirements.
6	B	ISO requires adjusting the audit program based on the importance of the process and the results of previous audits

Case 8: Answers

Sr.	*Answer*	*Reason/Explanation*
1	D	The organization repeatedly fixed the symptom (training) rather than addressing the underlying root cause, leading to recurring nonconformities.
2	B	Without identifying root causes, repeating the same training does not eliminate systemic issues.
3	C	Corrective action requires removing the root cause so the issue does not happen again.
4	C	ISO 27001 requires corrective actions to be documented, based on root cause analysis, proportional to risk, and verified for effectiveness.
5	A	Assuming that training alone resolves a recurring issue reflects confusion between correction and corrective action.
6	D	Controlled access and workflow changes address the underlying cause of document misuse, preventing recurrence—a core requirement of effective corrective action under ISO 27001.

Chapter 19

Practice paper

Answers and explanations

Before you start reading this section, let me pause you for a moment. Have you already finished answering all 100 questions in the Practice Paper? If not, please go back and do that first. Trust me, you'll learn far more that way.

This section is here to help you *reflect* on your answers, not replace the thinking process. Seeing the answers before attempting the questions won't add much value—it's like peeking at the results before running the race.

Once you've completed the paper, come back with your notes, compare your choices, and read the justifications carefully. Each explanation is short, practical, and designed to strengthen your understanding of ISO 27001 concepts.

Take this as your self-review session—the final step in consolidating everything you've learned through the book.

Sr.	*Answer*	*Reason/Explanation*
1	B	ISO 27001 defines the requirements for establishing, implementing, maintaining, and continually improving an ISMS that helps protect information assets effectively.
2	B	The official and authorized source for purchasing ISO 27001 is the ISO website (iso.org) or your national standards body's website.
3	C	ISO 27001 requires the ISMS scope to be documented and maintained as part of the organization's documented information to ensure clarity on what is covered and auditable.
4	A	According to ISO 27001, top management is responsible for establishing the information security policy to ensure it aligns with the organization's strategic direction and supports ISMS objectives.
5	A	Moving facilities to a low-flood-risk area eliminates the threat altogether, which is an example of risk avoidance—removing the source of risk rather than treating or transferring it.
6	A	ISO 27001:2022 includes 93 controls listed in Annex A, and all must be considered in the Statement of Applicability, with justification for inclusion or exclusion.
7	C	Insurance and outsourcing shift the financial or operational impact of a risk to another party, making them classic examples of risk transfer.
8	B	The Statement of Applicability records which Annex A controls are applicable and provides justification for each inclusion or exclusion, serving as key evidence of risk-based decision-making.
9	C	Residual risk is the level of risk that remains after controls or treatments have been applied to reduce or manage the original risk.

DOI: 10.1201/9781003744139-20

Sr.	*Answer*	*Reason/Explanation*
10	B	ISO 27002 is a guidance standard, not a certifiable one. Organizations can only be certified against ISO 27001, which specifies the requirements for an ISMS.
11	C	A certification body is an independent third party authorized to assess and certify an organization's management system for conformity with ISO 27001 requirements.
12	A	An ex-employee gaining unauthorized access represents a clear *threat*—an event or actor capable of exploiting vulnerabilities and causing harm to the organization's information assets.
13	A	Confidentiality ensures that sensitive information is accessed only by authorized individuals, protecting it from unauthorized disclosure or exposure.
14	C	ISO 27001 helps organizations establish, maintain, and continually improve a structured information security program aligned with business objectives and risk management.
15	C	Defined procedures and access control software are *preventive controls* designed to stop unauthorized access and reduce the likelihood of security incidents before they occur.
16	B	In the *Plan* phase of the PDCA cycle, an organization defines objectives, identifies risks, and plans appropriate controls and processes to achieve desired outcomes effectively.
17	D	While ISO 27001 defines requirements, integrating other frameworks like NIST can strengthen coverage, addressing emerging risks and controls not specifically detailed in ISO 27001.
18	C	A structured plan ensures all ISO 27001 requirements are addressed systematically, maintaining consistency, accountability, and completeness throughout ISMS implementation and certification preparation.
19	A	Availability refers to information being accessible when needed. Performance degradation, such as slow systems or downtime, directly affects the availability of information to authorized users.
20	C	ISO 27001 certification is granted only after an accredited certification body audits and confirms that the organization's ISMS meets all standard requirements.
21	C	"Context" in ISO 27001 refers to understanding internal and external factors that influence how the organization establishes, implements, and maintains its ISMS effectively.
22	B	Clause 4.3 of ISO 27001 requires the ISMS scope to be defined and maintained as documented information, clearly outlining boundaries and applicability
23	B	ISO 31000:2018 provides *guidelines* for risk management; it is not a certifiable requirement standard like ISO 27001.
24	A	Users must understand the information security policy, their ISMS role, and consequences of nonconformity. Internal audit findings are management-level information, not typically required for all users.
25	A	Clause 6 focuses on planning risks and objectives, while Clause 8 ensures those planned actions and controls are effectively implemented and operated.
26	B	Management review is the direct responsibility of top management in ISO 27001. It cannot be delegated, as it demonstrates leadership commitment and accountability for the ISMS's effectiveness.
27	C	ISO 27001 allows organizations to define their own risk assessment methodology, provided it is consistent, repeatable, and aligned with the organization's ISMS objectives.
28	C	ISO 27001 requires organizations to plan ISMS communications in advance—defining what, when, and by whom communication occurs—depending on context and audience
29	D	Unencrypted data is a *vulnerability*—a weakness that can be exploited by threats such as hackers or malware, leading to unauthorized access or data loss.

Sr.	*Answer*	*Reason/Explanation*
30	A	When segregation of duties isn't feasible, ISO 27001 allows compensating controls such as checks and balances to prevent misuse or unauthorized actions.
31	B	Integrity ensures information remains accurate, complete, and unaltered, safeguarding it from unauthorized modification or corruption.
32	C	Watching streaming media is a productivity issue, not an information security event. The other options relate directly to potential security breaches or system failures.
33	C	Independent reviews give an unbiased assessment of how well security controls function, helping identify gaps or weaknesses that internal teams might overlook.
34	A	A metro transit pass is personal or administrative, not an information security requirement. The other actions directly protect organizational information and assets during termination.
35	A	Uncontrolled changes can introduce vulnerabilities or disrupt operations. Control 8.32 ensures all changes are reviewed, approved, tested, and documented to maintain ISMS integrity and stability.
36	A	ISO 27005 provides guidelines for managing information security risks in a structured, consistent, and repeatable way, supporting ISO 27001 implementation.
37	D	ISO 27001 does not fix a specific timeframe for management reviews; they must occur at planned intervals determined by the organization's needs and ISMS performance.
38	C	ISO 27001 requires top management to establish an information security policy aligned with the organization's context, purpose, and strategic direction.
39	B	ISO 27001 specifies *requirements* for an ISMS, not implementation guidelines. Implementation guidance is provided in ISO 27002 and related standards.
40	B	Audit programs must evolve based on previous audit results and organizational changes. Keeping them unchanged contradicts ISO 27001's continual improvement approach.
41	B	Corrective action focuses on identifying and removing the root cause of a nonconformity to ensure it does not happen again.
42	A	ISO 27001 requires the *audit program* and *audit results* to be documented, not the audit plan itself. The plan guides activities but isn't mandatory documented information under the standard.
43	D	Implementing an ISO 27001-compliant ISMS demonstrates strong information security management, building trust and confidence among customers and stakeholders.
44	B	ISO 27001 is the certifiable standard in the ISO 27000 family, specifying formal requirements for establishing, implementing, maintaining, and continually improving an ISMS.
45	B	A management system provides a structured framework to achieve organizational objectives—such as quality, environment, or information security—through policies, processes, and continual improvement
46	D	The PDCA cycle is a continual improvement approach used in ISO 27001 to plan, implement, monitor, and improve the ISMS systematically.
47	C	ISO 27001 clearly assigns responsibility for the ISMS's effectiveness to top management, emphasizing leadership commitment, resource provision, and continual improvement
48	C	The ISMS scope must precisely define boundaries and applicability, reflecting the organization's context, operations, and information assets covered by the ISMS.

Sr.	*Answer*	*Reason/Explanation*
49	A	Top management commitment is essential for establishing, implementing, and sustaining an effective ISMS, ensuring resources, direction, and alignment with organizational goals.
50	B	ISO 27001 requires internal audits to be conducted at planned intervals, with frequency determined by process significance, changes, and outcomes of previous audits.
51	C	Records provide objective evidence that planned activities or procedures were carried out as intended, supporting compliance and traceability within the ISMS.
52	A	ISO 27001 requires the information security policy to include a commitment to continual improvement of the ISMS to enhance its effectiveness over time.
53	A	ISO 27001 mandates that the information security policy be communicated within the organization to ensure awareness and understanding among all relevant personnel.
54	B	The information security policy must be regularly reviewed and evaluated to ensure it remains relevant, effective, and aligned with organizational and ISMS objectives.
55	D	ISO 27001 requires information security objectives to be measurable, where practicable, to enable monitoring of progress and evaluation of ISMS effectiveness.
56	C	When the ISMS changes, ISO 27001 requires organizations to consider and evaluate potential consequences to ensure continued effectiveness and avoid introducing new risks.
57	B	Top management may delegate responsibility for ensuring ISMS conformity, but overall accountability for effectiveness and leadership commitment cannot be delegated.
58	B	ISO 27001 requires organizations to *determine* external and internal issues but does not mandate them to be documented.
59	A	A management system should reflect the organization's unique structure, processes, and context to ensure effective implementation and alignment with business objectives.
60	B	ISO 27001 specifically requires maintaining documented information for management review results, internal audit results, and measurable ISMS objectives.
61	A	ISO 27001 requires organizations to establish and apply a formal, systematic risk assessment process to identify, analyze, and evaluate information security risks.
62	D	All listed activities—monitoring performance, training and awareness, and reviewing residual risk—are essential ISMS requirements and cannot be excluded under ISO 27001.
63	A	Risk treatment is the process of determining how identified risks will be addressed and implementing the chosen treatment option, such as reducing, avoiding, transferring, or accepting the risk.
64	A	ISO 27001 requires organizations to ensure personnel competence through education, training, or experience relevant to their information security responsibilities.
65	A	Lack of awareness or training can lead to human errors or negligence, making untrained employees a significant information security risk within any organization.
66	D	Management review inputs must include feedback from interested parties, recommendations for improvement, and updates on risks, ensuring the ISMS remains effective and aligned with organizational needs.
67	C	ISO 27001 requires maintaining documented information on risk treatment outcomes to demonstrate that identified risks have been addressed appropriately.

Sr.	Answer	Reason/Explanation
68	D	ISO 27001 applies to protecting information in all forms—digital, paper-based, spoken, or otherwise—ensuring comprehensive information security management.
69	D	ISO 27001 requires documented information to be protected from loss of confidentiality, improper use, and loss of integrity to maintain trust and reliability of ISMS records.
70	C	ISO 27001 requires the policy to be documented, communicated internally, and made available to interested parties when appropriate—but not necessarily published on a corporate website.
71	C	In the *Check* phase of the PDCA cycle, organizations monitor, measure, and audit processes to evaluate performance and ensure objectives are being met.
72	A	Documented information serves as evidence of process performance and supports evaluation, helping identify areas for improvement within the ISMS.
73	B	The extent of documented information varies based on organizational size, complexity, and risk context.
74	B	ISO 27001 allows documented information in any format—electronic, paper, or other media—as long as it is properly controlled and accessible.
75	D	Risk identification aims to discover and describe potential events or situations that could positively or negatively affect the achievement of objectives.
76	B	Organizations should identify all relevant risks, whether controllable or not, to fully understand their context and decide on appropriate treatment or acceptance strategies.
77	A	ISO 27004 offers guidance on how to monitor, measure, analyze, and evaluate ISMS performance to support continual improvement and effectiveness assessment.
78	D	In the *Do* phase of the PDCA cycle, planned actions and controls are implemented to manage risks and achieve the defined objectives.
79	C	ISO 27001 requires every Annex A control to be evaluated, with justification for inclusion or exclusion documented in the Statement of Applicability.
80	D	Risk treatment options include avoiding risks, applying controls to reduce them, transferring them, or accepting them knowingly when they fall within acceptable limits.
81	B	A non-conformity is the failure to meet a specific ISO 27001 requirement.
82	B	ISO 27001 requires organizations to control and maintain documented information that is necessary for the effective operation of the ISMS.
83	D	ISO 27001 requires organizations to identify, analyze, and evaluate information security risks as part of a structured risk assessment process.
84	D	ISMS audits can help assess ISMS effectiveness, verify compliance with contractual and regulatory requirements, and even support decisions like selecting reliable service providers.
85	B	Risk evaluation helps prioritize and compare risks against criteria to support informed decision-making on treatment and resource allocation.
86	B	ISO 27001 requires monitoring and measurement at *planned intervals* determined by the organization, not at a fixed frequency like twice a year.
87	B	Organizations prioritize risks based on their potential impact and likelihood, focusing treatment on those with the highest combined effect.
88	D	ISO 27001 requires organizations to monitor, measure, analyze, and evaluate ISMS performance, conduct internal audits, and perform management reviews at planned intervals.
89	B	ISO 27001 requires management reviews to be conducted at planned intervals but does not prescribe a specific frequency. Organizations should determine the review schedule based on their needs and circumstances.
90	B	Corrective action focuses on identifying and eliminating the root cause of a nonconformity to prevent it from happening again.

Sr.	Answer	Reason/Explanation
91	A	In the Stage 1 audit, auditors review documented information to confirm the ISMS's readiness for the Stage 2 certification audit.
92	B	ISO develops international standards but does not conduct accreditation or certification. These activities are carried out by authorized accreditation and certification bodies.
93	C	Accreditation bodies formally recognize certification bodies, ensuring their competence to perform audits and issue ISO 27001 certifications.
94	C	An audit's main objective is to verify that the ISMS meets ISO 27001 requirements and operates as planned within the organization.
95	A	Risk appetite refers to the amount and type of risk an organization is willing to accept in pursuit of its objectives.
96	B	ISO 27001 allows exclusion of Annex A controls only when properly justified and documented in the Statement of Applicability.
97	C	The audit scope defines the boundaries and extent of the audit, including areas, processes, and activities to be covered.
98	C	Audit criteria are the set of policies, procedures, and requirements—such as ISO 27001 clauses and legal obligations—against which audit evidence is compared.
99	A	In the *Act* phase of the PDCA cycle, organizations take corrective and improvement actions based on audit findings and performance evaluations to enhance ISMS effectiveness.
100	B	ISO 19011:2018 provides *guidelines* for auditing management systems; it is not a requirement or certifiable standard.

Bibliography

[1] ISO/IEC 27001:2022, Information security, cybersecurity and privacy protection — Information.
[2] ISO 9001:2015, Quality management systems — Requirements.
[3] ISO 14001:2015, Environmental management systems — Requirements with guidance for use.
[4] ISO 19011:2018, Guidelines for auditing management systems.
[5] ISO/IEC 27000:2018, Information technology — Security techniques — Information security management systems — Overview and vocabulary.
[6] ISO/IEC 27007:2020, Information security, cybersecurity and privacy protection — Guidelines for information security management systems auditing.
[7] ISO/IEC 27002:2022, Information security, cybersecurity and privacy protection — Information security controls.
[8] ISO 13485:2016, Medical devices — Quality management systems — Requirements for regulatory purposes.
[9] ISO/IEC 27003, Information technology — Security techniques — Information security management systems — Guidance.
[10] ISO/IEC 27004, Information technology — Security techniques — Information security management — Monitoring, measurement, analysis and evaluation.
[11] ISO/IEC 27005, Information security, cybersecurity and privacy protection — Guidance on managing information security risks.
[12] ISO/IEC 27006-1:2024, Information security, cybersecurity and privacy protection — Requirements for bodies providing audit and certification of information security management systems.
[13] ISO/IEC TS 27008, Information technology — Security techniques — Guidelines for the assessment of information security controls.
[14] ISO/IEC 27009:2020, Information security, cybersecurity and privacy protection — Sector-specific application of ISO/IEC 27001 — Requirements (Withdrawn).
[15] ISO/IEC 27010:2015, Information technology — Security techniques — Information security management for inter-sector and inter-organizational communications.
[16] ISO/IEC 27011, Information technology — Security techniques — Code of practice for Information security controls based on ISO/IEC 27002 for telecommunications organizations.
[17] ISO/IEC 27013:2021/Amd 1:2024, Information security, cybersecurity and privacy protection — Guidance on the integrated implementation of ISO/IEC 27001 and ISO/IEC 20000-1.
[18] ISO/IEC 27014:2020, Information security, cybersecurity and privacy protection — Governance of information security.
[19] ISO/IEC TR 27016, Information technology — Security techniques — Information security management — Organizational economics.
[20] ISO/IEC 27017, Information technology — Security techniques — Code of practice for information security controls based on ISO/IEC 27002 for cloud services.
[21] ISO/IEC 27018, Information technology — Security techniques — Code of practice for protection of personally identifiable information (PII) in public clouds acting as PII processors.

[22] ISO/IEC 27019, Information technology — Security techniques — Information security controls for the energy utility industry.
[23] ISO/IEC 27021:2017, Information technology — Security techniques — Competence requirements for information security management systems professionals.
[24] ISO 45001:2018, Occupational health and safety management systems — Requirements with guidance for use.
[25] ISO 22301:2019, Security and resilience — Business continuity management systems — Requirements.
[26] ISO 31000:2018, Risk management — Guidelines.
[27] ISO/IEC 21827:2008, Information technology — Security techniques — Systems Security Engineering — Capability Maturity Model® (SSE-CMM®).
[28] ISO 31073:2022, Risk management — Vocabulary.
[29] IEC 31010:2019, Risk management — Risk assessment techniques.
[30] ISO/IEC TS 27110:2021, Information technology, cybersecurity and privacy protection — Cybersecurity framework development guidelines.

For Product Safety Concerns and Information please contact our EU
representative GPSR@taylorandfrancis.com
Taylor & Francis Verlag GmbH, Kaufingerstraße 24, 80331 München, Germany

www.ingramcontent.com/pod-product-compliance
Ingram Content Group UK Ltd.
Pitfield, Milton Keynes, MK11 3LW, UK
UKHW052051230926
475702UK00025B/1095
9781041249023